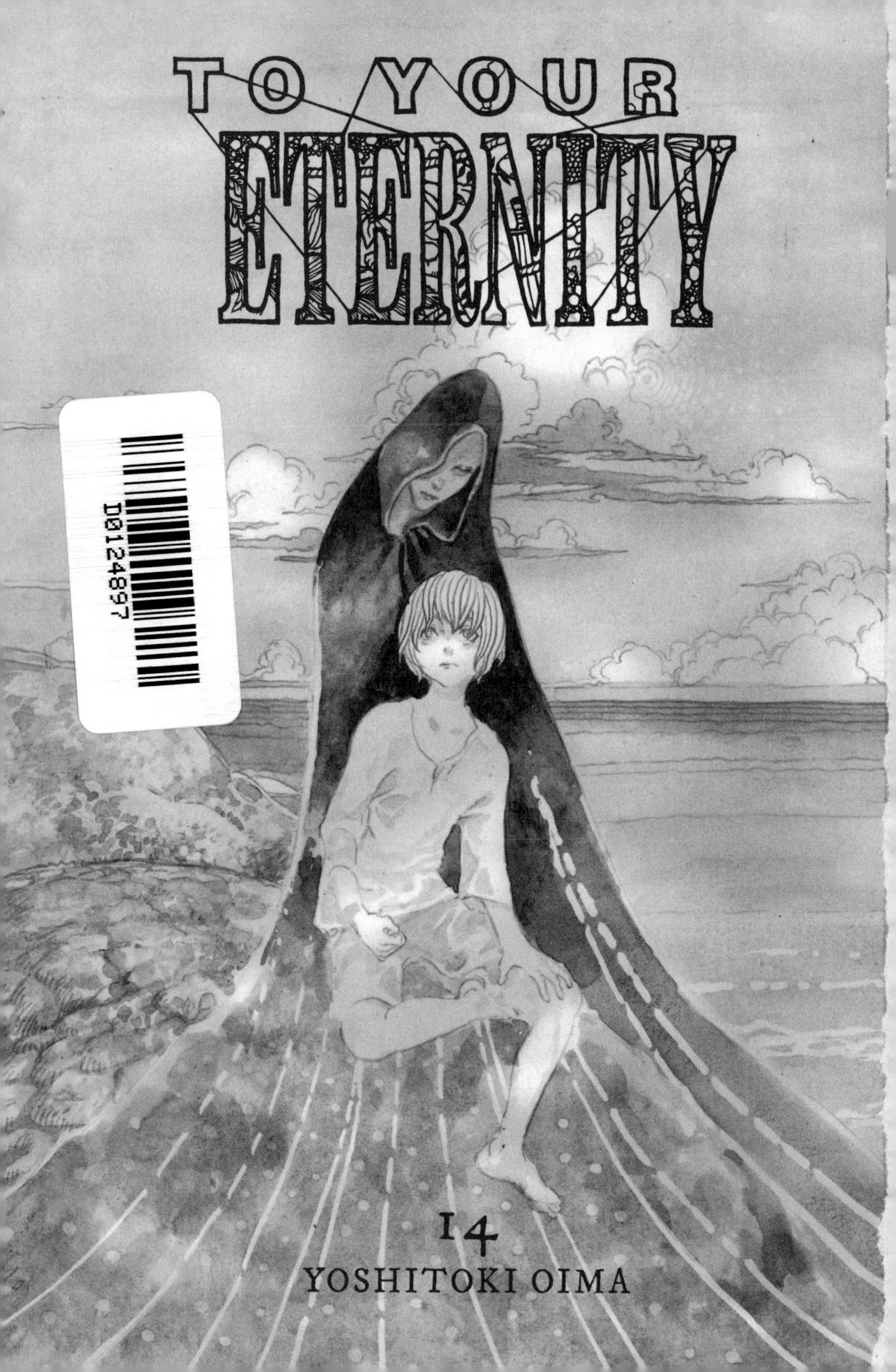
TO YOUR
ETERNITY
14
YOSHITOKI OIMA

# THE STORY SO FAR

All of Fushi's vessels were stolen, reducing him to a powerless orb once more.

With Renril on the verge of destruction from the Nokkers' ferocious attack,
Bon gave his life in a secret plan to reawaken Fushi.

After acquiring Bon's vessel, Fushi gained the power to see the dead, and
brought his fallen comrades back to life to initiate a counteroffensive.
It eventually succeeded, and the Nokkers were finally routed!

A few centuries later...
Fushi continued to fight and exterminate the Nokkers on his own in order
to bring his friends back to a peaceful world... Before he knew it, the world
before him had indeed become a beautiful, stimulating, and peaceful place.

After running into a boy named Yuki, Fushi and his
now-resurrected friends began to gleefully freeload at Yuki's house.

But then Fushi met a girl: Mizuha, a descendant of Hayase.
After Mizuha killed her mother, she turned to Fushi for help...

# CHARACTERS

## Fushi

An immortal being who can transform into acquired vessels. After learning to control his senses, he spread roots over the surface of the world and eliminated the Nokkers. Was given the power of reconnection by the Beholder.

## Mizuha

Second-year junior high school student. Descendant of Hayase. A girl with both beauty and brains who can accomplish anything perfectly. Knows the legends about Fushi and is interested in him.

## Yuki Aoki

First-year junior high school student. Vice President of the Occult Research Club. Always curious. Found Fushi at the beach and took him home. Likes Mizuha.

# COMRADES RESURRECTED IN THE MODERN WORLD

Tonari

Gugu

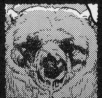
Oniguma

March

Iddy

Bonchien Nicoli
la Tasty Peach Uralis

Horse

Ligard

Hairo Rich

Kai Renald Rawle

Messar Robin Bastar

## Occult Research Club Members

The Brains, Senba (left), and the Brawn, Tamaki (right). Both are first-year students.

## Mizuha's Mother

Descendant of Hayase, but cut off the rest of her family. Dotes on her daughter.

## Yuki's Family

Fushi and friends live with them. Aiko is Yuki's capable little sister. Kazumitsu is a grandfather who can't say no to his grandchildren.

## Hanna

Second-year in junior high. Mizuha's friend. President of the Handicrafts (Occult Research) Club.

## Nokker

Their true forms, called fye, are similar to souls. They oppose Fushi and the Beholder for standing in their way. They were completely wiped out by Fushi following the battle of Renril.

## The Beholder

Created Fushi in order to preserve the world. Always watching Fushi from nearby. Grants Fushi the power of reconnection after he defeats the Nokkers, then tells him to celebrate.

# CONTENTS

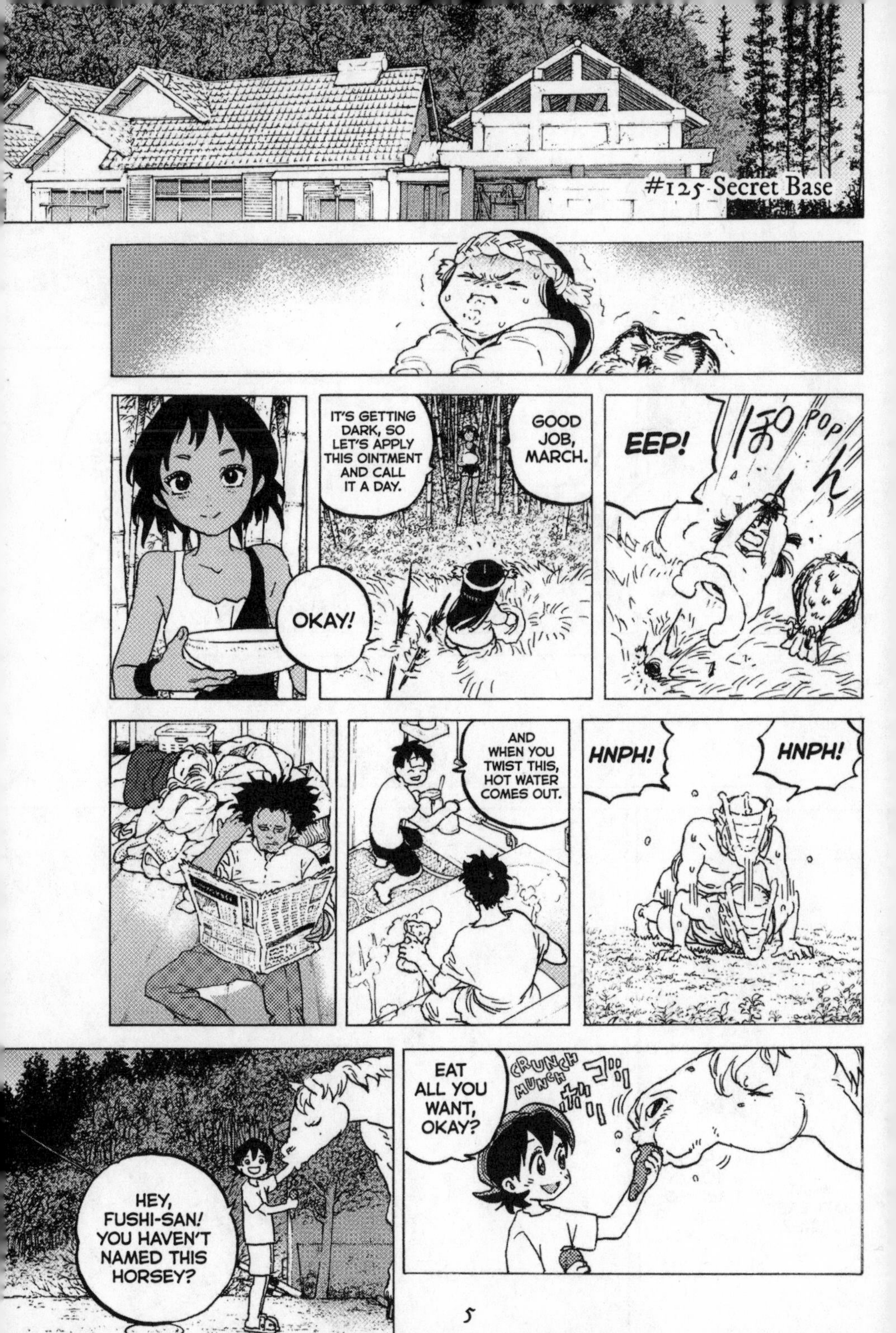
#125 Secret Base
EEP!
ぽん POP
GOOD JOB, MARCH.
IT'S GETTING DARK, SO LET'S APPLY THIS OINTMENT AND CALL IT A DAY.
OKAY!
HNPH!
HNPH!
AND WHEN YOU TWIST THIS, HOT WATER COMES OUT.
EAT ALL YOU WANT, OKAY?
CRUNCH MUNCH
HEY, FUSHI-SAN! YOU HAVEN'T NAMED THIS HORSEY?

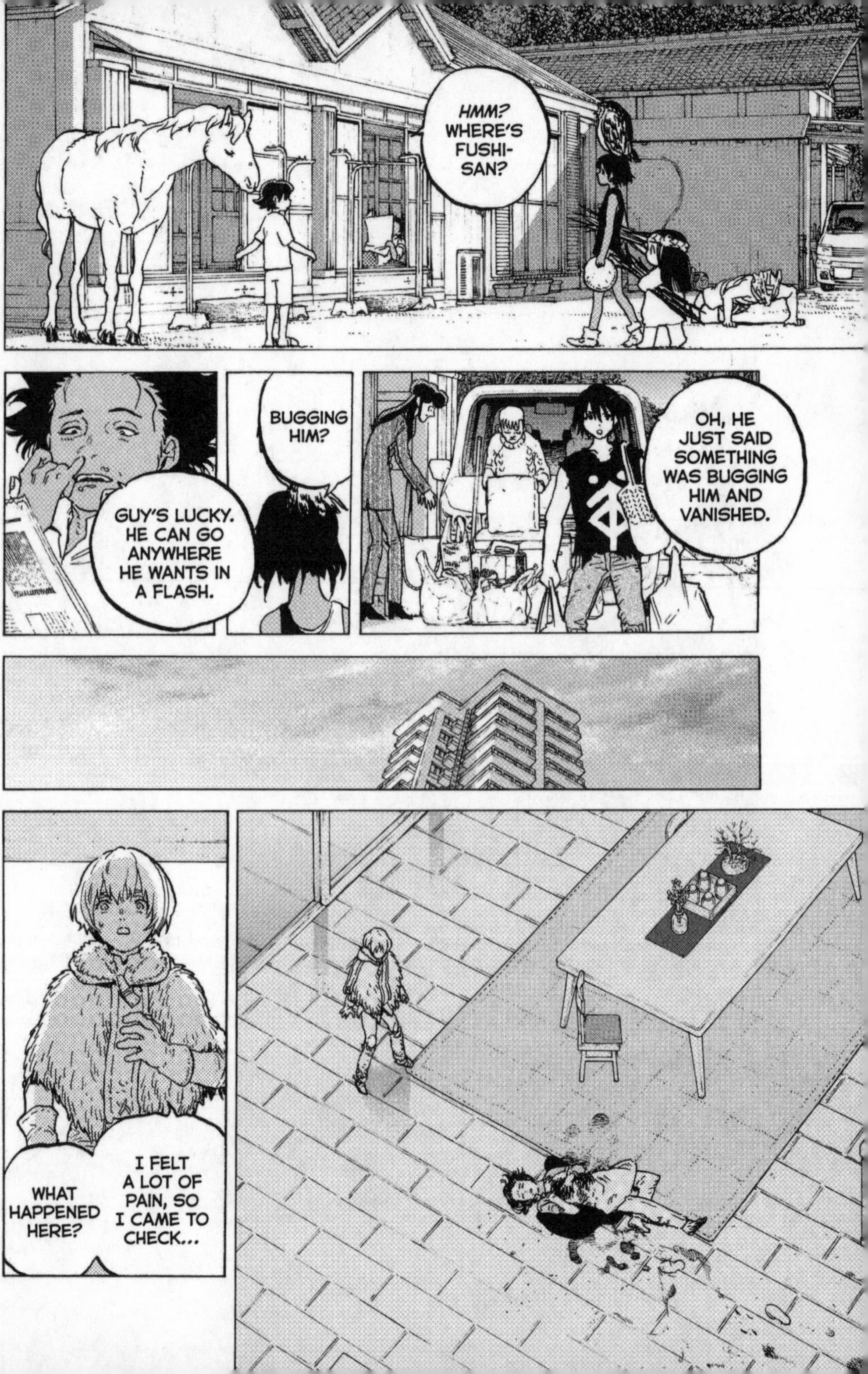
HMM? WHERE'S FUSHI-SAN?
OH, HE JUST SAID SOMETHING WAS BUGGING HIM AND VANISHED.
BUGGING HIM?
GUY'S LUCKY. HE CAN GO ANYWHERE HE WANTS IN A FLASH.
I FELT A LOT OF PAIN, SO I CAME TO CHECK...
WHAT HAPPENED HERE?

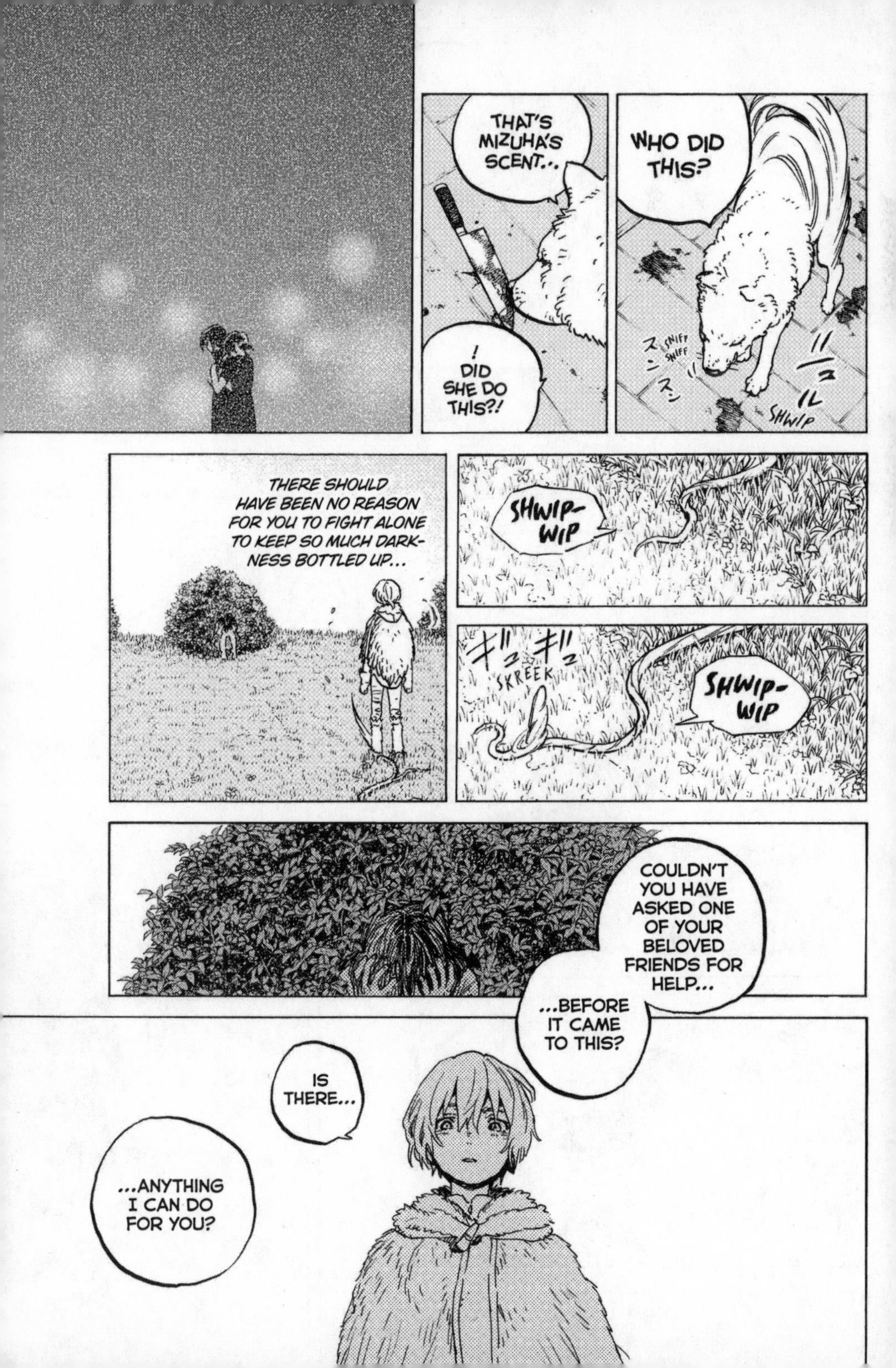
WHO DID THIS?
SNIFF SNIFF
SHWIP
THAT'S MIZUHA'S SCENT...
! DID SHE DO THIS?!
SHWIP-WIP
SKREEK
SHWIP-WIP
THERE SHOULD HAVE BEEN NO REASON FOR YOU TO FIGHT ALONE TO KEEP SO MUCH DARKNESS BOTTLED UP...
COULDN'T YOU HAVE ASKED ONE OF YOUR BELOVED FRIENDS FOR HELP...
...BEFORE IT CAME TO THIS?
IS THERE...
...ANYTHING I CAN DO FOR YOU?

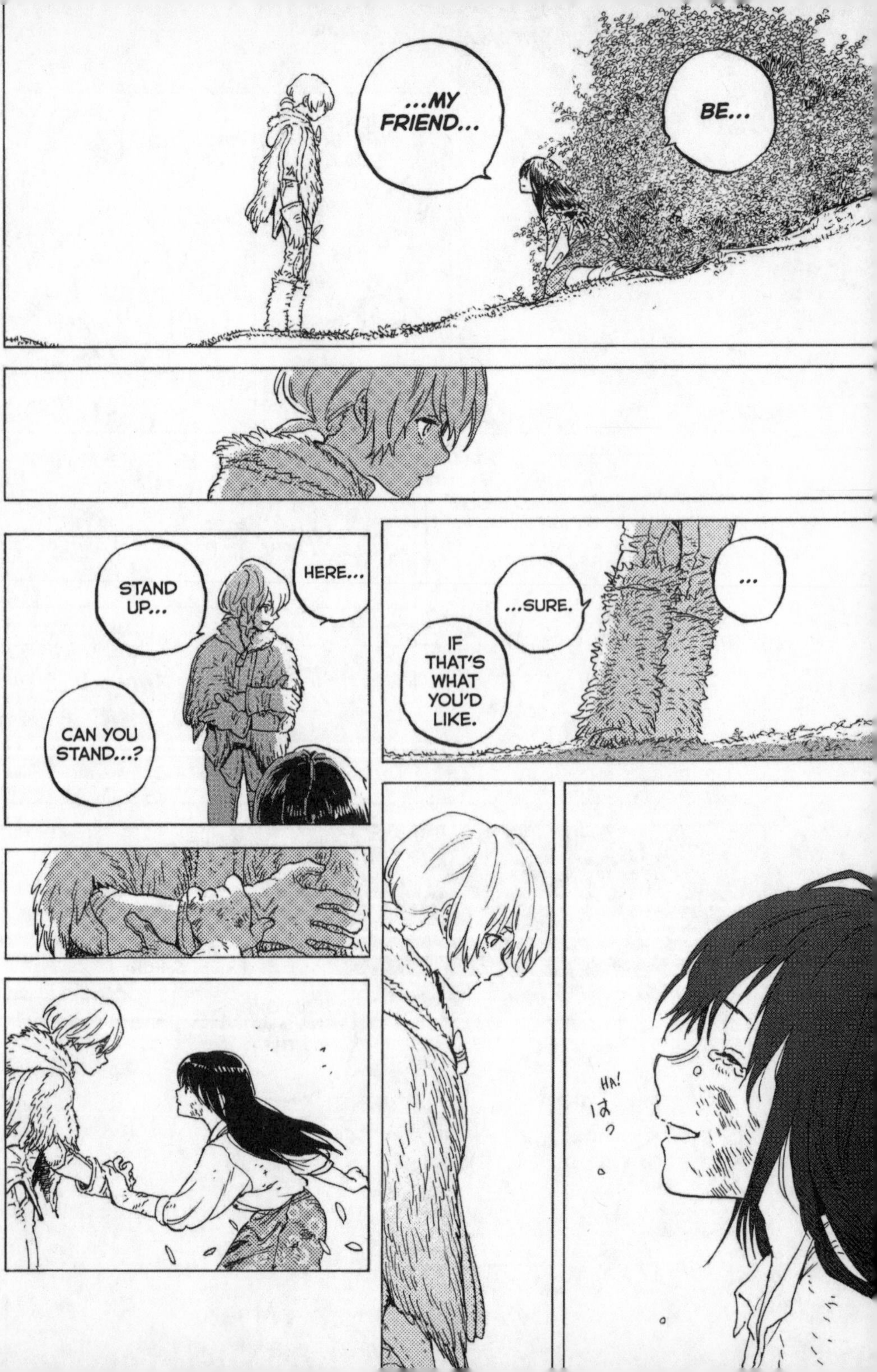
BE...
...MY FRIEND...
...
...SURE.
IF THAT'S WHAT YOU'D LIKE.
HERE...
STAND UP...
CAN YOU STAND...?
HA!
はっ

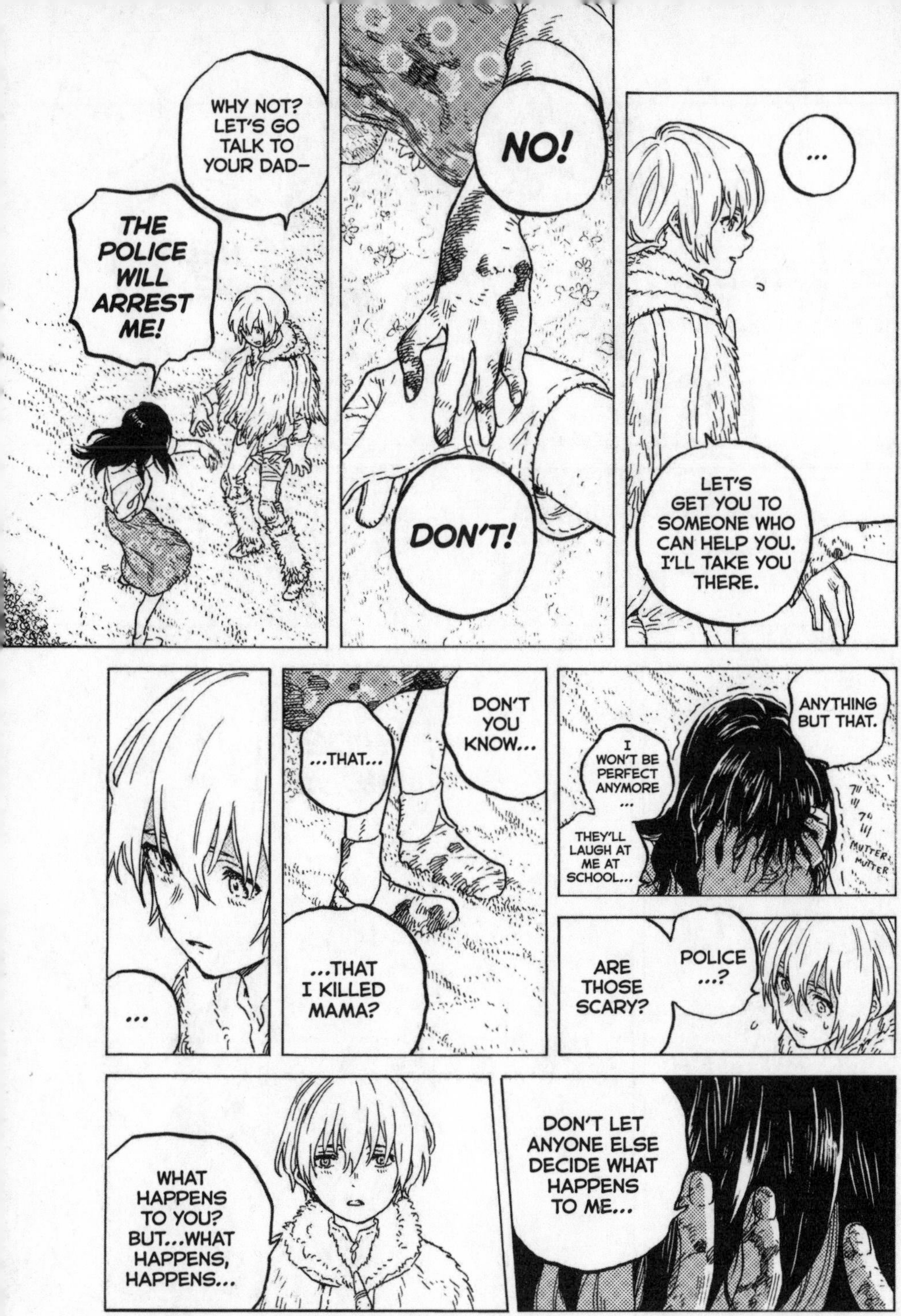
...
LET'S GET YOU TO SOMEONE WHO CAN HELP YOU. I'LL TAKE YOU THERE.
NO!
DON'T!
WHY NOT? LET'S GO TALK TO YOUR DAD—
THE POLICE WILL ARREST ME!
ANYTHING BUT THAT.
I WON'T BE PERFECT ANYMORE...
THEY'LL LAUGH AT ME AT SCHOOL...
MUTTER MUTTER
POLICE...?
ARE THOSE SCARY?
DON'T YOU KNOW...
...THAT...
...THAT I KILLED MAMA?
...
DON'T LET ANYONE ELSE DECIDE WHAT HAPPENS TO ME...
WHAT HAPPENS TO YOU? BUT...WHAT HAPPENS, HAPPENS...

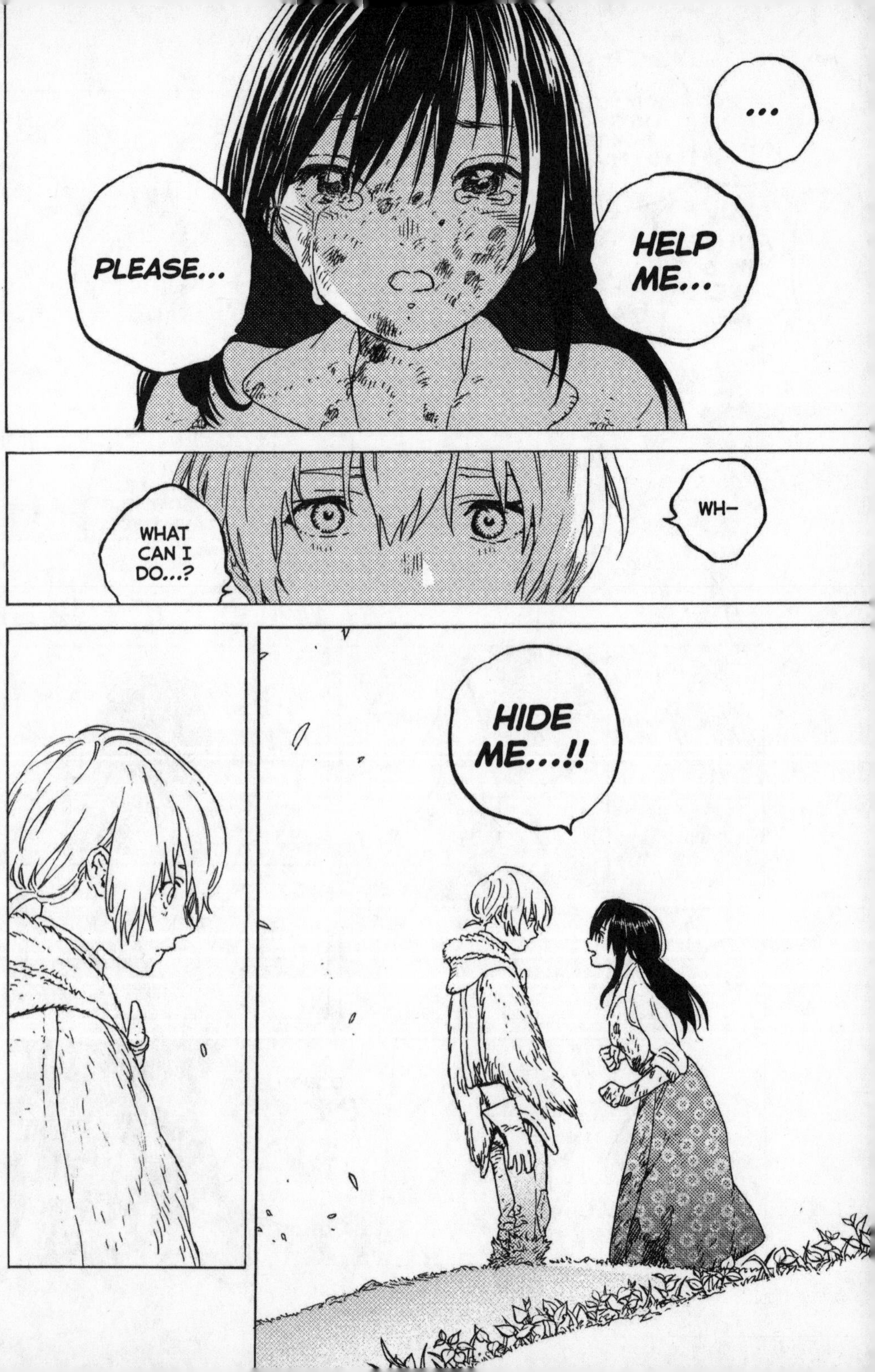
...
HELP ME...
PLEASE...
WH–
WHAT CAN I DO...?
HIDE ME...!!

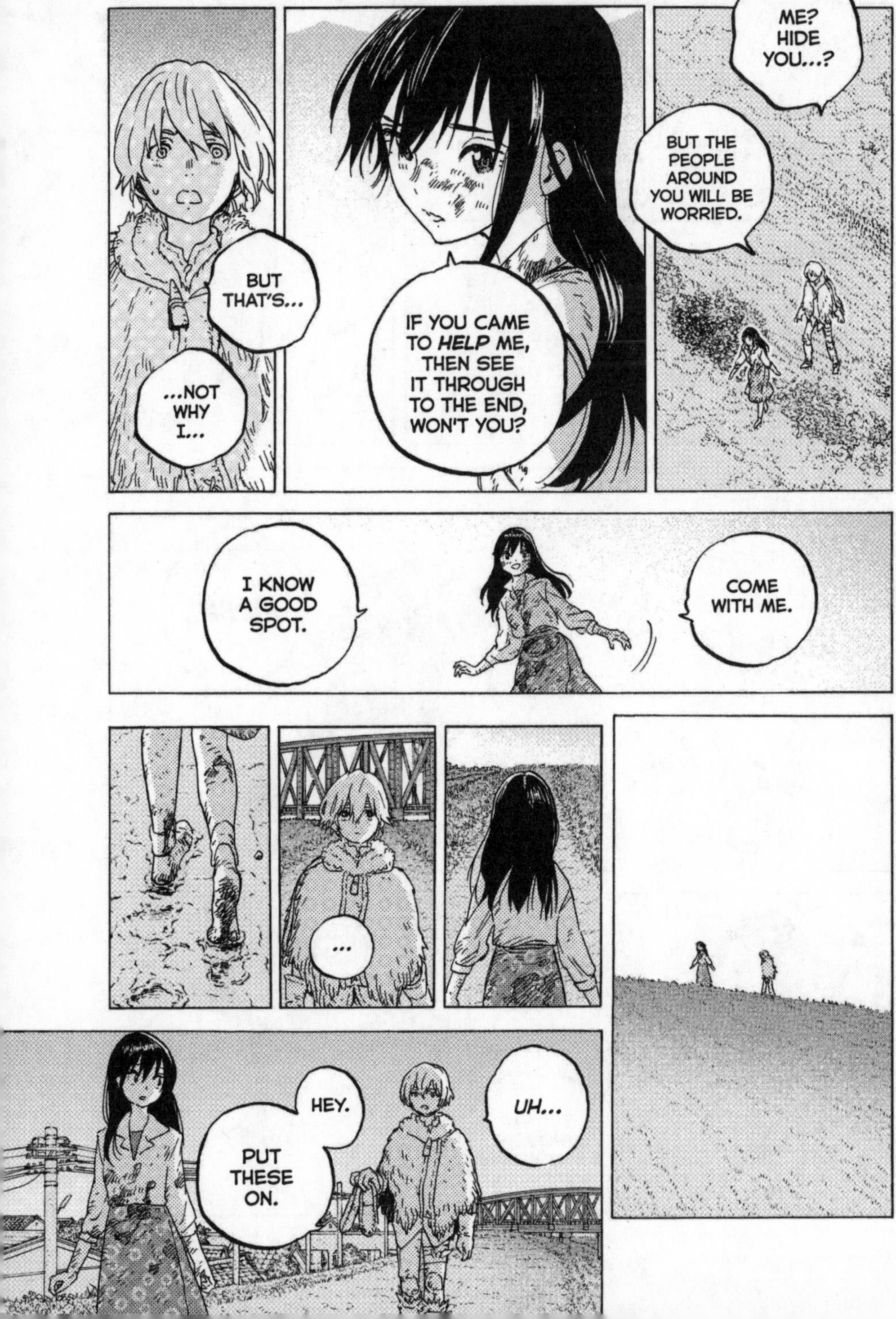
ME? HIDE YOU...?
BUT THE PEOPLE AROUND YOU WILL BE WORRIED.
IF YOU CAME TO *HELP* ME, THEN SEE IT THROUGH TO THE END, WON'T YOU?
BUT THAT'S...
...NOT WHY I...
COME WITH ME.
I KNOW A GOOD SPOT.
...
UH...
HEY.
PUT THESE ON.

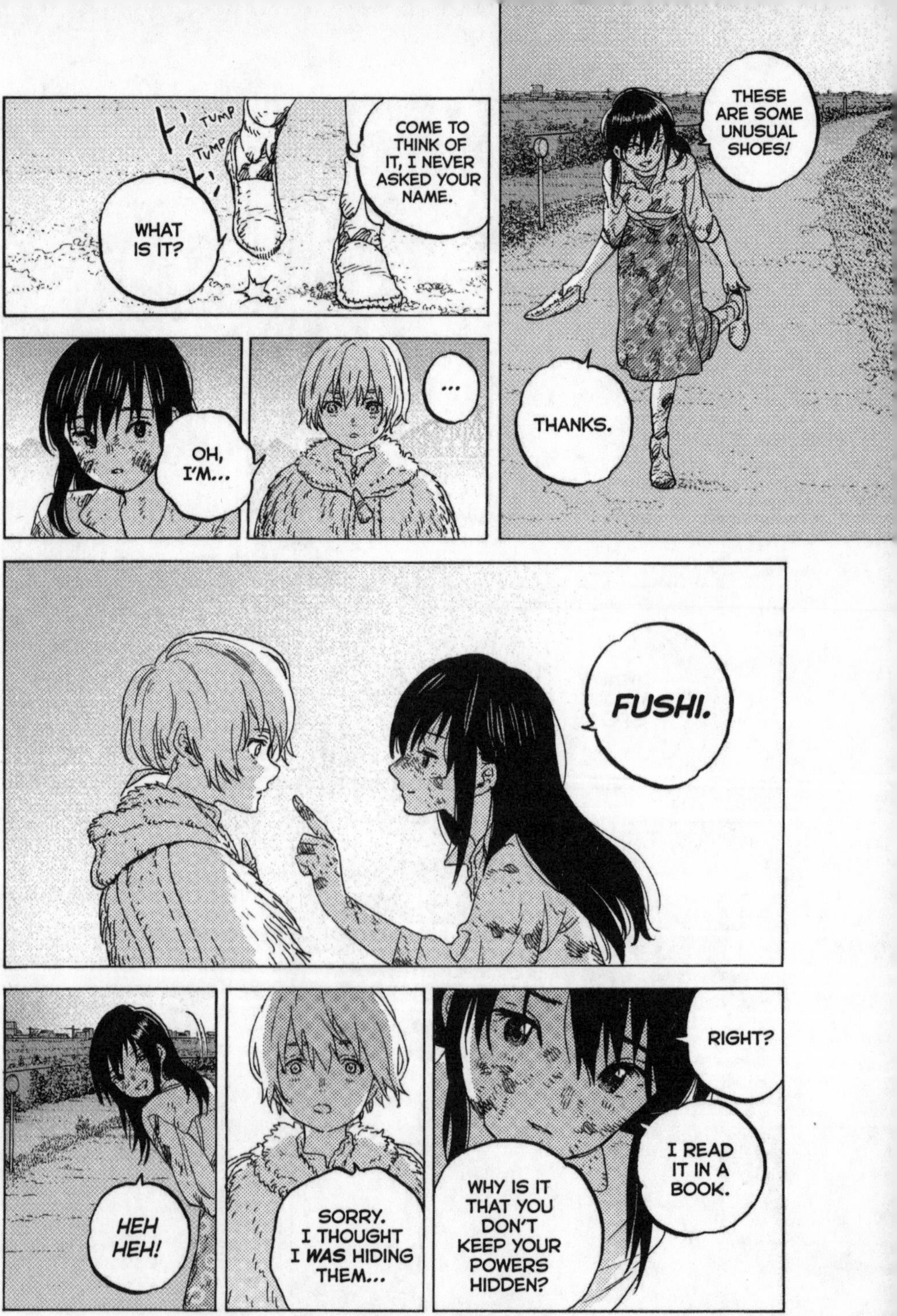
THESE ARE SOME UNUSUAL SHOES!
THANKS.
COME TO THINK OF IT, I NEVER ASKED YOUR NAME.
TUMP
TUMP
WHAT IS IT?
...
OH, I'M...
FUSHI.
RIGHT?
I READ IT IN A BOOK.
WHY IS IT THAT YOU DON'T KEEP YOUR POWERS HIDDEN?
SORRY. I THOUGHT I *WAS* HIDING THEM...
HEH HEH!

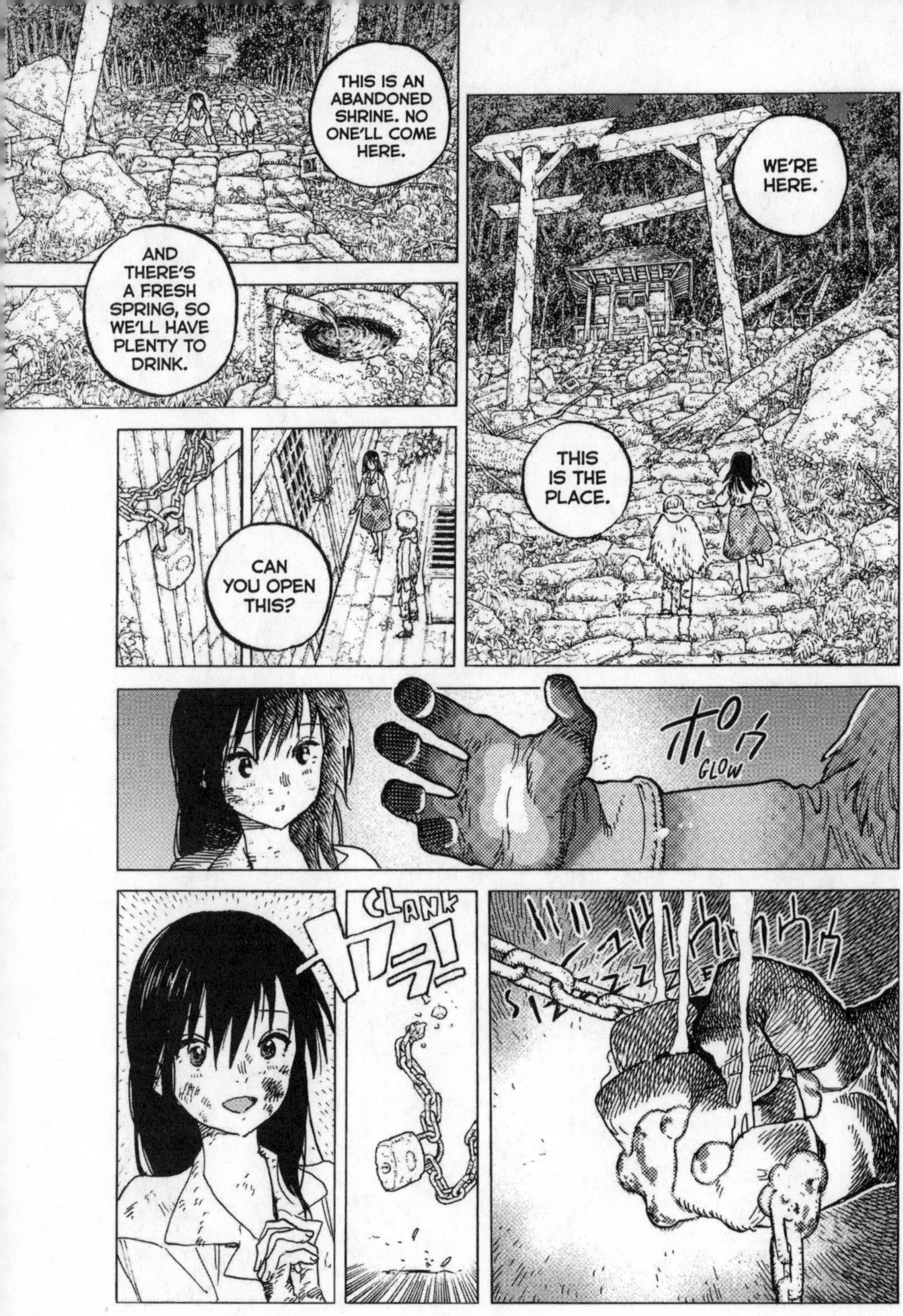
WE'RE HERE.
THIS IS THE PLACE.
THIS IS AN ABANDONED SHRINE. NO ONE'LL COME HERE.
AND THERE'S A FRESH SPRING, SO WE'LL HAVE PLENTY TO DRINK.
CAN YOU OPEN THIS?
ポゥ
GLOW
SIZZLE
CLANK

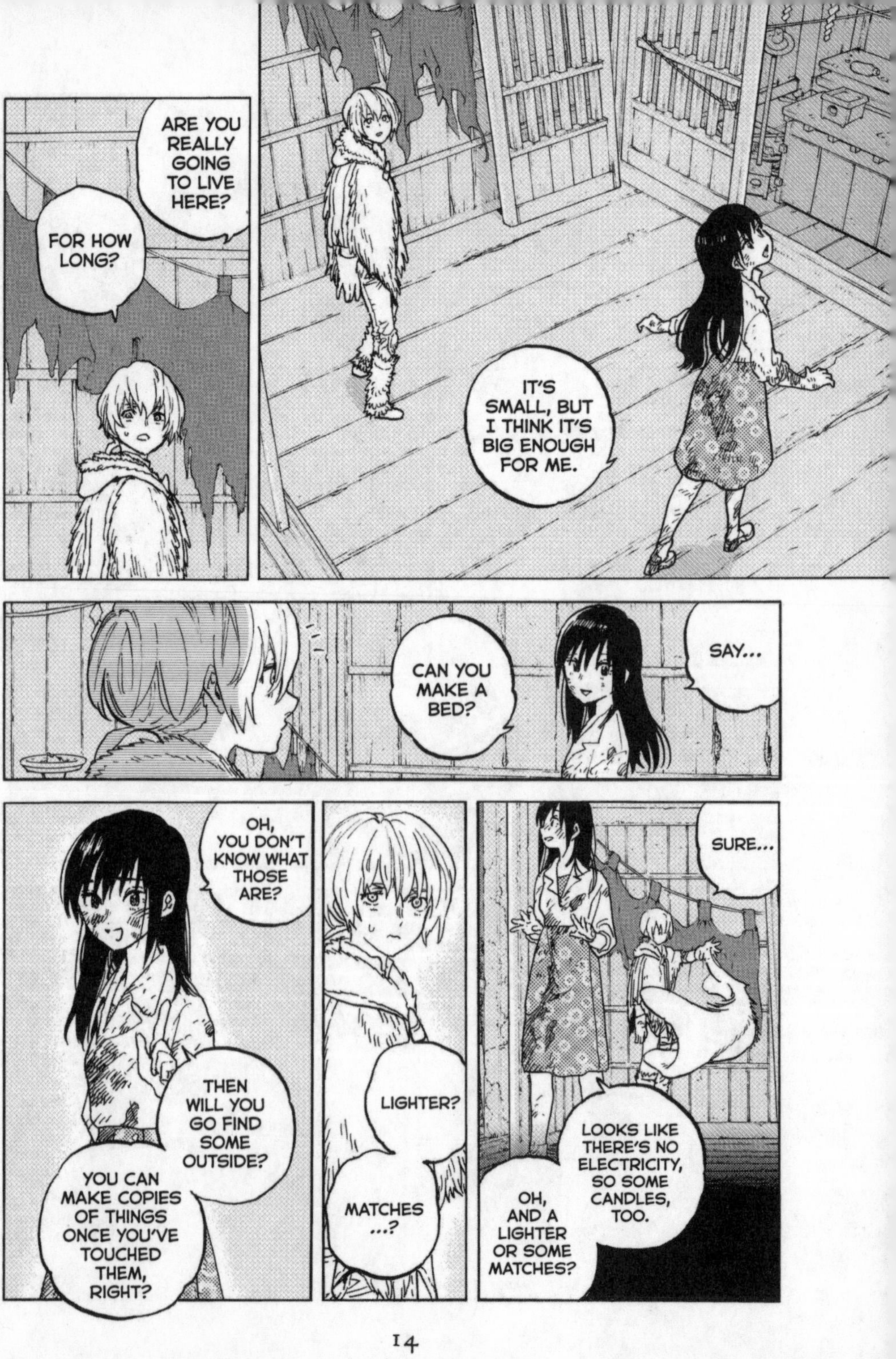
IT'S SMALL, BUT I THINK IT'S BIG ENOUGH FOR ME.
ARE YOU REALLY GOING TO LIVE HERE?
FOR HOW LONG?
SAY...
CAN YOU MAKE A BED?
SURE...
LOOKS LIKE THERE'S NO ELECTRICITY, SO SOME CANDLES, TOO.
OH, AND A LIGHTER OR SOME MATCHES?
LIGHTER?
MATCHES ...?
OH, YOU DON'T KNOW WHAT THOSE ARE?
THEN WILL YOU GO FIND SOME OUTSIDE?
YOU CAN MAKE COPIES OF THINGS ONCE YOU'VE TOUCHED THEM, RIGHT?

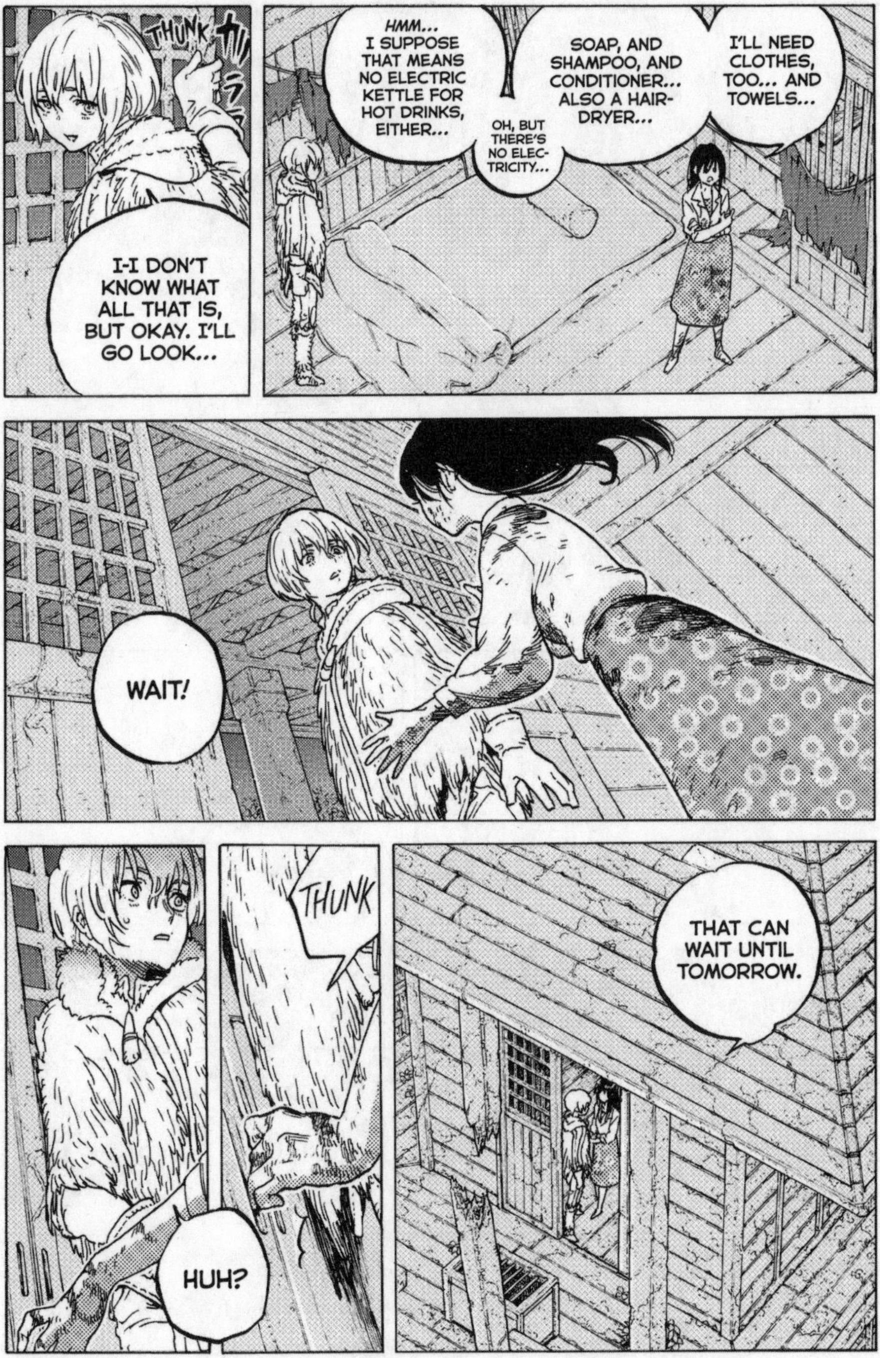
I'LL NEED CLOTHES, TOO... AND TOWELS...
SOAP, AND SHAMPOO, AND CONDITIONER... ALSO A HAIR-DRYER...
OH, BUT THERE'S NO ELECTRICITY...
HMM... I SUPPOSE THAT MEANS NO ELECTRIC KETTLE FOR HOT DRINKS, EITHER...
THUNK
I-I DON'T KNOW WHAT ALL THAT IS, BUT OKAY. I'LL GO LOOK...
WAIT!
THAT CAN WAIT UNTIL TOMORROW.
THUNK
HUH?

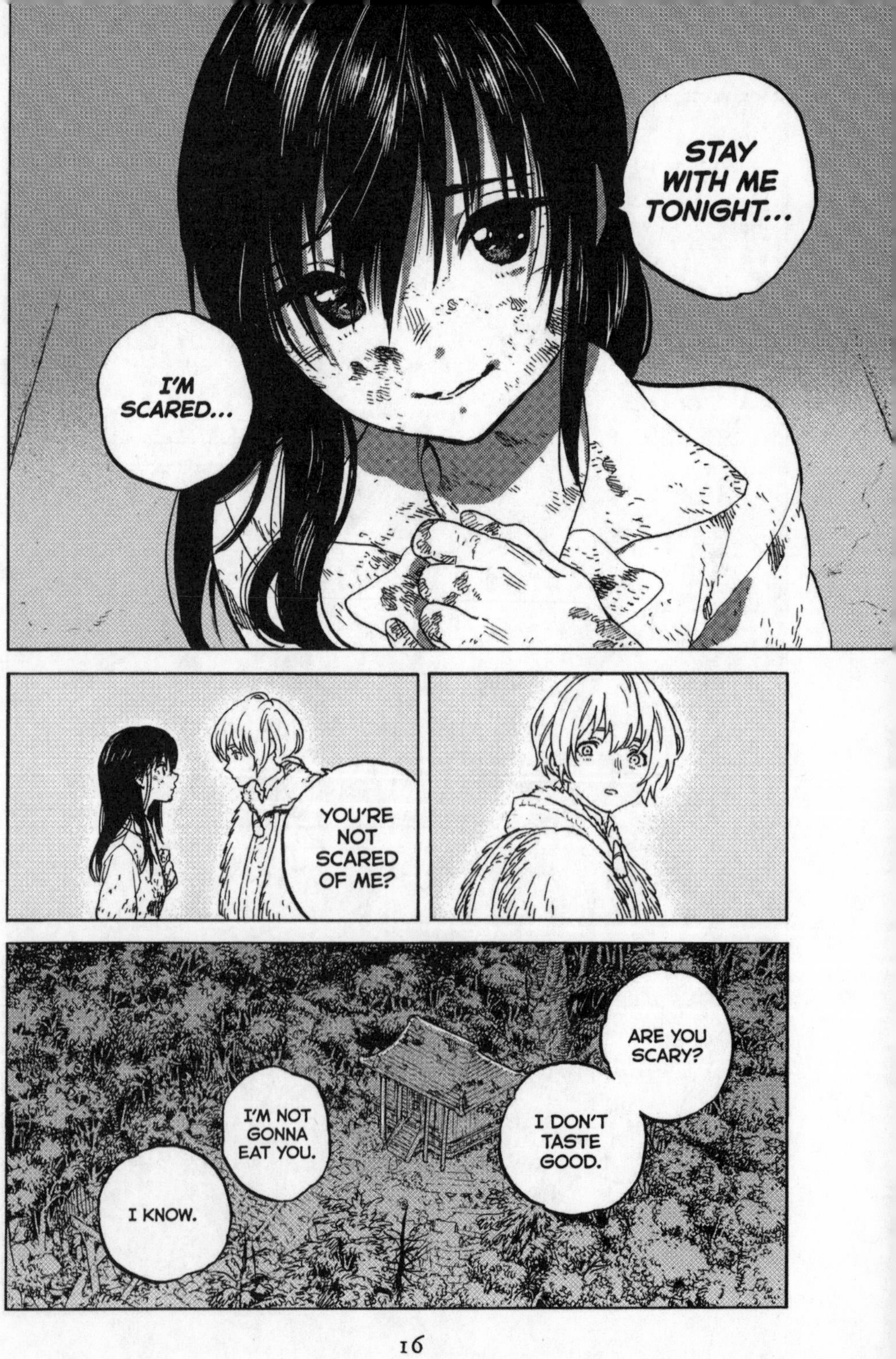
STAY WITH ME TONIGHT...
I'M SCARED...
YOU'RE NOT SCARED OF ME?
ARE YOU SCARY?
I DON'T TASTE GOOD.
I'M NOT GONNA EAT YOU.
I KNOW.

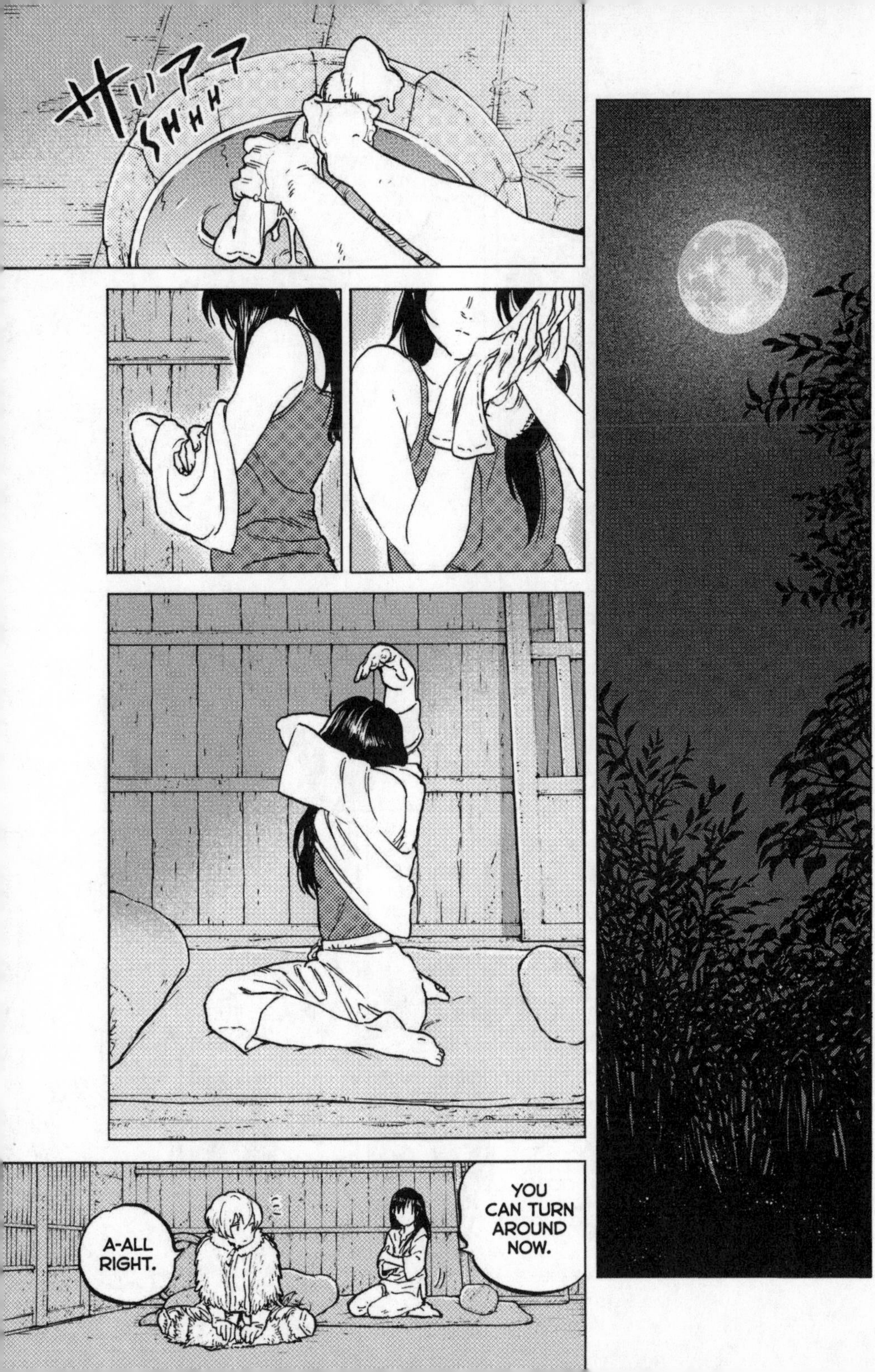
サリアア
SHHH
YOU CAN TURN AROUND NOW.
A-ALL RIGHT.

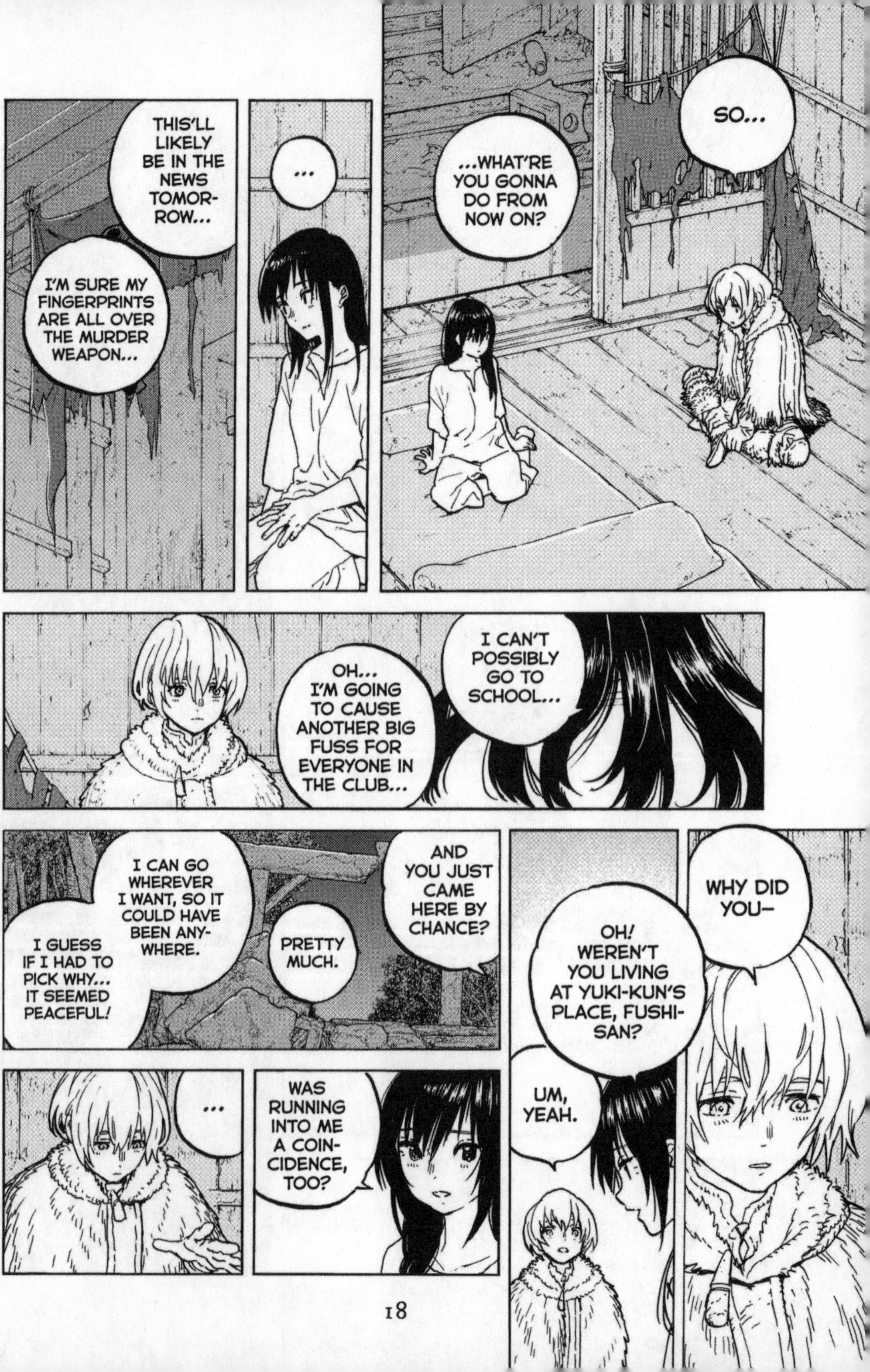
SO...
...WHAT'RE YOU GONNA DO FROM NOW ON?
...
THIS'LL LIKELY BE IN THE NEWS TOMOR-ROW...
I'M SURE MY FINGERPRINTS ARE ALL OVER THE MURDER WEAPON...
I CAN'T POSSIBLY GO TO SCHOOL...
OH... I'M GOING TO CAUSE ANOTHER BIG FUSS FOR EVERYONE IN THE CLUB...
WHY DID YOU—
OH! WEREN'T YOU LIVING AT YUKI-KUN'S PLACE, FUSHI-SAN?
UM, YEAH.
AND YOU JUST CAME HERE BY CHANCE?
PRETTY MUCH.
I CAN GO WHEREVER I WANT, SO IT COULD HAVE BEEN ANY-WHERE.
I GUESS IF I HAD TO PICK WHY... IT SEEMED PEACEFUL!
WAS RUNNING INTO ME A COINCIDENCE, TOO?
...

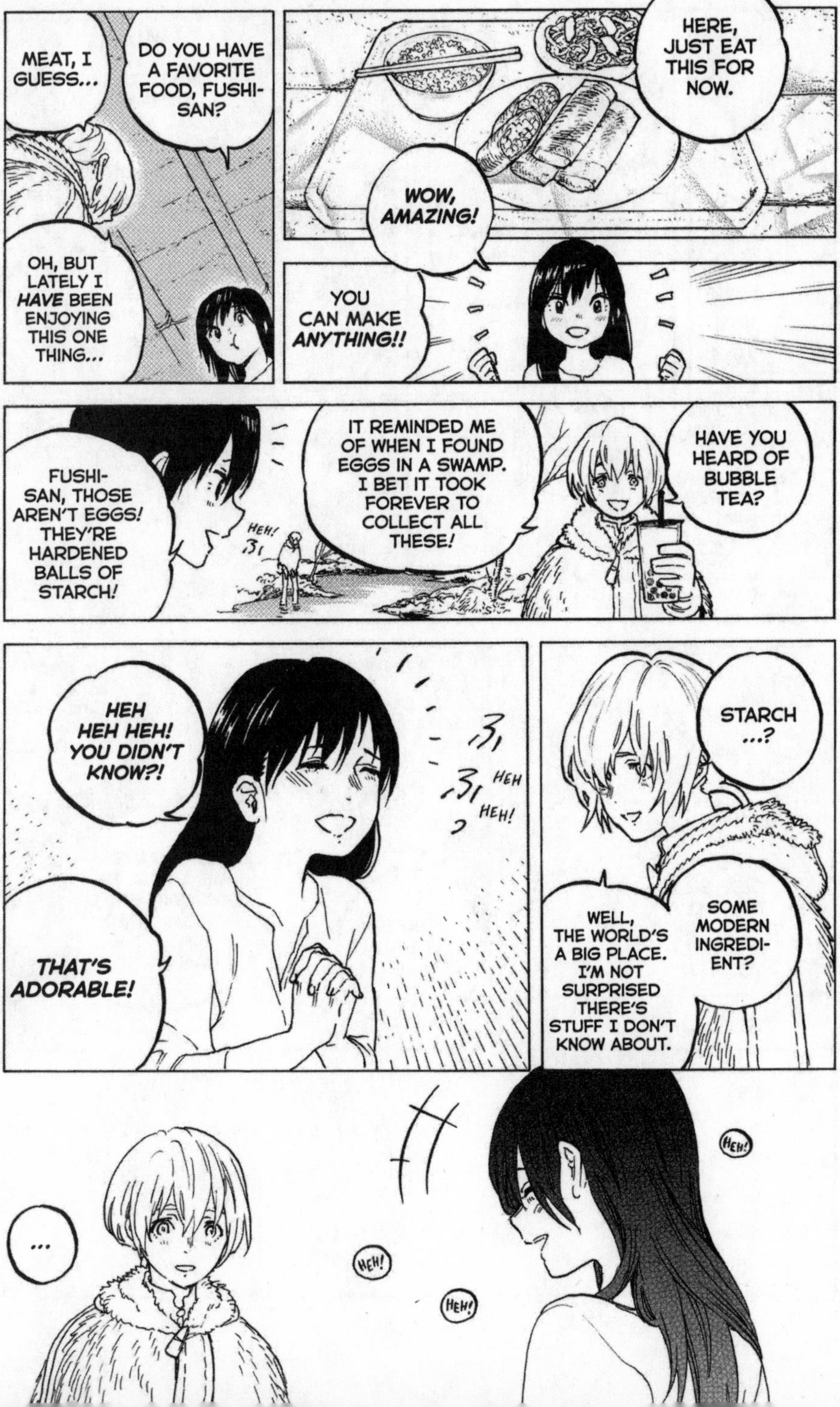

HERE, JUST EAT THIS FOR NOW.
WOW, AMAZING!
YOU CAN MAKE ANYTHING!!
DO YOU HAVE A FAVORITE FOOD, FUSHI-SAN?
MEAT, I GUESS...
OH, BUT LATELY I HAVE BEEN ENJOYING THIS ONE THING...
HAVE YOU HEARD OF BUBBLE TEA?
IT REMINDED ME OF WHEN I FOUND EGGS IN A SWAMP. I BET IT TOOK FOREVER TO COLLECT ALL THESE!
HEH!
FUSHI-SAN, THOSE AREN'T EGGS! THEY'RE HARDENED BALLS OF STARCH!
STARCH ...?
SOME MODERN INGREDIENT?
WELL, THE WORLD'S A BIG PLACE. I'M NOT SURPRISED THERE'S STUFF I DON'T KNOW ABOUT.
HEH HEH HEH! YOU DIDN'T KNOW?!
HEH
HEH!
THAT'S ADORABLE!
HEH!
HEH!
HEH!
...

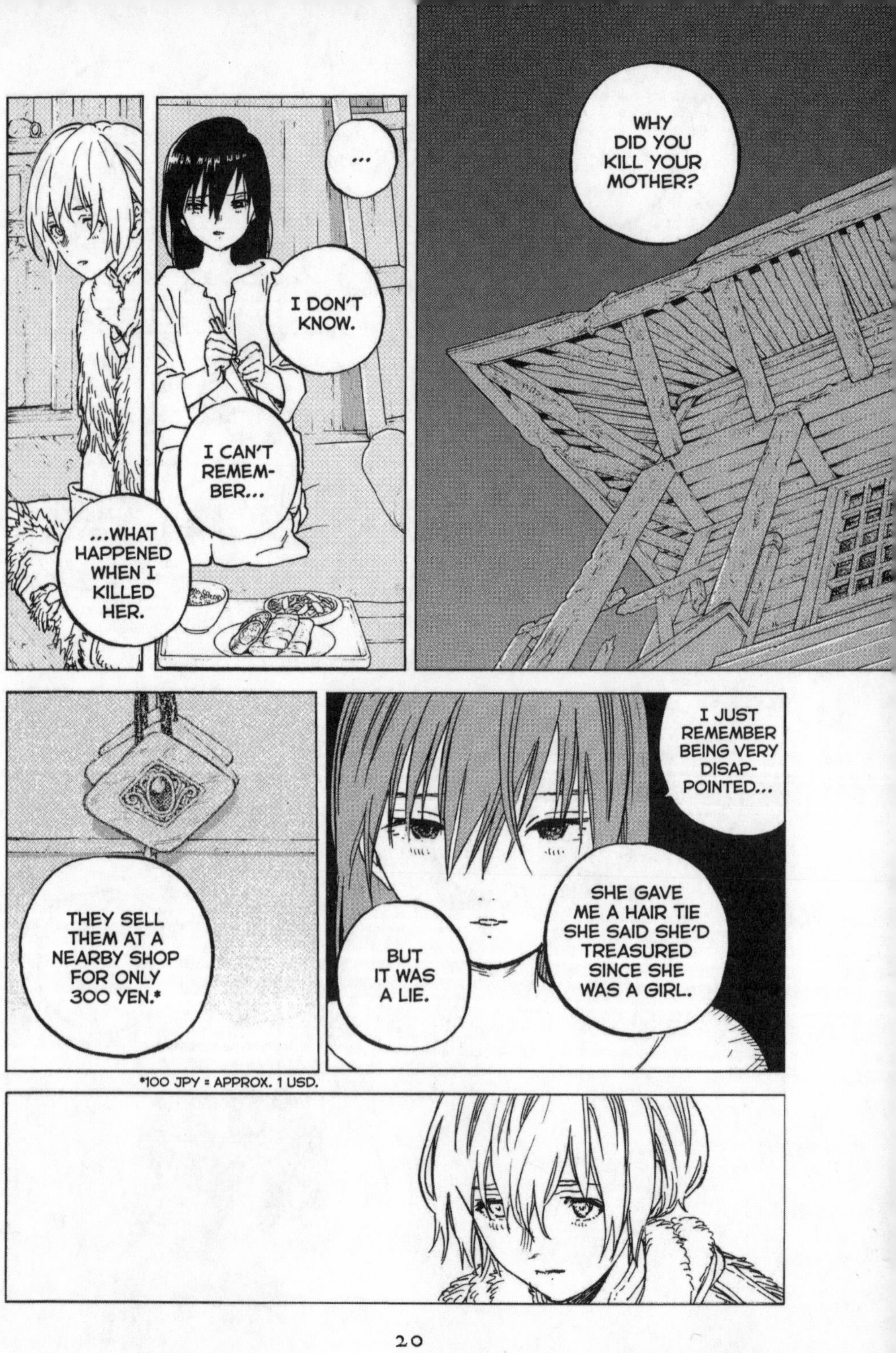
WHY DID YOU KILL YOUR MOTHER?
...
I DON'T KNOW.
I CAN'T REMEMBER...
...WHAT HAPPENED WHEN I KILLED HER.
I JUST REMEMBER BEING VERY DISAPPOINTED...
SHE GAVE ME A HAIR TIE SHE SAID SHE'D TREASURED SINCE SHE WAS A GIRL.
BUT IT WAS A LIE.
THEY SELL THEM AT A NEARBY SHOP FOR ONLY 300 YEN.*

*100 JPY = APPROX. 1 USD.

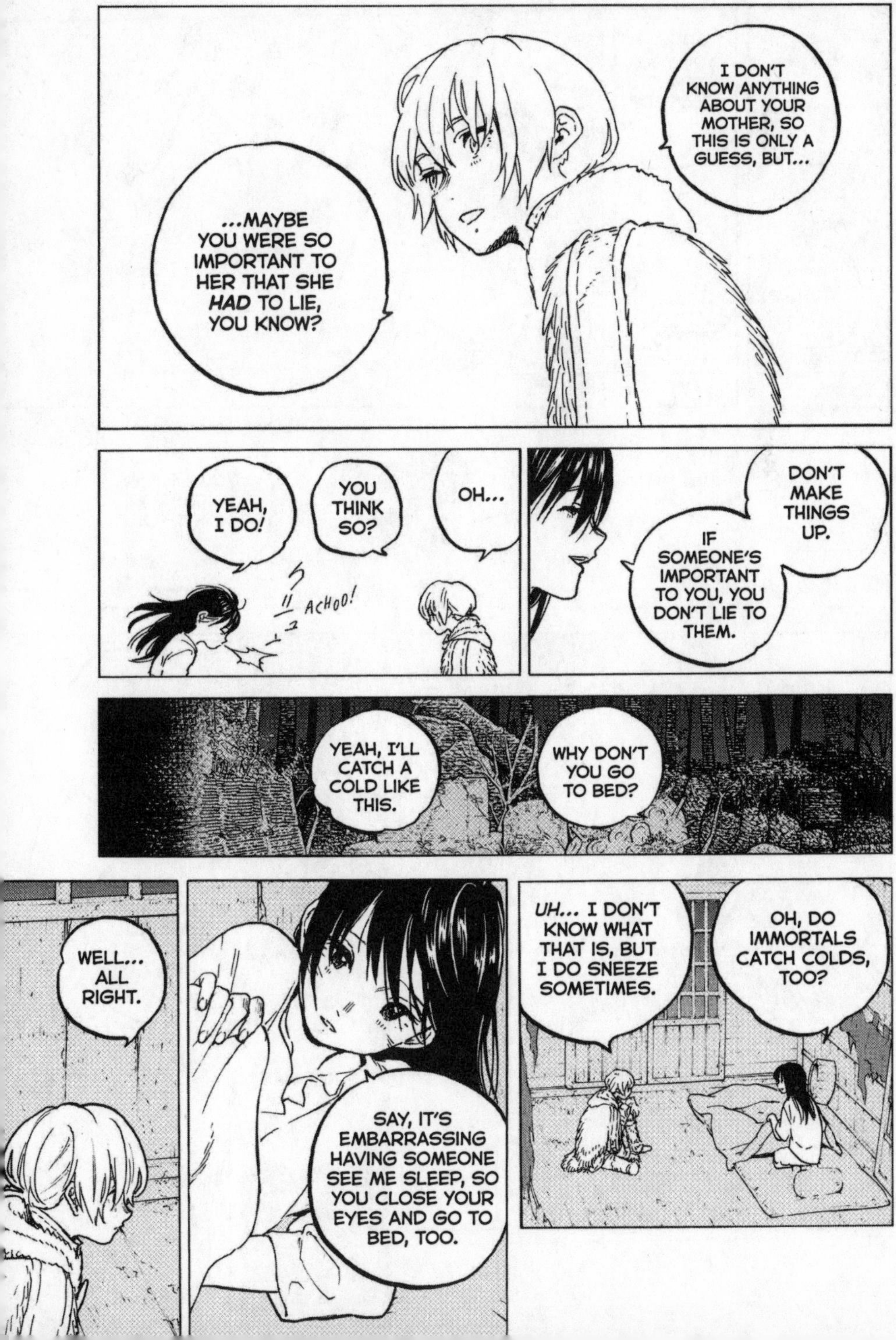
I DON'T KNOW ANYTHING ABOUT YOUR MOTHER, SO THIS IS ONLY A GUESS, BUT...
...MAYBE YOU WERE SO IMPORTANT TO HER THAT SHE *HAD* TO LIE, YOU KNOW?
DON'T MAKE THINGS UP.
IF SOMEONE'S IMPORTANT TO YOU, YOU DON'T LIE TO THEM.
OH...
YOU THINK SO?
YEAH, I DO!
ACHOO!
WHY DON'T YOU GO TO BED?
YEAH, I'LL CATCH A COLD LIKE THIS.
OH, DO IMMORTALS CATCH COLDS, TOO?
*UH...* I DON'T KNOW WHAT THAT IS, BUT I DO SNEEZE SOMETIMES.
SAY, IT'S EMBARRASSING HAVING SOMEONE SEE ME SLEEP, SO YOU CLOSE YOUR EYES AND GO TO BED, TOO.
WELL... ALL RIGHT.

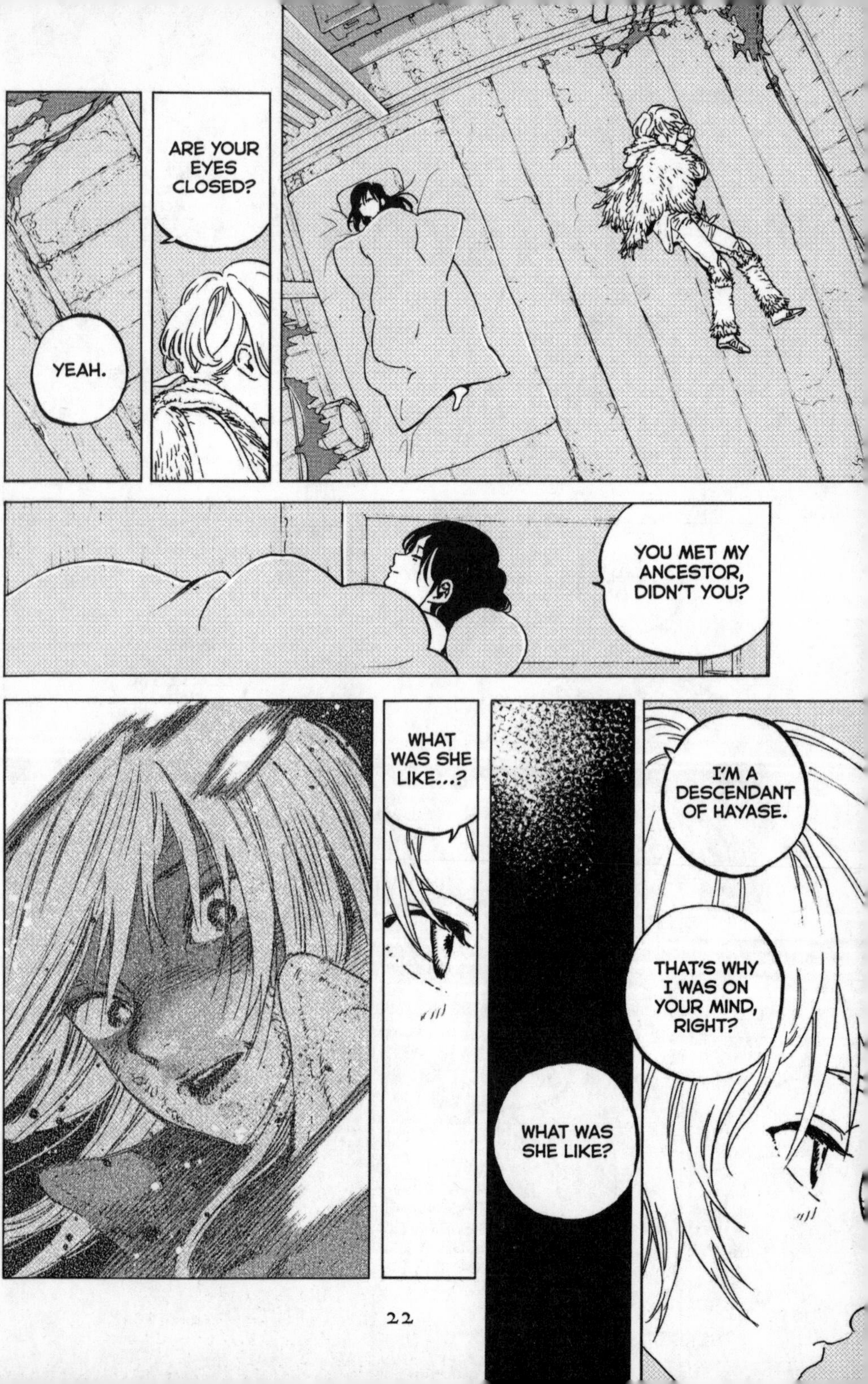
ARE YOUR EYES CLOSED?
YEAH.
YOU MET MY ANCESTOR, DIDN'T YOU?
I'M A DESCENDANT OF HAYASE.
THAT'S WHY I WAS ON YOUR MIND, RIGHT?
WHAT WAS SHE LIKE?
WHAT WAS SHE LIKE...?

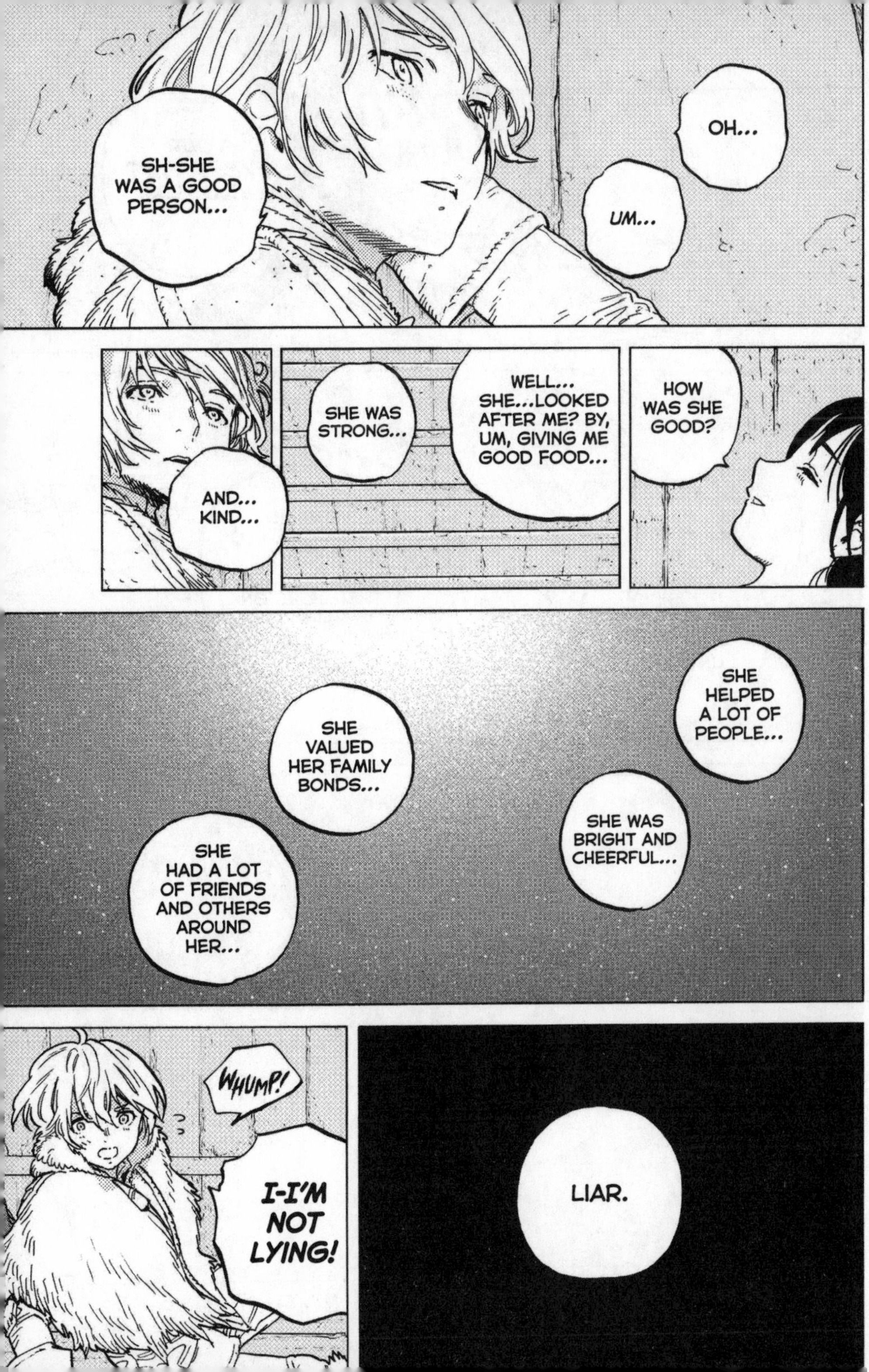
OH...
UM...
SH-SHE WAS A GOOD PERSON...
HOW WAS SHE GOOD?
WELL... SHE...LOOKED AFTER ME? BY, UM, GIVING ME GOOD FOOD...
SHE WAS STRONG...
AND... KIND...
SHE HELPED A LOT OF PEOPLE...
SHE VALUED HER FAMILY BONDS...
SHE WAS BRIGHT AND CHEERFUL...
SHE HAD A LOT OF FRIENDS AND OTHERS AROUND HER...
LIAR.
WHUMP!
I-I'M NOT LYING!

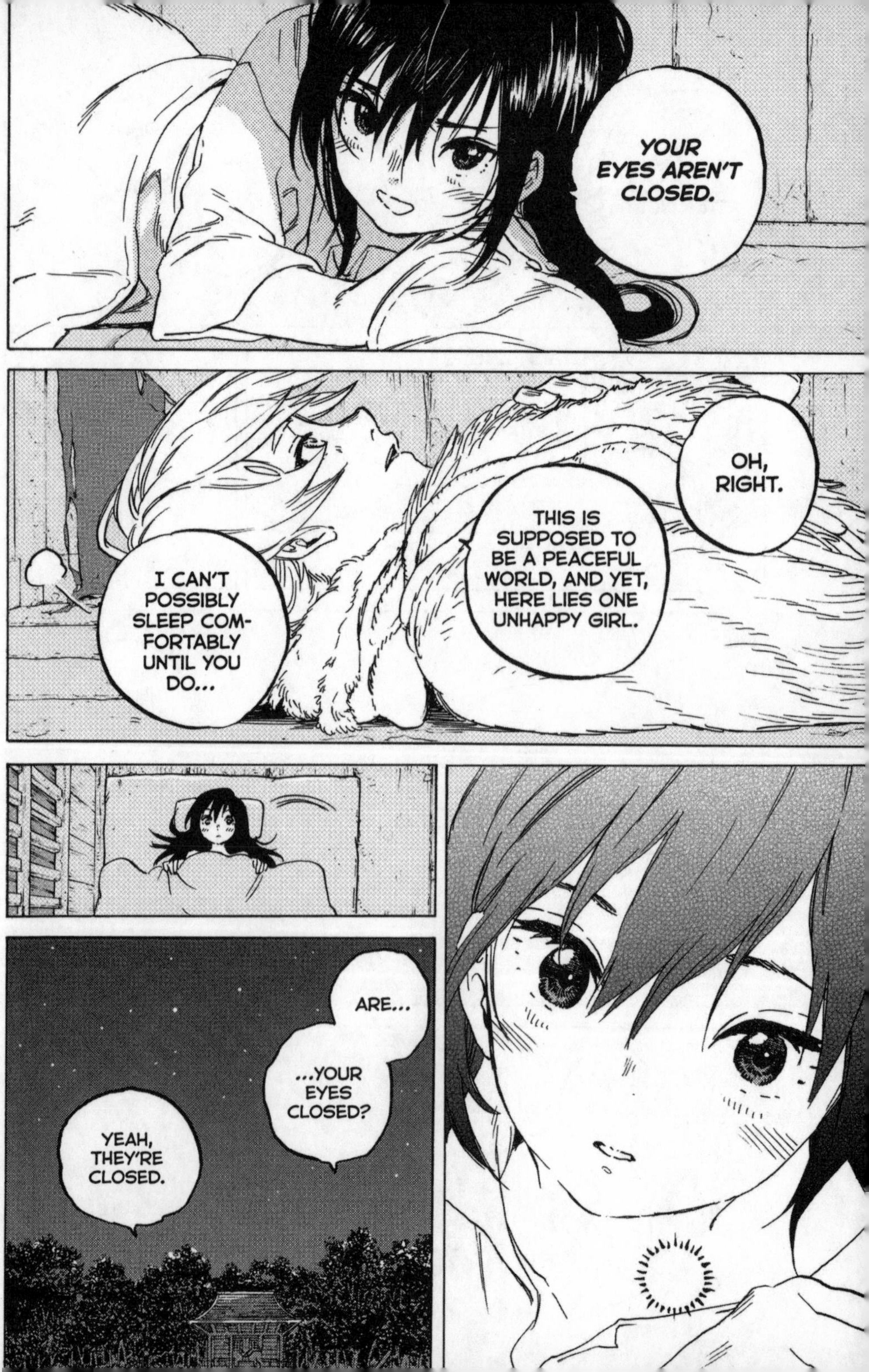
YOUR EYES AREN'T CLOSED.
OH, RIGHT.
THIS IS SUPPOSED TO BE A PEACEFUL WORLD, AND YET, HERE LIES ONE UNHAPPY GIRL.
I CAN'T POSSIBLY SLEEP COMFORTABLY UNTIL YOU DO...
ARE...
...YOUR EYES CLOSED?
YEAH, THEY'RE CLOSED.

TO YOUR

ETERNITY

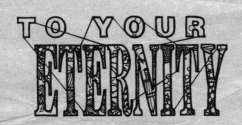

TO YOUR ETERNITY

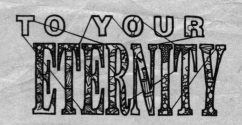

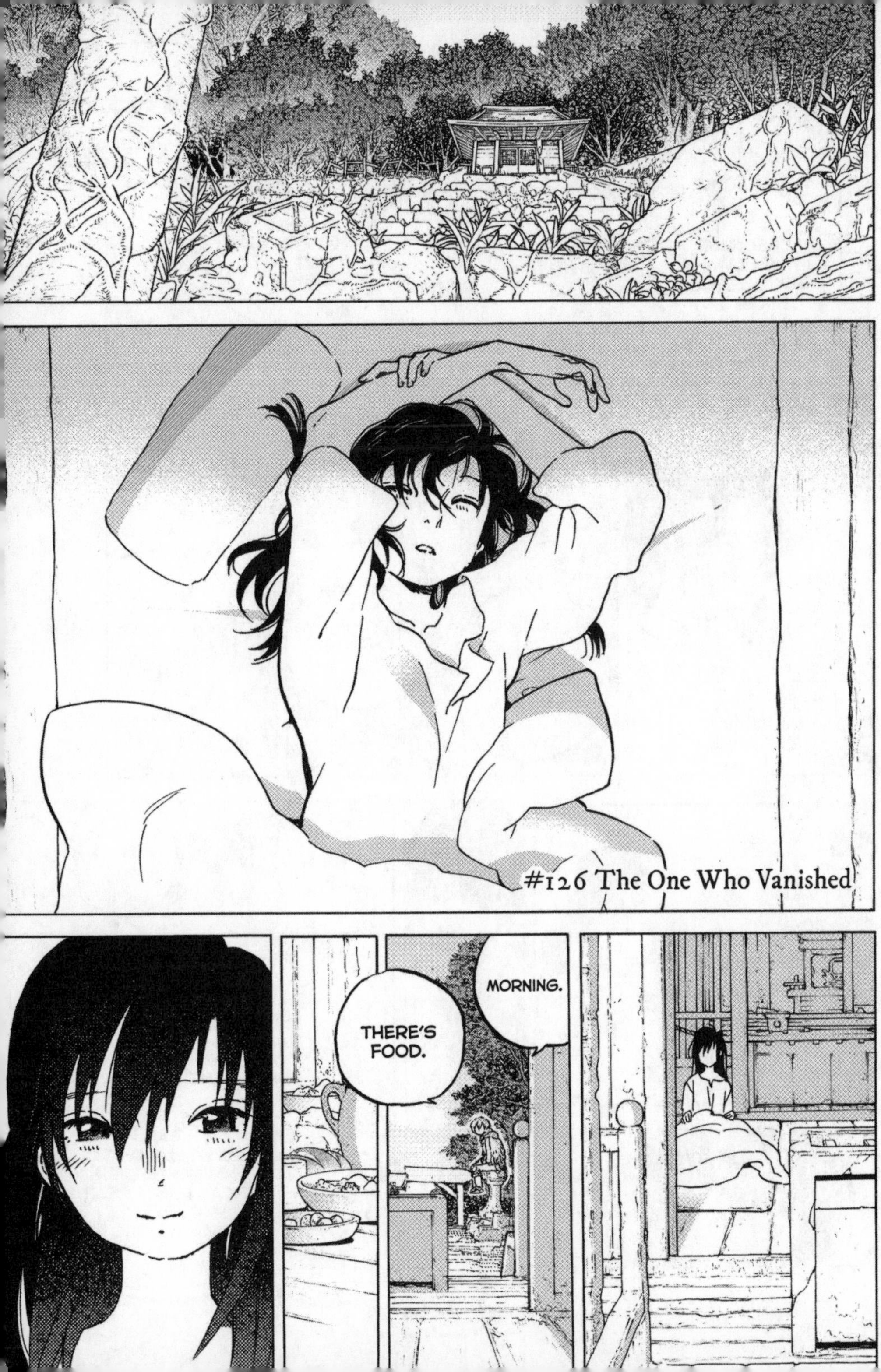
#126 The One Who Vanished
MORNING.
THERE'S FOOD.

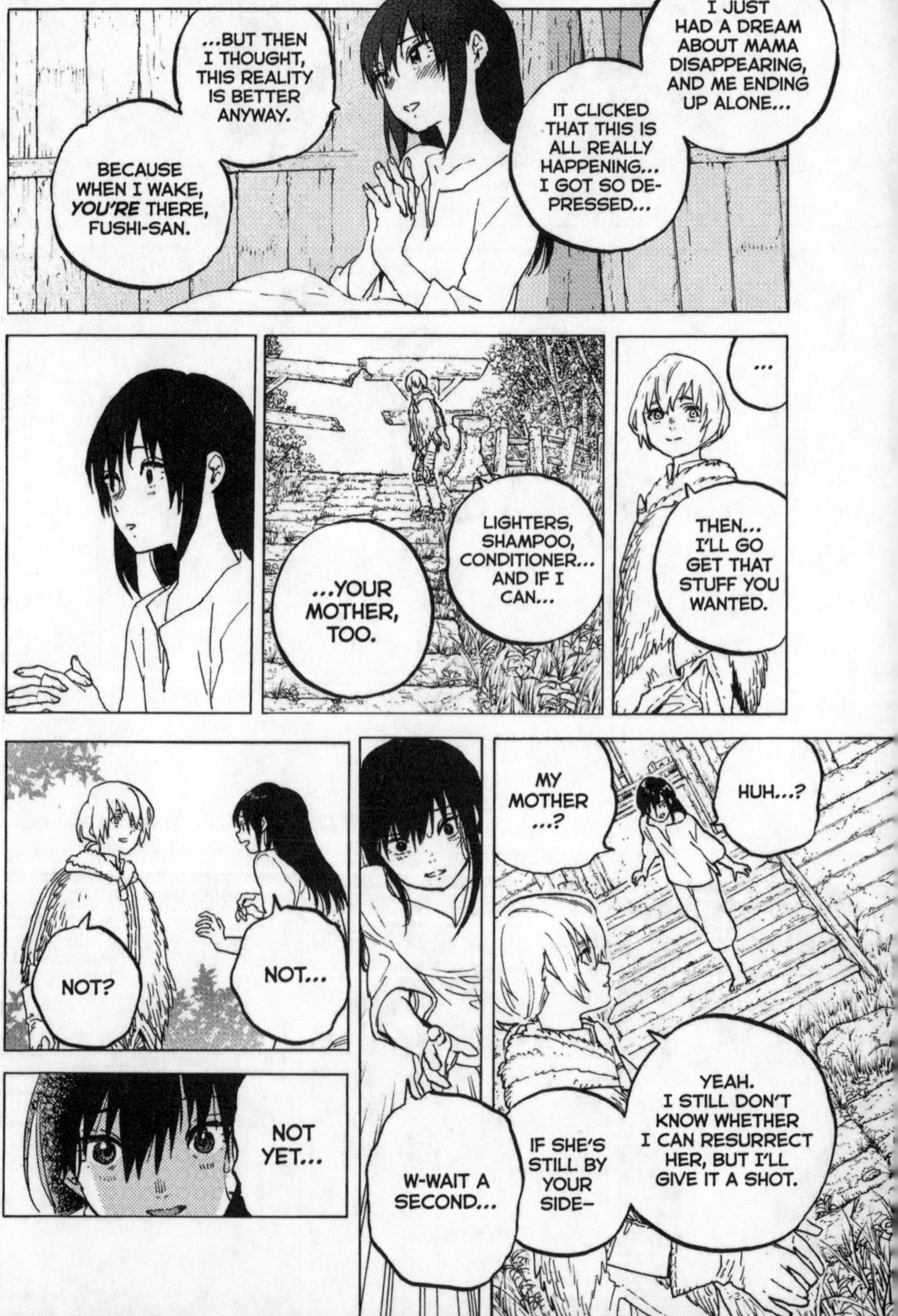
I JUST HAD A DREAM ABOUT MAMA DISAPPEARING, AND ME ENDING UP ALONE...
IT CLICKED THAT THIS IS ALL REALLY HAPPENING... I GOT SO DE-PRESSED...
...BUT THEN I THOUGHT, THIS REALITY IS BETTER ANYWAY.
BECAUSE WHEN I WAKE, *YOU'RE* THERE, FUSHI-SAN.
...
THEN... I'LL GO GET THAT STUFF YOU WANTED.
LIGHTERS, SHAMPOO, CONDITIONER... AND IF I CAN...
...YOUR MOTHER, TOO.
HUH...?
MY MOTHER ...?
YEAH. I STILL DON'T KNOW WHETHER I CAN RESURRECT HER, BUT I'LL GIVE IT A SHOT.
IF SHE'S STILL BY YOUR SIDE–
W-WAIT A SECOND...
NOT...
NOT?
NOT YET...

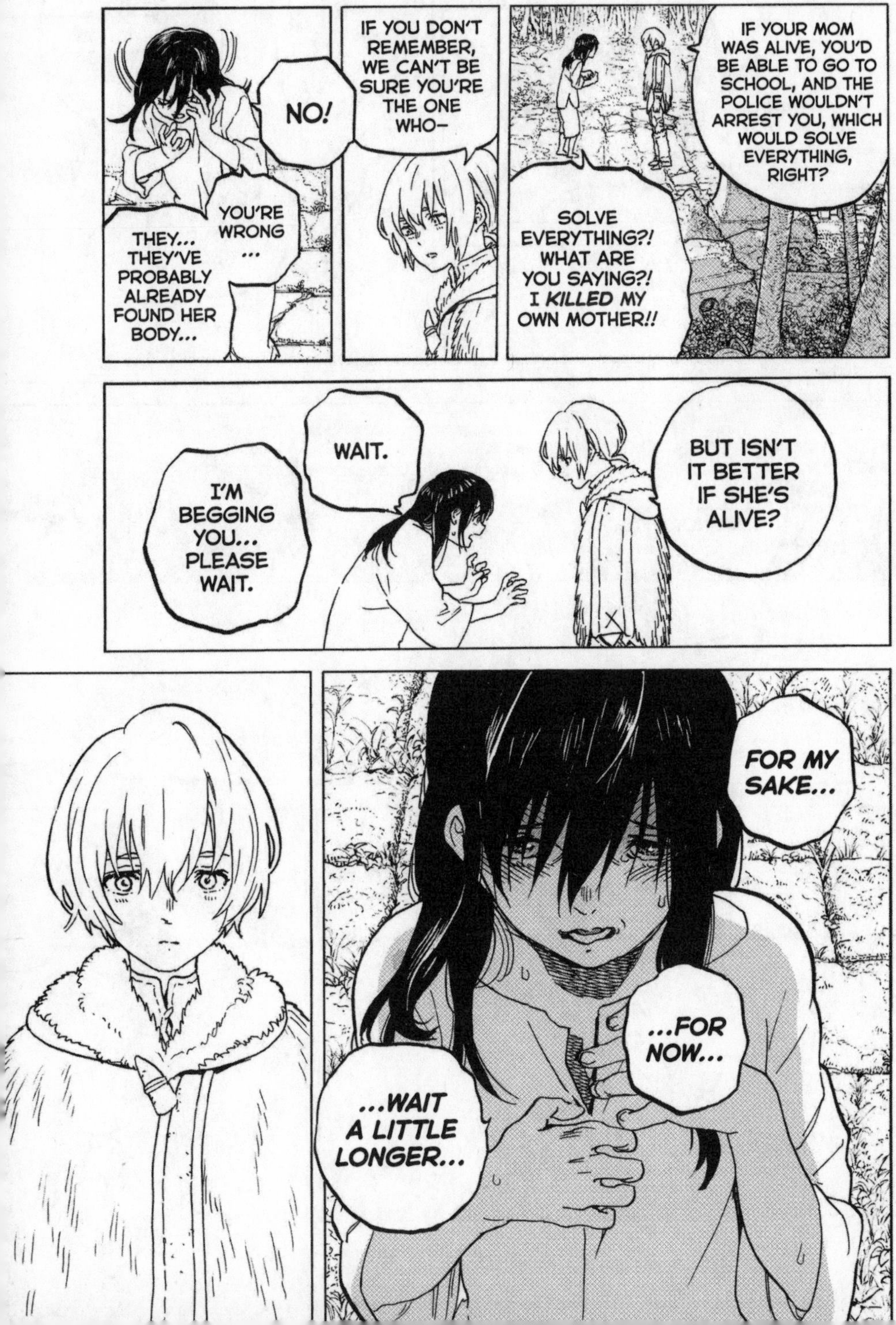
IF YOUR MOM WAS ALIVE, YOU'D BE ABLE TO GO TO SCHOOL, AND THE POLICE WOULDN'T ARREST YOU, WHICH WOULD SOLVE EVERYTHING, RIGHT?
SOLVE EVERYTHING?! WHAT ARE YOU SAYING?! I *KILLED* MY OWN MOTHER!!
IF YOU DON'T REMEMBER, WE CAN'T BE SURE YOU'RE THE ONE WHO–
NO!
YOU'RE WRONG ...
THEY... THEY'VE PROBABLY ALREADY FOUND HER BODY...
BUT ISN'T IT BETTER IF SHE'S ALIVE?
WAIT.
I'M BEGGING YOU... PLEASE WAIT.
*FOR MY SAKE...*
*...FOR NOW...*
*...WAIT A LITTLE LONGER...*

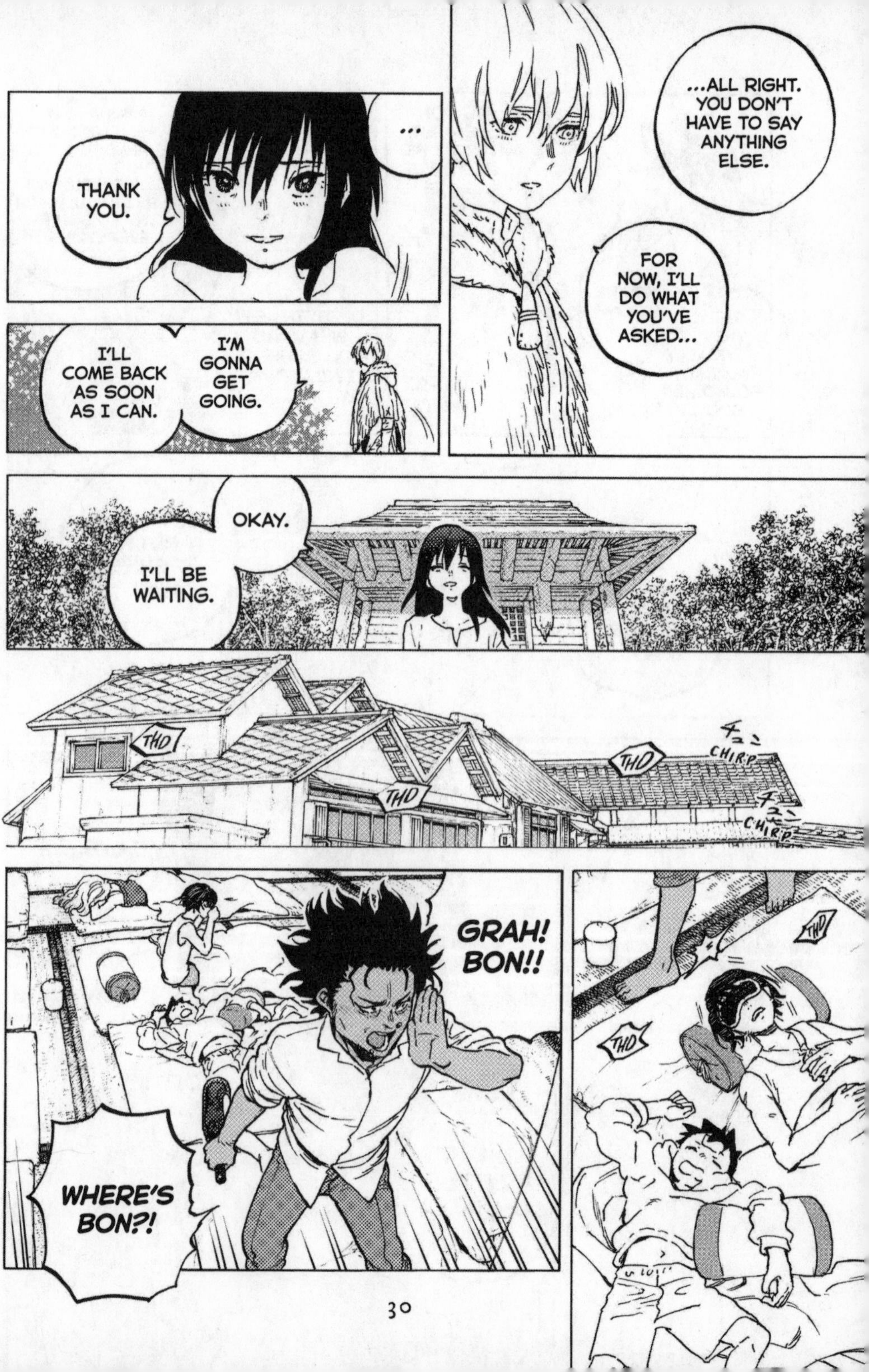
...ALL RIGHT. YOU DON'T HAVE TO SAY ANYTHING ELSE.
FOR NOW, I'LL DO WHAT YOU'VE ASKED...
...
THANK YOU.
I'M GONNA GET GOING.
I'LL COME BACK AS SOON AS I CAN.
OKAY.
I'LL BE WAITING.
CHIRP
CHIRP
THD
THD
THD
THD
THD
GRAH! BON!!
WHERE'S BON?!

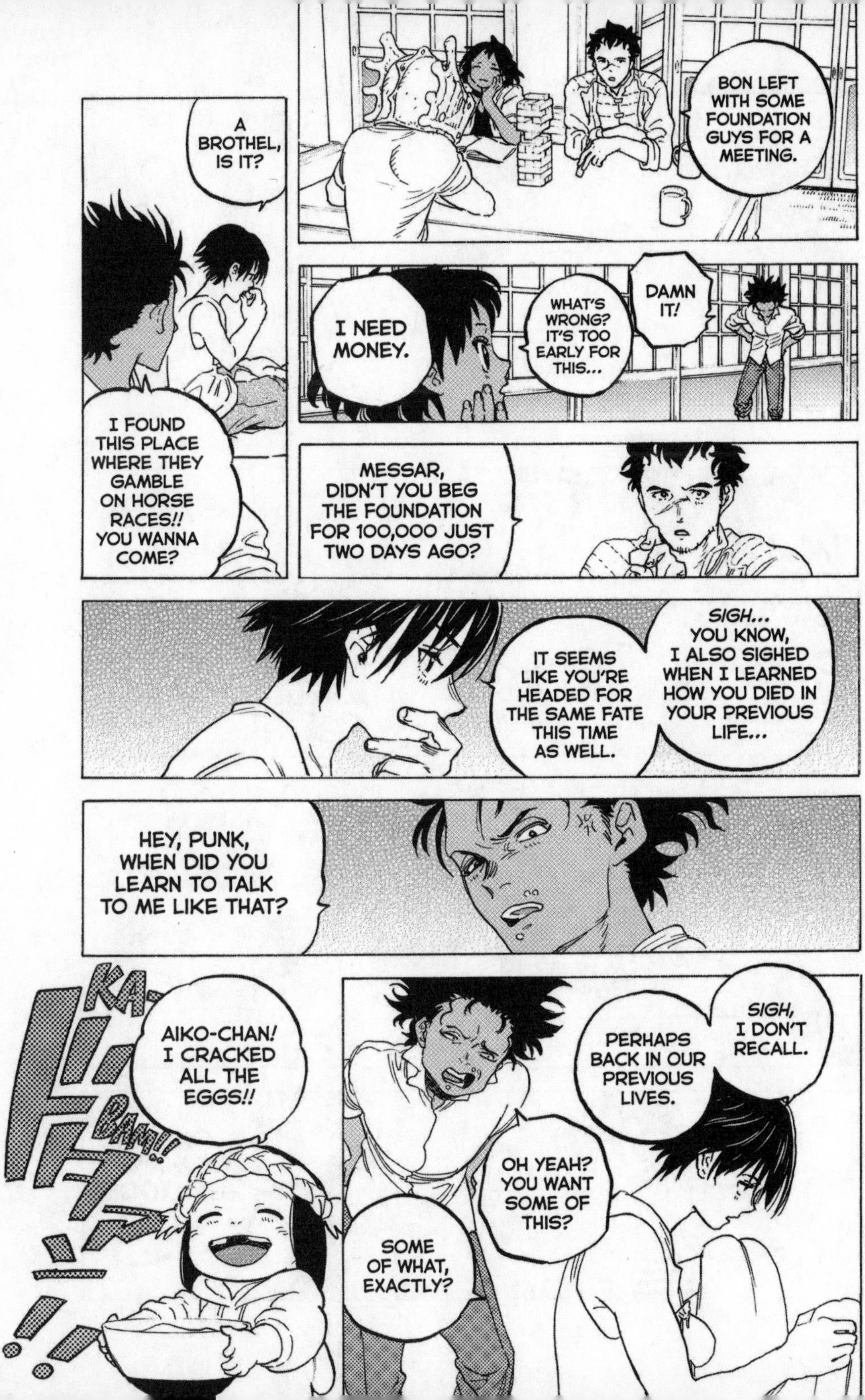

BON LEFT WITH SOME FOUNDATION GUYS FOR A MEETING.
DAMN IT!
WHAT'S WRONG? IT'S TOO EARLY FOR THIS...
I NEED MONEY.
MESSAR, DIDN'T YOU BEG THE FOUNDATION FOR 100,000 JUST TWO DAYS AGO?
A BROTHEL, IS IT?
I FOUND THIS PLACE WHERE THEY GAMBLE ON HORSE RACES!! YOU WANNA COME?
SIGH... YOU KNOW, I ALSO SIGHED WHEN I LEARNED HOW YOU DIED IN YOUR PREVIOUS LIFE...
IT SEEMS LIKE YOU'RE HEADED FOR THE SAME FATE THIS TIME AS WELL.
HEY, PUNK, WHEN DID YOU LEARN TO TALK TO ME LIKE THAT?
SIGH, I DON'T RECALL.
PERHAPS BACK IN OUR PREVIOUS LIVES.
OH YEAH? YOU WANT SOME OF THIS?
SOME OF WHAT, EXACTLY?
KA-
BAM!!
AIKO-CHAN! I CRACKED ALL THE EGGS!!

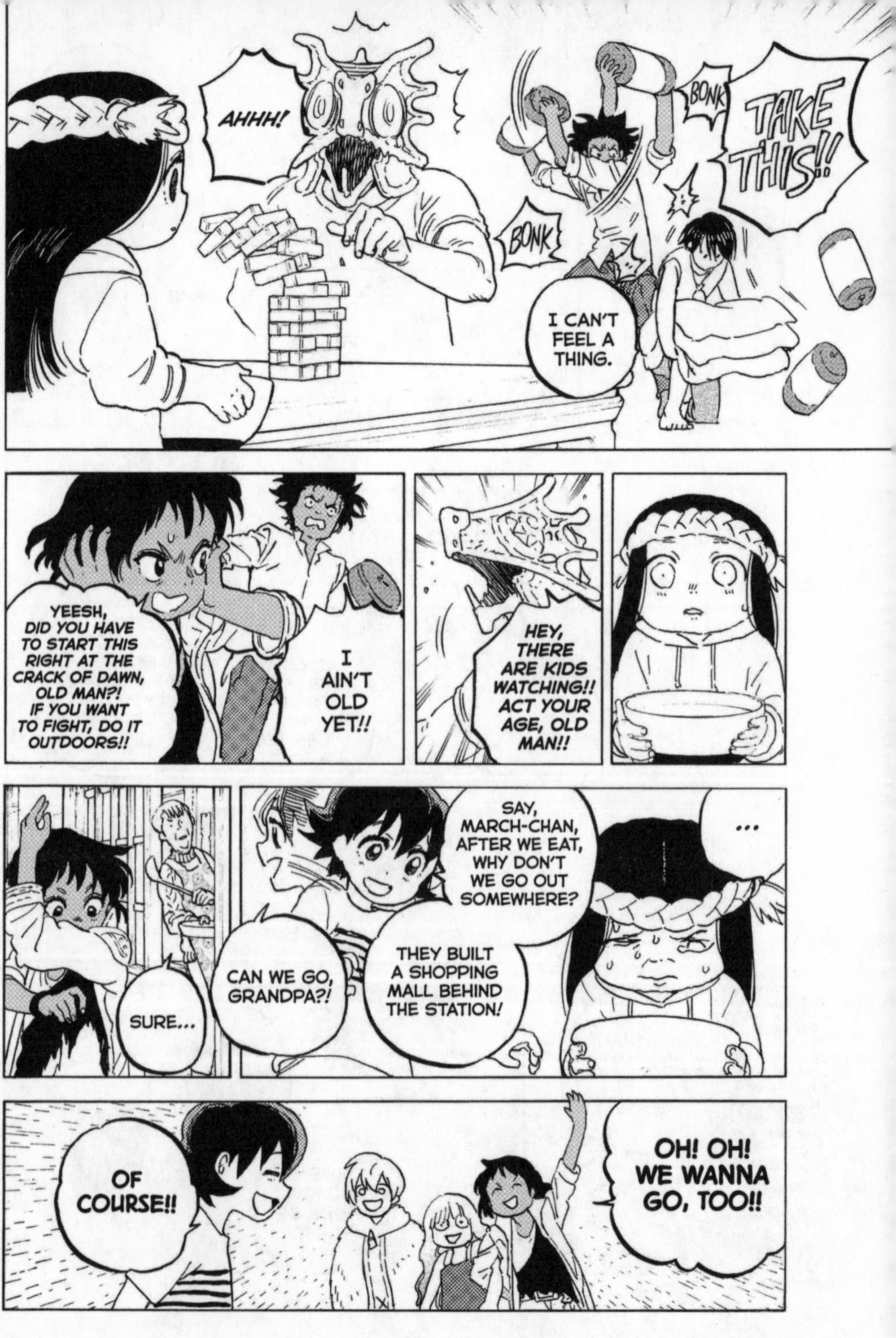
TAKE THIS!!
BONK
AHHH!
BONK
I CAN'T FEEL A THING.
HEY, THERE ARE KIDS WATCHING!! ACT YOUR AGE, OLD MAN!!
YEESH, DID YOU HAVE TO START THIS RIGHT AT THE CRACK OF DAWN, OLD MAN?! IF YOU WANT TO FIGHT, DO IT OUTDOORS!!
I AIN'T OLD YET!!
...
SAY, MARCH-CHAN, AFTER WE EAT, WHY DON'T WE GO OUT SOMEWHERE?
THEY BUILT A SHOPPING MALL BEHIND THE STATION!
CAN WE GO, GRANDPA?!
SURE...
OH! OH! WE WANNA GO, TOO!!
OF COURSE!!

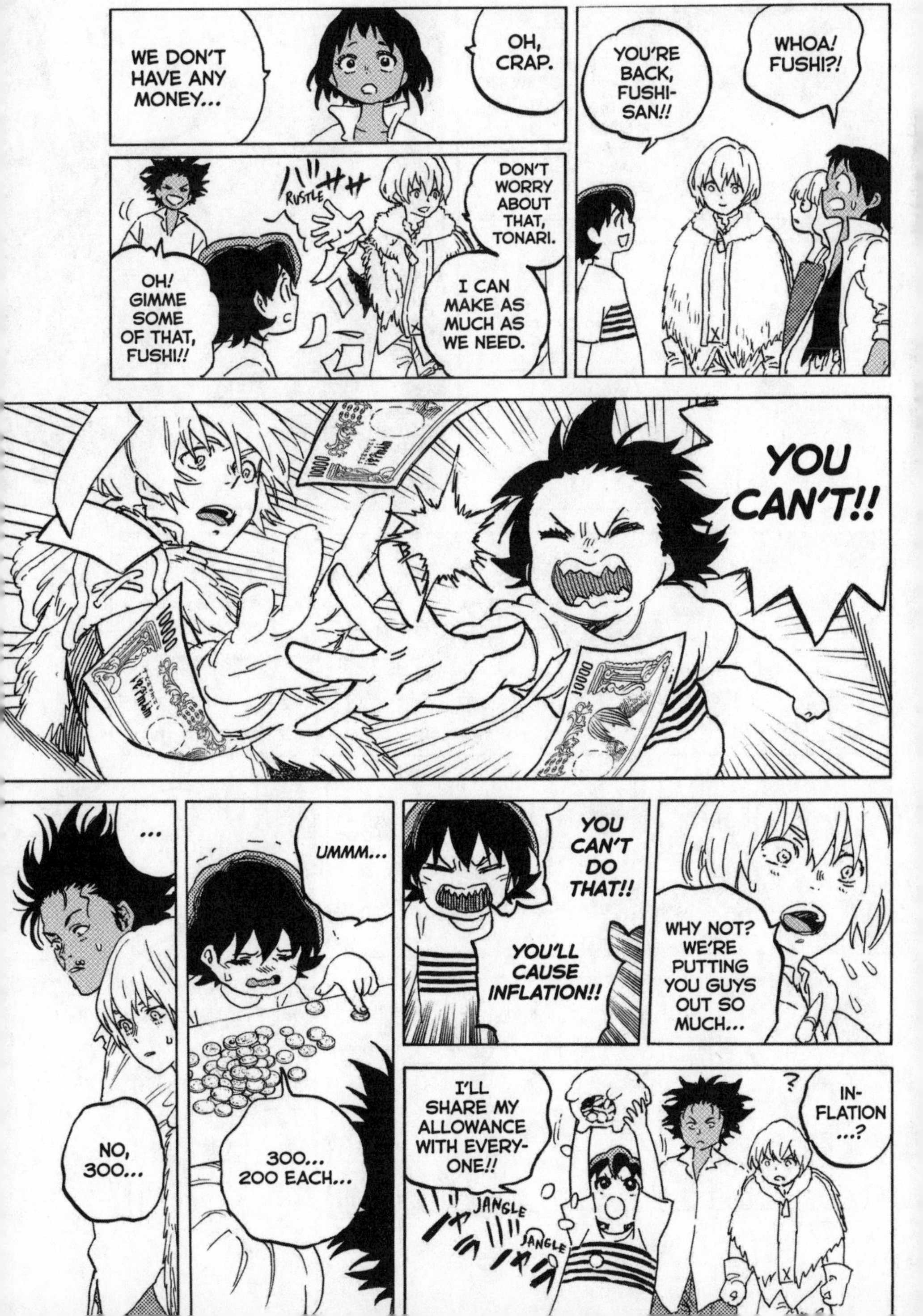
WHOA! FUSHI?!
YOU'RE BACK, FUSHI-SAN!!
OH, CRAP.
WE DON'T HAVE ANY MONEY...
DON'T WORRY ABOUT THAT, TONARI.
I CAN MAKE AS MUCH AS WE NEED.
RUSTLE
OH! GIMME SOME OF THAT, FUSHI!!
YOU CAN'T!!
WHY NOT? WE'RE PUTTING YOU GUYS OUT SO MUCH...
YOU CAN'T DO THAT!!
YOU'LL CAUSE INFLATION!!
IN-FLATION ...?
I'LL SHARE MY ALLOWANCE WITH EVERY-ONE!!
JANGLE
JANGLE
UMMM...
300... 200 EACH...
...
NO, 300...

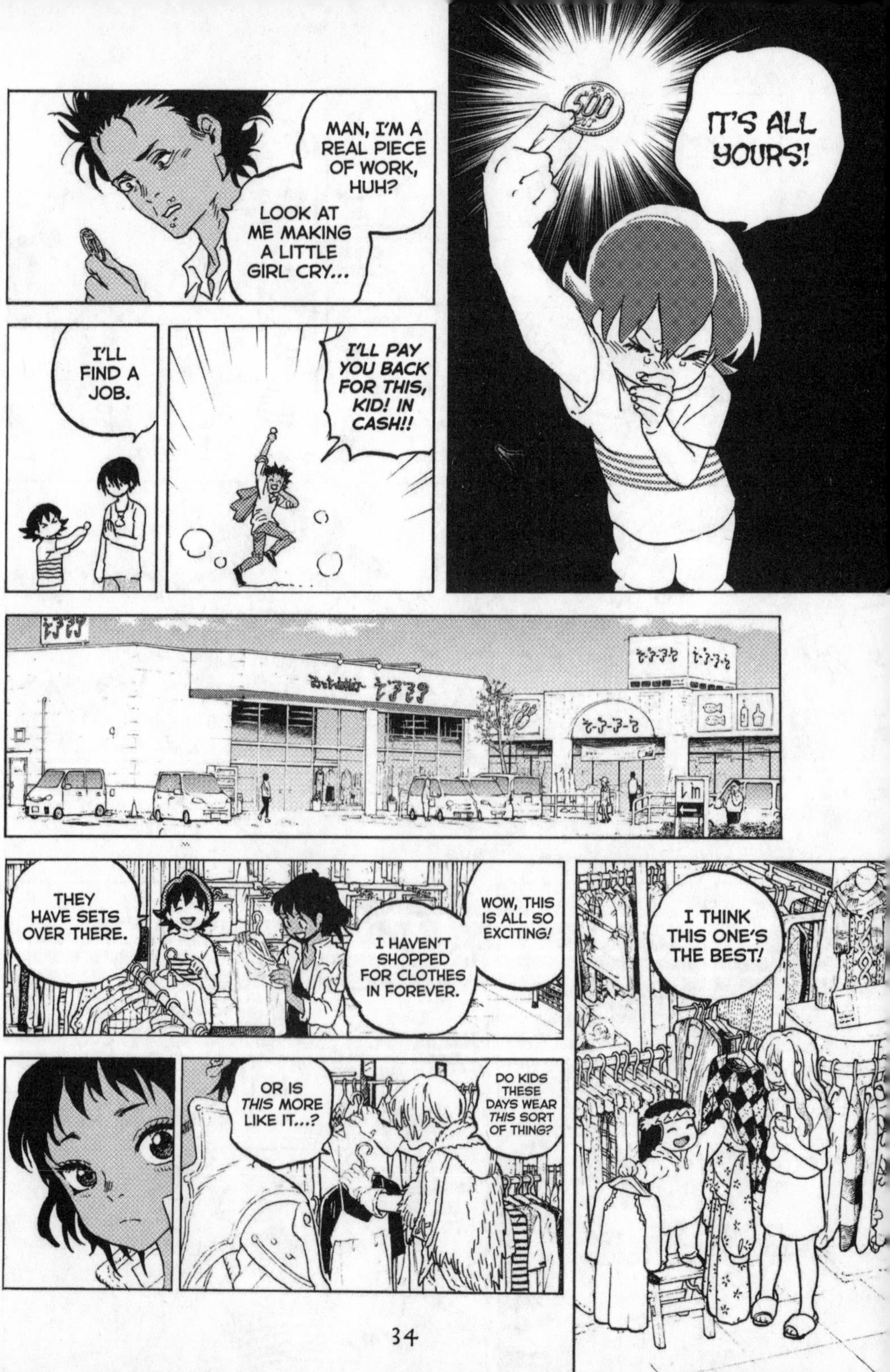
IT'S ALL YOURS!
MAN, I'M A REAL PIECE OF WORK, HUH?
LOOK AT ME MAKING A LITTLE GIRL CRY...
I'LL PAY YOU BACK FOR THIS, KID! IN CASH!!
I'LL FIND A JOB.
I THINK THIS ONE'S THE BEST!
WOW, THIS IS ALL SO EXCITING!
I HAVEN'T SHOPPED FOR CLOTHES IN FOREVER.
THEY HAVE SETS OVER THERE.
DO KIDS THESE DAYS WEAR *THIS* SORT OF THING?
OR IS *THIS* MORE LIKE IT...?

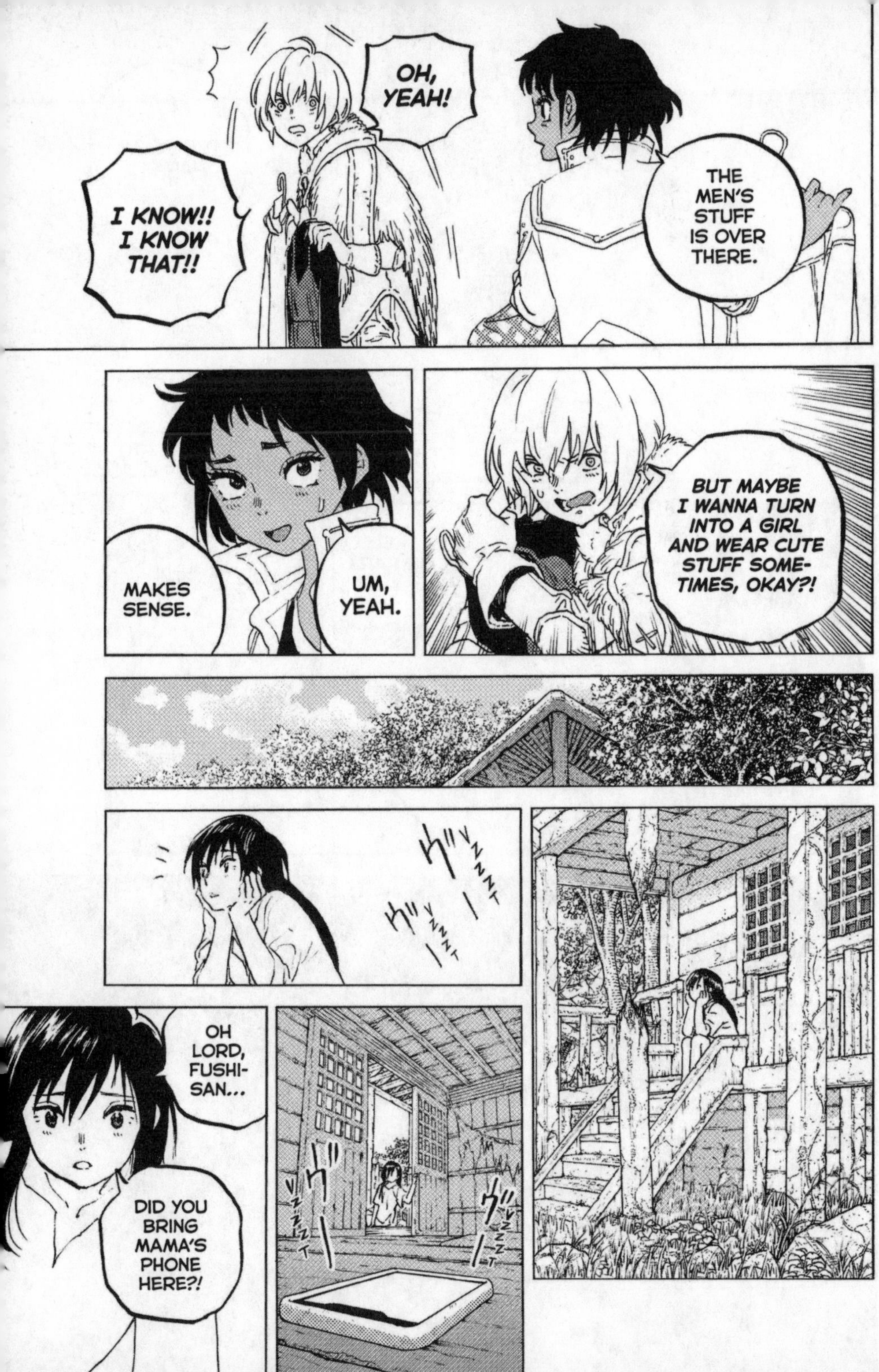
THE MEN'S STUFF IS OVER THERE.
OH, YEAH!
I KNOW!! I KNOW THAT!!
BUT MAYBE I WANNA TURN INTO A GIRL AND WEAR CUTE STUFF SOME-TIMES, OKAY?!
UM, YEAH.
MAKES SENSE.
VZZZT
VZZZT
VZZZT
VZZZT
OH LORD, FUSHI-SAN...
DID YOU BRING MAMA'S PHONE HERE?!

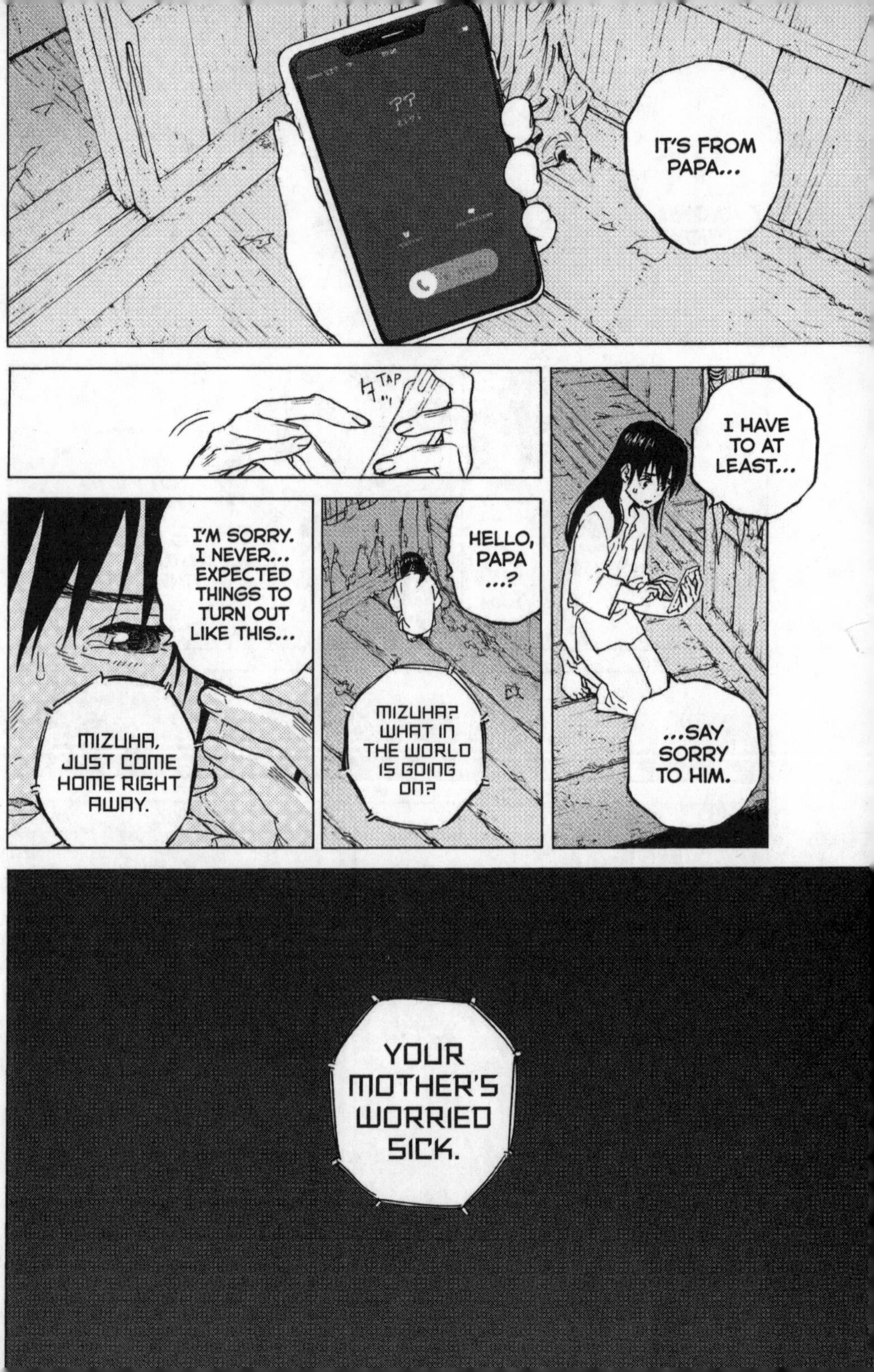
IT'S FROM PAPA...
I HAVE TO AT LEAST...
...SAY SORRY TO HIM.
TAP
HELLO, PAPA ...?
MIZUHA? WHAT IN THE WORLD IS GOING ON?
I'M SORRY. I NEVER... EXPECTED THINGS TO TURN OUT LIKE THIS...
MIZUHA, JUST COME HOME RIGHT AWAY.
YOUR MOTHER'S WORRIED SICK.

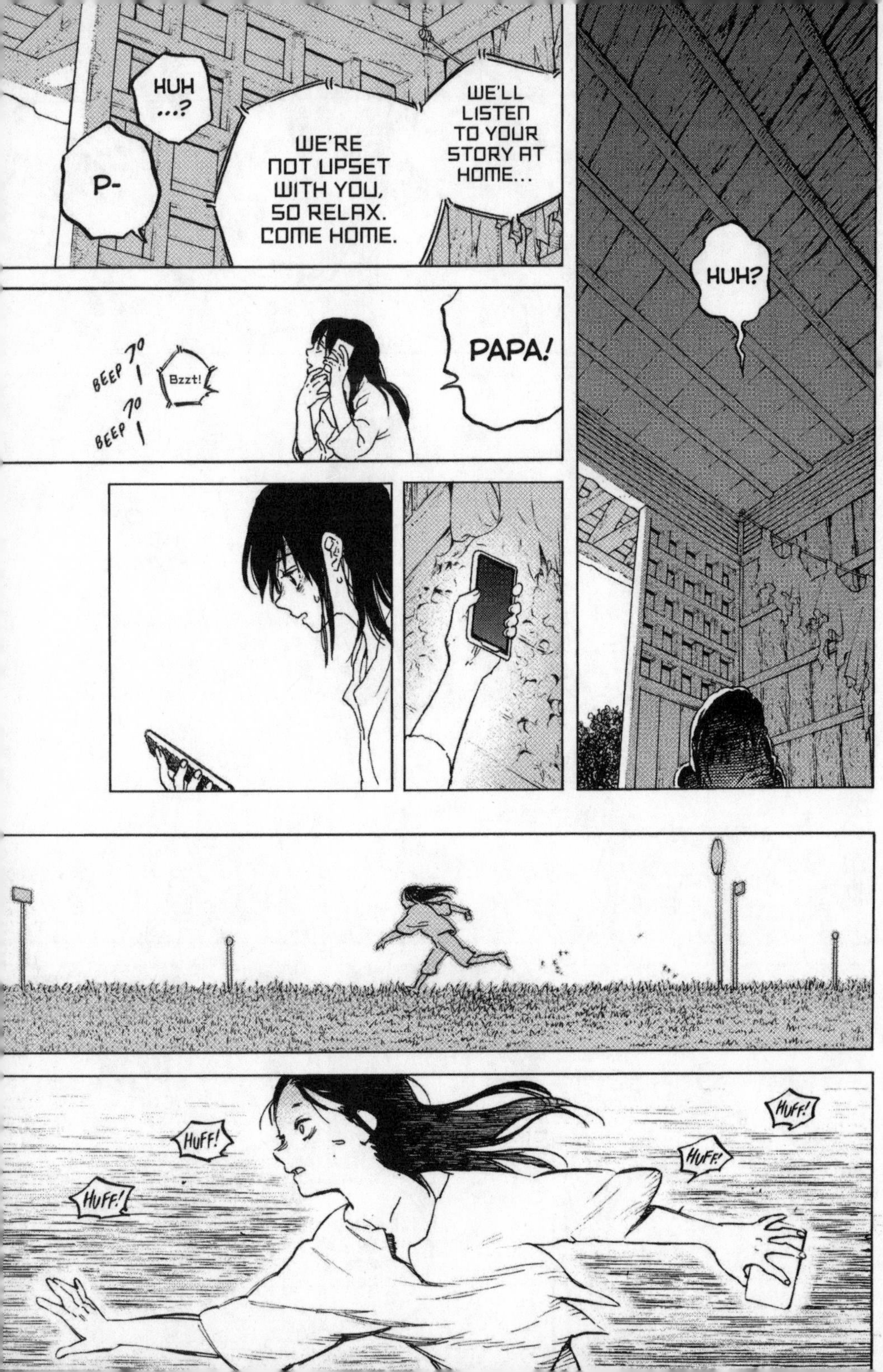
HUH?
WE'LL LISTEN TO YOUR STORY AT HOME...
WE'RE NOT UPSET WITH YOU, SO RELAX. COME HOME.
HUH ...?
P-
PAPA!
Bzzt!
BEEP
BEEP
HUFF!
HUFF!
HUFF!
HUFF!

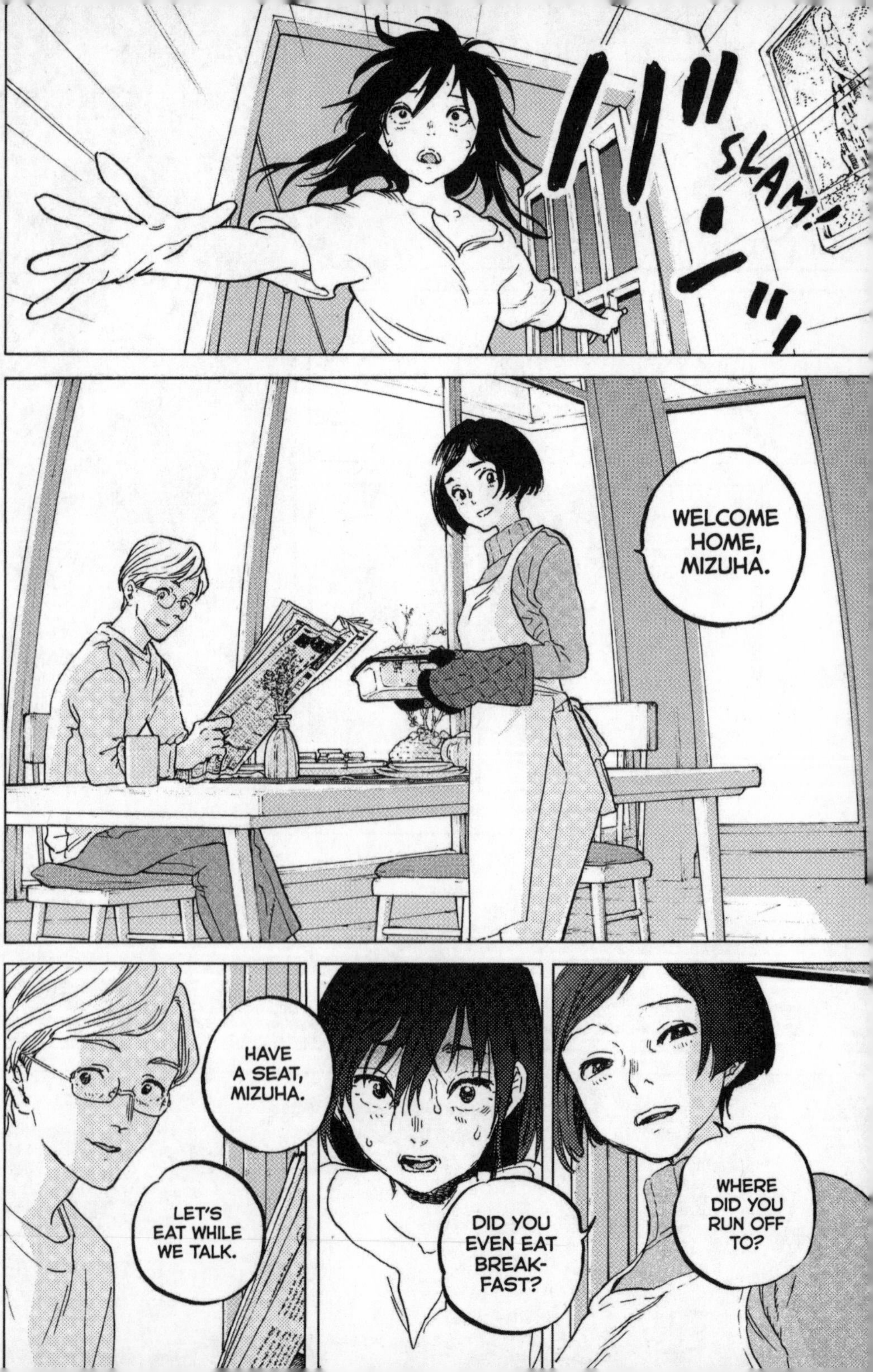
SLAM!!
WELCOME HOME, MIZUHA.
WHERE DID YOU RUN OFF TO?
DID YOU EVEN EAT BREAK-FAST?
HAVE A SEAT, MIZUHA.
LET'S EAT WHILE WE TALK.

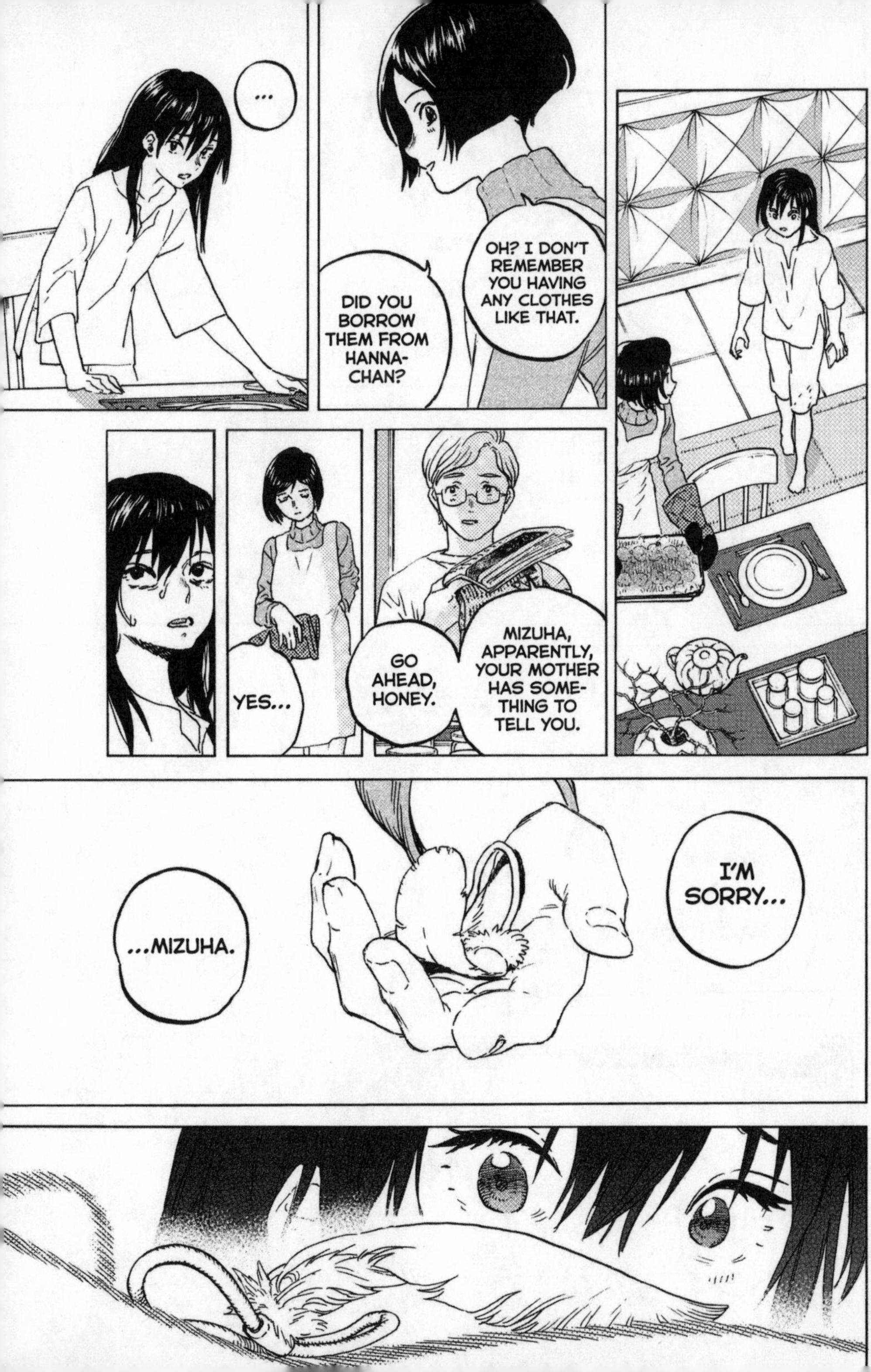
OH? I DON'T REMEMBER YOU HAVING ANY CLOTHES LIKE THAT.
DID YOU BORROW THEM FROM HANNA-CHAN?
...
MIZUHA, APPARENTLY, YOUR MOTHER HAS SOME-THING TO TELL YOU.
GO AHEAD, HONEY.
YES...
I'M SORRY...
...MIZUHA.

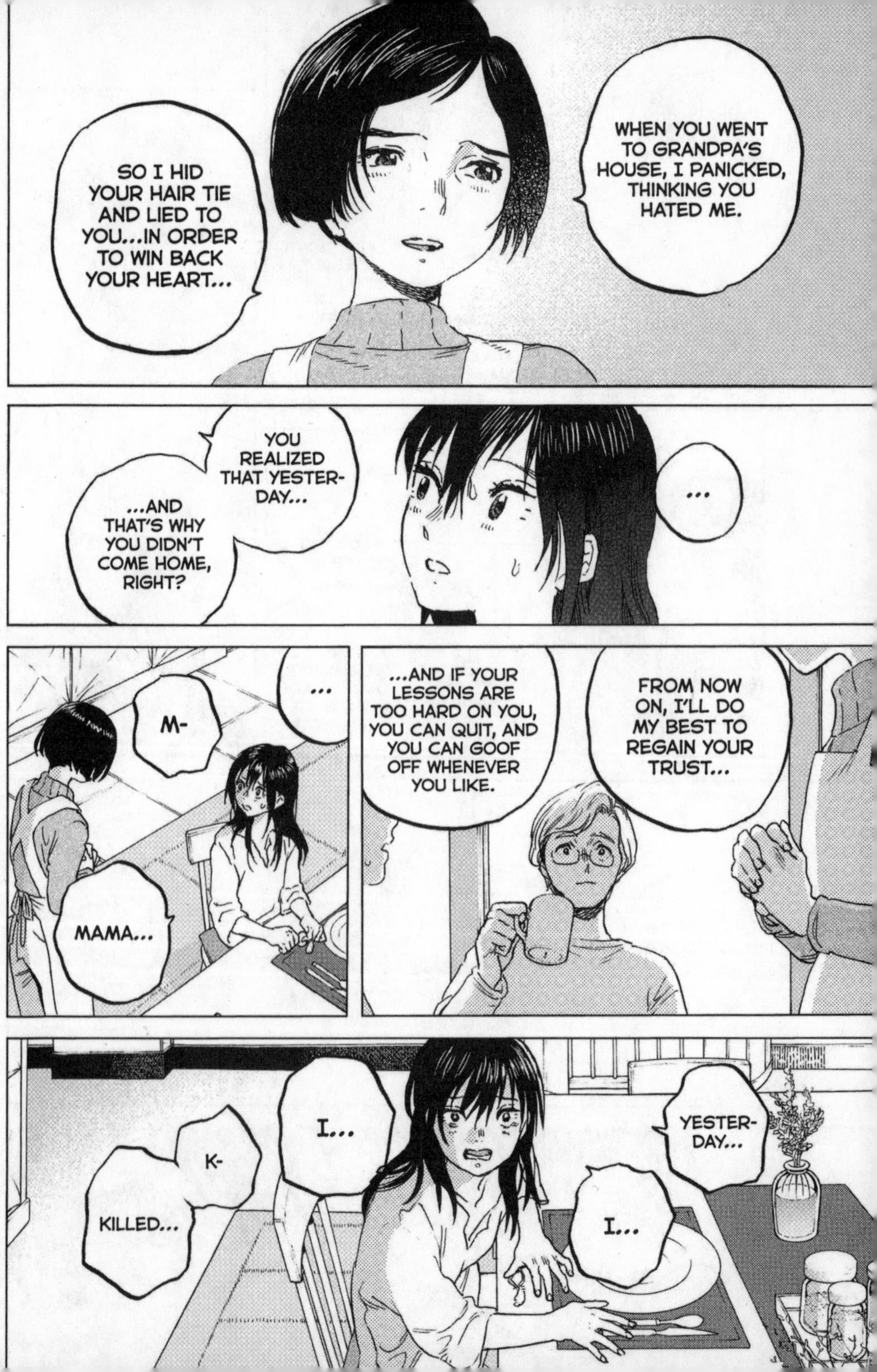
WHEN YOU WENT TO GRANDPA'S HOUSE, I PANICKED, THINKING YOU HATED ME.
SO I HID YOUR HAIR TIE AND LIED TO YOU...IN ORDER TO WIN BACK YOUR HEART...
...
YOU REALIZED THAT YESTER-DAY...
...AND THAT'S WHY YOU DIDN'T COME HOME, RIGHT?
FROM NOW ON, I'LL DO MY BEST TO REGAIN YOUR TRUST...
...AND IF YOUR LESSONS ARE TOO HARD ON YOU, YOU CAN QUIT, AND YOU CAN GOOF OFF WHENEVER YOU LIKE.
...
M-
MAMA...
YESTER-DAY...
I...
I...
K-
KILLED...

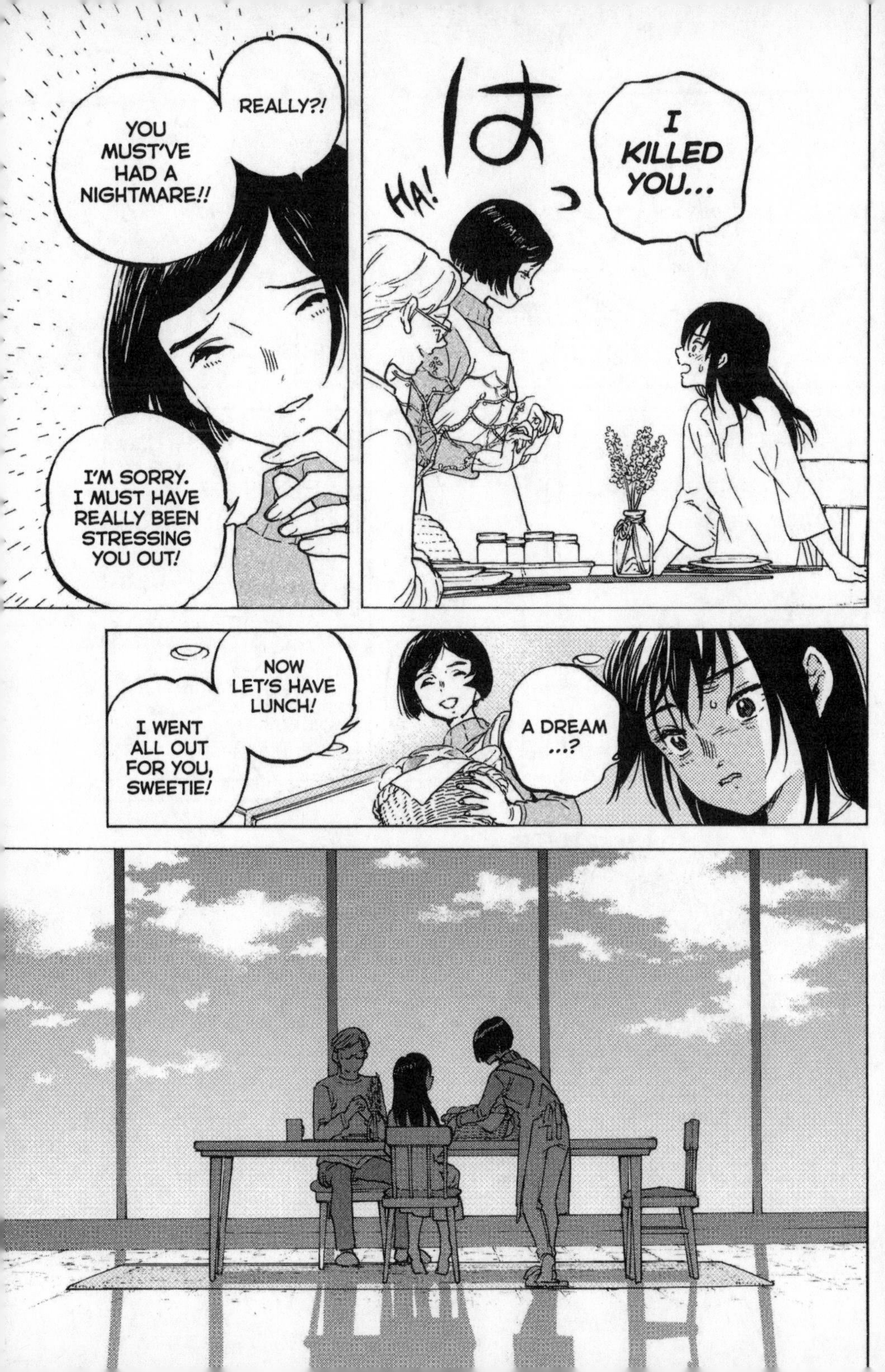
I KILLED YOU...
はっ
HA!
REALLY?!
YOU MUST'VE HAD A NIGHTMARE!!
I'M SORRY. I MUST HAVE REALLY BEEN STRESSING YOU OUT!
A DREAM ...?
NOW LET'S HAVE LUNCH!
I WENT ALL OUT FOR YOU, SWEETIE!

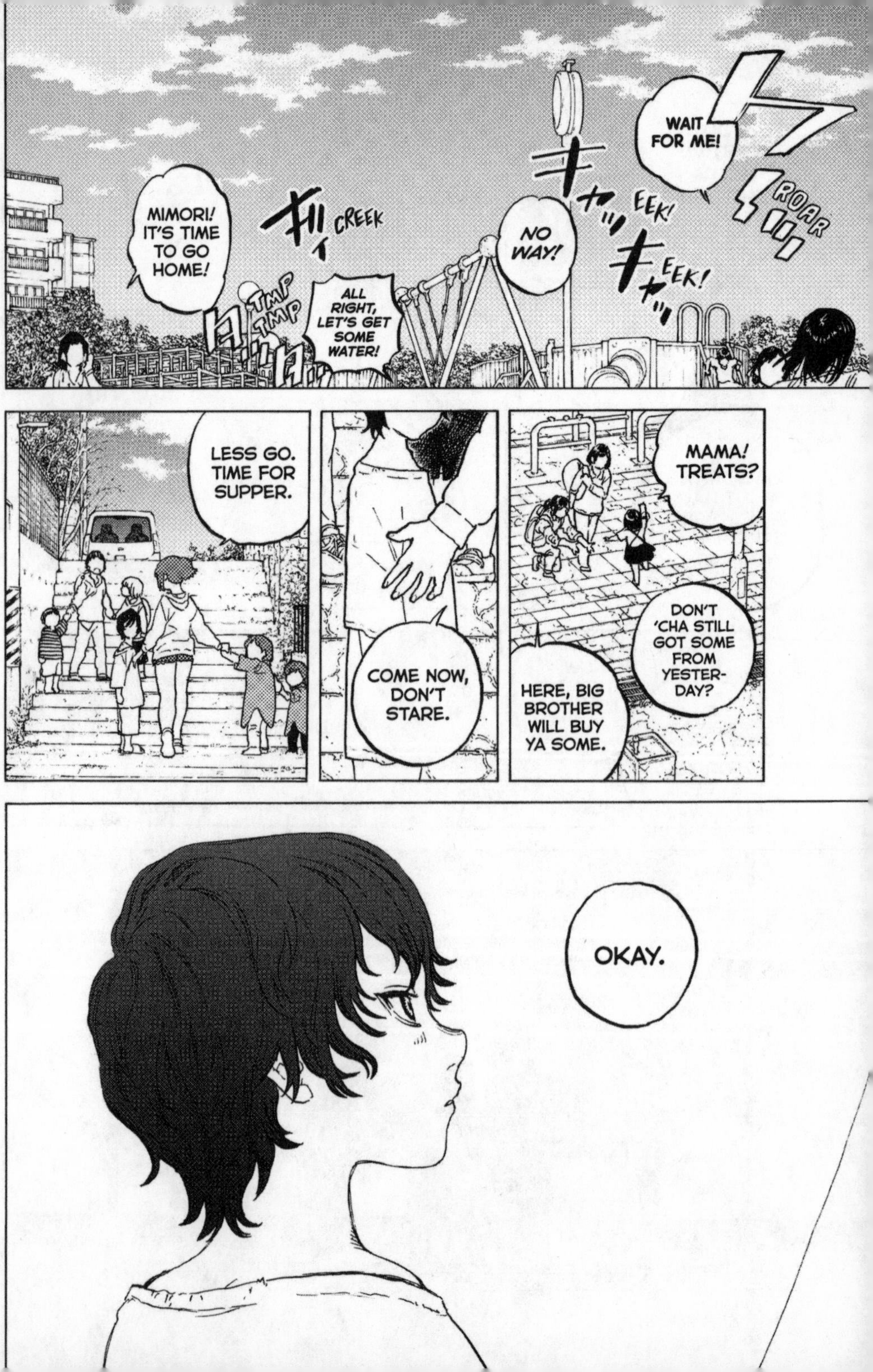
WAIT FOR ME!
ROAR
EEK!
EEK!
NO WAY!
ALL RIGHT, LET'S GET SOME WATER!
CREEK
TMP TMP
MIMORI! IT'S TIME TO GO HOME!
MAMA! TREATS?
DON'T 'CHA STILL GOT SOME FROM YESTER-DAY?
HERE, BIG BROTHER WILL BUY YA SOME.
COME NOW, DON'T STARE.
LESS GO. TIME FOR SUPPER.
OKAY.

TO YOUR ETERNITY

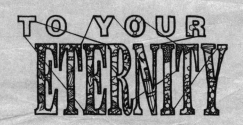

TO YOUR

ETERNITY

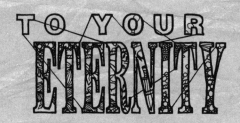

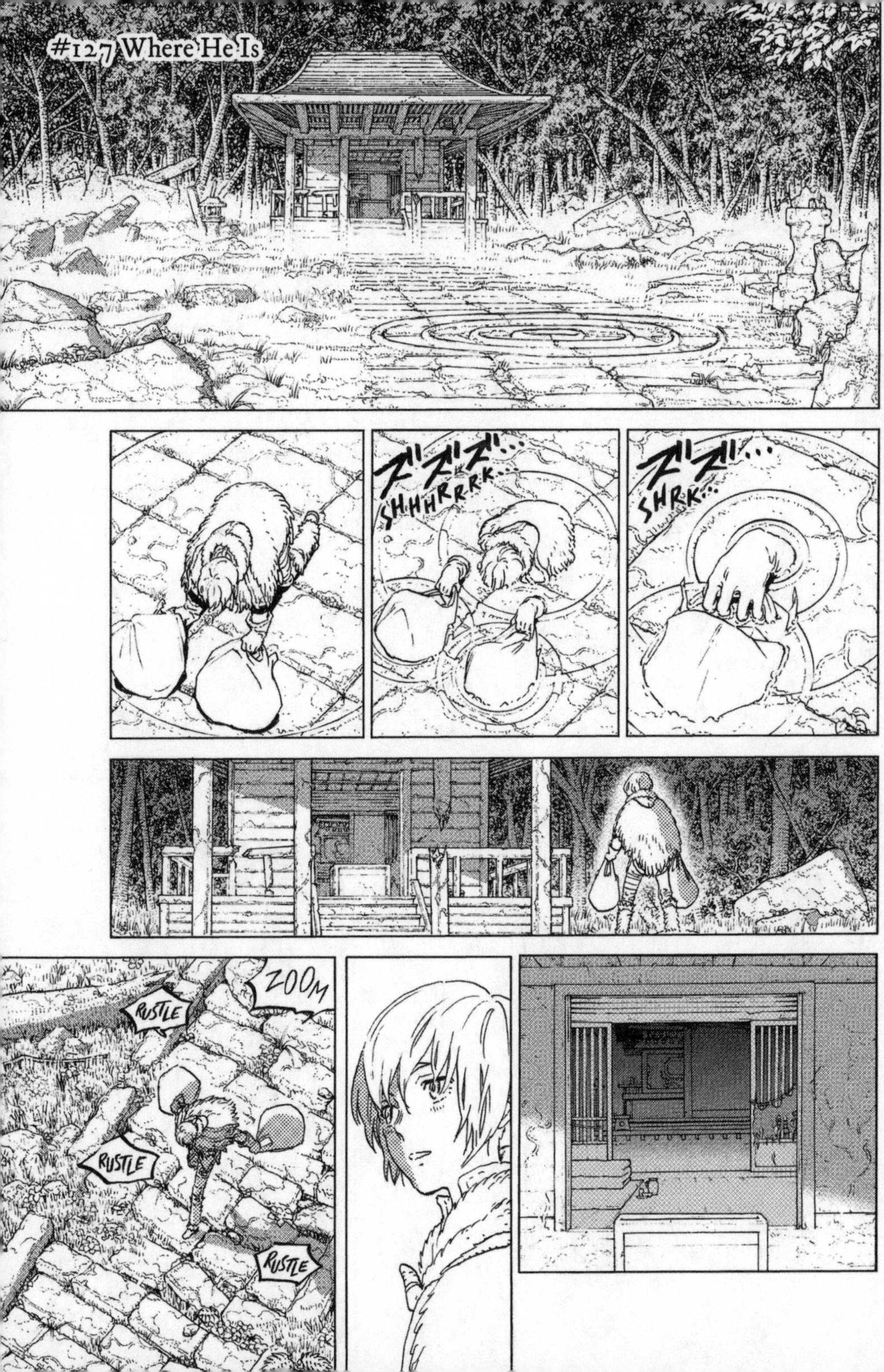
#127 Where He Is
ズズ…
SHRK…
ズズズ…
SHHHRRRK…
ZOOM
RUSTLE
RUSTLE
RUSTLE

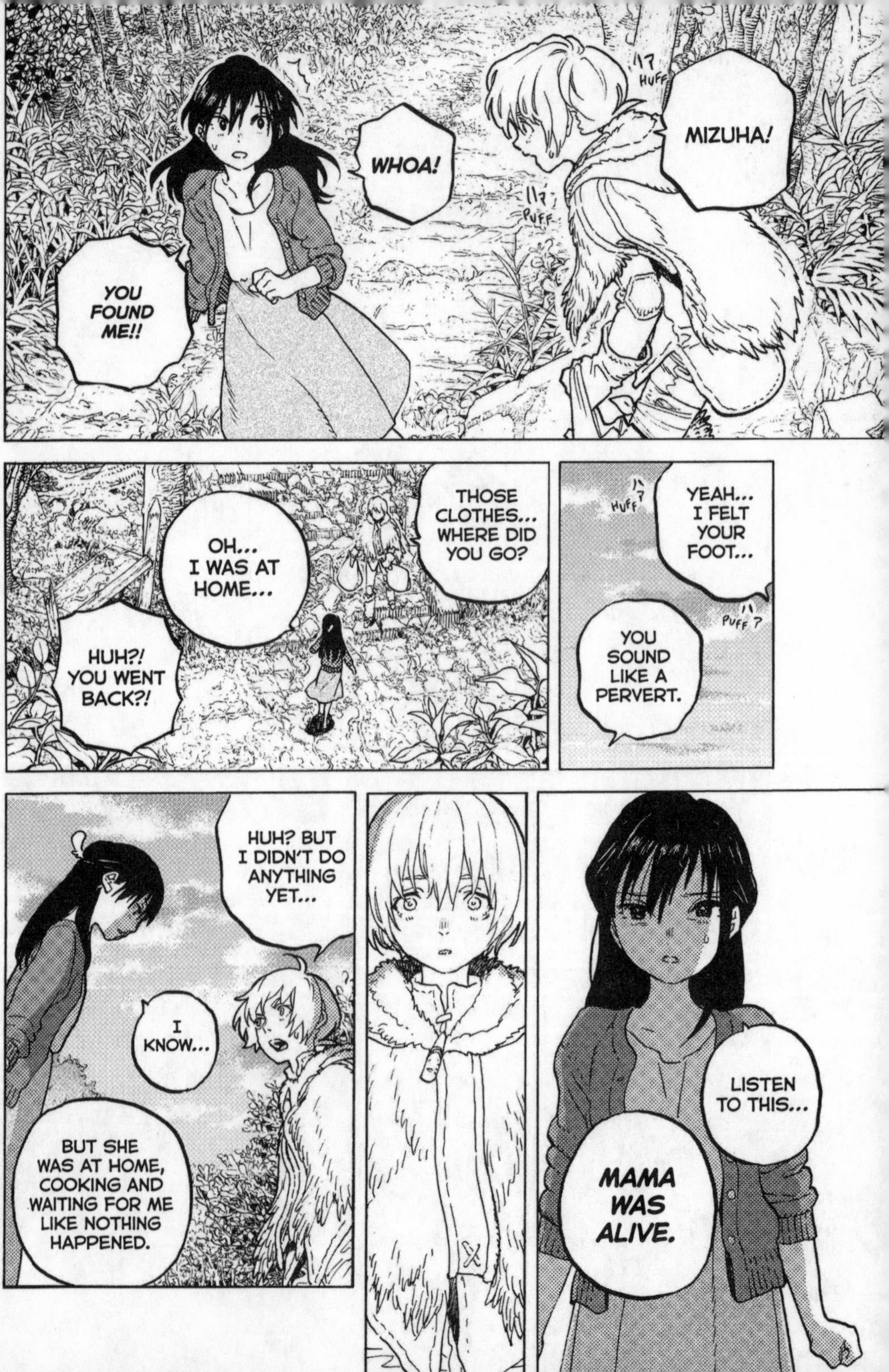
HUFF
MIZUHA!
PUFF
WHOA!
YOU FOUND ME!!
HUFF
YEAH... I FELT YOUR FOOT...
PUFF ?
YOU SOUND LIKE A PERVERT.
THOSE CLOTHES... WHERE DID YOU GO?
OH... I WAS AT HOME...
HUH?! YOU WENT BACK?!
LISTEN TO THIS...
MAMA WAS ALIVE.
HUH? BUT I DIDN'T DO ANYTHING YET...
I KNOW...
BUT SHE WAS AT HOME, COOKING AND WAITING FOR ME LIKE NOTHING HAPPENED.

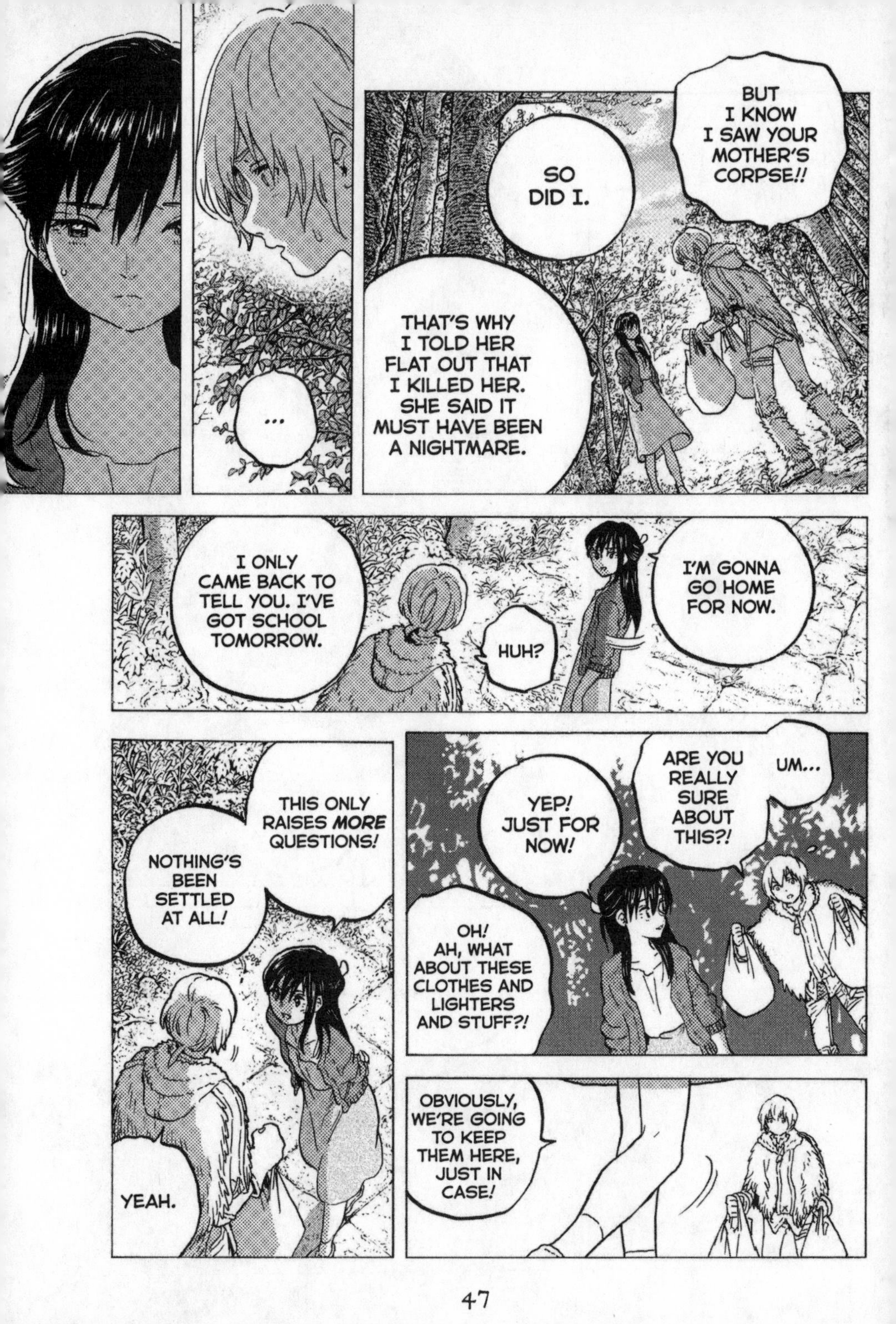
BUT I KNOW I SAW YOUR MOTHER'S CORPSE!!
SO DID I.
THAT'S WHY I TOLD HER FLAT OUT THAT I KILLED HER. SHE SAID IT MUST HAVE BEEN A NIGHTMARE.
...
I'M GONNA GO HOME FOR NOW.
HUH?
I ONLY CAME BACK TO TELL YOU. I'VE GOT SCHOOL TOMORROW.
UM...
ARE YOU REALLY SURE ABOUT THIS?!
YEP! JUST FOR NOW!
OH! AH, WHAT ABOUT THESE CLOTHES AND LIGHTERS AND STUFF?!
OBVIOUSLY, WE'RE GOING TO KEEP THEM HERE, JUST IN CASE!
THIS ONLY RAISES *MORE* QUESTIONS!
NOTHING'S BEEN SETTLED AT ALL!
YEAH.

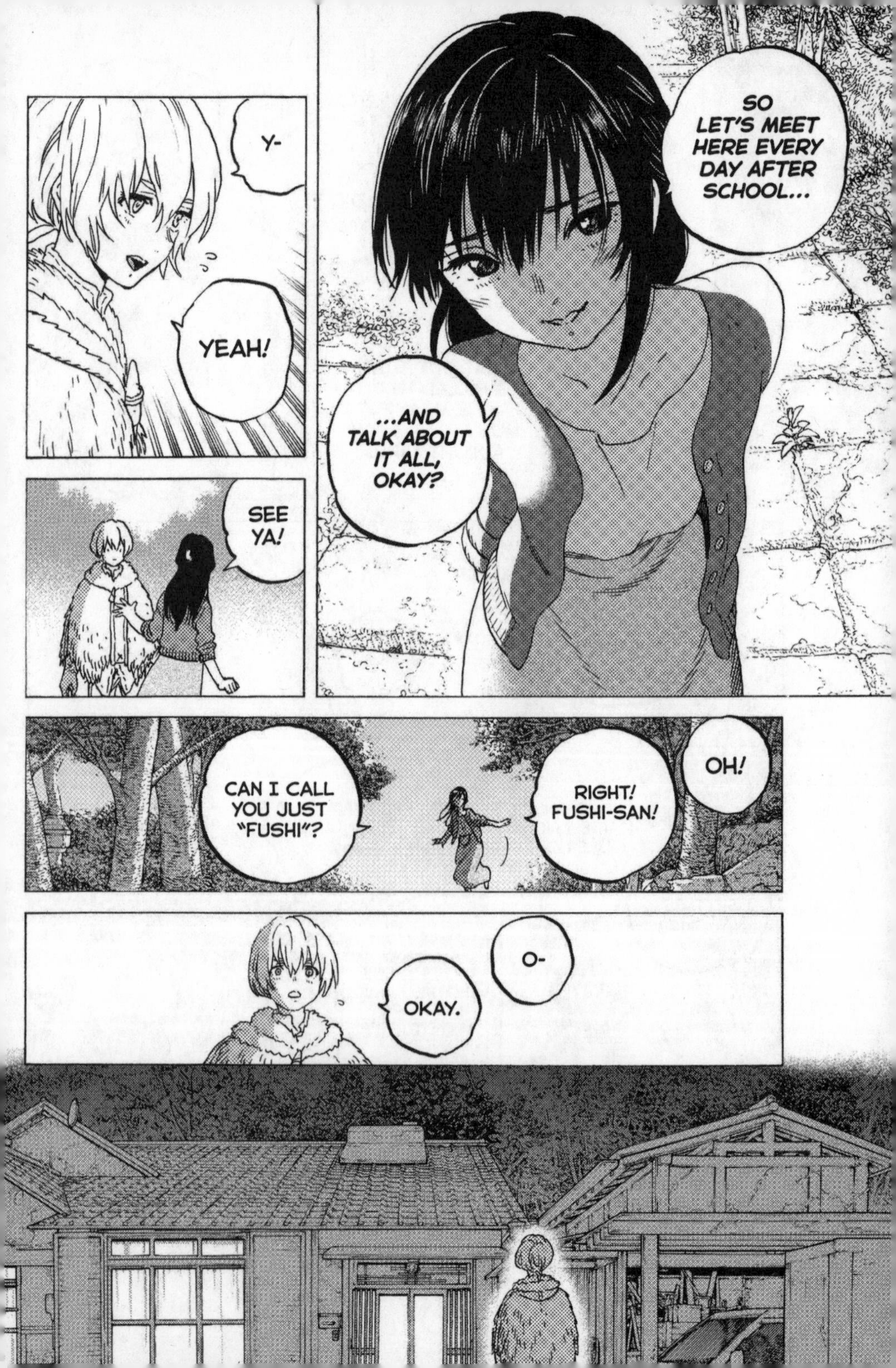
SO LET'S MEET HERE EVERY DAY AFTER SCHOOL...
...AND TALK ABOUT IT ALL, OKAY?
Y-
YEAH!
SEE YA!
OH!
RIGHT! FUSHI-SAN!
CAN I CALL YOU JUST "FUSHI"?
O-
OKAY.

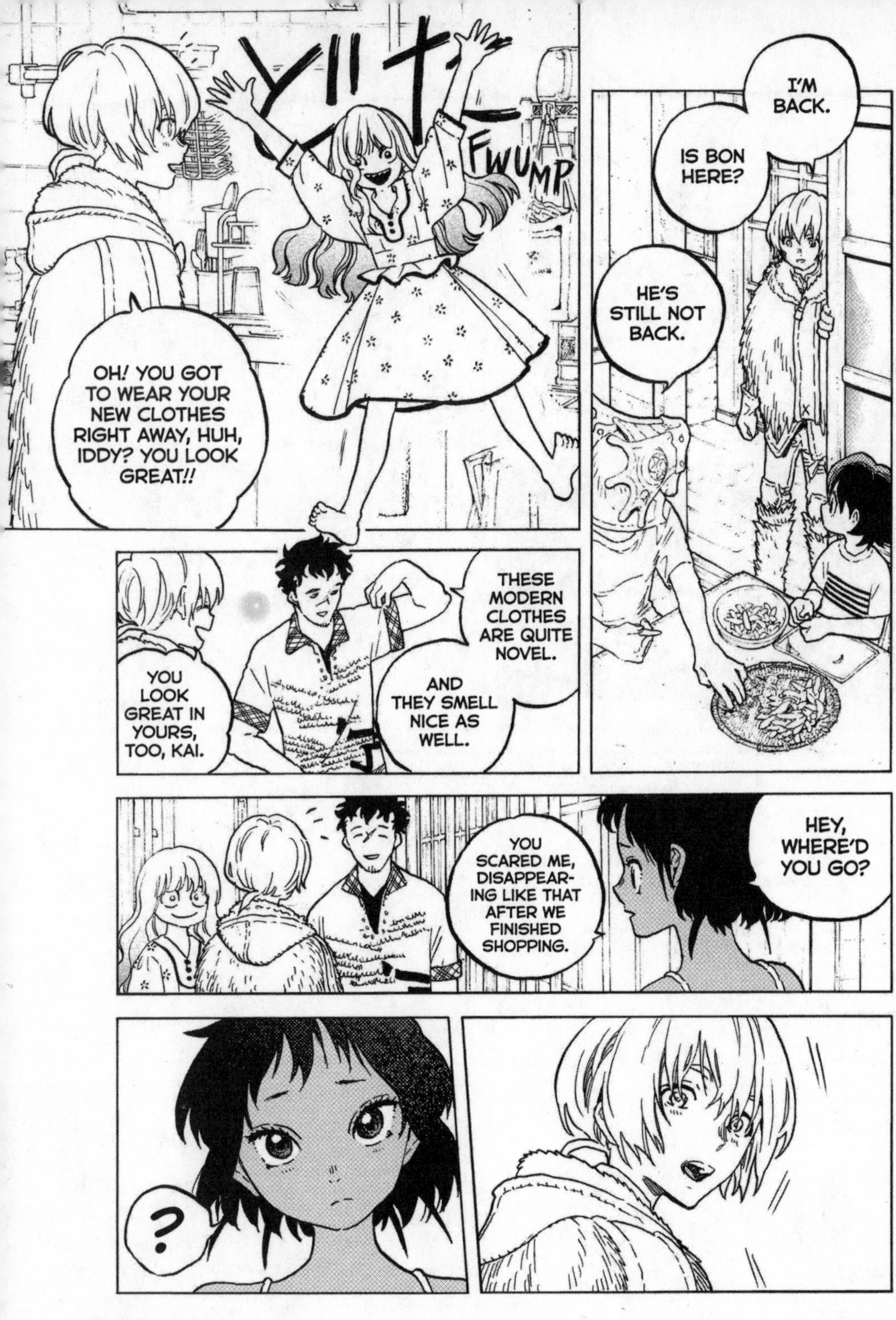
I'M BACK.
IS BON HERE?
HE'S STILL NOT BACK.
FWUMP
OH! YOU GOT TO WEAR YOUR NEW CLOTHES RIGHT AWAY, HUH, IDDY? YOU LOOK GREAT!!
THESE MODERN CLOTHES ARE QUITE NOVEL.
AND THEY SMELL NICE AS WELL.
YOU LOOK GREAT IN YOURS, TOO, KAI.
HEY, WHERE'D YOU GO?
YOU SCARED ME, DISAPPEARING LIKE THAT AFTER WE FINISHED SHOPPING.
?

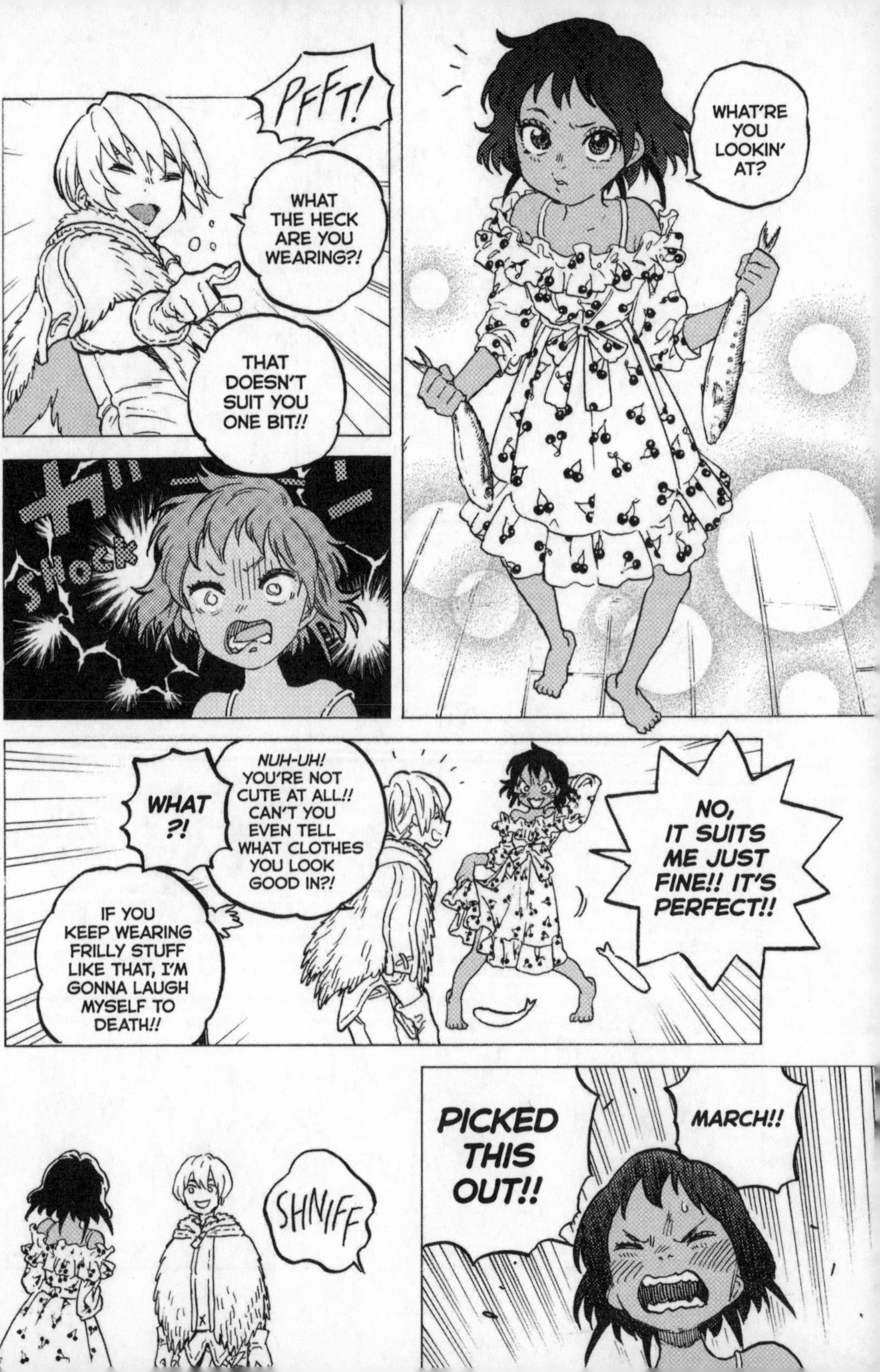
WHAT'RE YOU LOOKIN' AT?
PFFT!
WHAT THE HECK ARE YOU WEARING?!
THAT DOESN'T SUIT YOU ONE BIT!!
SHOCK
NO, IT SUITS ME JUST FINE!! IT'S PERFECT!!
NUH-UH! YOU'RE NOT CUTE AT ALL!! CAN'T YOU EVEN TELL WHAT CLOTHES YOU LOOK GOOD IN?!
WHAT?!
IF YOU KEEP WEARING FRILLY STUFF LIKE THAT, I'M GONNA LAUGH MYSELF TO DEATH!!
MARCH!!
PICKED THIS OUT!!
SHNIFF

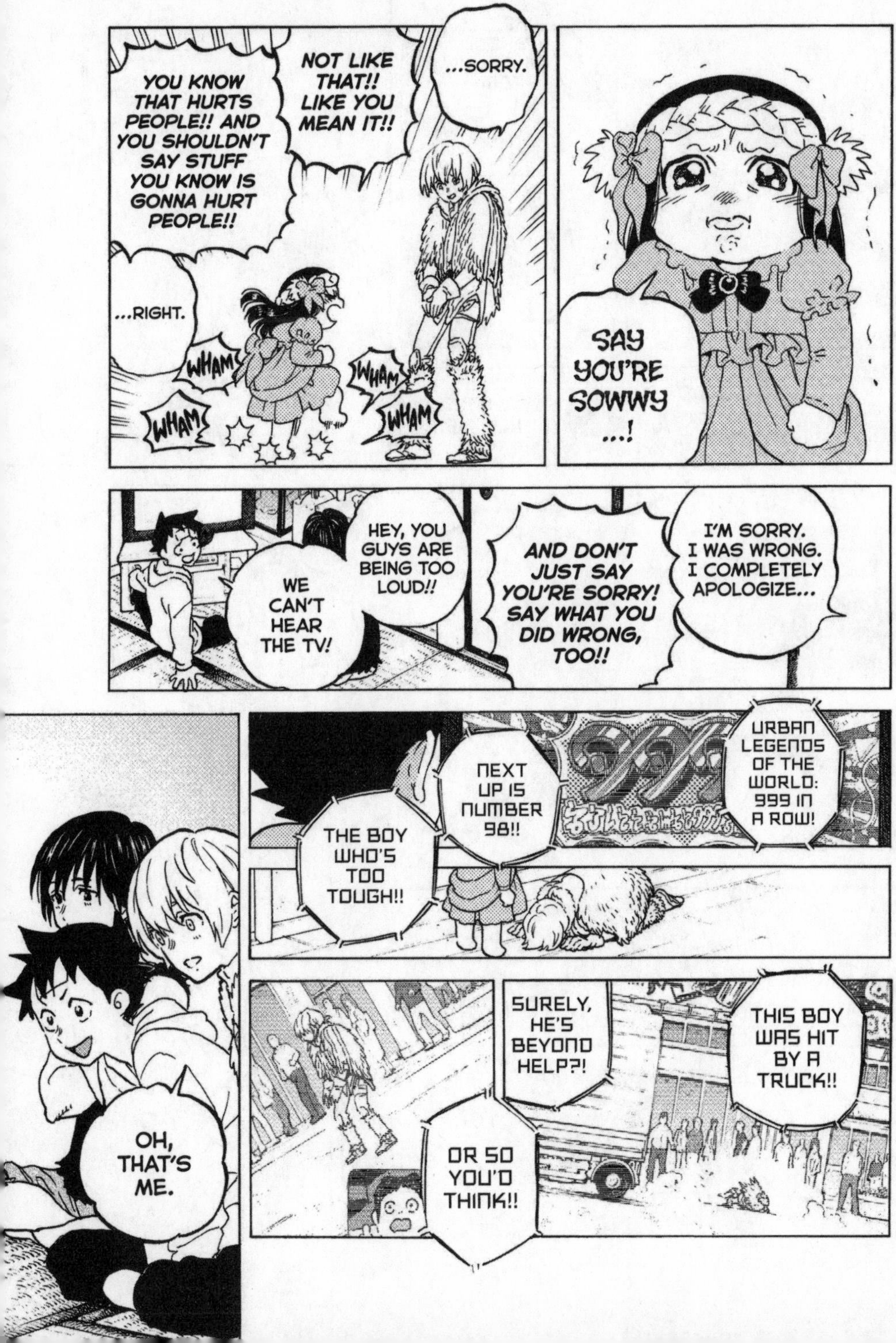
SAY YOU'RE SOWWY ...!
...SORRY.
NOT LIKE THAT!! LIKE YOU MEAN IT!!
YOU KNOW THAT HURTS PEOPLE!! AND YOU SHOULDN'T SAY STUFF YOU KNOW IS GONNA HURT PEOPLE!!
...RIGHT.
WHAM
WHAM
WHAM
WHAM
I'M SORRY. I WAS WRONG. I COMPLETELY APOLOGIZE...
AND DON'T JUST SAY YOU'RE SORRY! SAY WHAT YOU DID WRONG, TOO!!
HEY, YOU GUYS ARE BEING TOO LOUD!!
WE CAN'T HEAR THE TV!
URBAN LEGENDS OF THE WORLD: 999 IN A ROW!
NEXT UP IS NUMBER 98!!
THE BOY WHO'S TOO TOUGH!!
THIS BOY WAS HIT BY A TRUCK!!
SURELY, HE'S BEYOND HELP?!
OR SO YOU'D THINK!!
OH, THAT'S ME.

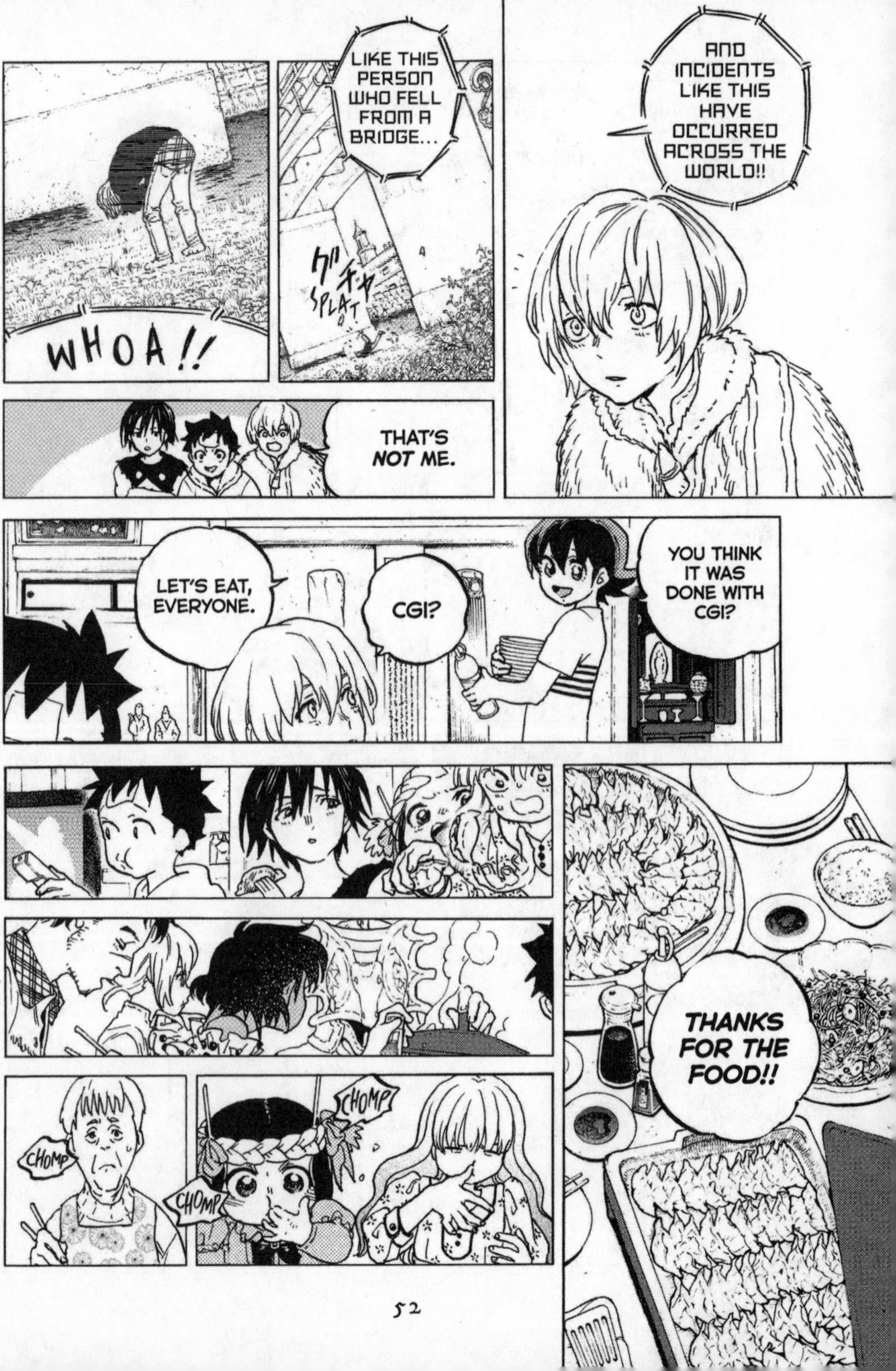
AND INCIDENTS LIKE THIS HAVE OCCURRED ACROSS THE WORLD!!
LIKE THIS PERSON WHO FELL FROM A BRIDGE...
グチャ
SPLAT
WHOA!!
THAT'S *NOT* ME.
YOU THINK IT WAS DONE WITH CGI?
CGI?
LET'S EAT, EVERYONE.
THANKS FOR THE FOOD!!
CHOMP
CHOMP
CHOMP

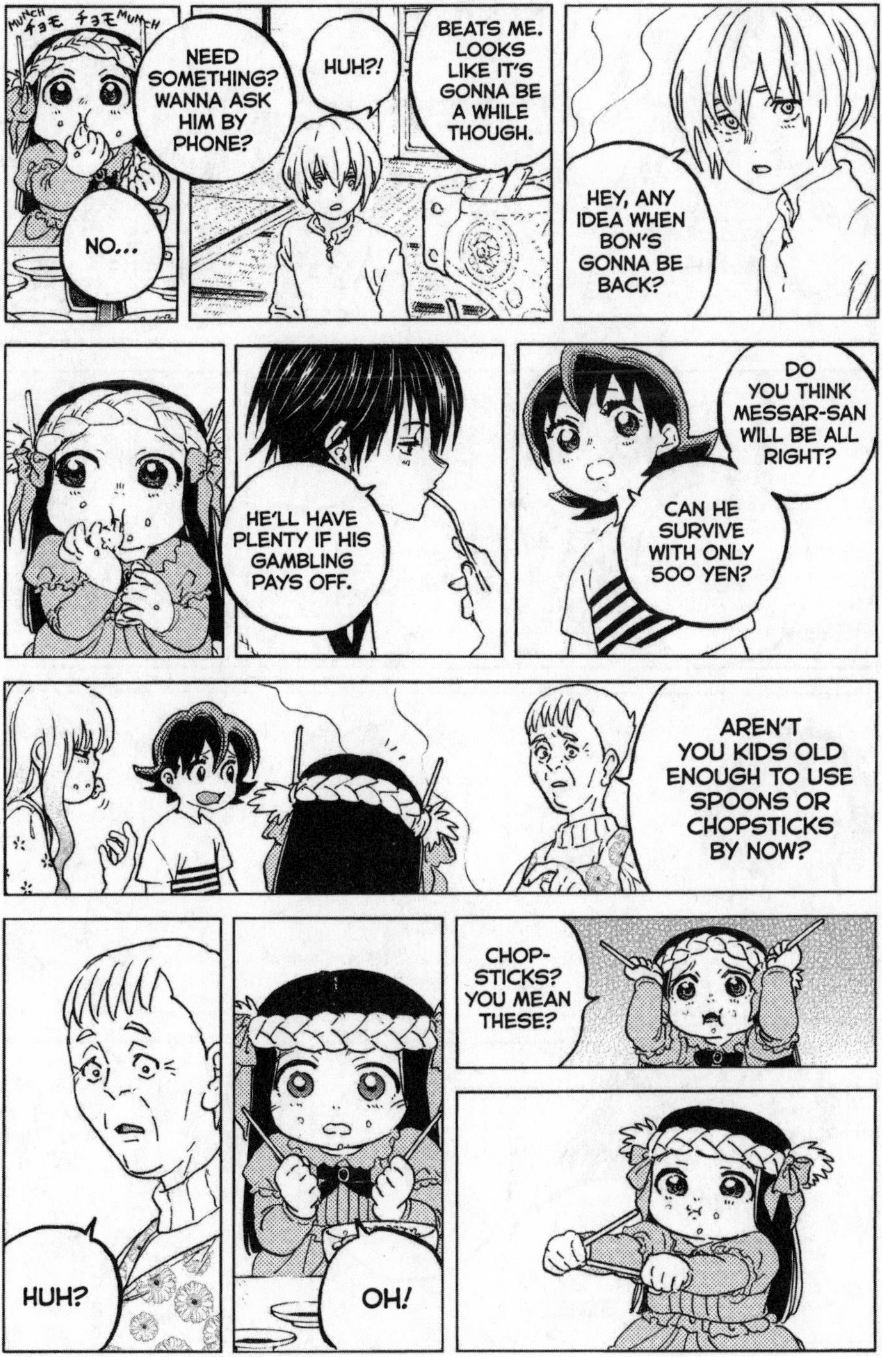

HEY, ANY IDEA WHEN BON'S GONNA BE BACK?
BEATS ME. LOOKS LIKE IT'S GONNA BE A WHILE THOUGH.
HUH?!
MUNCH チョモ チョモ MUNCH
NEED SOMETHING? WANNA ASK HIM BY PHONE?
NO...
DO YOU THINK MESSAR-SAN WILL BE ALL RIGHT?
CAN HE SURVIVE WITH ONLY 500 YEN?
HE'LL HAVE PLENTY IF HIS GAMBLING PAYS OFF.
AREN'T YOU KIDS OLD ENOUGH TO USE SPOONS OR CHOPSTICKS BY NOW?
CHOP-STICKS? YOU MEAN THESE?
OH!
HUH?

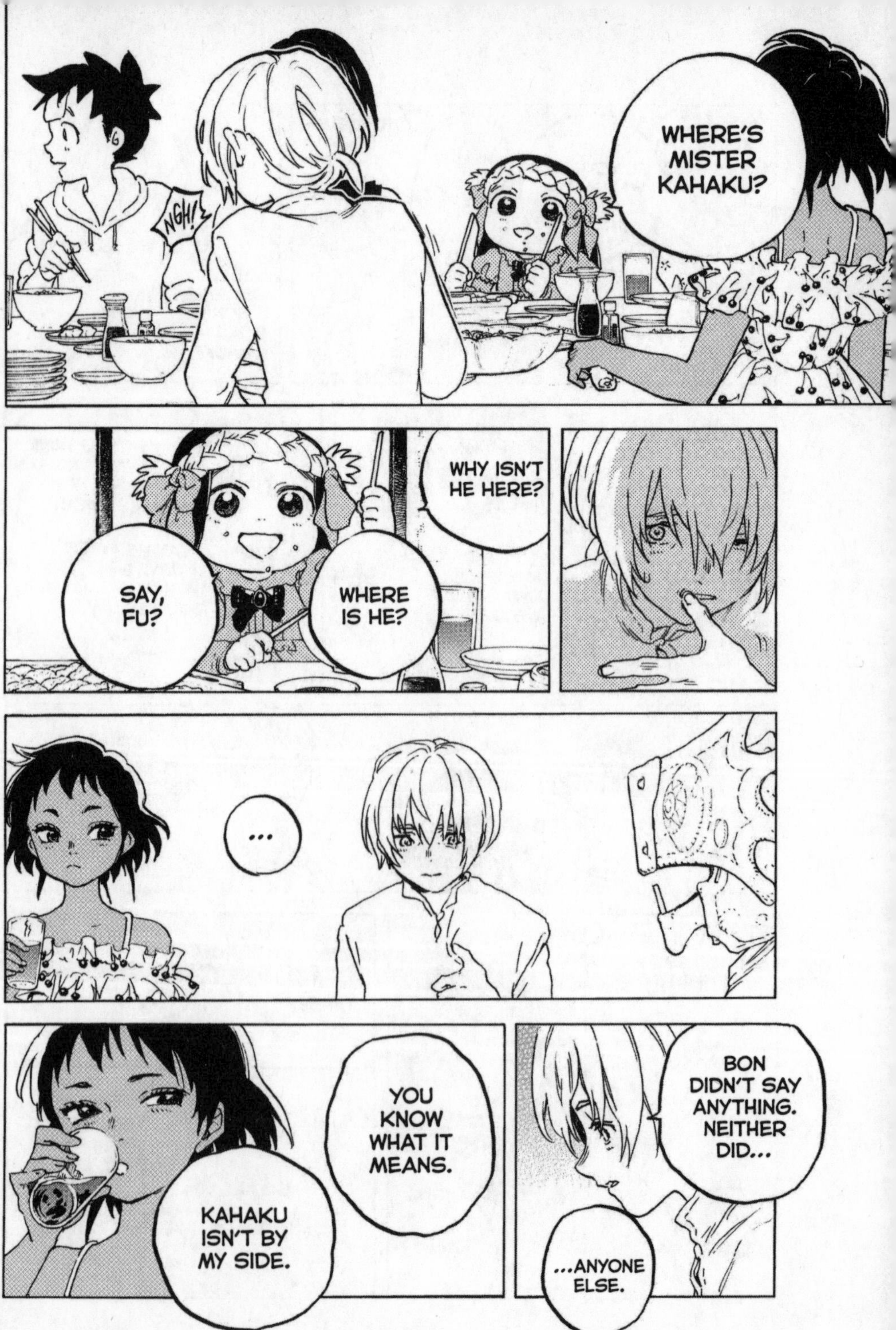
WHERE'S MISTER KAHAKU?
NGH!
WHY ISN'T HE HERE?
WHERE IS HE?
SAY, FU?
...
BON DIDN'T SAY ANYTHING. NEITHER DID...
...ANYONE ELSE.
YOU KNOW WHAT IT MEANS.
KAHAKU ISN'T BY MY SIDE.

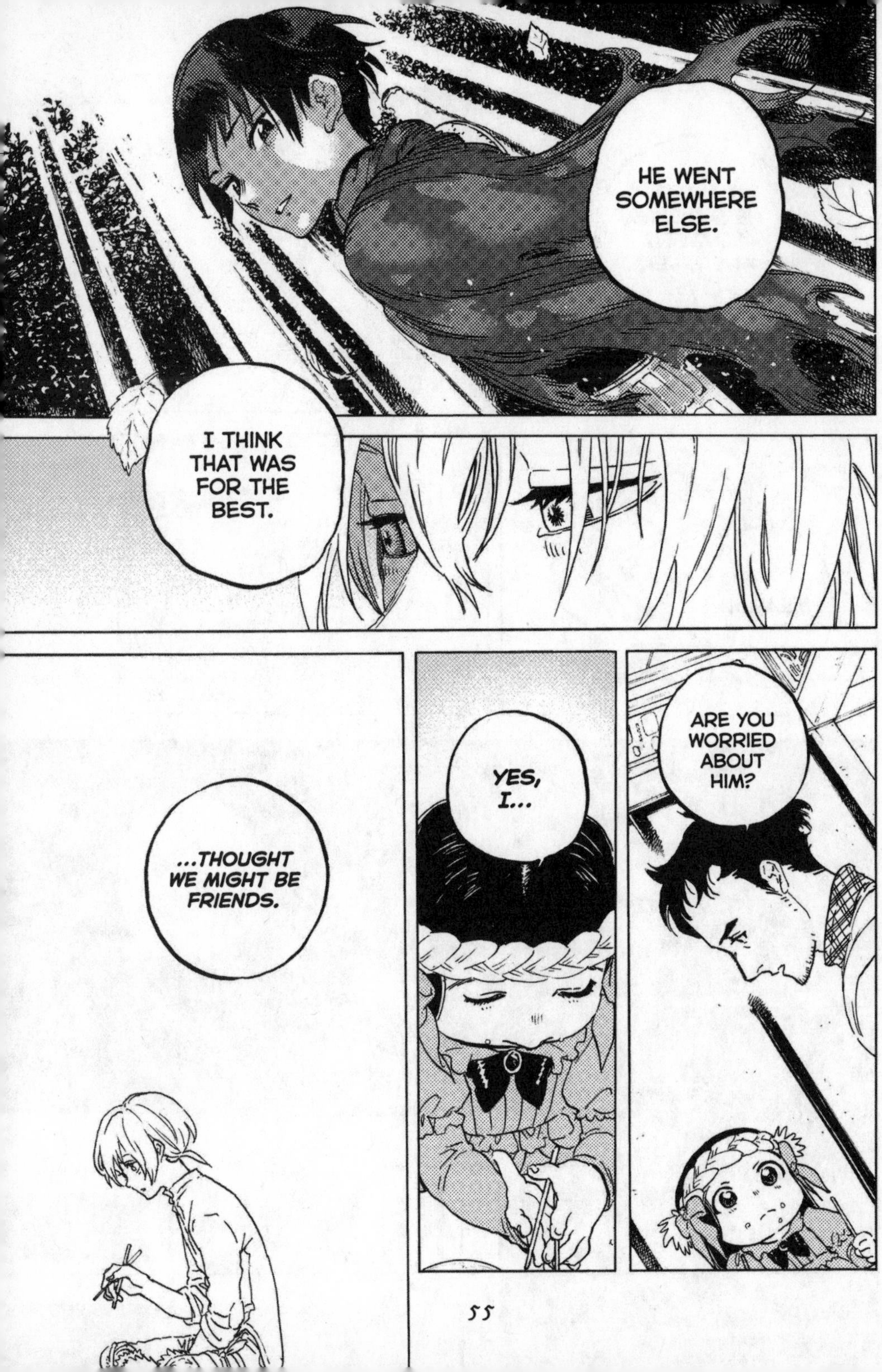
HE WENT SOMEWHERE ELSE.
I THINK THAT WAS FOR THE BEST.
ARE YOU WORRIED ABOUT HIM?
YES, I...
...THOUGHT WE MIGHT BE FRIENDS.

HUH.

I HOPE HE'S DOING ALL RIGHT, WHEREVER HE IS.

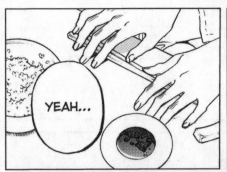

YEAH...

I HOPE SO...

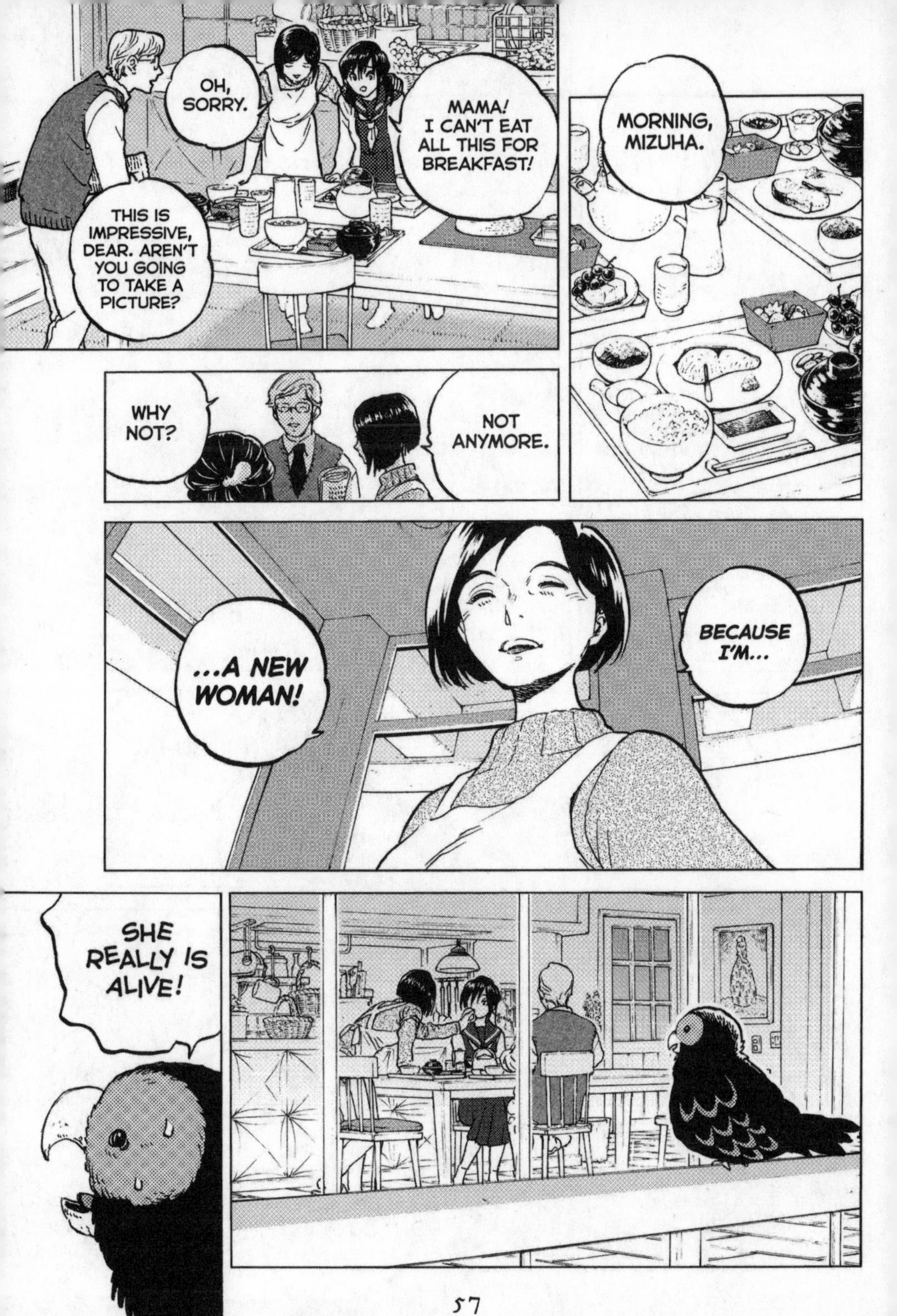
MORNING, MIZUHA.
MAMA! I CAN'T EAT ALL THIS FOR BREAKFAST!
OH, SORRY.
THIS IS IMPRESSIVE, DEAR. AREN'T YOU GOING TO TAKE A PICTURE?
NOT ANYMORE.
WHY NOT?
BECAUSE I'M...
...A NEW WOMAN!
SHE REALLY IS ALIVE!

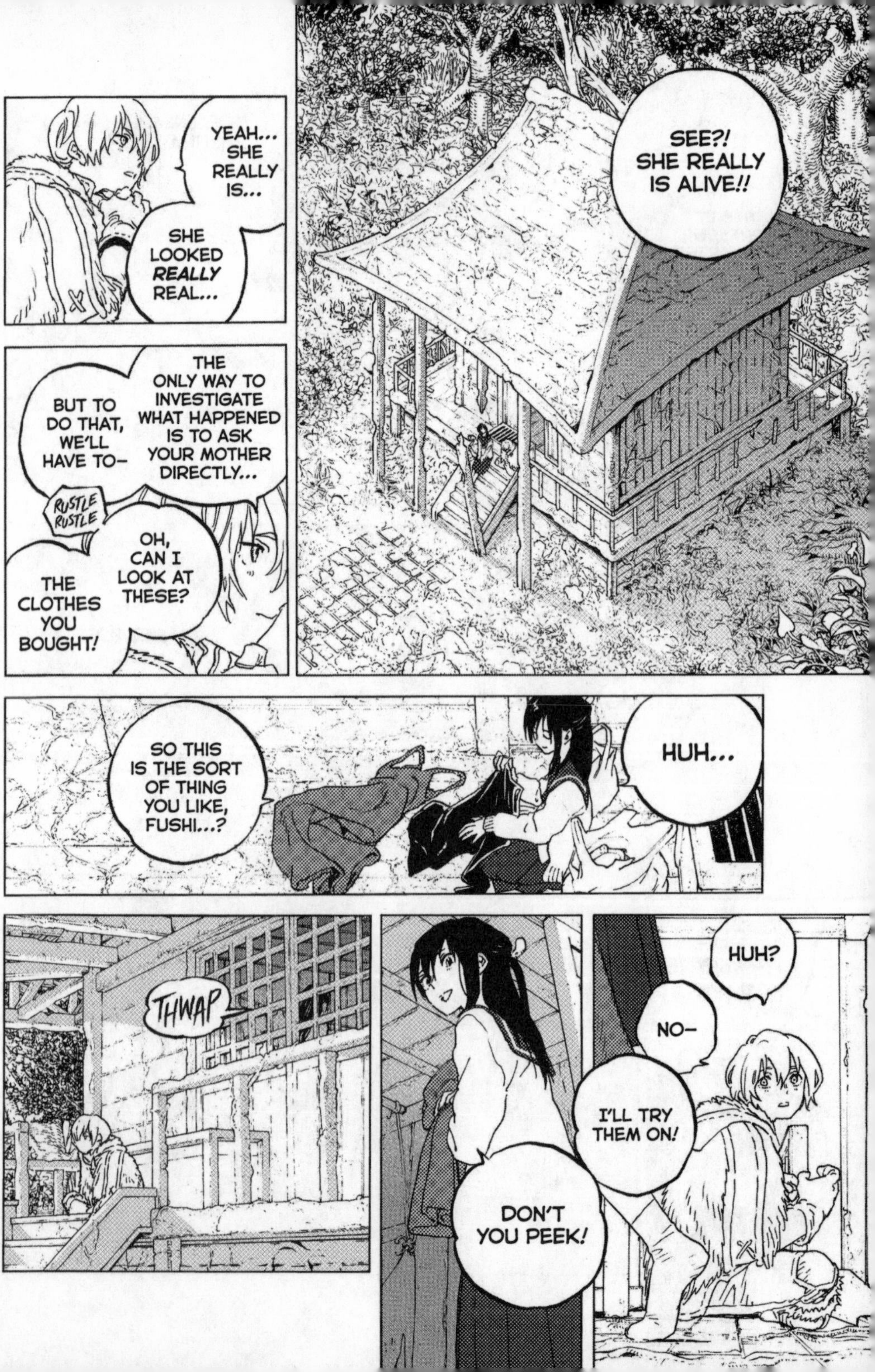
SEE?! SHE REALLY IS ALIVE!!
YEAH... SHE REALLY IS...
SHE LOOKED *REALLY* REAL...
THE ONLY WAY TO INVESTIGATE WHAT HAPPENED IS TO ASK YOUR MOTHER DIRECTLY...
BUT TO DO THAT, WE'LL HAVE TO–
RUSTLE RUSTLE
OH, CAN I LOOK AT THESE?
THE CLOTHES YOU BOUGHT!
HUH...
SO THIS IS THE SORT OF THING YOU LIKE, FUSHI...?
HUH?
NO–
I'LL TRY THEM ON!
DON'T YOU PEEK!
THWAP

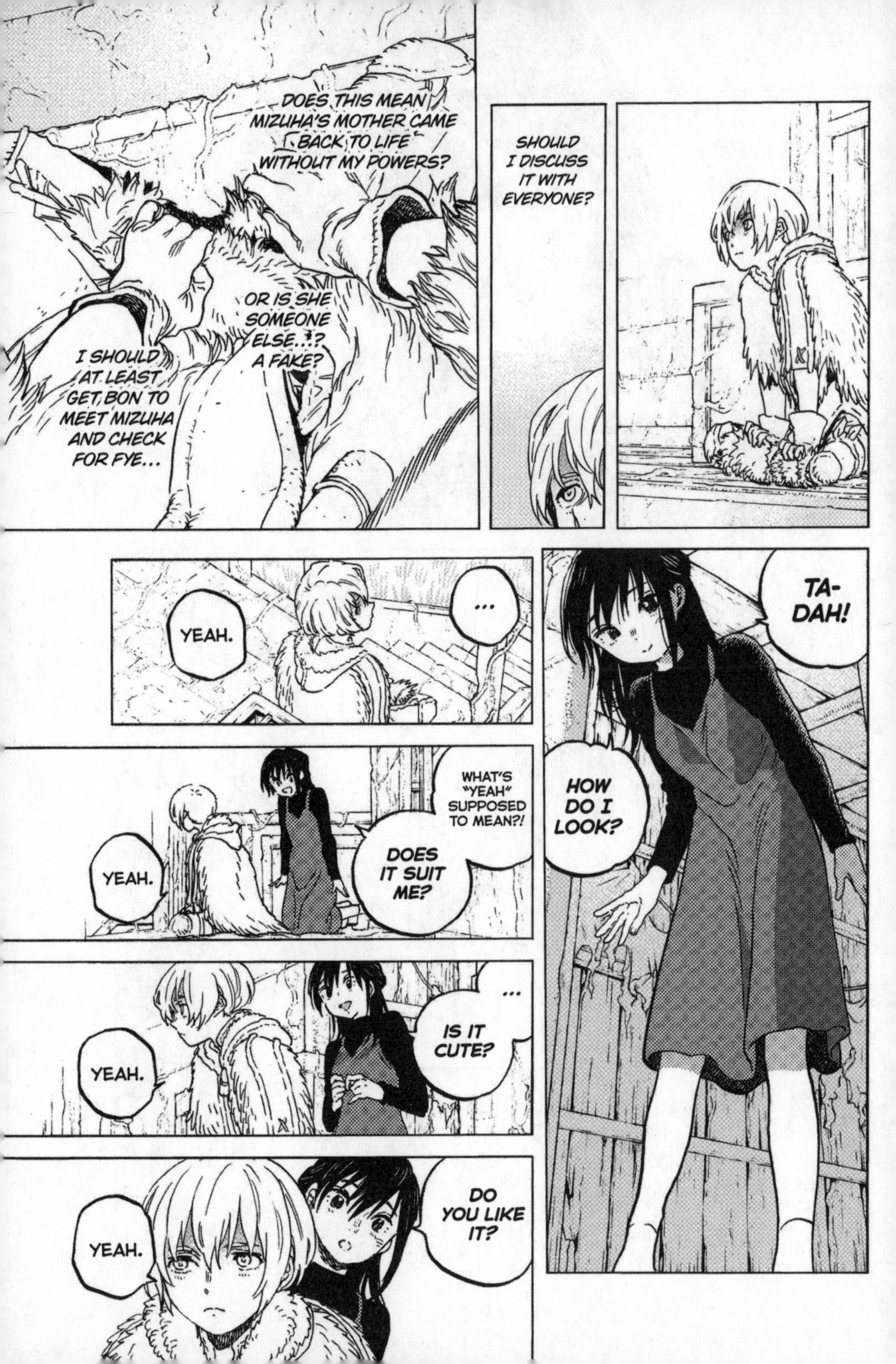
SHOULD I DISCUSS IT WITH EVERYONE?
DOES THIS MEAN MIZUHA'S MOTHER CAME BACK TO LIFE WITHOUT MY POWERS?
OR IS SHE SOMEONE ELSE...? A FAKE?
I SHOULD AT LEAST GET BON TO MEET MIZUHA AND CHECK FOR FYE...
TA-DAH!
HOW DO I LOOK?
...
YEAH.
WHAT'S "YEAH" SUPPOSED TO MEAN?!
DOES IT SUIT ME?
YEAH.
... IS IT CUTE?
YEAH.
DO YOU LIKE IT?
YEAH.

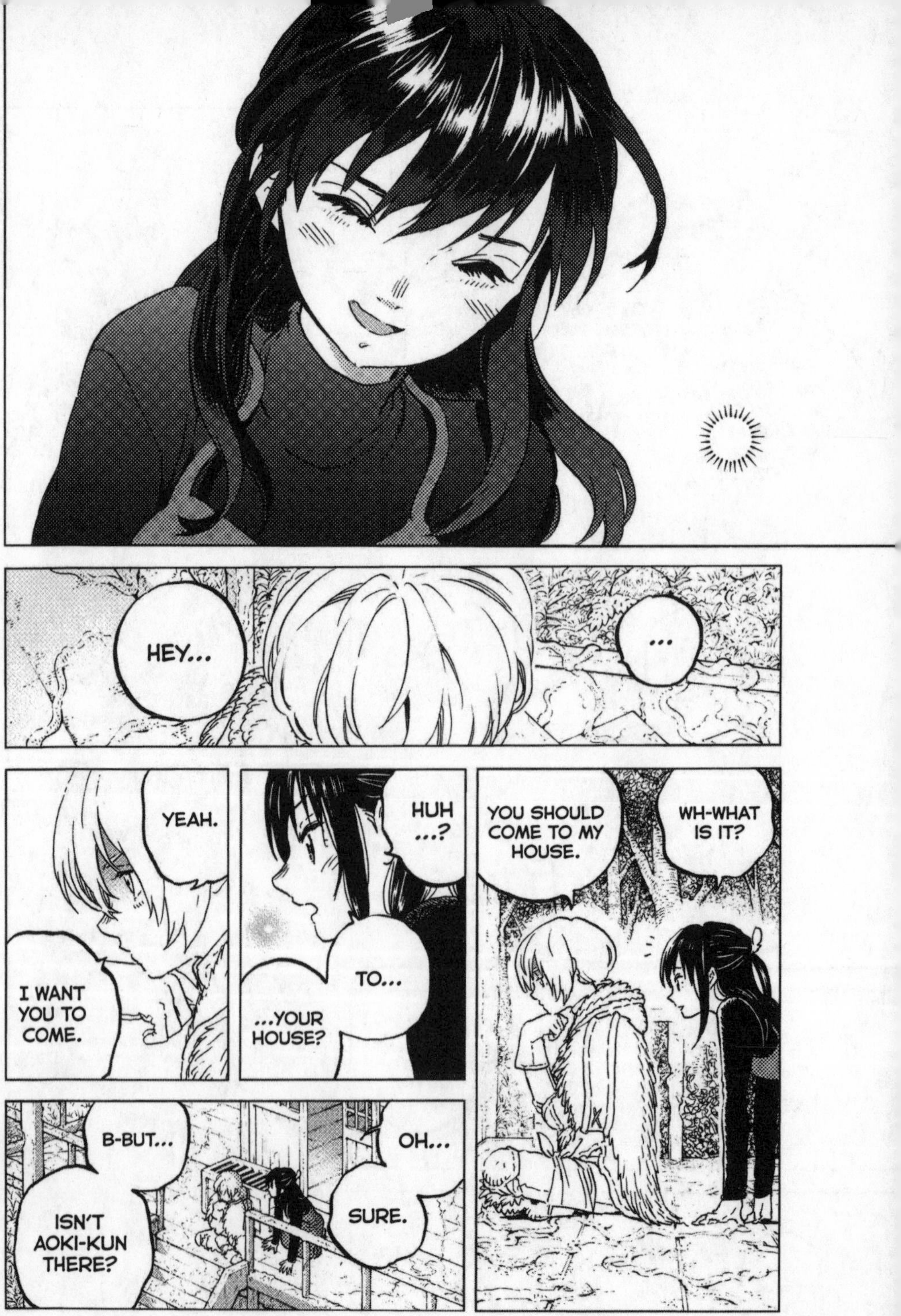

...
HEY...
WH-WHAT IS IT?
YOU SHOULD COME TO MY HOUSE.
HUH ...?
TO...
...YOUR HOUSE?
YEAH.
I WANT YOU TO COME.
OH... SURE.
B-BUT...
ISN'T AOKI-KUN THERE?

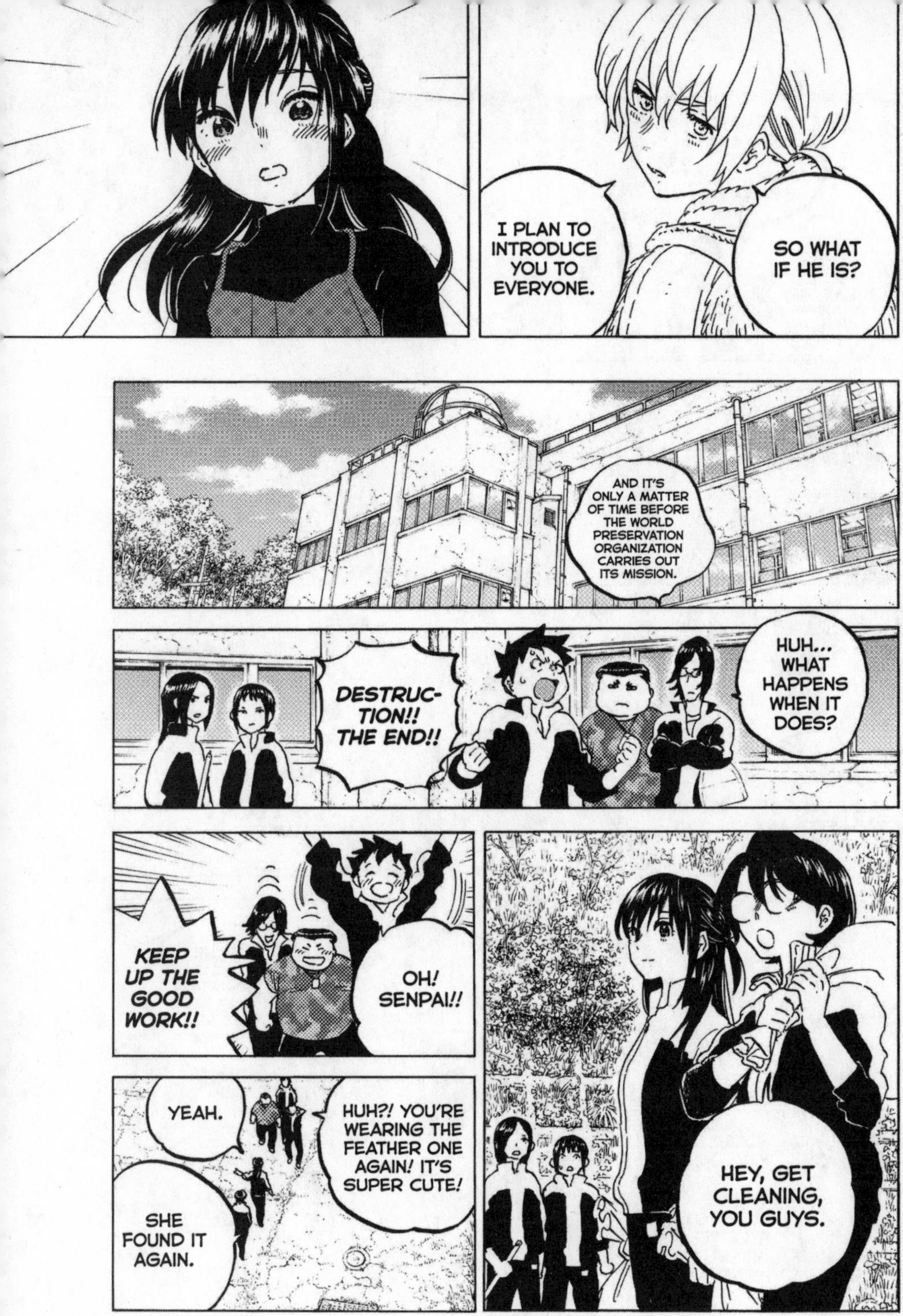
SO WHAT IF HE IS?
I PLAN TO INTRODUCE YOU TO EVERYONE.
AND IT'S ONLY A MATTER OF TIME BEFORE THE WORLD PRESERVATION ORGANIZATION CARRIES OUT ITS MISSION.
HUH... WHAT HAPPENS WHEN IT DOES?
DESTRUCTION!! THE END!!
HEY, GET CLEANING, YOU GUYS.
OH! SENPAI!!
KEEP UP THE GOOD WORK!!
HUH?! YOU'RE WEARING THE FEATHER ONE AGAIN! IT'S SUPER CUTE!
YEAH.
SHE FOUND IT AGAIN.

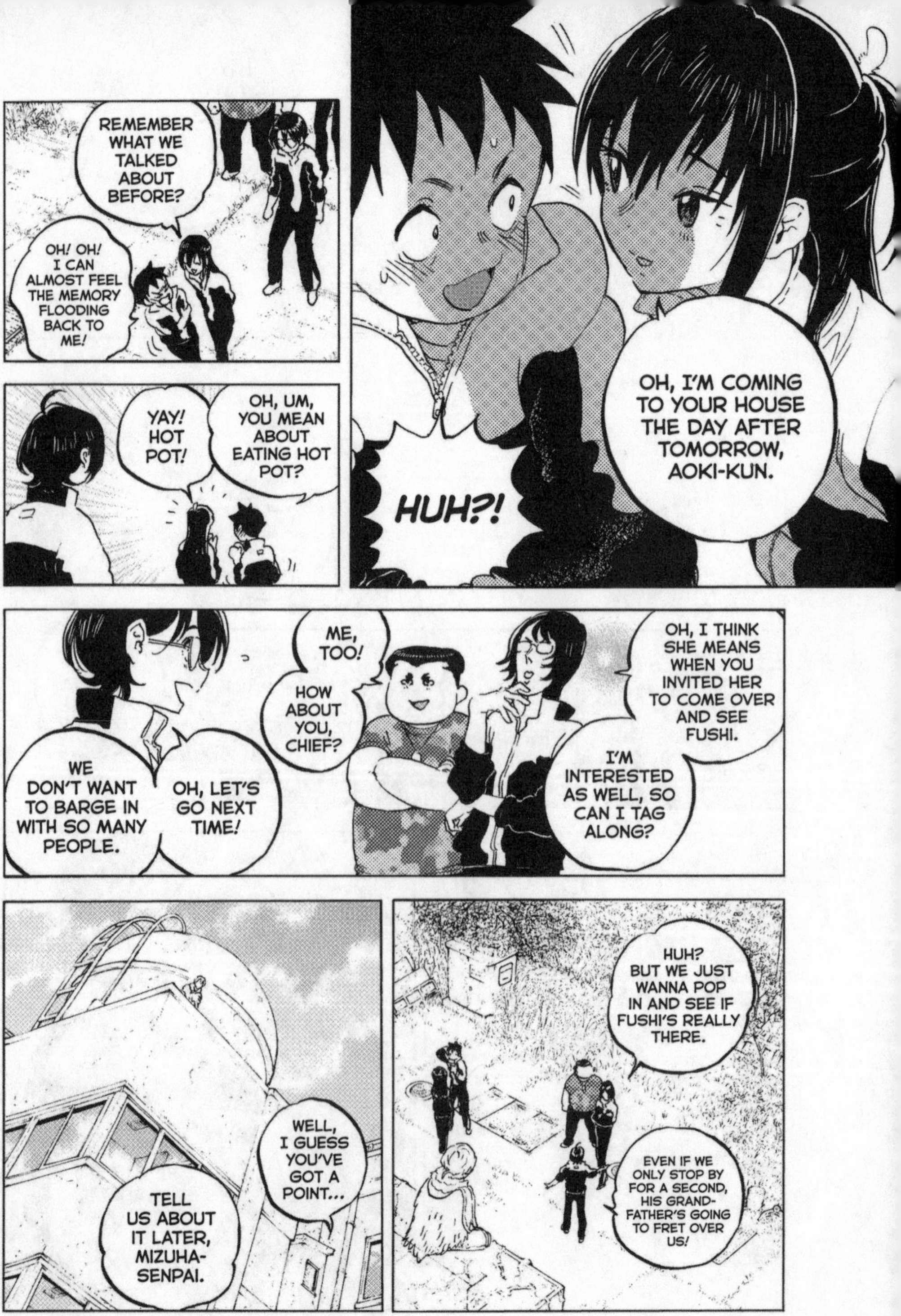
OH, I'M COMING TO YOUR HOUSE THE DAY AFTER TOMORROW, AOKI-KUN.
HUH?!
REMEMBER WHAT WE TALKED ABOUT BEFORE?
OH! OH! I CAN ALMOST FEEL THE MEMORY FLOODING BACK TO ME!
OH, UM, YOU MEAN ABOUT EATING HOT POT?
YAY! HOT POT!
OH, I THINK SHE MEANS WHEN YOU INVITED HER TO COME OVER AND SEE FUSHI.
I'M INTERESTED AS WELL, SO CAN I TAG ALONG?
ME, TOO!
HOW ABOUT YOU, CHIEF?
OH, LET'S GO NEXT TIME!
WE DON'T WANT TO BARGE IN WITH SO MANY PEOPLE.
HUH? BUT WE JUST WANNA POP IN AND SEE IF FUSHI'S REALLY THERE.
EVEN IF WE ONLY STOP BY FOR A SECOND, HIS GRAND-FATHER'S GOING TO FRET OVER US!
WELL, I GUESS YOU'VE GOT A POINT...
TELL US ABOUT IT LATER, MIZUHA-SENPAI.

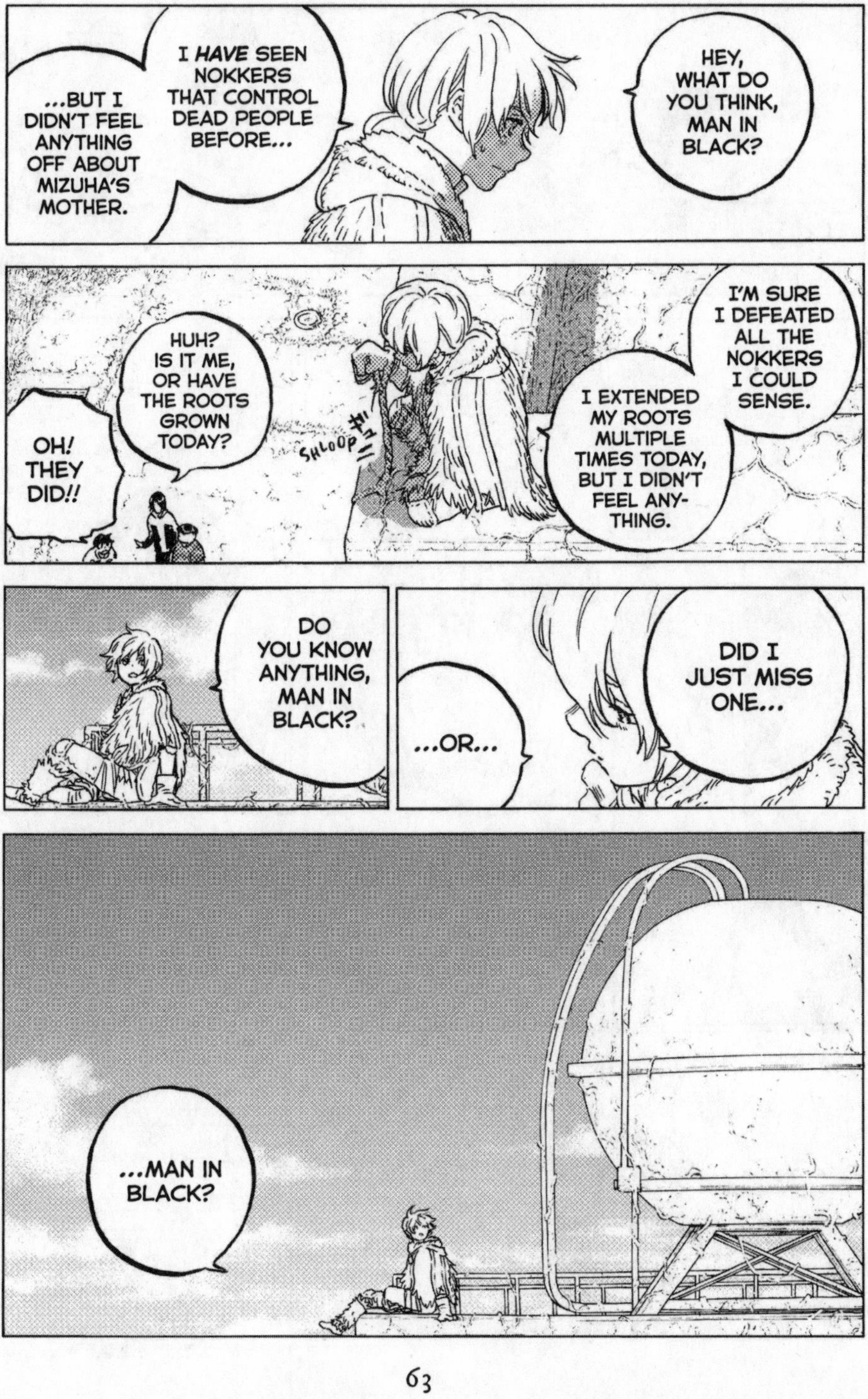

HEY, WHAT DO YOU THINK, MAN IN BLACK?
I *HAVE* SEEN NOKKERS THAT CONTROL DEAD PEOPLE BEFORE...
...BUT I DIDN'T FEEL ANYTHING OFF ABOUT MIZUHA'S MOTHER.
I'M SURE I DEFEATED ALL THE NOKKERS I COULD SENSE.
I EXTENDED MY ROOTS MULTIPLE TIMES TODAY, BUT I DIDN'T FEEL ANY-THING.
SHLOOP
HUH? IS IT ME, OR HAVE THE ROOTS GROWN TODAY?
OH! THEY DID!!
DID I JUST MISS ONE...
...OR...
DO YOU KNOW ANYTHING, MAN IN BLACK?
...MAN IN BLACK?

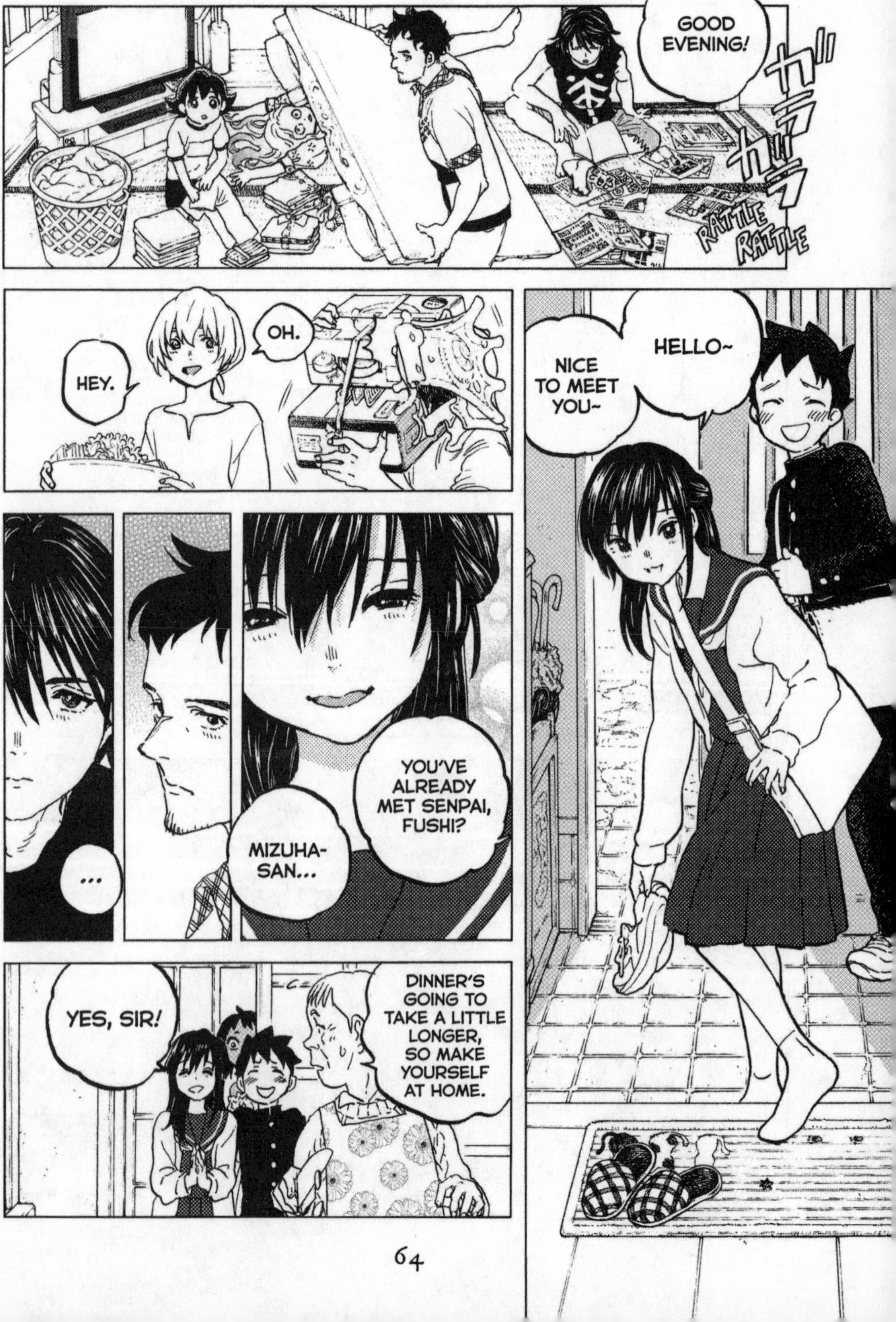
GOOD EVENING!
RATTLE RATTLE
HELLO~
NICE TO MEET YOU~
OH.
HEY.
YOU'VE ALREADY MET SENPAI, FUSHI?
MIZUHA-SAN...
...
DINNER'S GOING TO TAKE A LITTLE LONGER, SO MAKE YOURSELF AT HOME.
YES, SIR!

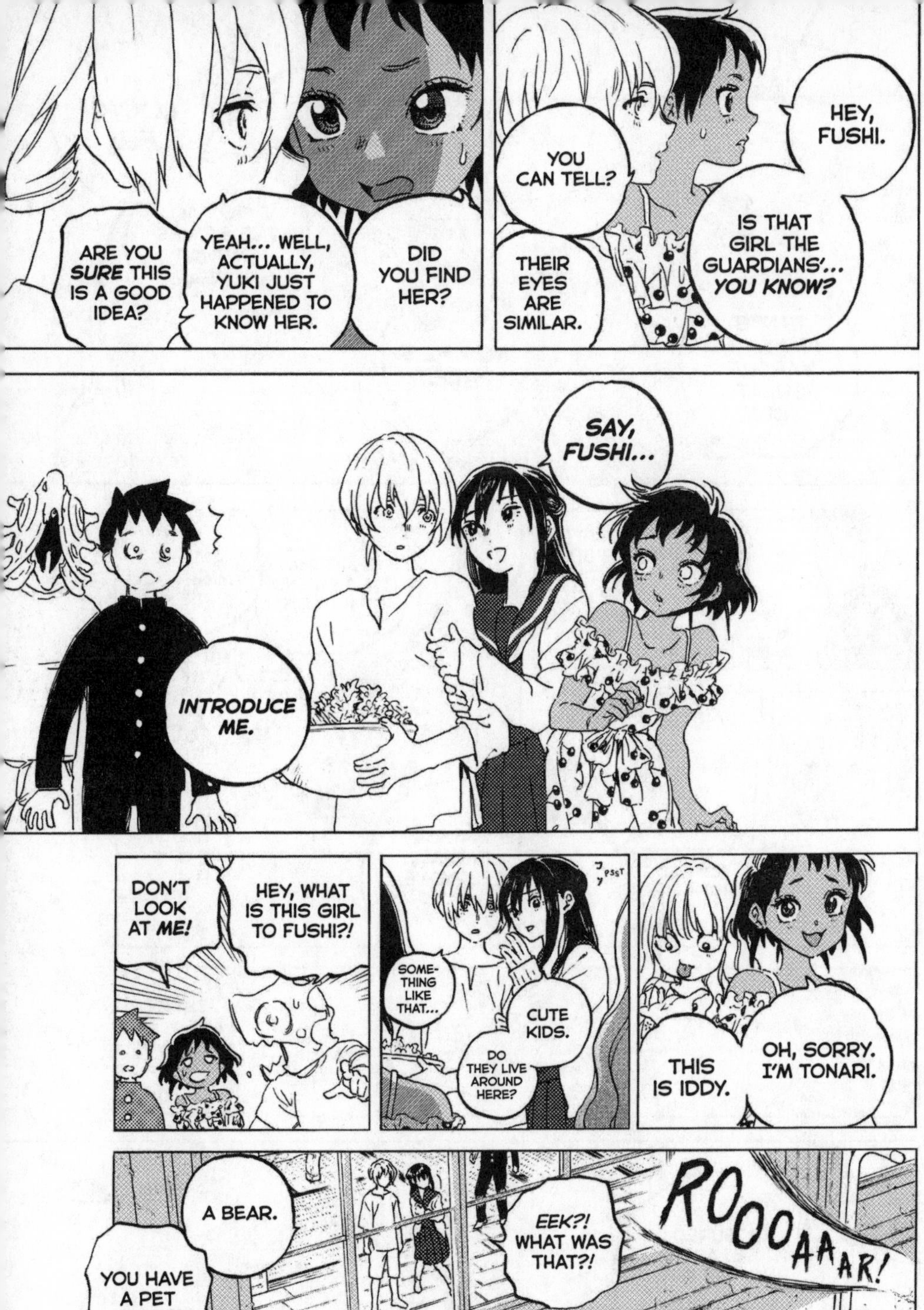
HEY, FUSHI.
IS THAT GIRL THE GUARDIANS'... *YOU KNOW?*
YOU CAN TELL?
THEIR EYES ARE SIMILAR.
DID YOU FIND HER?
YEAH... WELL, ACTUALLY, YUKI JUST HAPPENED TO KNOW HER.
ARE YOU *SURE* THIS IS A GOOD IDEA?
*SAY, FUSHI...*
*INTRODUCE ME.*
OH, SORRY. I'M TONARI.
THIS IS IDDY.
PSST
CUTE KIDS.
DO THEY LIVE AROUND HERE?
SOMETHING LIKE THAT...
HEY, WHAT IS THIS GIRL TO FUSHI?!
DON'T LOOK AT *ME!*
ROOOAAAR!
*EEK?!* WHAT WAS THAT?!
A BEAR.
YOU HAVE A PET BEAR?!

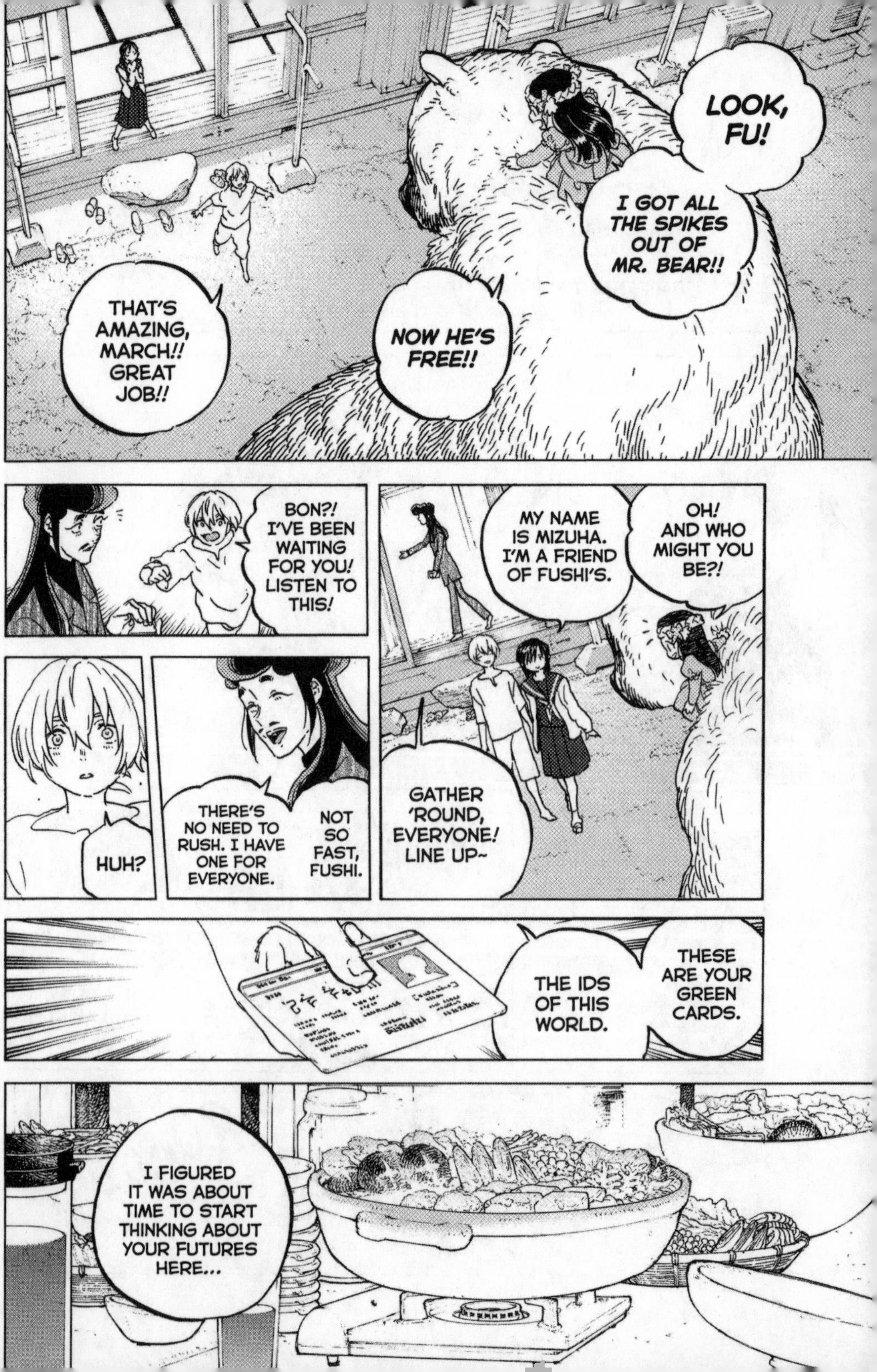
LOOK, FU!
I GOT ALL THE SPIKES OUT OF MR. BEAR!!
NOW HE'S FREE!!
THAT'S AMAZING, MARCH!! GREAT JOB!!
OH! AND WHO MIGHT YOU BE?!
MY NAME IS MIZUHA. I'M A FRIEND OF FUSHI'S.
GATHER 'ROUND, EVERYONE! LINE UP~
BON?! I'VE BEEN WAITING FOR YOU! LISTEN TO THIS!
NOT SO FAST, FUSHI.
THERE'S NO NEED TO RUSH. I HAVE ONE FOR EVERYONE.
HUH?
THESE ARE YOUR GREEN CARDS.
THE IDS OF THIS WORLD.
I FIGURED IT WAS ABOUT TIME TO START THINKING ABOUT YOUR FUTURES HERE...

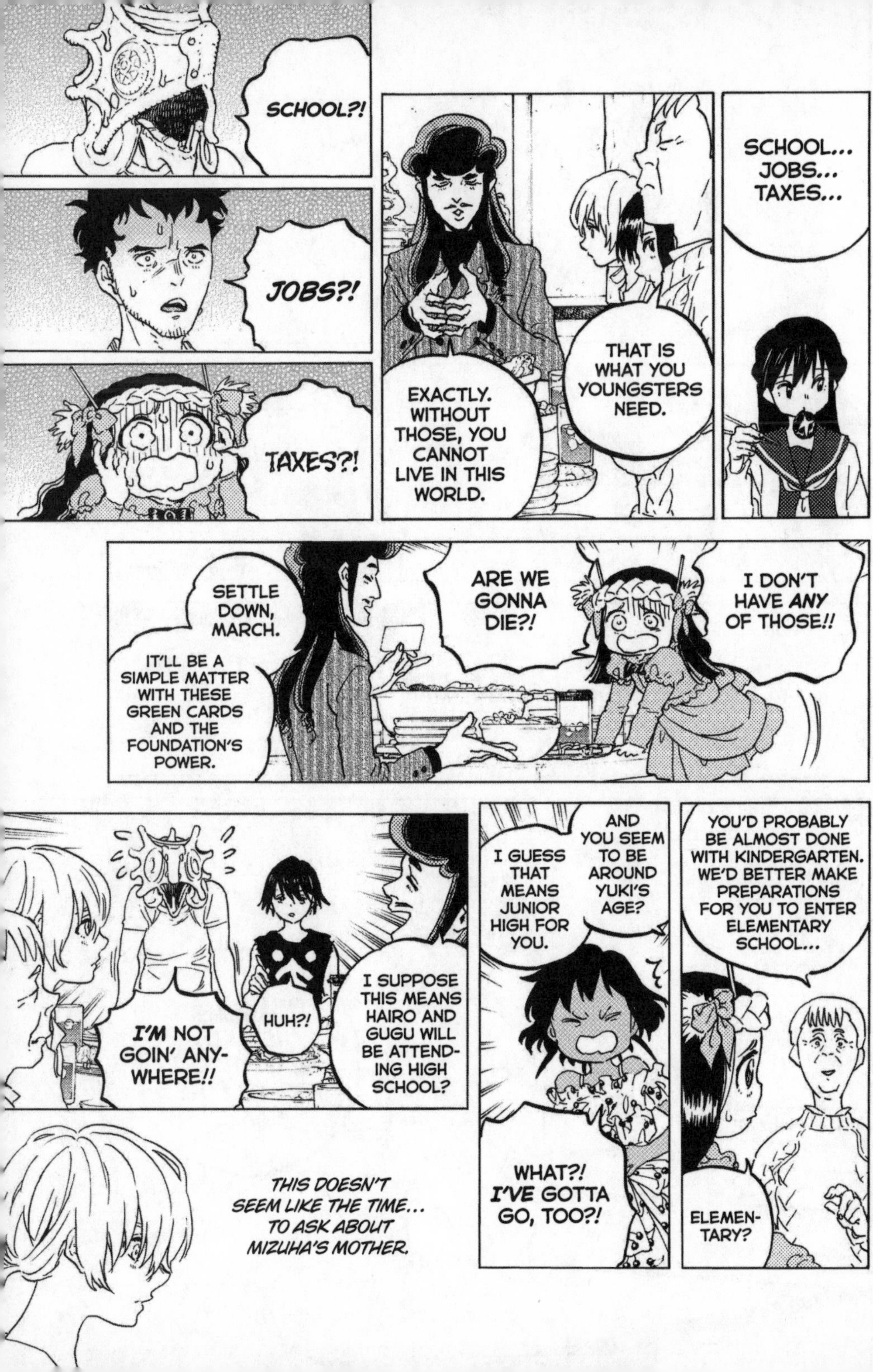
SCHOOL... JOBS... TAXES...
THAT IS WHAT YOU YOUNGSTERS NEED.
EXACTLY. WITHOUT THOSE, YOU CANNOT LIVE IN THIS WORLD.
SCHOOL?!
JOBS?!
TAXES?!
I DON'T HAVE *ANY* OF THOSE!!
ARE WE GONNA DIE?!
SETTLE DOWN, MARCH.
IT'LL BE A SIMPLE MATTER WITH THESE GREEN CARDS AND THE FOUNDATION'S POWER.
YOU'D PROBABLY BE ALMOST DONE WITH KINDERGARTEN. WE'D BETTER MAKE PREPARATIONS FOR YOU TO ENTER ELEMENTARY SCHOOL...
ELEMENTARY?
AND YOU SEEM TO BE AROUND YUKI'S AGE?
I GUESS THAT MEANS JUNIOR HIGH FOR YOU.
WHAT?! *I'VE* GOTTA GO, TOO?!
I SUPPOSE THIS MEANS HAIRO AND GUGU WILL BE ATTENDING HIGH SCHOOL?
HUH?!
*I'M* NOT GOIN' ANYWHERE!!
THIS DOESN'T SEEM LIKE THE TIME... TO ASK ABOUT MIZUHA'S MOTHER.

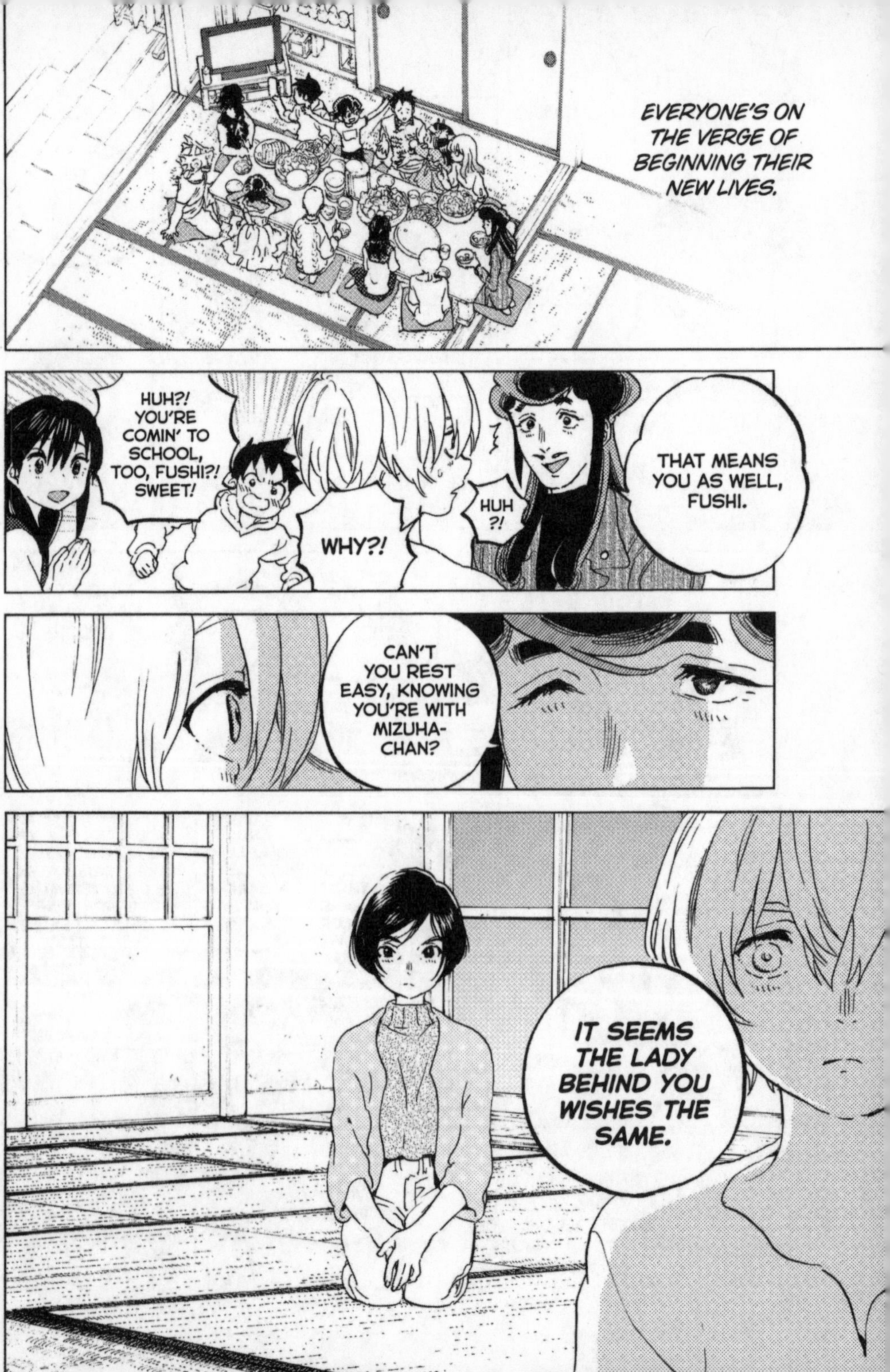
EVERYONE'S ON THE VERGE OF BEGINNING THEIR NEW LIVES.
THAT MEANS YOU AS WELL, FUSHI.
HUH?!
WHY?!
HUH?! YOU'RE COMIN' TO SCHOOL, TOO, FUSHI?! SWEET!
CAN'T YOU REST EASY, KNOWING YOU'RE WITH MIZUHA-CHAN?
IT SEEMS THE LADY BEHIND YOU WISHES THE SAME.

TO YOUR ETERNITY

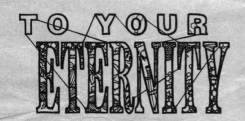

1 ¥500
¥1000

1 ¥399
¥798

1 ¥490
¥980

1 ¥490
¥980

1 ¥99

¥1,978

¥2,175

50%

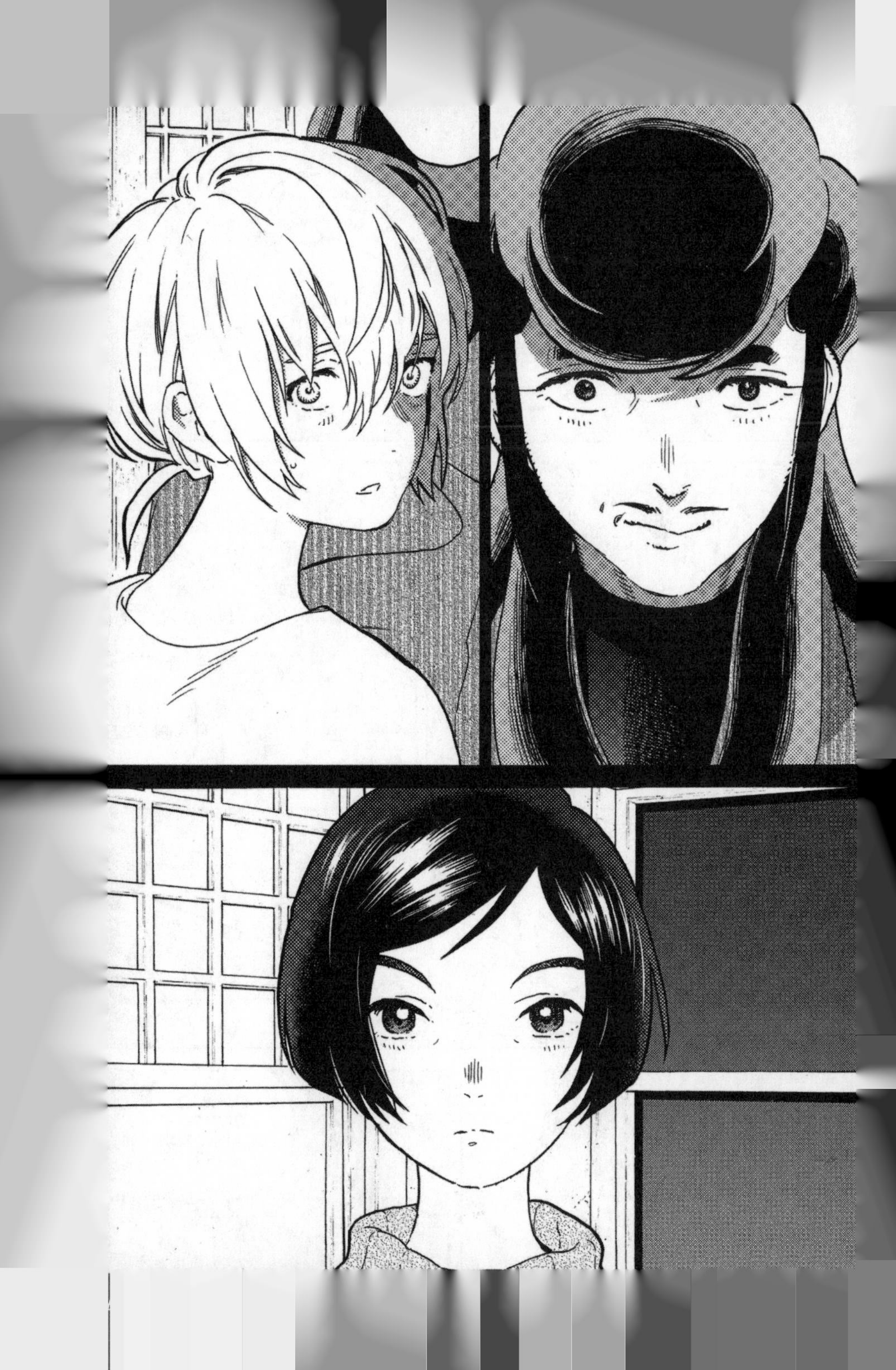

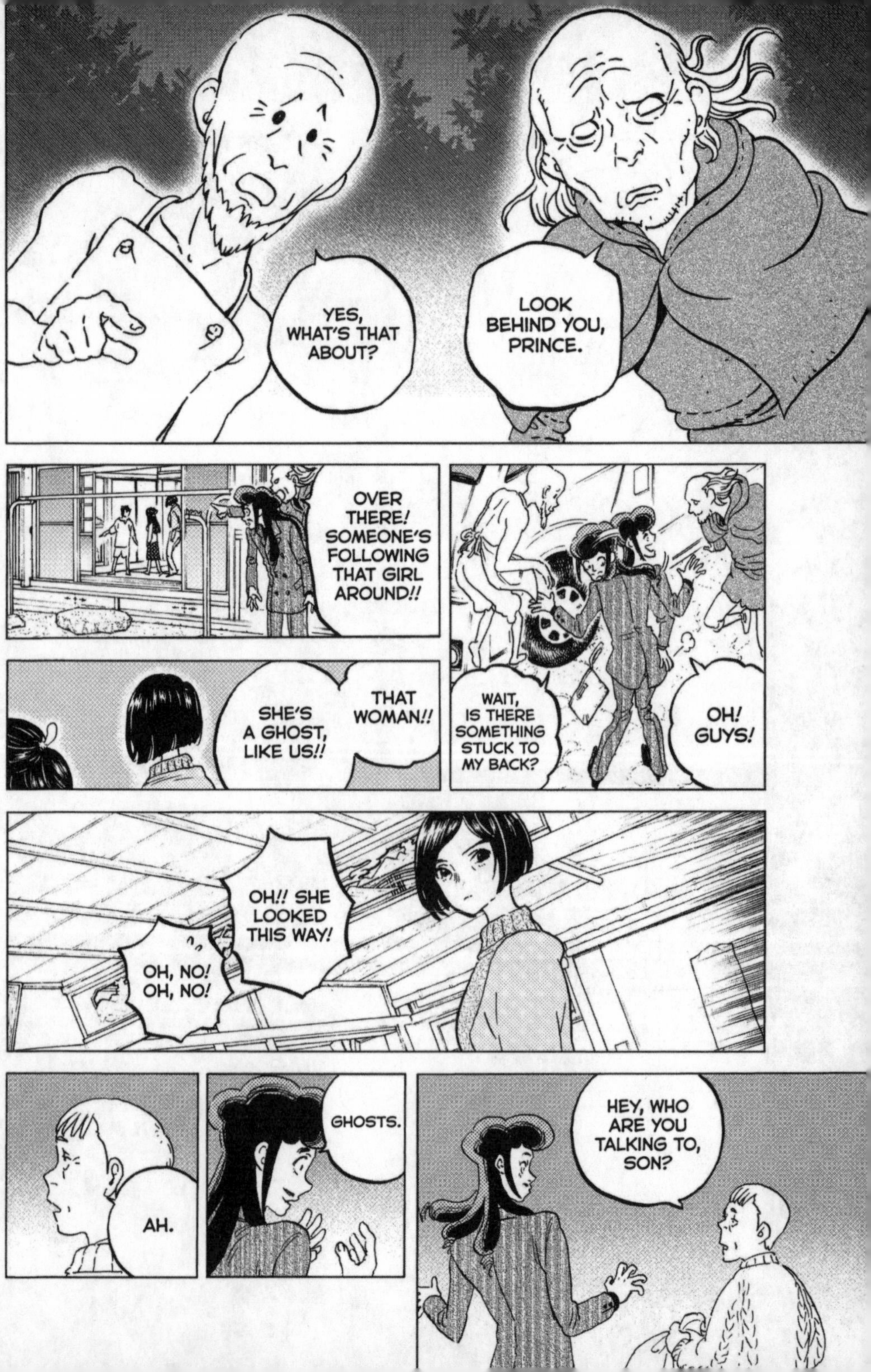
LOOK BEHIND YOU, PRINCE.
YES, WHAT'S THAT ABOUT?
OH! GUYS!
WAIT, IS THERE SOMETHING STUCK TO MY BACK?
OVER THERE! SOMEONE'S FOLLOWING THAT GIRL AROUND!!
THAT WOMAN!!
SHE'S A GHOST, LIKE US!!
OH!! SHE LOOKED THIS WAY!
OH, NO! OH, NO!
HEY, WHO ARE YOU TALKING TO, SON?
GHOSTS.
AH.

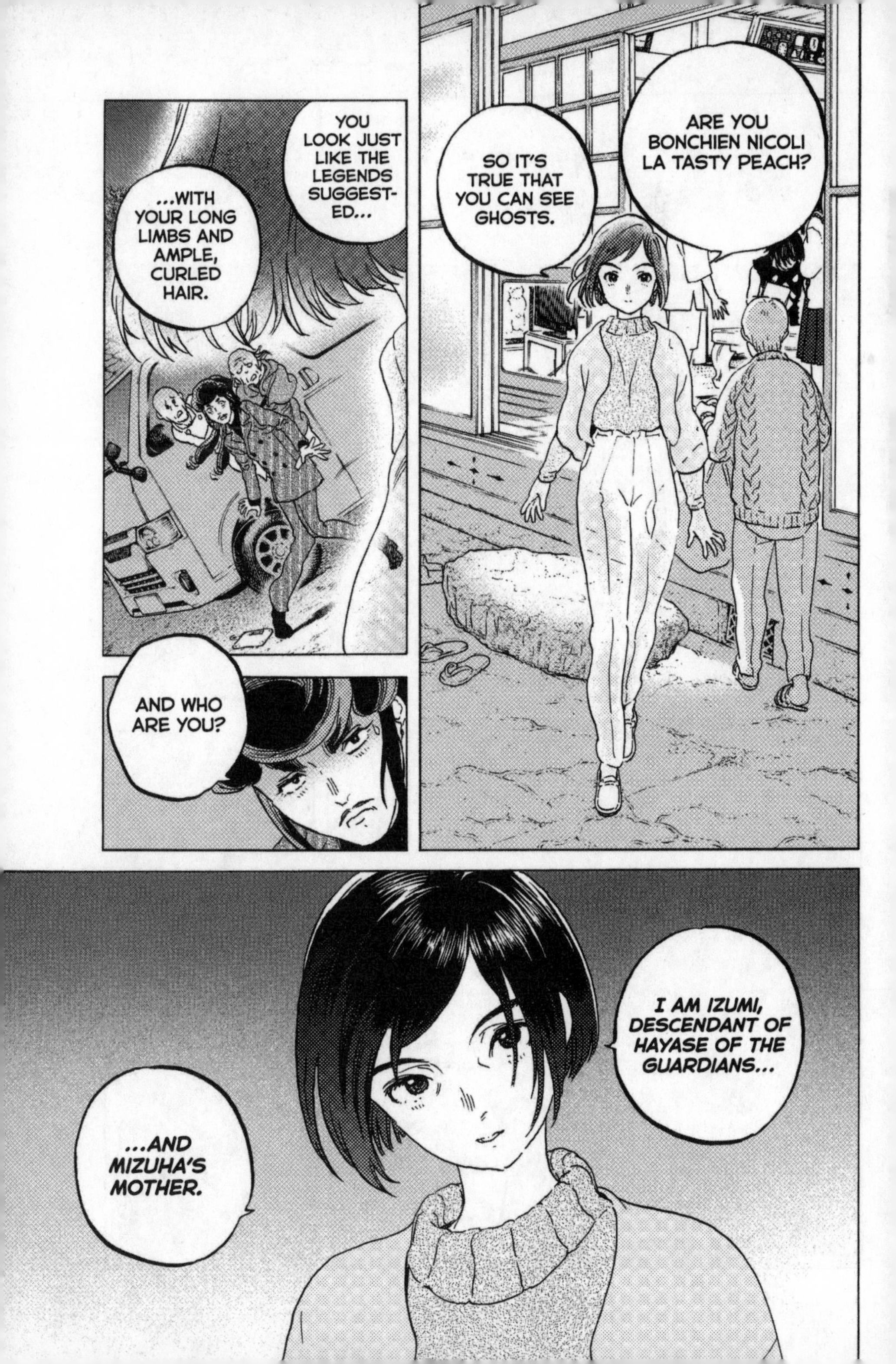
ARE YOU BONCHIEN NICOLI LA TASTY PEACH?
SO IT'S TRUE THAT YOU CAN SEE GHOSTS.
YOU LOOK JUST LIKE THE LEGENDS SUGGEST-ED...
...WITH YOUR LONG LIMBS AND AMPLE, CURLED HAIR.
AND WHO ARE YOU?
I AM IZUMI, DESCENDANT OF HAYASE OF THE GUARDIANS...
...AND MIZUHA'S MOTHER.

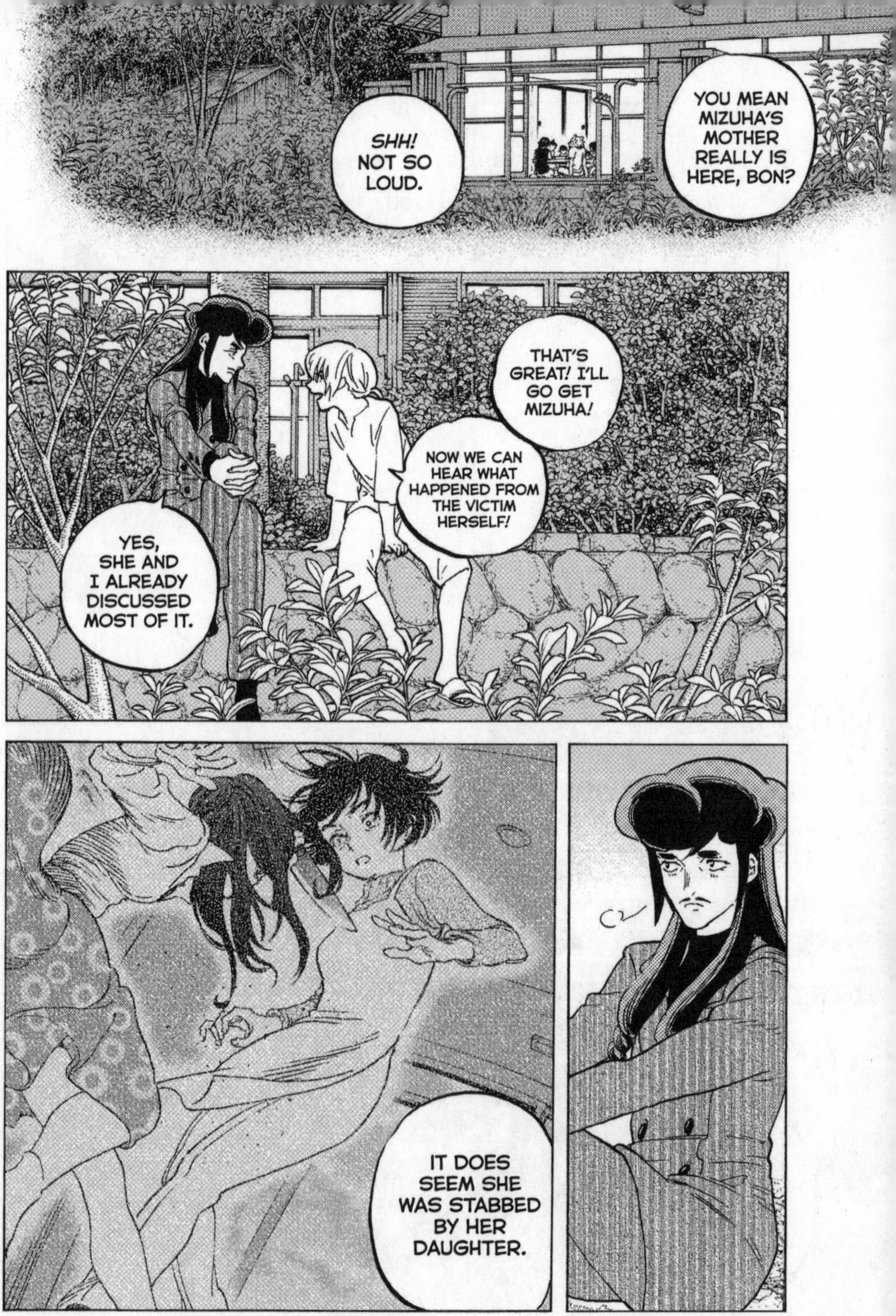
YOU MEAN MIZUHA'S MOTHER REALLY IS HERE, BON?
SHH! NOT SO LOUD.
THAT'S GREAT! I'LL GO GET MIZUHA!
NOW WE CAN HEAR WHAT HAPPENED FROM THE VICTIM HERSELF!
YES, SHE AND I ALREADY DISCUSSED MOST OF IT.
IT DOES SEEM SHE WAS STABBED BY HER DAUGHTER.

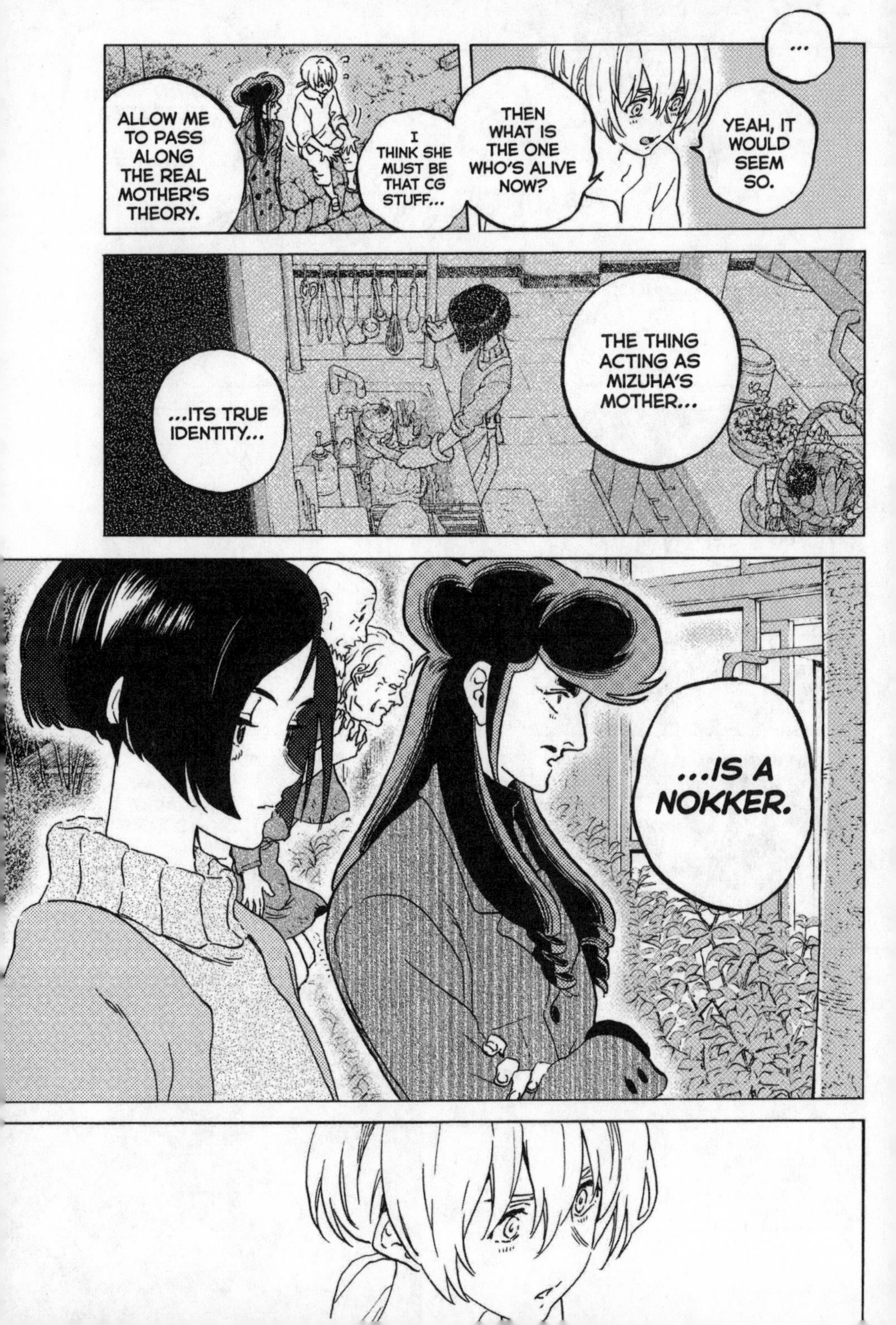
...
YEAH, IT WOULD SEEM SO.
THEN WHAT IS THE ONE WHO'S ALIVE NOW?
I THINK SHE MUST BE THAT CG STUFF...
ALLOW ME TO PASS ALONG THE REAL MOTHER'S THEORY.
THE THING ACTING AS MIZUHA'S MOTHER...
...ITS TRUE IDENTITY...
...IS A NOKKER.

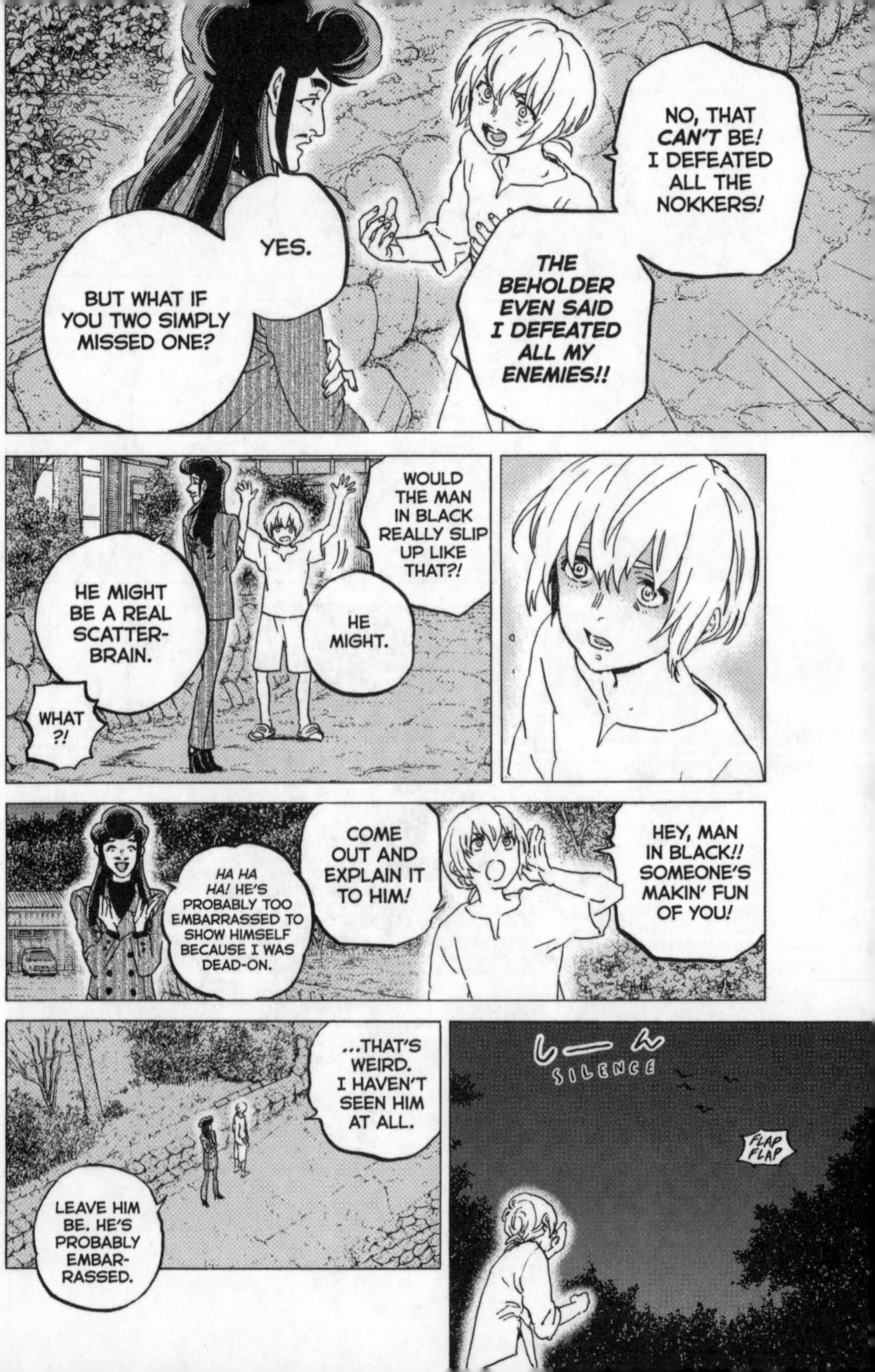
NO, THAT CAN'T BE! I DEFEATED ALL THE NOKKERS!
THE BEHOLDER EVEN SAID I DEFEATED ALL MY ENEMIES!!
YES.
BUT WHAT IF YOU TWO SIMPLY MISSED ONE?
WOULD THE MAN IN BLACK REALLY SLIP UP LIKE THAT?!
HE MIGHT.
HE MIGHT BE A REAL SCATTER-BRAIN.
WHAT ?!
HEY, MAN IN BLACK!! SOMEONE'S MAKIN' FUN OF YOU!
COME OUT AND EXPLAIN IT TO HIM!
HA HA HA! HE'S PROBABLY TOO EMBARRASSED TO SHOW HIMSELF BECAUSE I WAS DEAD-ON.
しーん
SILENCE
FLAP FLAP
...THAT'S WEIRD. I HAVEN'T SEEN HIM AT ALL.
LEAVE HIM BE. HE'S PROBABLY EMBARRASSED.

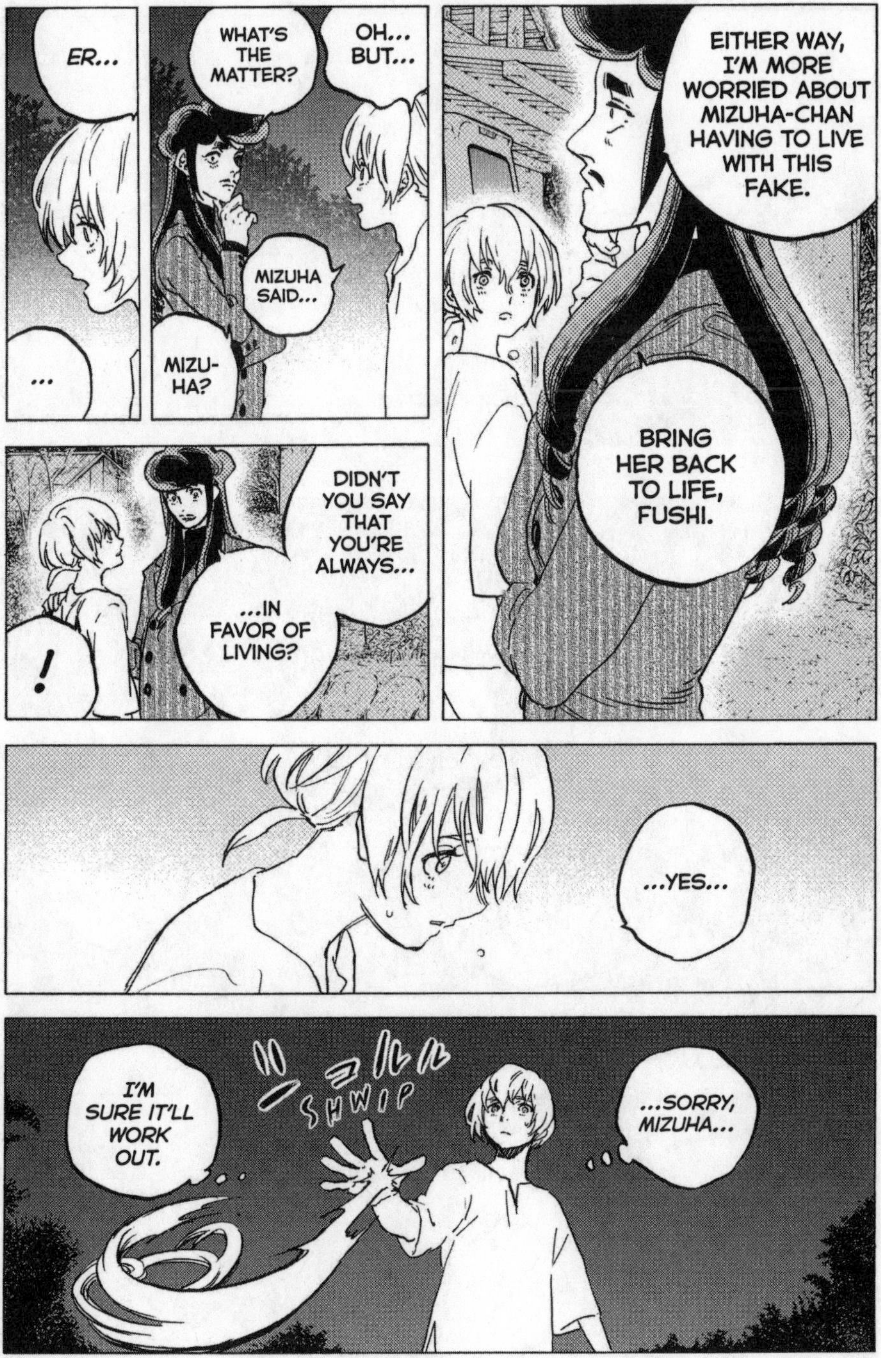
EITHER WAY, I'M MORE WORRIED ABOUT MIZUHA-CHAN HAVING TO LIVE WITH THIS FAKE.
BRING HER BACK TO LIFE, FUSHI.
OH... BUT...
WHAT'S THE MATTER?
MIZUHA SAID...
MIZU-HA?
ER...
...
DIDN'T YOU SAY THAT YOU'RE ALWAYS...
...IN FAVOR OF LIVING?
!
...YES...
...SORRY, MIZUHA...
SHWIP
I'M SURE IT'LL WORK OUT.

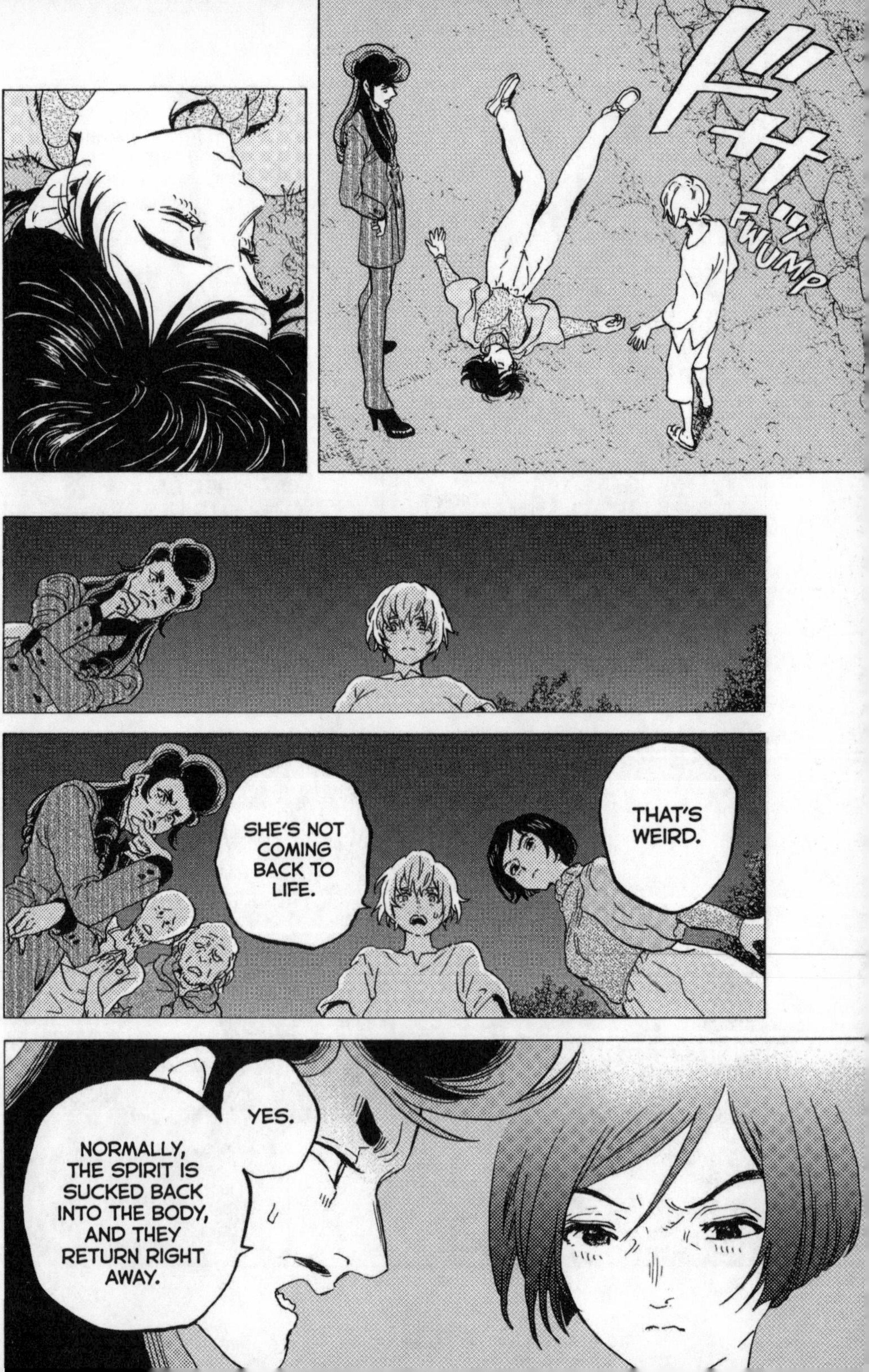
FWUMP
THAT'S WEIRD.
SHE'S NOT COMING BACK TO LIFE.
YES.
NORMALLY, THE SPIRIT IS SUCKED BACK INTO THE BODY, AND THEY RETURN RIGHT AWAY.

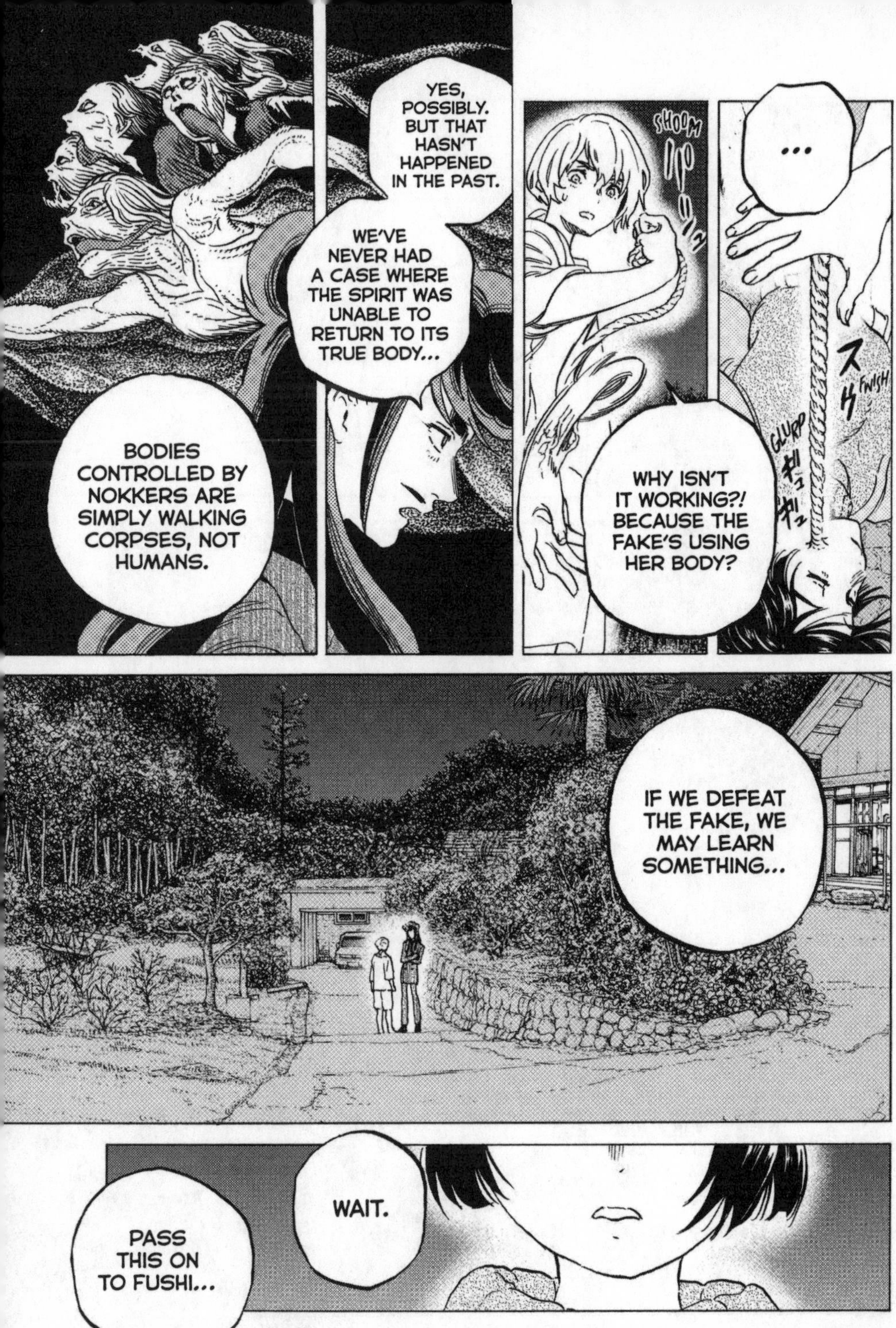
...
FWISH
GLURP
SHOOM
WHY ISN'T IT WORKING?! BECAUSE THE FAKE'S USING HER BODY?
YES, POSSIBLY. BUT THAT HASN'T HAPPENED IN THE PAST.
WE'VE NEVER HAD A CASE WHERE THE SPIRIT WAS UNABLE TO RETURN TO ITS TRUE BODY...
BODIES CONTROLLED BY NOKKERS ARE SIMPLY WALKING CORPSES, NOT HUMANS.
IF WE DEFEAT THE FAKE, WE MAY LEARN SOMETHING...
WAIT.
PASS THIS ON TO FUSHI...

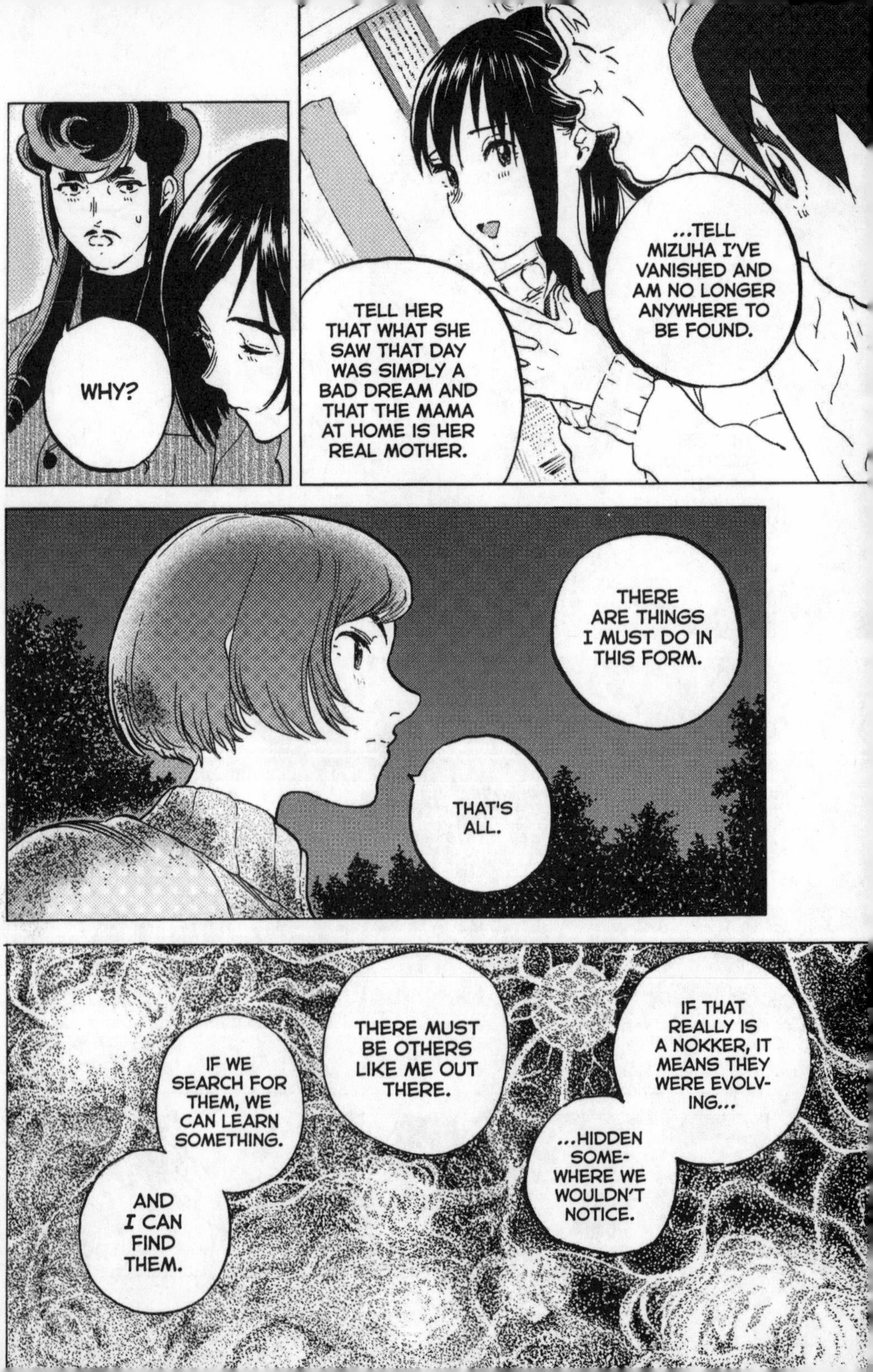
...TELL MIZUHA I'VE VANISHED AND AM NO LONGER ANYWHERE TO BE FOUND.
TELL HER THAT WHAT SHE SAW THAT DAY WAS SIMPLY A BAD DREAM AND THAT THE MAMA AT HOME IS HER REAL MOTHER.
WHY?
THERE ARE THINGS I MUST DO IN THIS FORM.
THAT'S ALL.
IF THAT REALLY IS A NOKKER, IT MEANS THEY WERE EVOLV-ING...
...HIDDEN SOME-WHERE WE WOULDN'T NOTICE.
THERE MUST BE OTHERS LIKE ME OUT THERE.
IF WE SEARCH FOR THEM, WE CAN LEARN SOMETHING.
AND *I* CAN FIND THEM.

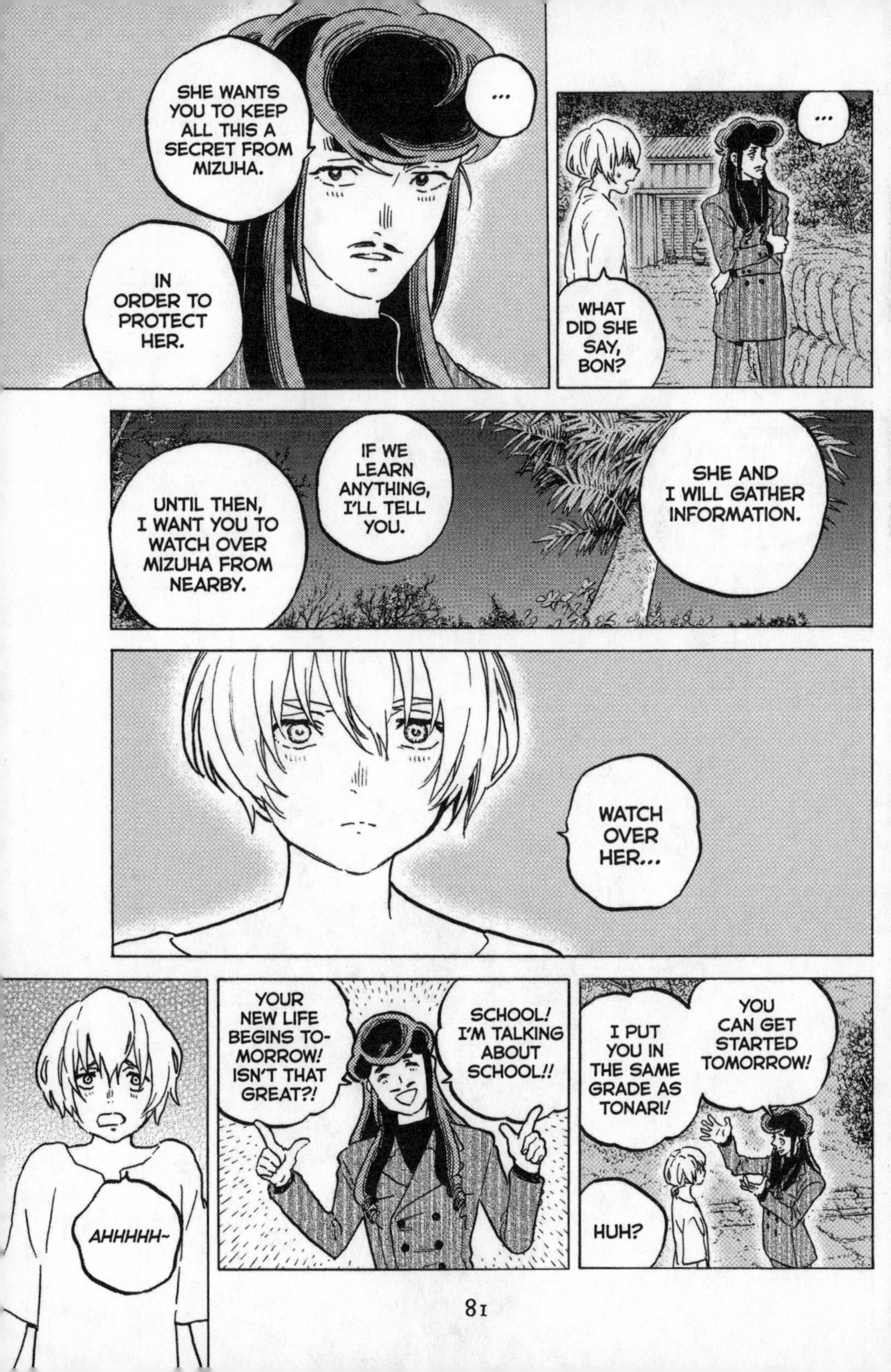
...
WHAT DID SHE SAY, BON?
...
SHE WANTS YOU TO KEEP ALL THIS A SECRET FROM MIZUHA.
IN ORDER TO PROTECT HER.
SHE AND I WILL GATHER INFORMATION.
IF WE LEARN ANYTHING, I'LL TELL YOU.
UNTIL THEN, I WANT YOU TO WATCH OVER MIZUHA FROM NEARBY.
WATCH OVER HER...
YOU CAN GET STARTED TOMORROW!
I PUT YOU IN THE SAME GRADE AS TONARI!
HUH?
SCHOOL! I'M TALKING ABOUT SCHOOL!!
YOUR NEW LIFE BEGINS TO-MORROW! ISN'T THAT GREAT?!
AHHHHH~

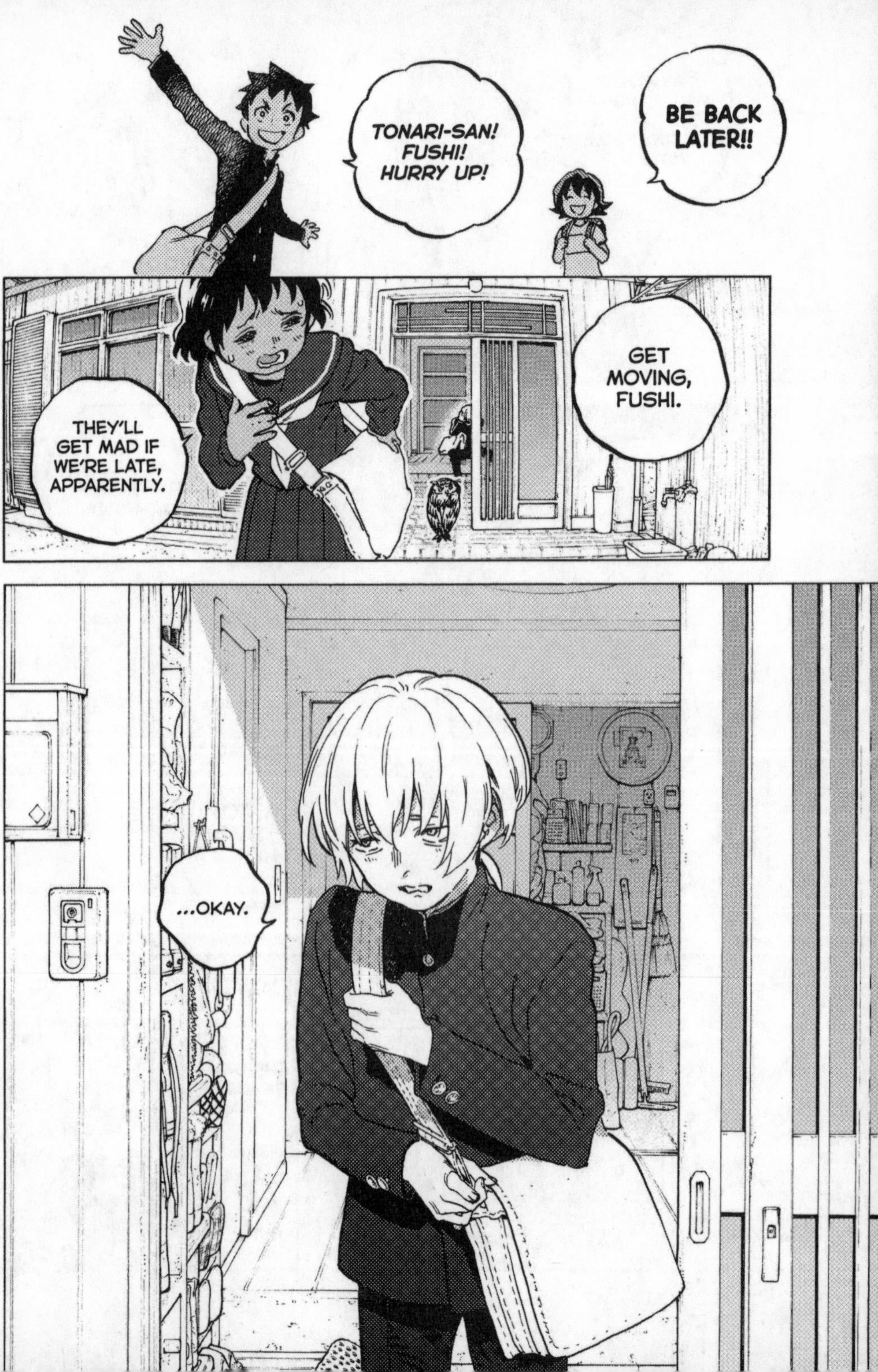
BE BACK LATER!!
TONARI-SAN! FUSHI! HURRY UP!
GET MOVING, FUSHI.
THEY'LL GET MAD IF WE'RE LATE, APPARENTLY.
...OKAY.

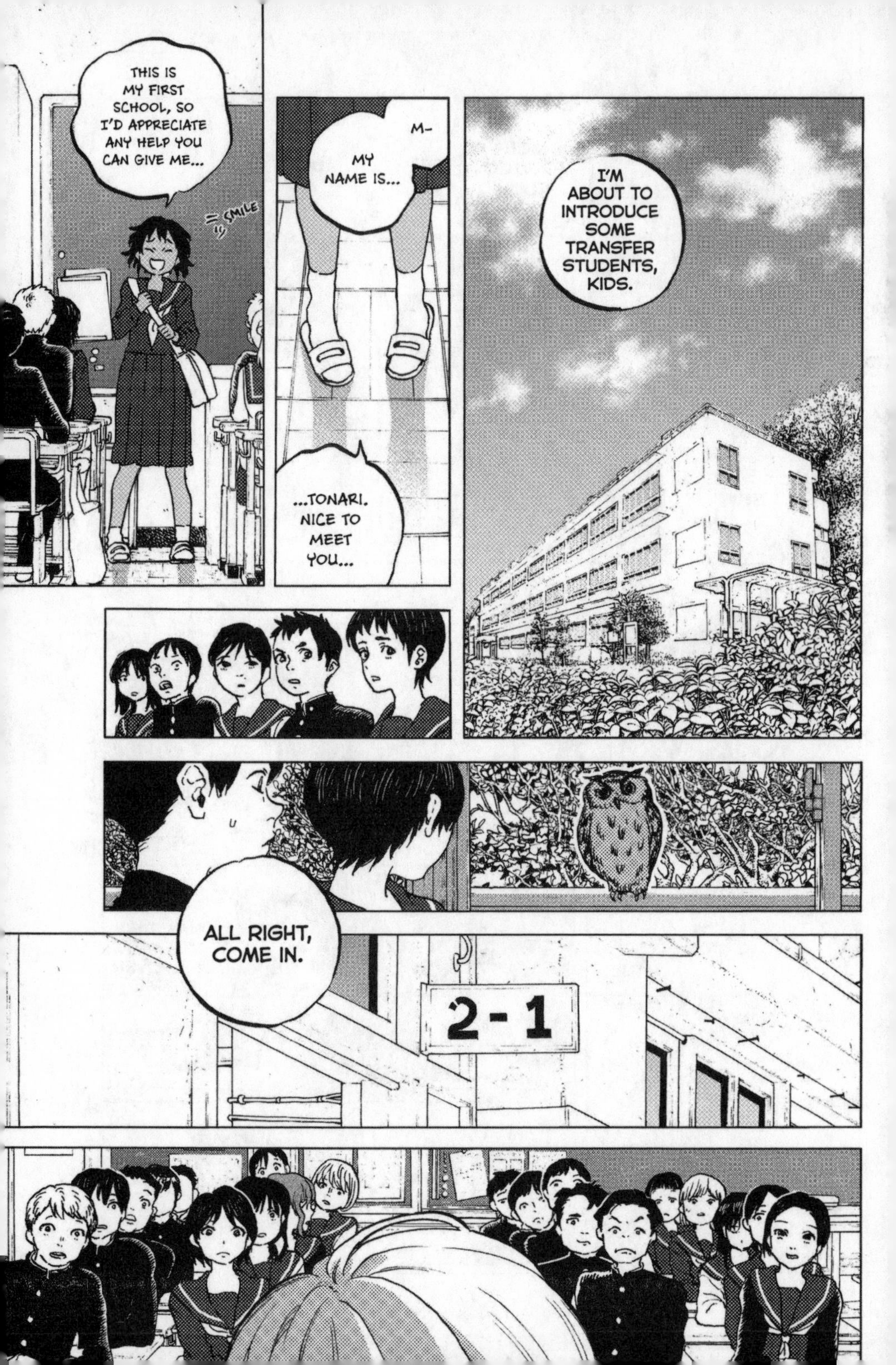
I'M ABOUT TO INTRODUCE SOME TRANSFER STUDENTS, KIDS.
M-
MY NAME IS...
...TONARI. NICE TO MEET YOU...
THIS IS MY FIRST SCHOOL, SO I'D APPRECIATE ANY HELP YOU CAN GIVE ME...
SMILE
ALL RIGHT, COME IN.
2-1

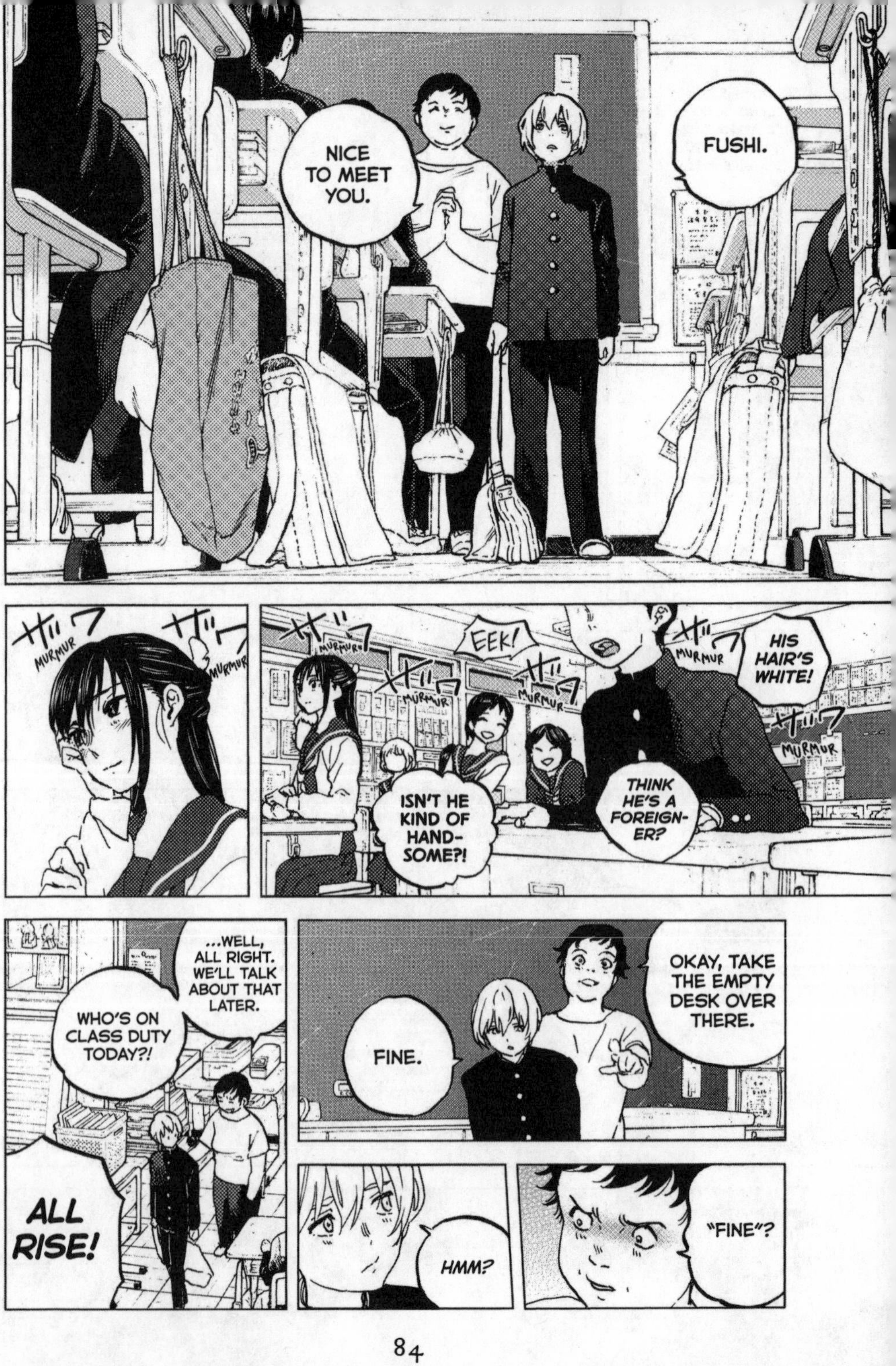
FUSHI.
NICE TO MEET YOU.
MURMUR
HIS HAIR'S WHITE!
EEK!
MURMUR
MURMUR
MURMUR
THINK HE'S A FOREIGNER?
ISN'T HE KIND OF HANDSOME?!
MURMUR
MURMUR
MURMUR
OKAY, TAKE THE EMPTY DESK OVER THERE.
FINE.
"FINE"?
HMM?
...WELL, ALL RIGHT. WE'LL TALK ABOUT THAT LATER.
WHO'S ON CLASS DUTY TODAY?!
ALL RISE!

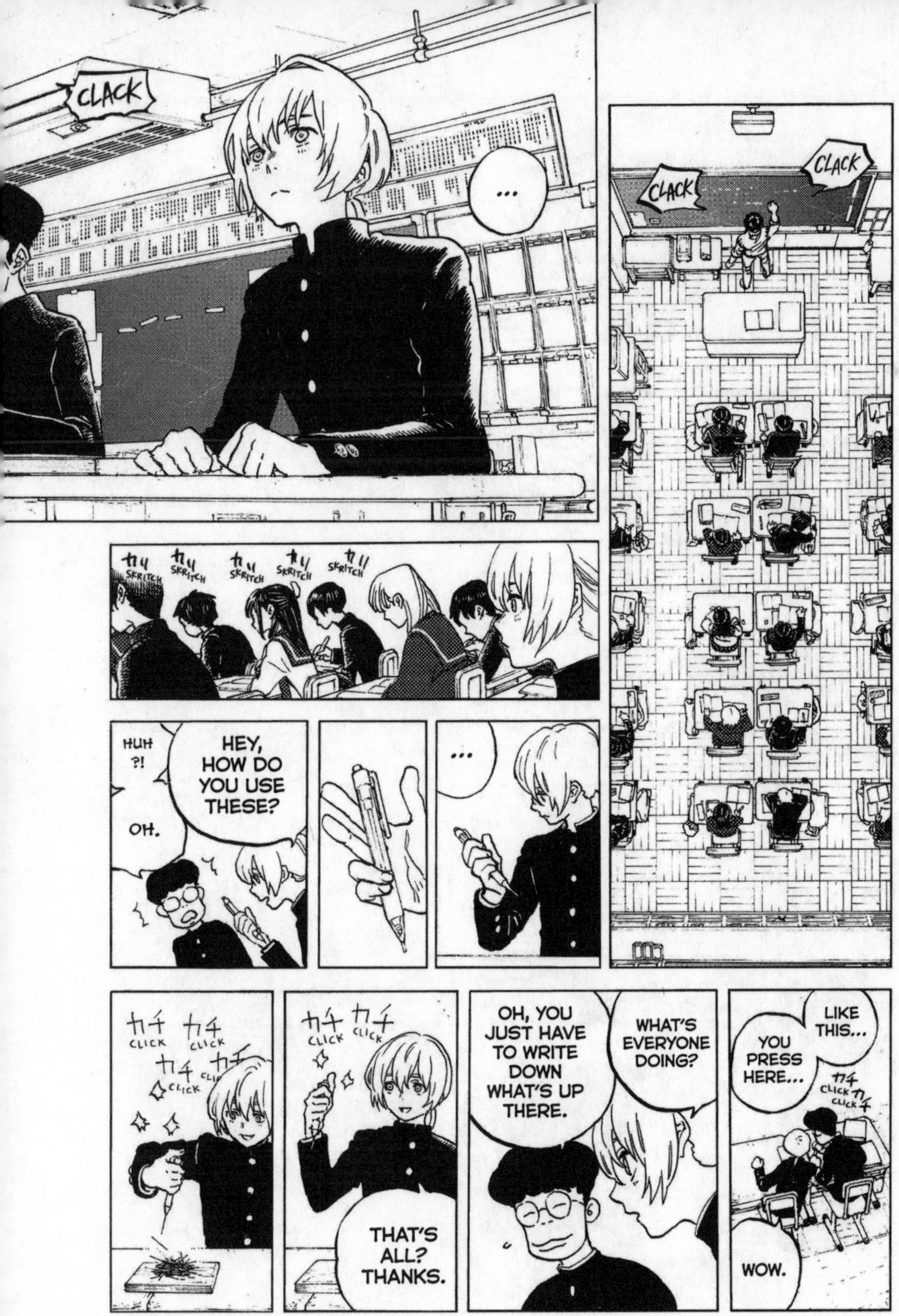
CLACK
CLACK
CLACK
...
カリ SKRITCH
カリ SKRITCH
カリ SKRITCH
カリ SKRITCH
カリ SKRITCH
...
HEY, HOW DO YOU USE THESE?
HUH ?!
OH.
LIKE THIS...
YOU PRESS HERE...
カチ CLICK カチ CLICK
WOW.
WHAT'S EVERYONE DOING?
OH, YOU JUST HAVE TO WRITE DOWN WHAT'S UP THERE.
カチ CLICK カチ CLICK
THAT'S ALL? THANKS.
カチ CLICK カチ CLICK
カチ CLICK カチ CLICK

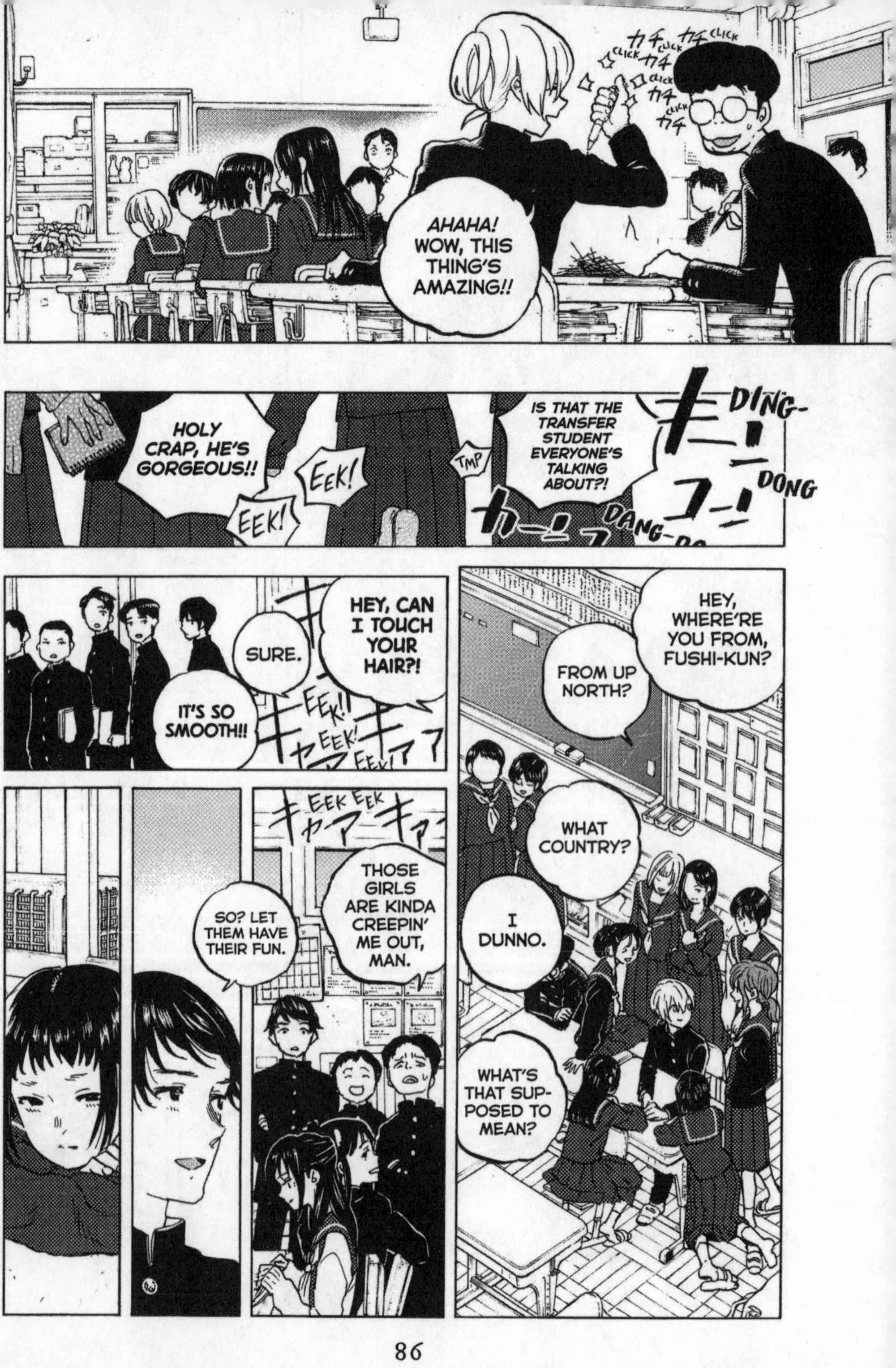
CLICK CLICK CLICK CLICK CLICK
AHAHA! WOW, THIS THING'S AMAZING!!
DING-
DONG
IS THAT THE TRANSFER STUDENT EVERYONE'S TALKING ABOUT?!
TMP
EEK!
EEK!
HOLY CRAP, HE'S GORGEOUS!!
HEY, WHERE'RE YOU FROM, FUSHI-KUN?
FROM UP NORTH?
WHAT COUNTRY?
I DUNNO.
WHAT'S THAT SUP-POSED TO MEAN?
HEY, CAN I TOUCH YOUR HAIR?!
SURE.
IT'S SO SMOOTH!!
EEK!! EEK! EEK!
EEK EEK
THOSE GIRLS ARE KINDA CREEPIN' ME OUT, MAN.
SO? LET THEM HAVE THEIR FUN.

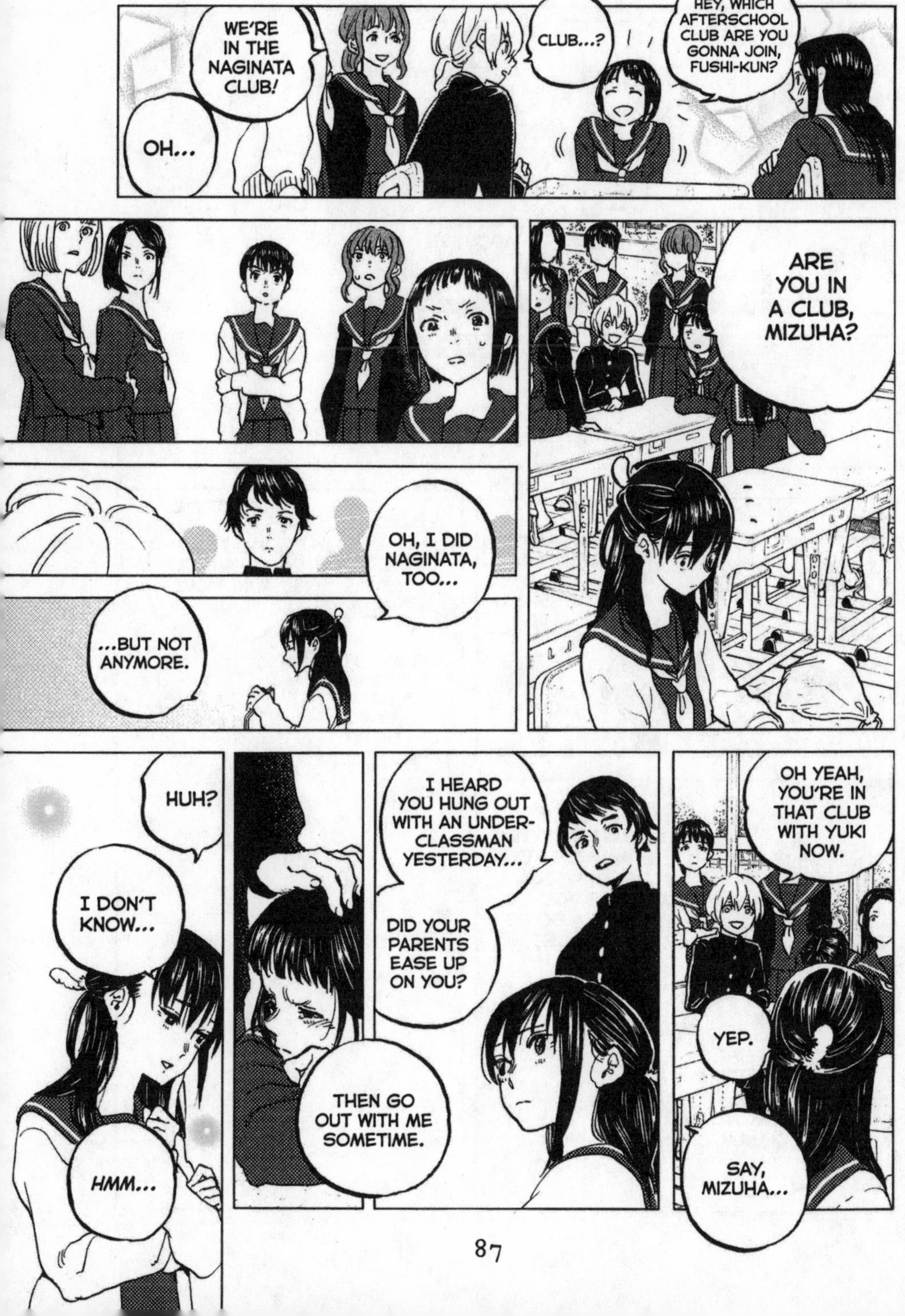
HEY, WHICH AFTERSCHOOL CLUB ARE YOU GONNA JOIN, FUSHI-KUN?
CLUB...?
WE'RE IN THE NAGINATA CLUB!
OH...
ARE YOU IN A CLUB, MIZUHA?
OH, I DID NAGINATA, TOO...
...BUT NOT ANYMORE.
OH YEAH, YOU'RE IN THAT CLUB WITH YUKI NOW.
YEP.
SAY, MIZUHA...
I HEARD YOU HUNG OUT WITH AN UNDER-CLASSMAN YESTERDAY...
DID YOUR PARENTS EASE UP ON YOU?
THEN GO OUT WITH ME SOMETIME.
HUH?
I DON'T KNOW...
HMM...

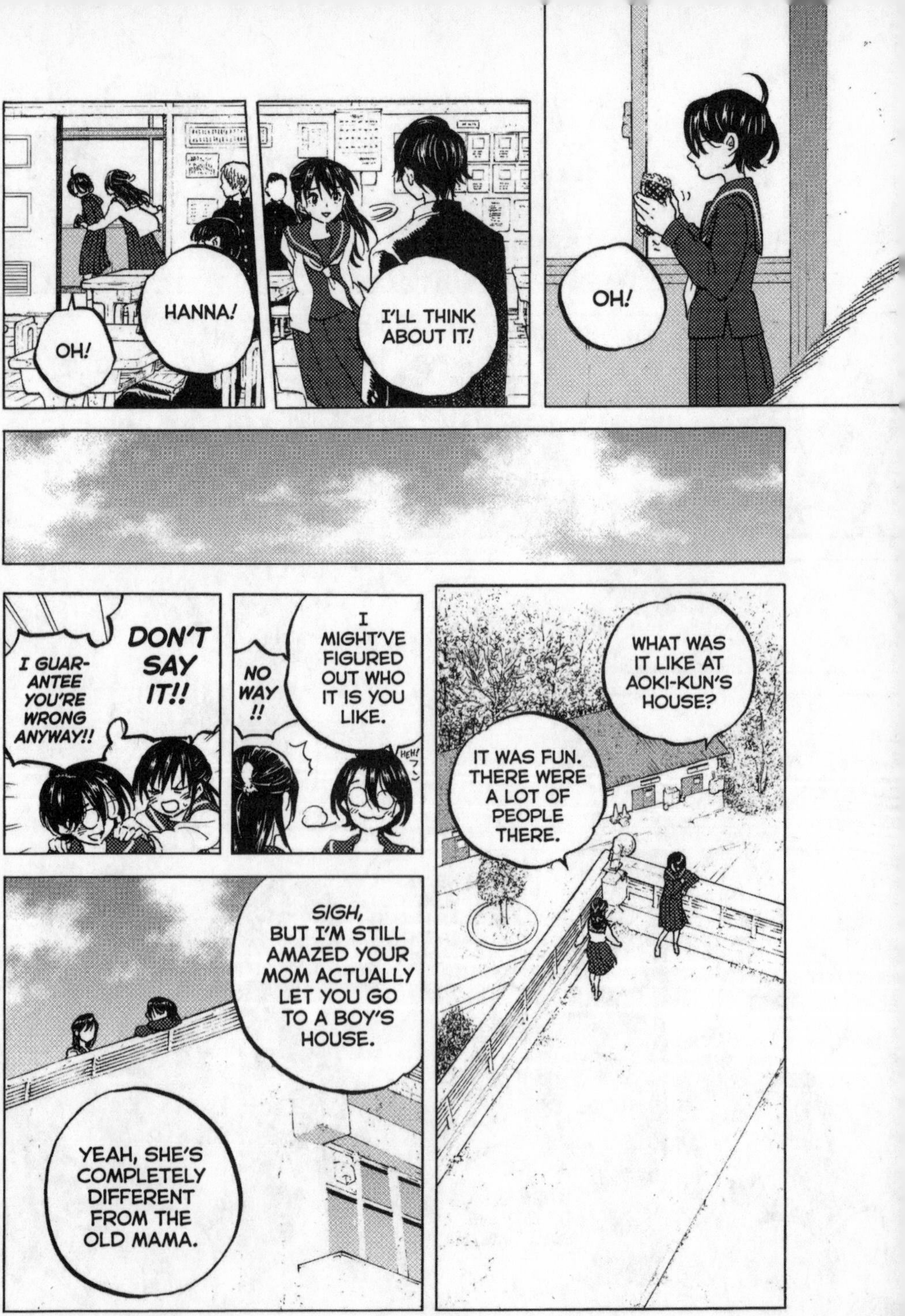
OH!
I'LL THINK ABOUT IT!
HANNA!
OH!
WHAT WAS IT LIKE AT AOKI-KUN'S HOUSE?
IT WAS FUN. THERE WERE A LOT OF PEOPLE THERE.
I MIGHT'VE FIGURED OUT WHO IT IS YOU LIKE.
HEH!
NO WAY!!
DON'T SAY IT!!
I GUARANTEE YOU'RE WRONG ANYWAY!!
SIGH, BUT I'M STILL AMAZED YOUR MOM ACTUALLY LET YOU GO TO A BOY'S HOUSE.
YEAH, SHE'S COMPLETELY DIFFERENT FROM THE OLD MAMA.

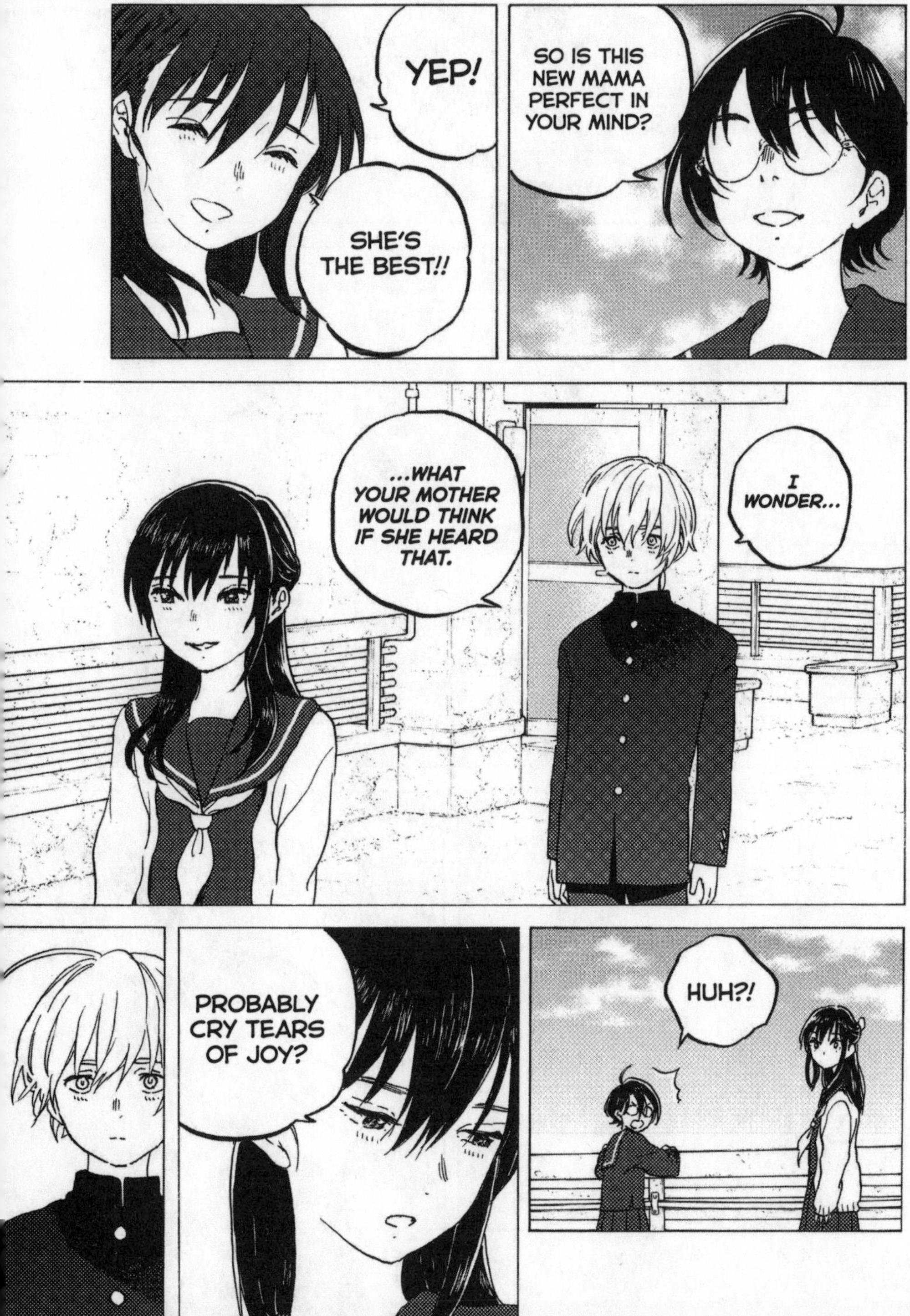
SO IS THIS NEW MAMA PERFECT IN YOUR MIND?
YEP!
SHE'S THE BEST!!
I WONDER...
...WHAT YOUR MOTHER WOULD THINK IF SHE HEARD THAT.
HUH?!
PROBABLY CRY TEARS OF JOY?

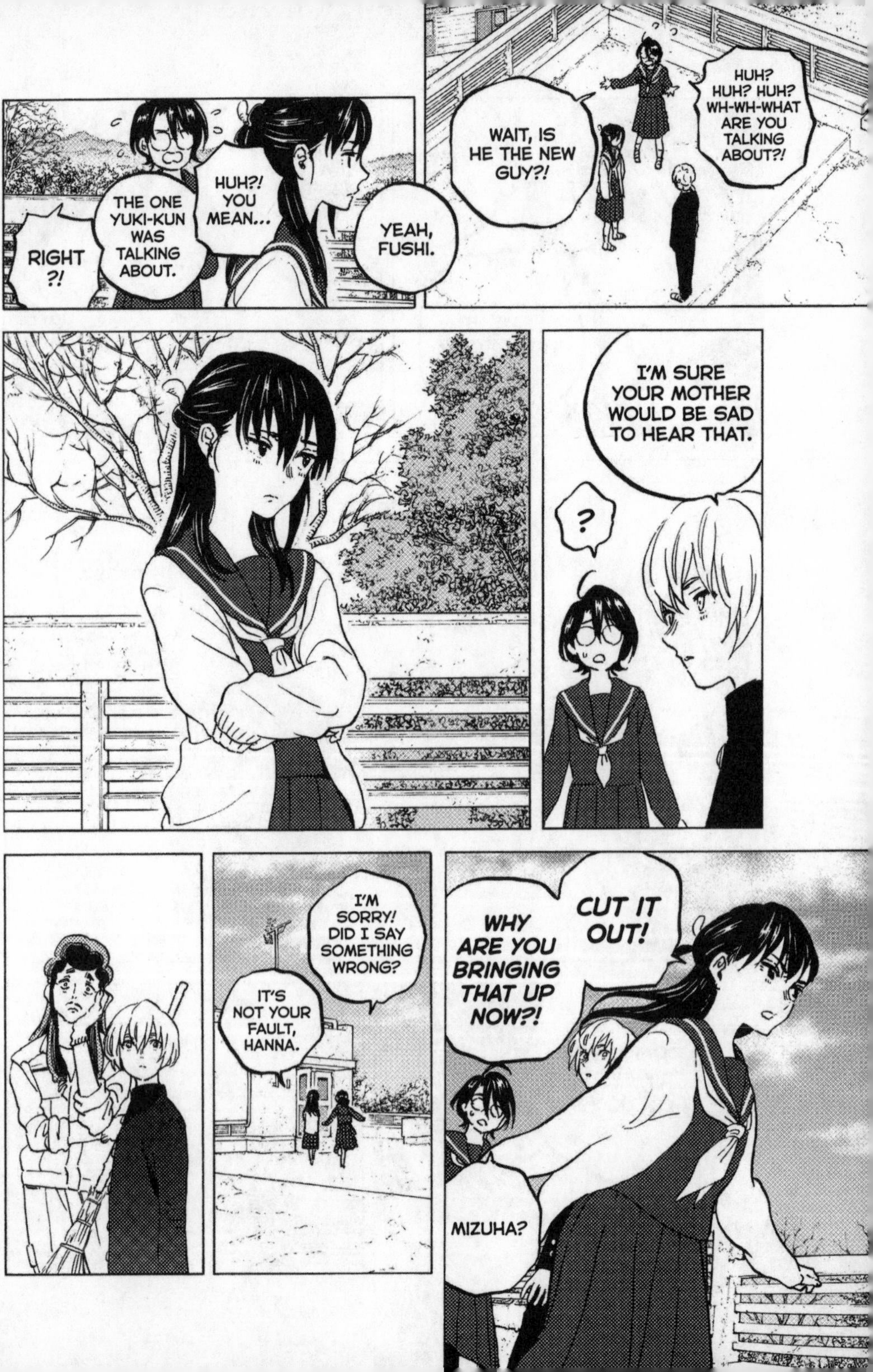
HUH? HUH? HUH? WH-WH-WHAT ARE YOU TALKING ABOUT?!
WAIT, IS HE THE NEW GUY?!
YEAH, FUSHI.
HUH?! YOU MEAN...
THE ONE YUKI-KUN WAS TALKING ABOUT.
RIGHT ?!
I'M SURE YOUR MOTHER WOULD BE SAD TO HEAR THAT.
?
CUT IT OUT!
WHY ARE YOU BRINGING THAT UP NOW?!
MIZUHA?
I'M SORRY! DID I SAY SOMETHING WRONG?
IT'S NOT YOUR FAULT, HANNA.

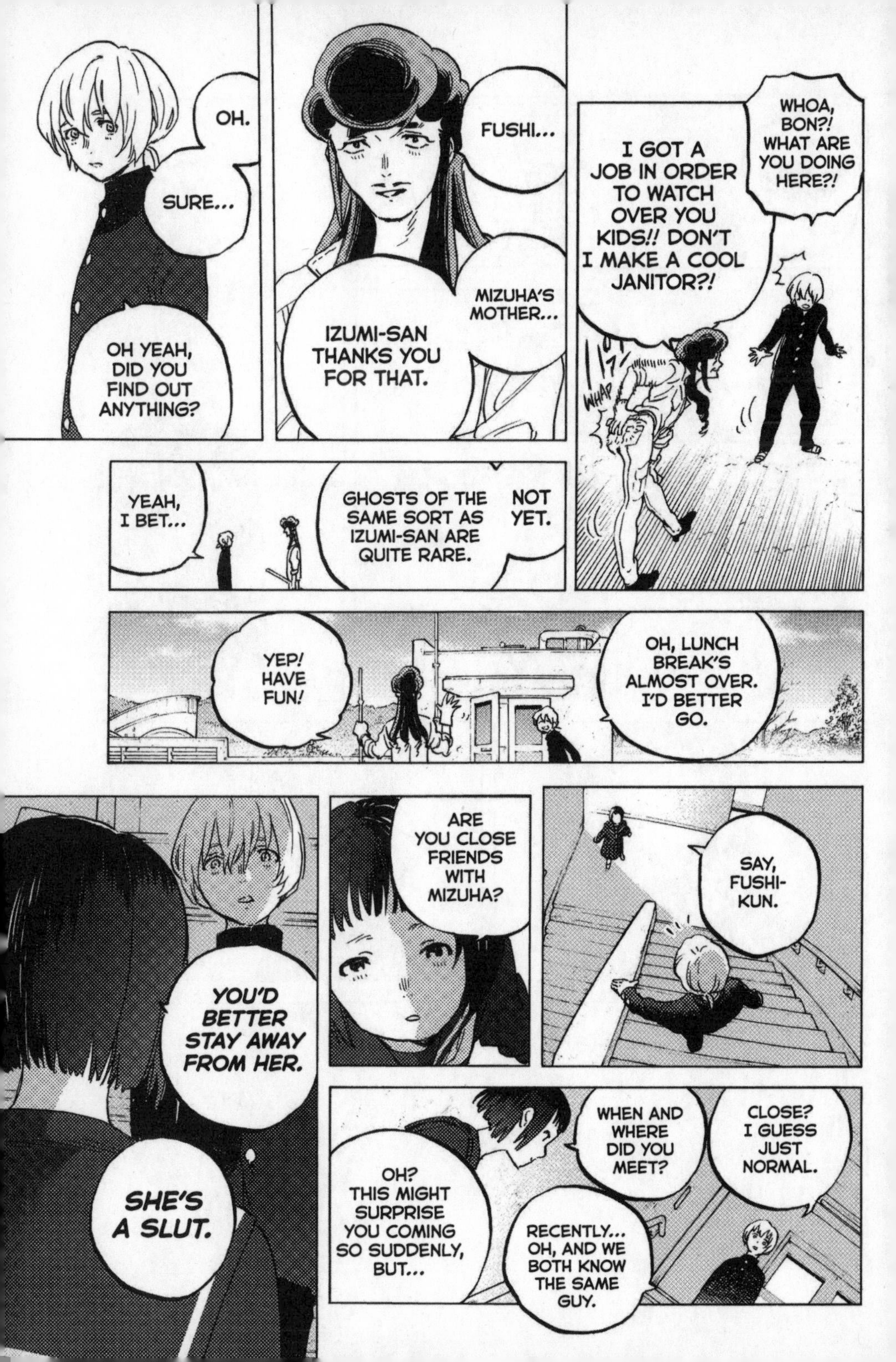
WHOA, BON?! WHAT ARE YOU DOING HERE?!
I GOT A JOB IN ORDER TO WATCH OVER YOU KIDS!! DON'T I MAKE A COOL JANITOR?!
WHAP
FUSHI...
MIZUHA'S MOTHER...
IZUMI-SAN THANKS YOU FOR THAT.
OH.
SURE...
OH YEAH, DID YOU FIND OUT ANYTHING?
NOT YET.
GHOSTS OF THE SAME SORT AS IZUMI-SAN ARE QUITE RARE.
YEAH, I BET...
OH, LUNCH BREAK'S ALMOST OVER. I'D BETTER GO.
YEP! HAVE FUN!
SAY, FUSHI-KUN.
ARE YOU CLOSE FRIENDS WITH MIZUHA?
CLOSE? I GUESS JUST NORMAL.
WHEN AND WHERE DID YOU MEET?
RECENTLY... OH, AND WE BOTH KNOW THE SAME GUY.
OH? THIS MIGHT SURPRISE YOU COMING SO SUDDENLY, BUT...
YOU'D BETTER STAY AWAY FROM HER.
SHE'S A SLUT.

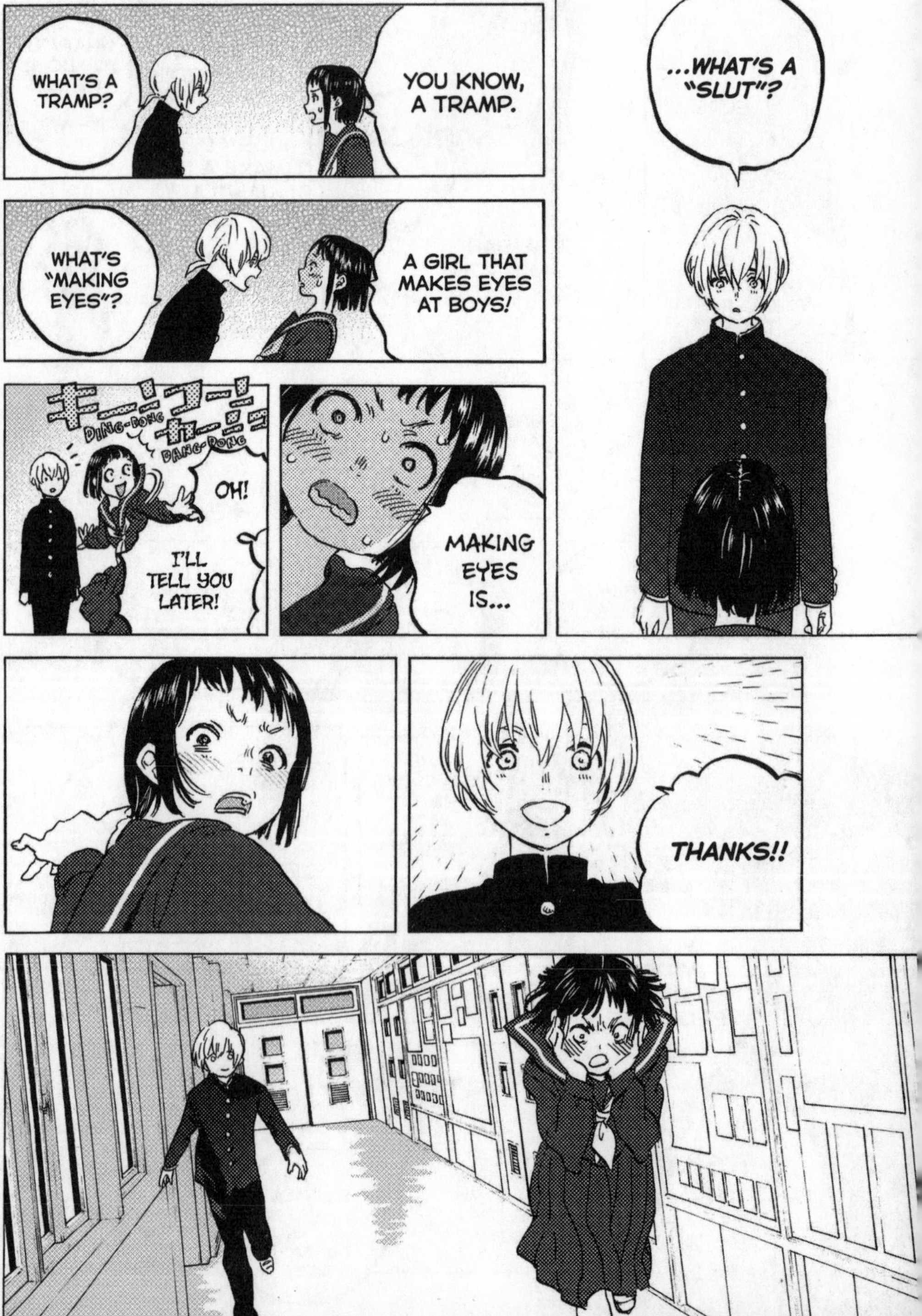
...WHAT'S A "SLUT"?
YOU KNOW, A TRAMP.
WHAT'S A TRAMP?
A GIRL THAT MAKES EYES AT BOYS!
WHAT'S "MAKING EYES"?
MAKING EYES IS...
DING-DONG
DANG-DONG
OH!
I'LL TELL YOU LATER!
THANKS!!

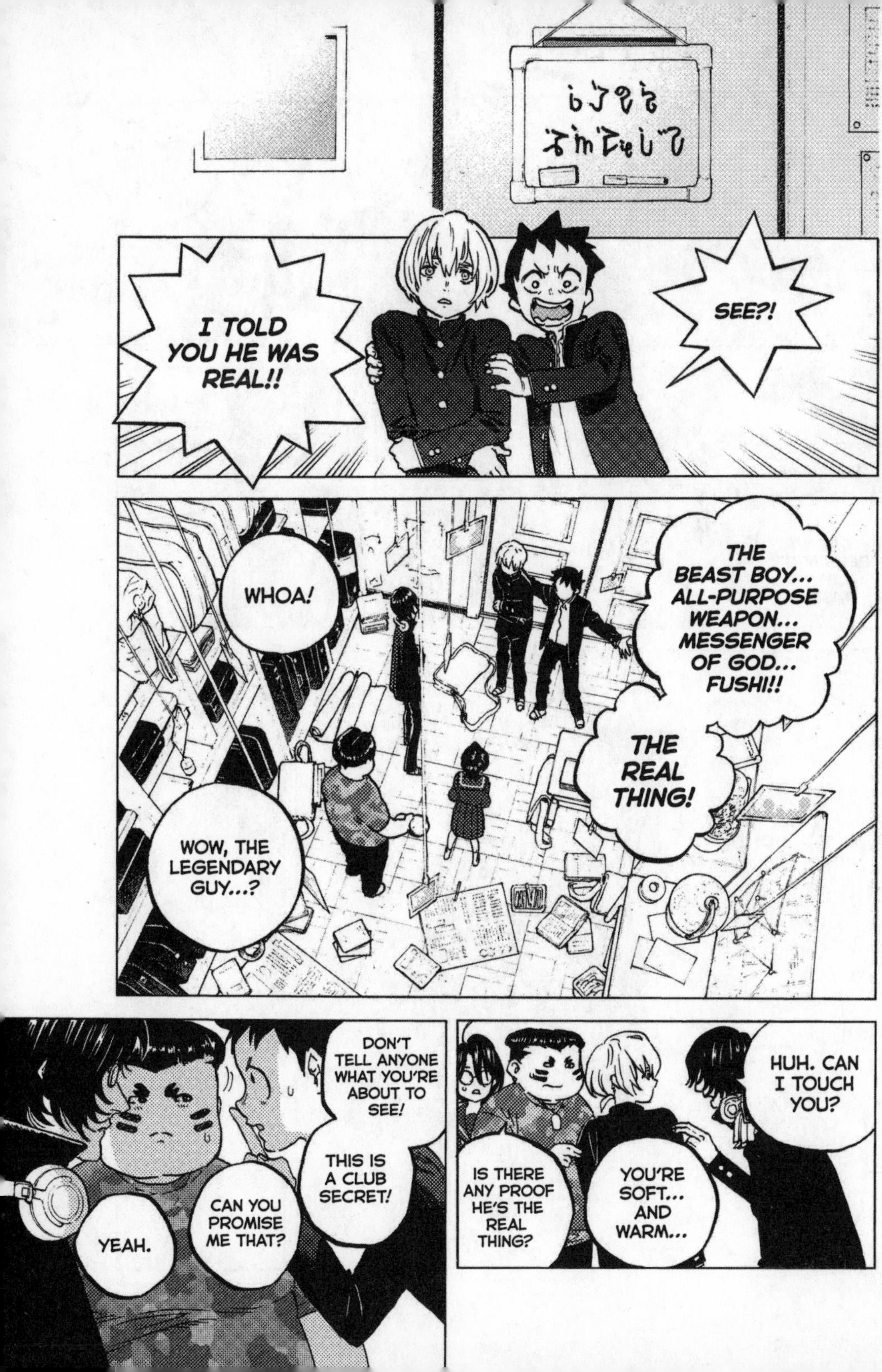
SEE?!
I TOLD YOU HE WAS REAL!!
THE BEAST BOY... ALL-PURPOSE WEAPON... MESSENGER OF GOD... FUSHI!!
THE REAL THING!
WHOA!
WOW, THE LEGENDARY GUY...?
HUH. CAN I TOUCH YOU?
YOU'RE SOFT... AND WARM...
IS THERE ANY PROOF HE'S THE REAL THING?
DON'T TELL ANYONE WHAT YOU'RE ABOUT TO SEE!
THIS IS A CLUB SECRET!
CAN YOU PROMISE ME THAT?
YEAH.

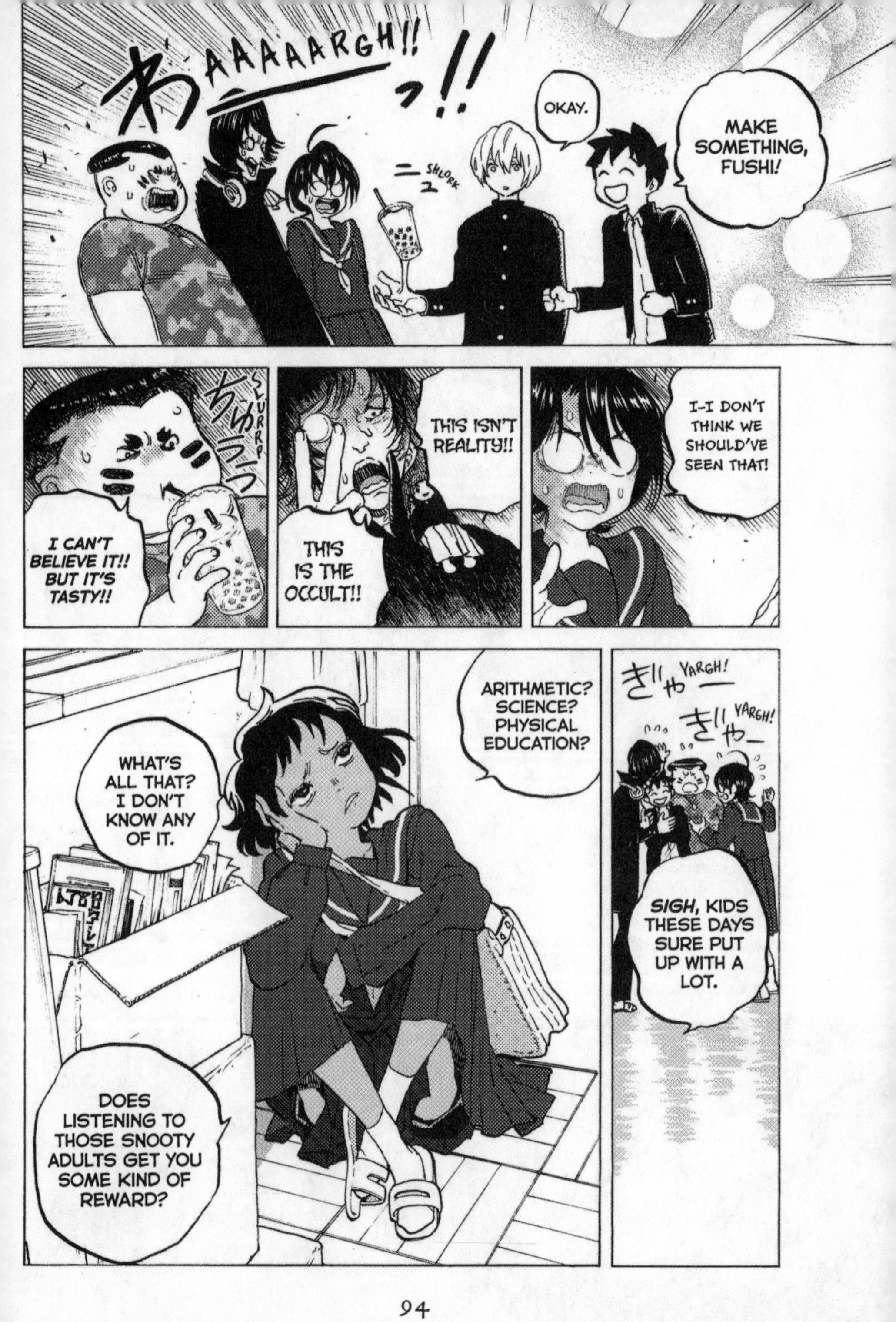
MAKE SOMETHING, FUSHI!
OKAY.
SHLORK
AAAAAARGH!!
I-I DON'T THINK WE SHOULD'VE SEEN THAT!
THIS ISN'T REALITY!!
THIS IS THE OCCULT!!
SLURRP
I CAN'T BELIEVE IT!! BUT IT'S TASTY!!
YARGH!
YARGH!
*SIGH*, KIDS THESE DAYS SURE PUT UP WITH A LOT.
ARITHMETIC? SCIENCE? PHYSICAL EDUCATION?
WHAT'S ALL THAT? I DON'T KNOW ANY OF IT.
DOES LISTENING TO THOSE SNOOTY ADULTS GET YOU SOME KIND OF REWARD?

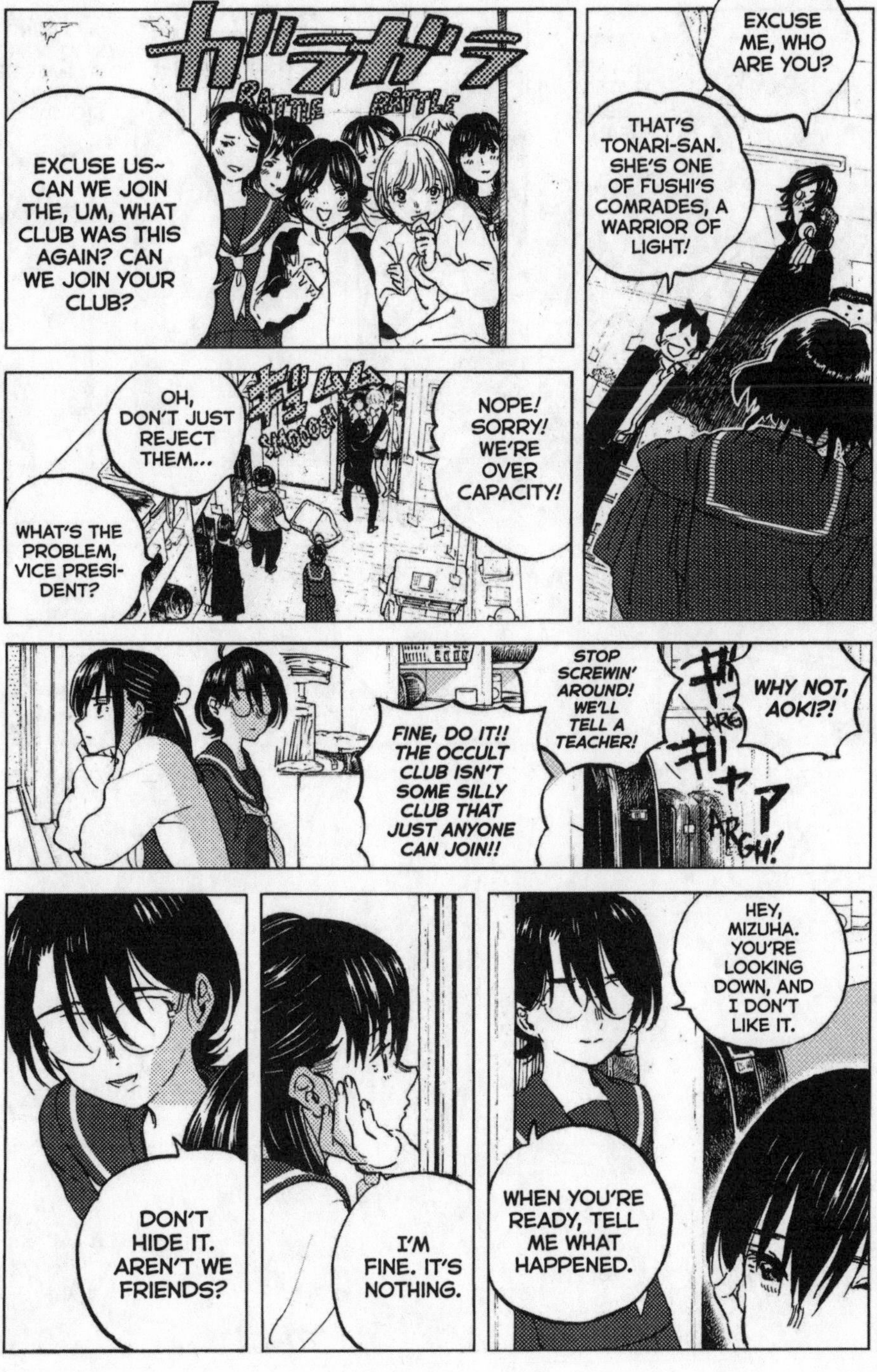
EXCUSE ME, WHO ARE YOU?
THAT'S TONARI-SAN. SHE'S ONE OF FUSHI'S COMRADES, A WARRIOR OF LIGHT!
ガラガラ
RATTLE RATTLE
EXCUSE US~ CAN WE JOIN THE, UM, WHAT CLUB WAS THIS AGAIN? CAN WE JOIN YOUR CLUB?
NOPE! SORRY! WE'RE OVER CAPACITY!
OH, DON'T JUST REJECT THEM...
WHAT'S THE PROBLEM, VICE PRESIDENT?
WHY NOT, AOKI?!
ARG
ARGH!
STOP SCREWIN' AROUND! WE'LL TELL A TEACHER!
FINE, DO IT!! THE OCCULT CLUB ISN'T SOME SILLY CLUB THAT JUST ANYONE CAN JOIN!!
HEY, MIZUHA. YOU'RE LOOKING DOWN, AND I DON'T LIKE IT.
WHEN YOU'RE READY, TELL ME WHAT HAPPENED.
I'M FINE. IT'S NOTHING.
DON'T HIDE IT. AREN'T WE FRIENDS?

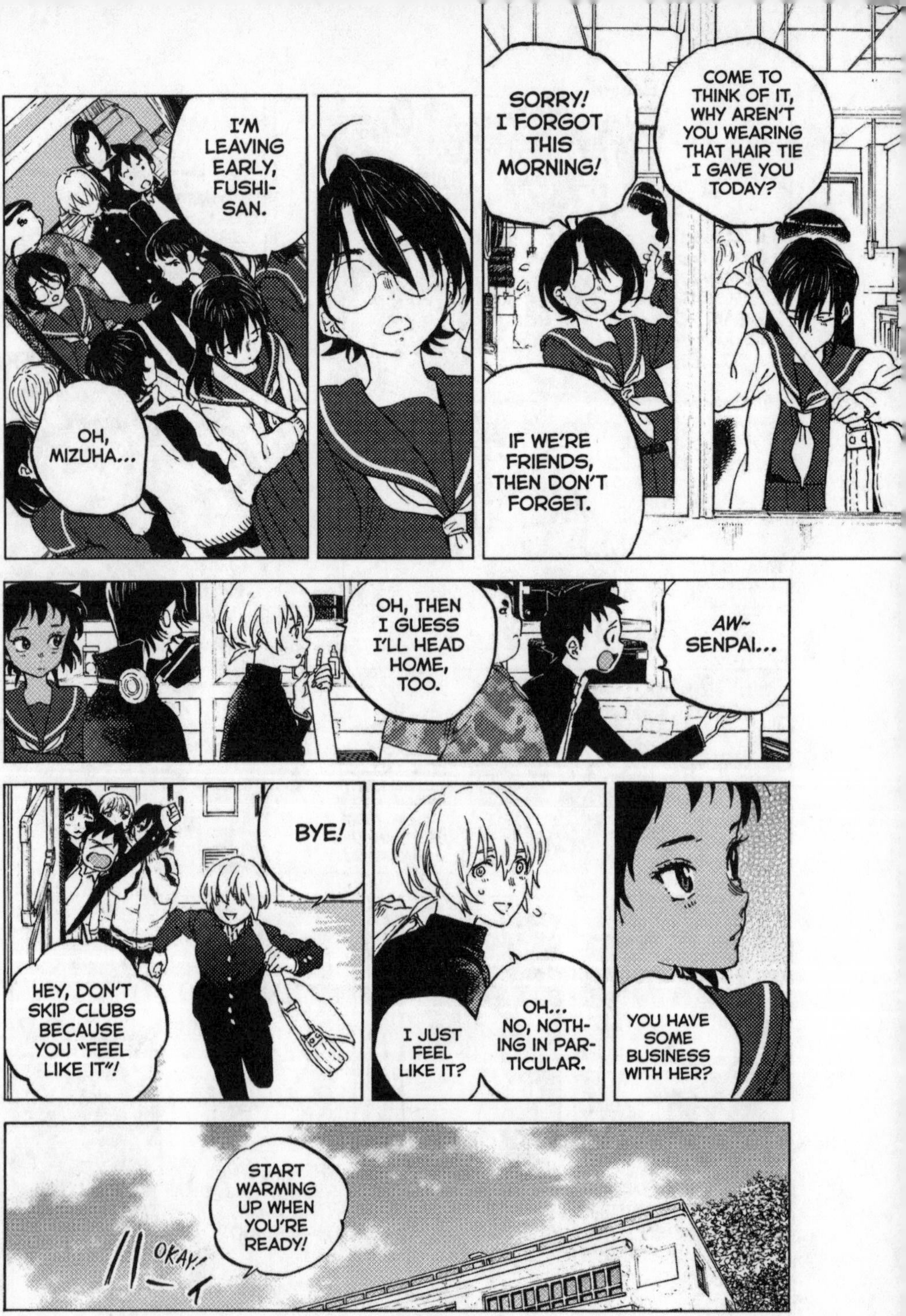
COME TO THINK OF IT, WHY AREN'T YOU WEARING THAT HAIR TIE I GAVE YOU TODAY?
SORRY! I FORGOT THIS MORNING!
IF WE'RE FRIENDS, THEN DON'T FORGET.
I'M LEAVING EARLY, FUSHI-SAN.
OH, MIZUHA...
AW~ SENPAI...
OH, THEN I GUESS I'LL HEAD HOME, TOO.
YOU HAVE SOME BUSINESS WITH HER?
OH... NO, NOTHING IN PARTICULAR.
I JUST FEEL LIKE IT?
BYE!
HEY, DON'T SKIP CLUBS BECAUSE YOU "FEEL LIKE IT"!
START WARMING UP WHEN YOU'RE READY!
OKAY!

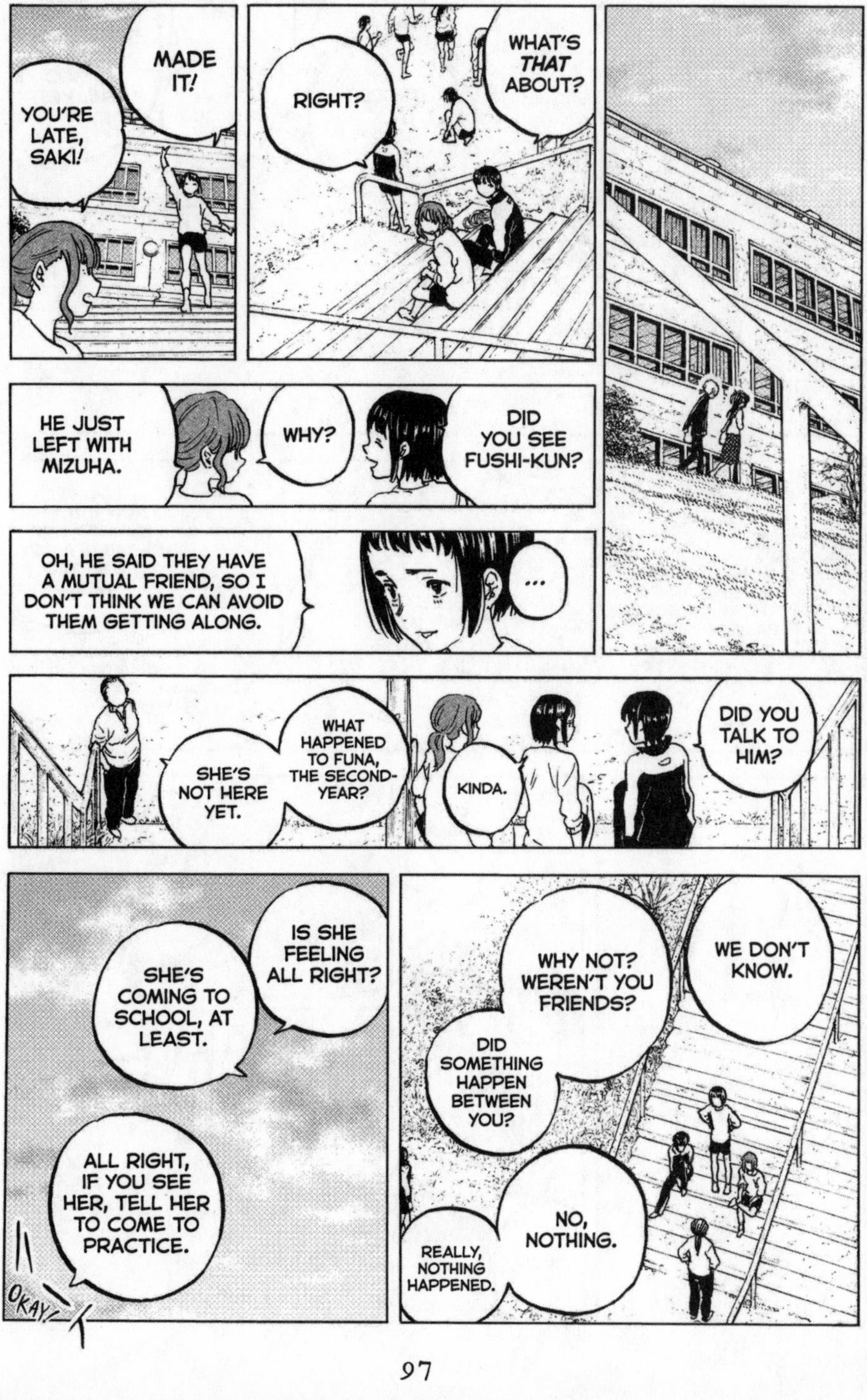
WHAT'S *THAT* ABOUT?
RIGHT?
MADE IT!
YOU'RE LATE, SAKI!
DID YOU SEE FUSHI-KUN?
WHY?
HE JUST LEFT WITH MIZUHA.
...
OH, HE SAID THEY HAVE A MUTUAL FRIEND, SO I DON'T THINK WE CAN AVOID THEM GETTING ALONG.
DID YOU TALK TO HIM?
KINDA.
WHAT HAPPENED TO FUNA, THE SECOND-YEAR?
SHE'S NOT HERE YET.
WE DON'T KNOW.
WHY NOT? WEREN'T YOU FRIENDS?
DID SOMETHING HAPPEN BETWEEN YOU?
NO, NOTHING.
REALLY, NOTHING HAPPENED.
IS SHE FEELING ALL RIGHT?
SHE'S COMING TO SCHOOL, AT LEAST.
ALL RIGHT, IF YOU SEE HER, TELL HER TO COME TO PRACTICE.
OKAY!

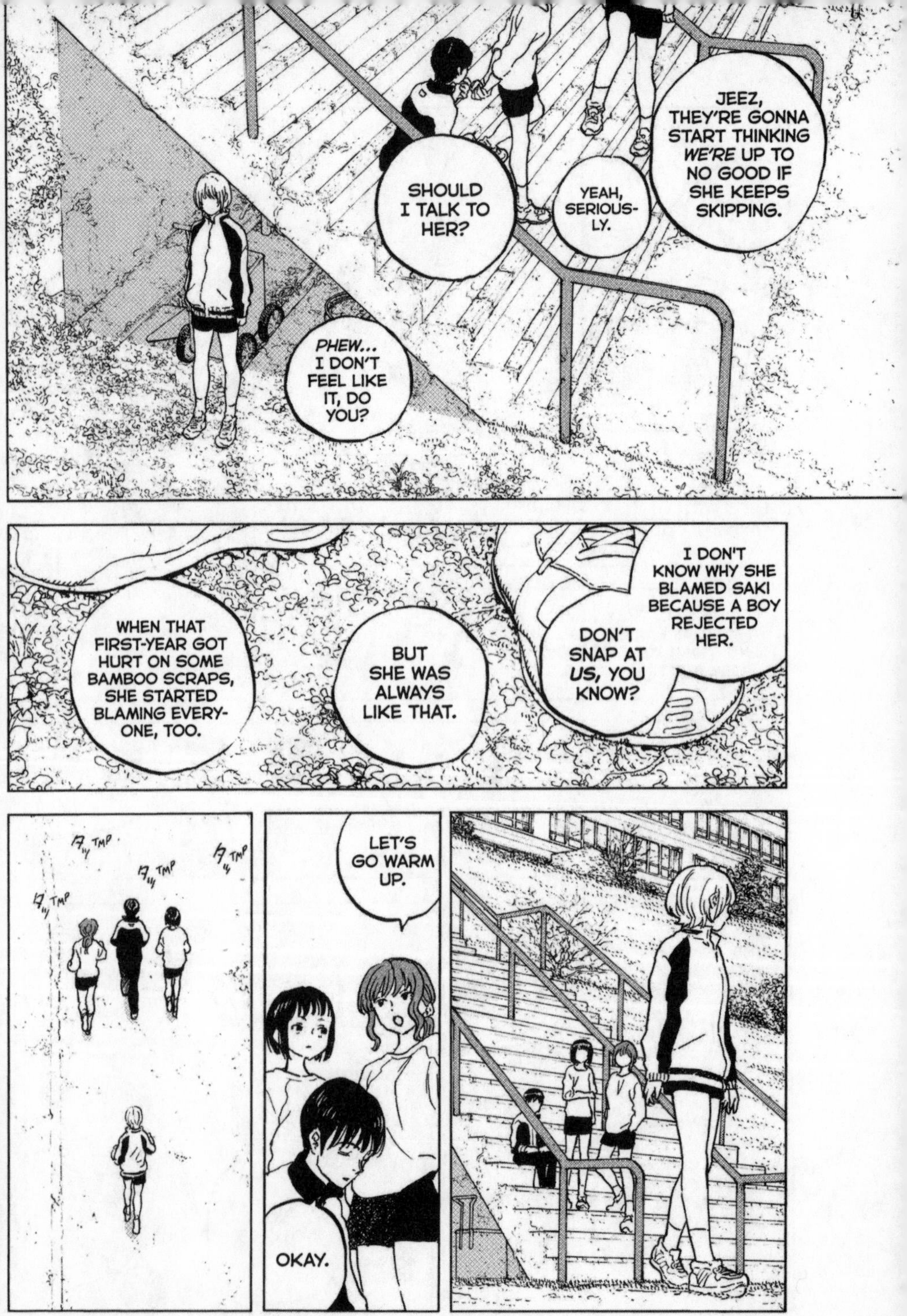
JEEZ, THEY'RE GONNA START THINKING *WE'RE* UP TO NO GOOD IF SHE KEEPS SKIPPING.
YEAH, SERIOUS-LY.
SHOULD I TALK TO HER?
*PHEW...* I DON'T FEEL LIKE IT, DO YOU?
I DON'T KNOW WHY SHE BLAMED SAKI BECAUSE A BOY REJECTED HER.
DON'T SNAP AT *US*, YOU KNOW?
BUT SHE WAS ALWAYS LIKE THAT.
WHEN THAT FIRST-YEAR GOT HURT ON SOME BAMBOO SCRAPS, SHE STARTED BLAMING EVERY-ONE, TOO.
LET'S GO WARM UP.
OKAY.
タッ TMP
タッ TMP
タッ TMP
タッ TMP

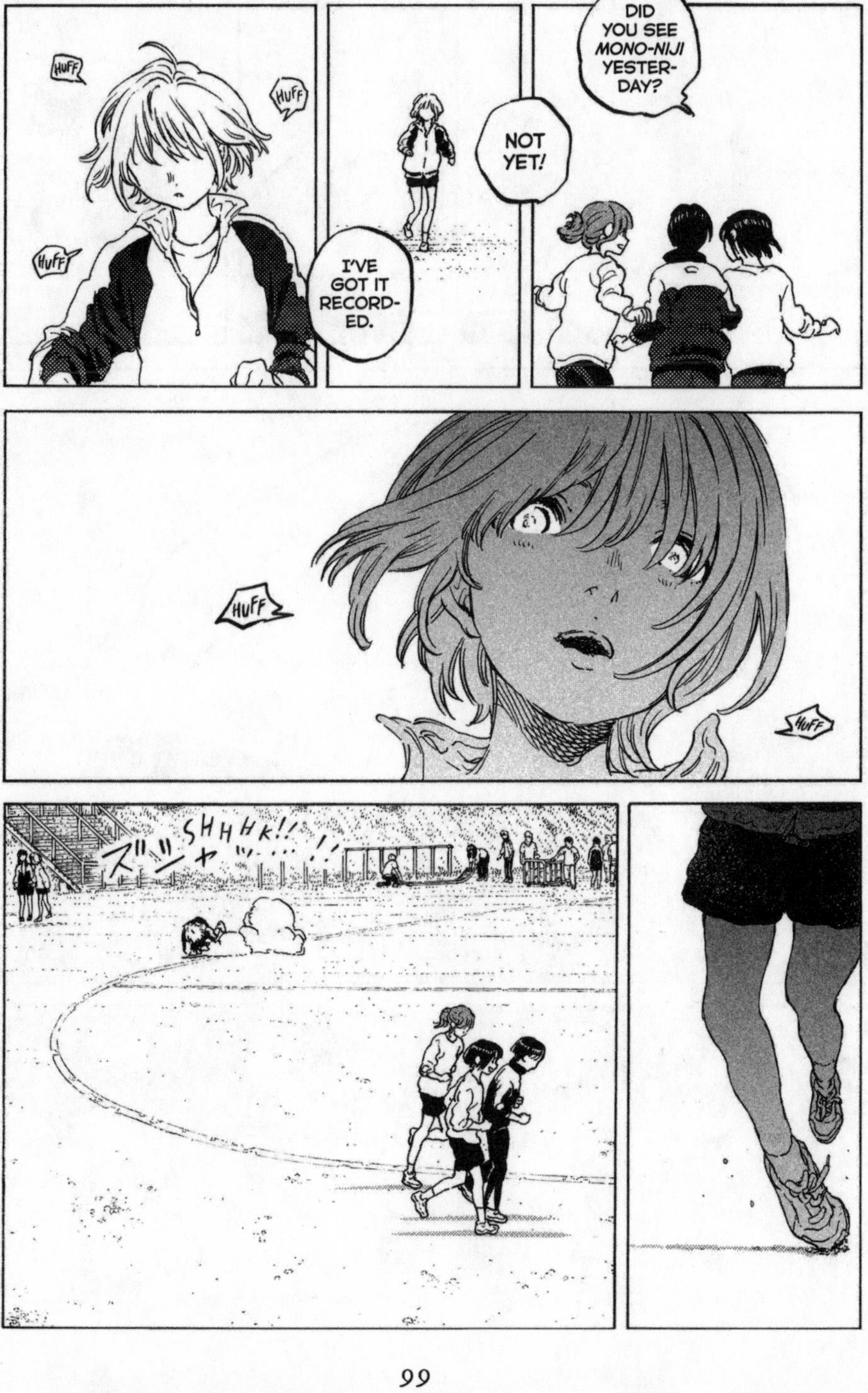
DID YOU SEE MONO-NIJI YESTER-DAY?
NOT YET!
I'VE GOT IT RECORD-ED.
HUFF
HUFF
HUFF
HUFF
HUFF
SHHHK!!

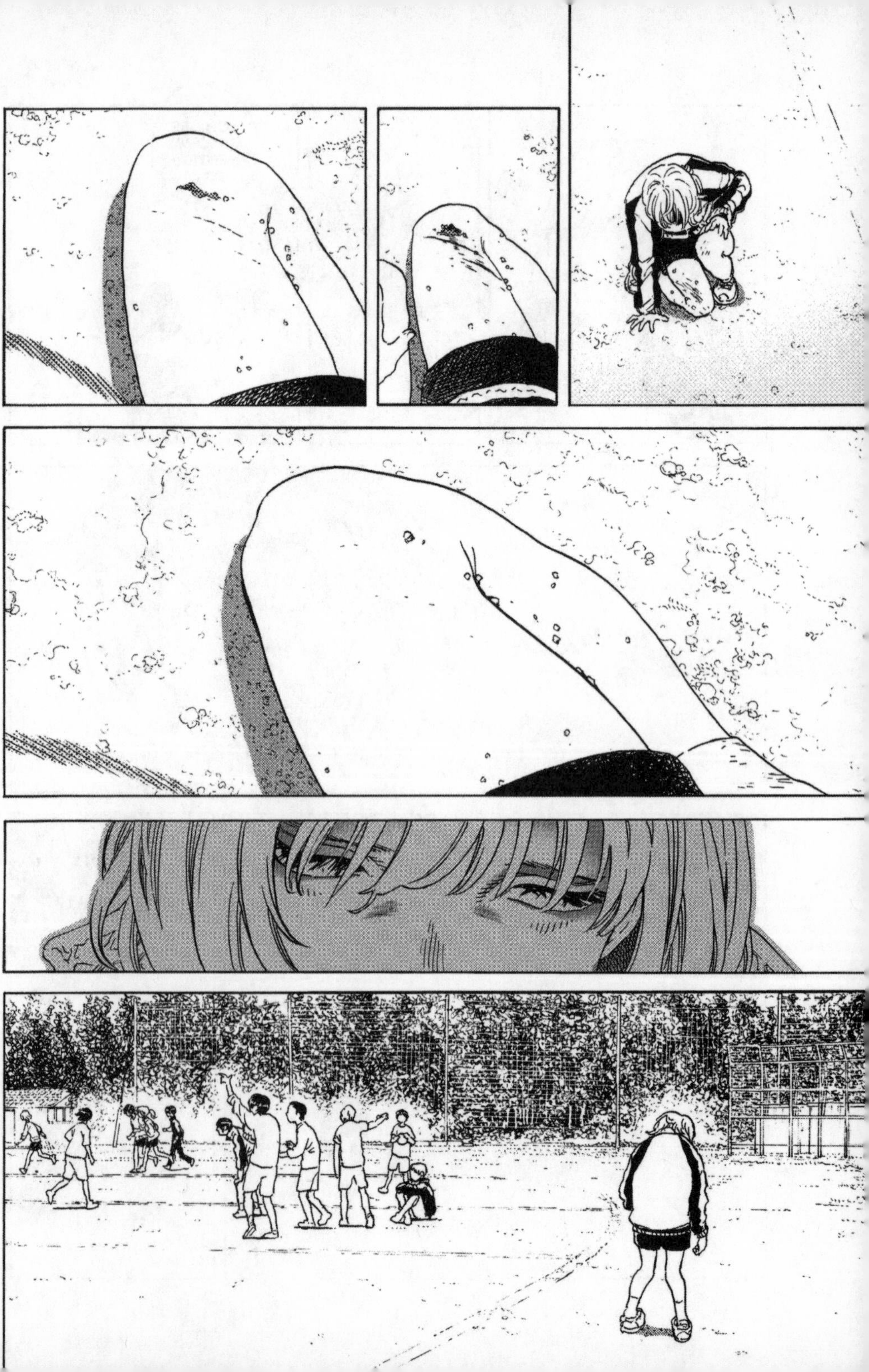

TO YOUR

ETERNITY

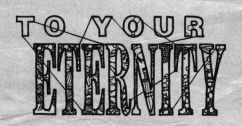

**Minamoto Junior High School's Four Precepts**

1. Be as pure and proper as spring water.

2. Be someone whose heart is as big as the sea.

3. Be ever-changing like the river.

4. Be as tranquil as a still pond.

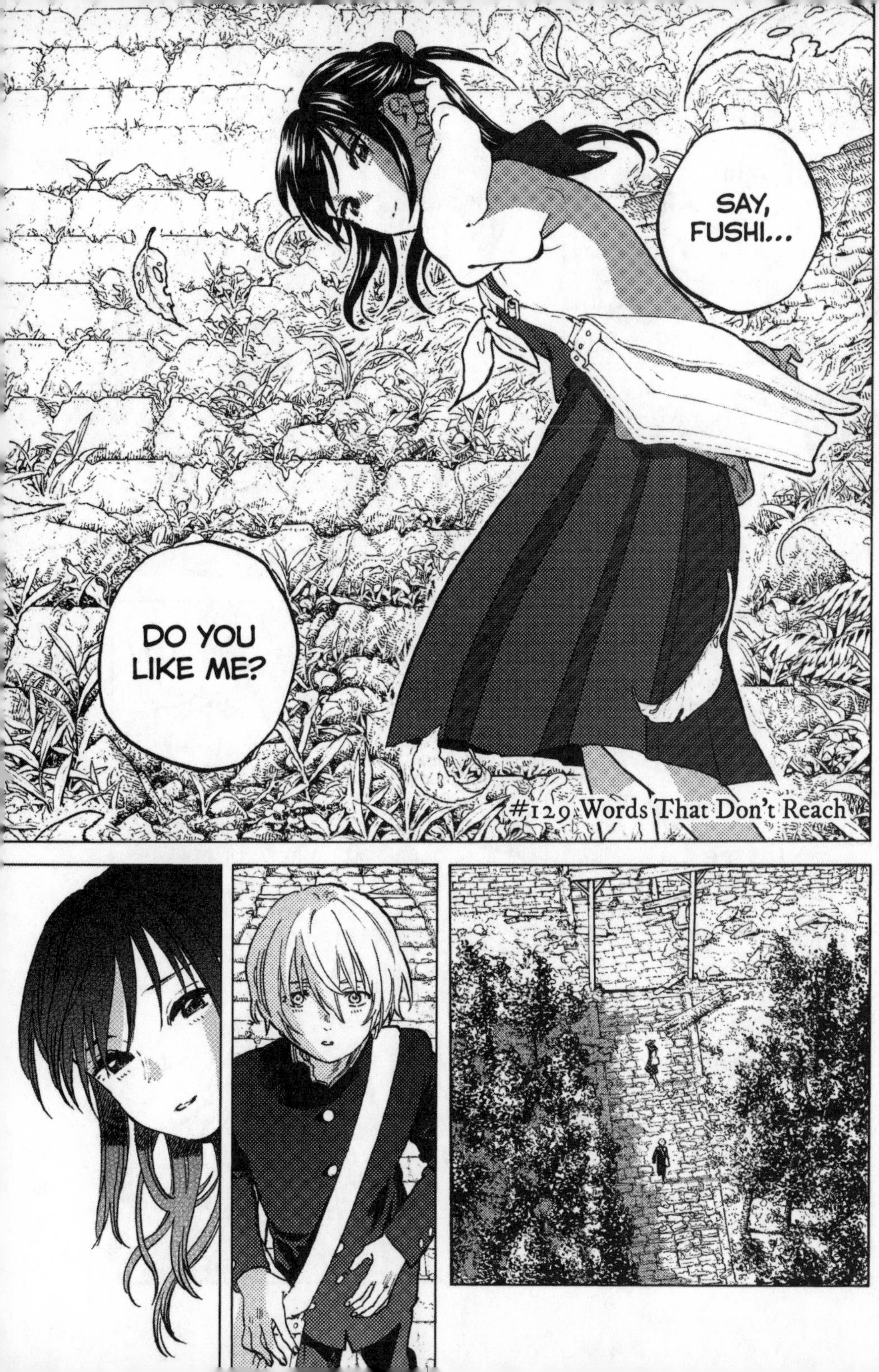
SAY, FUSHI...
DO YOU LIKE ME?
#129 Words That Don't Reach

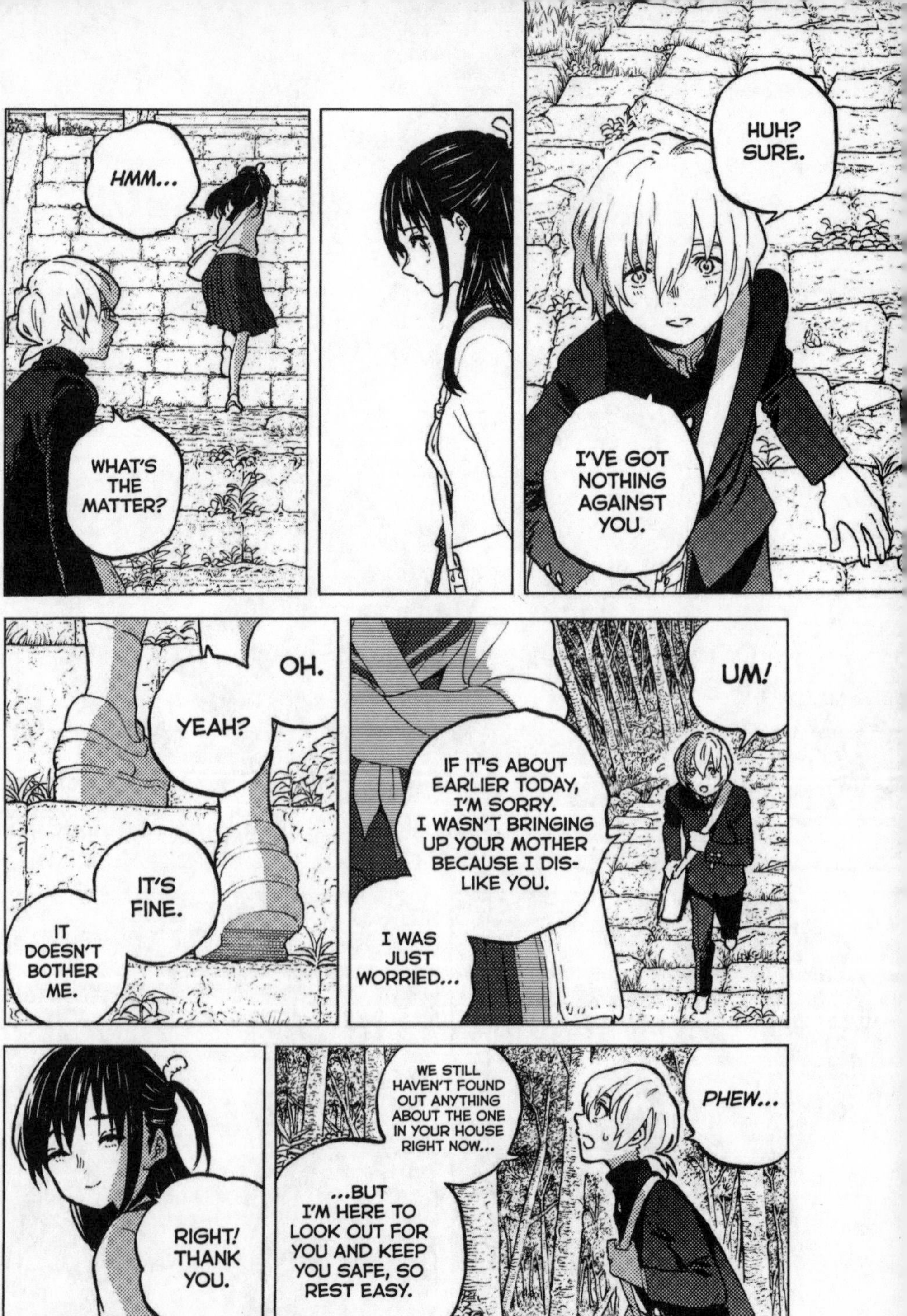
HUH? SURE.
I'VE GOT NOTHING AGAINST YOU.
HMM...
WHAT'S THE MATTER?
UM!
IF IT'S ABOUT EARLIER TODAY, I'M SORRY. I WASN'T BRINGING UP YOUR MOTHER BECAUSE I DIS-LIKE YOU.
I WAS JUST WORRIED...
OH.
YEAH?
IT'S FINE.
IT DOESN'T BOTHER ME.
PHEW...
WE STILL HAVEN'T FOUND OUT ANYTHING ABOUT THE ONE IN YOUR HOUSE RIGHT NOW...
...BUT I'M HERE TO LOOK OUT FOR YOU AND KEEP YOU SAFE, SO REST EASY.
RIGHT! THANK YOU.

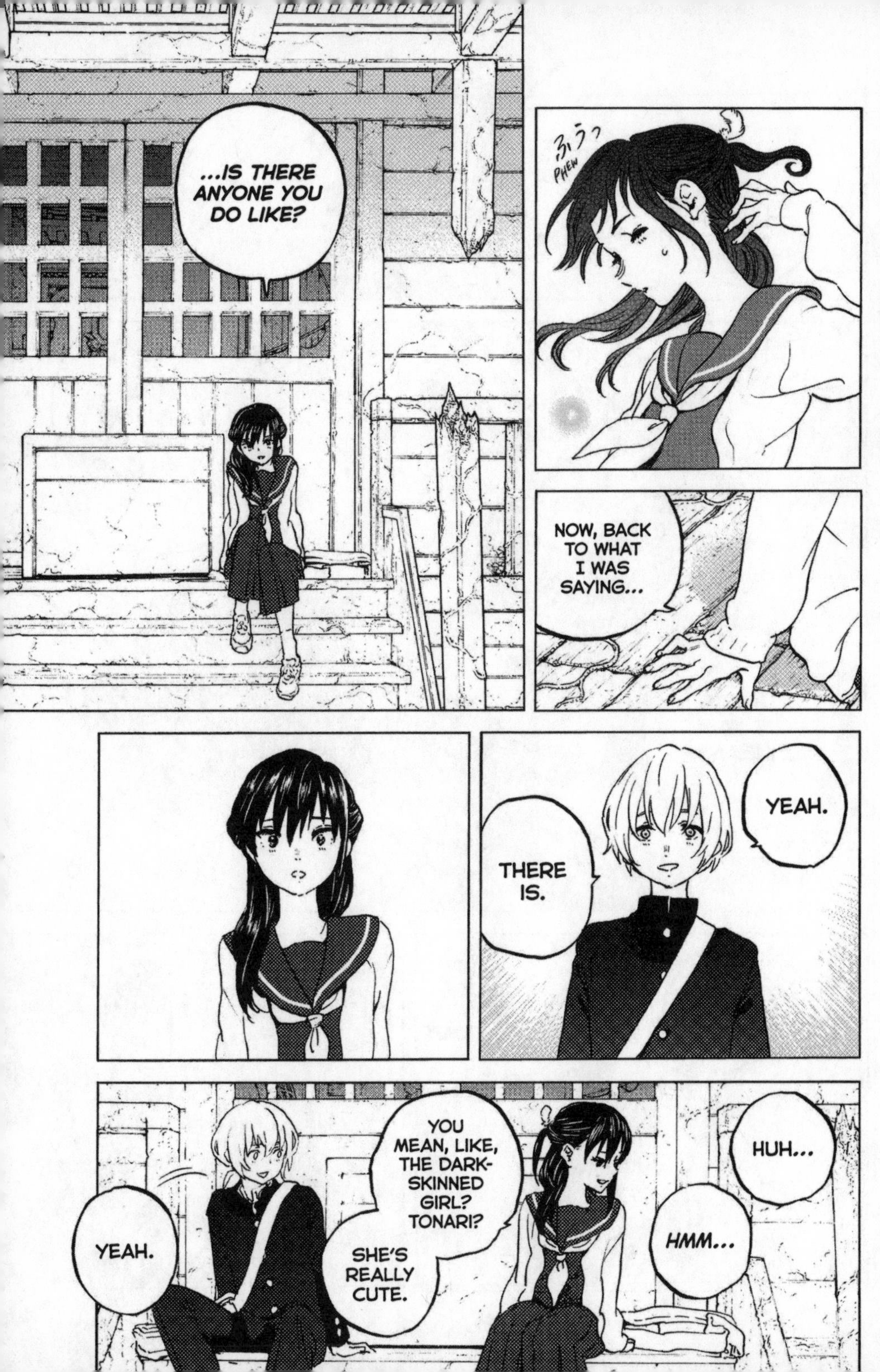
ふうっ
PHEW
NOW, BACK TO WHAT I WAS SAYING...
...IS THERE ANYONE YOU DO LIKE?
YEAH.
THERE IS.
HUH...
HMM...
YOU MEAN, LIKE, THE DARK-SKINNED GIRL? TONARI?
SHE'S REALLY CUTE.
YEAH.

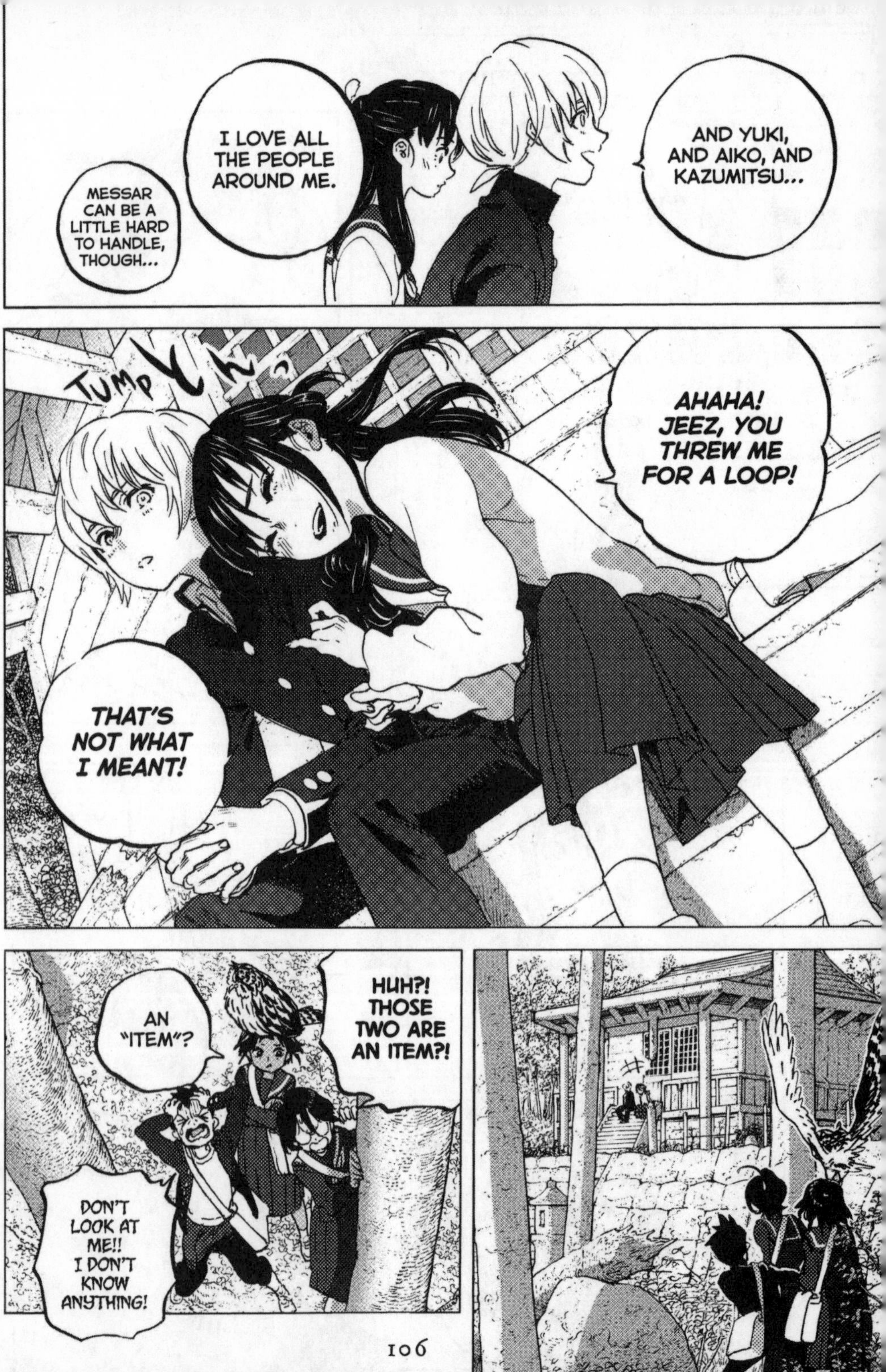
AND YUKI, AND AIKO, AND KAZUMITSU...
I LOVE ALL THE PEOPLE AROUND ME.
MESSAR CAN BE A LITTLE HARD TO HANDLE, THOUGH...
AHAHA! JEEZ, YOU THREW ME FOR A LOOP!
TUMP YUH
THAT'S NOT WHAT I MEANT!
HUH?! THOSE TWO ARE AN ITEM?!
AN "ITEM"?
DON'T LOOK AT ME!! I DON'T KNOW ANYTHING!

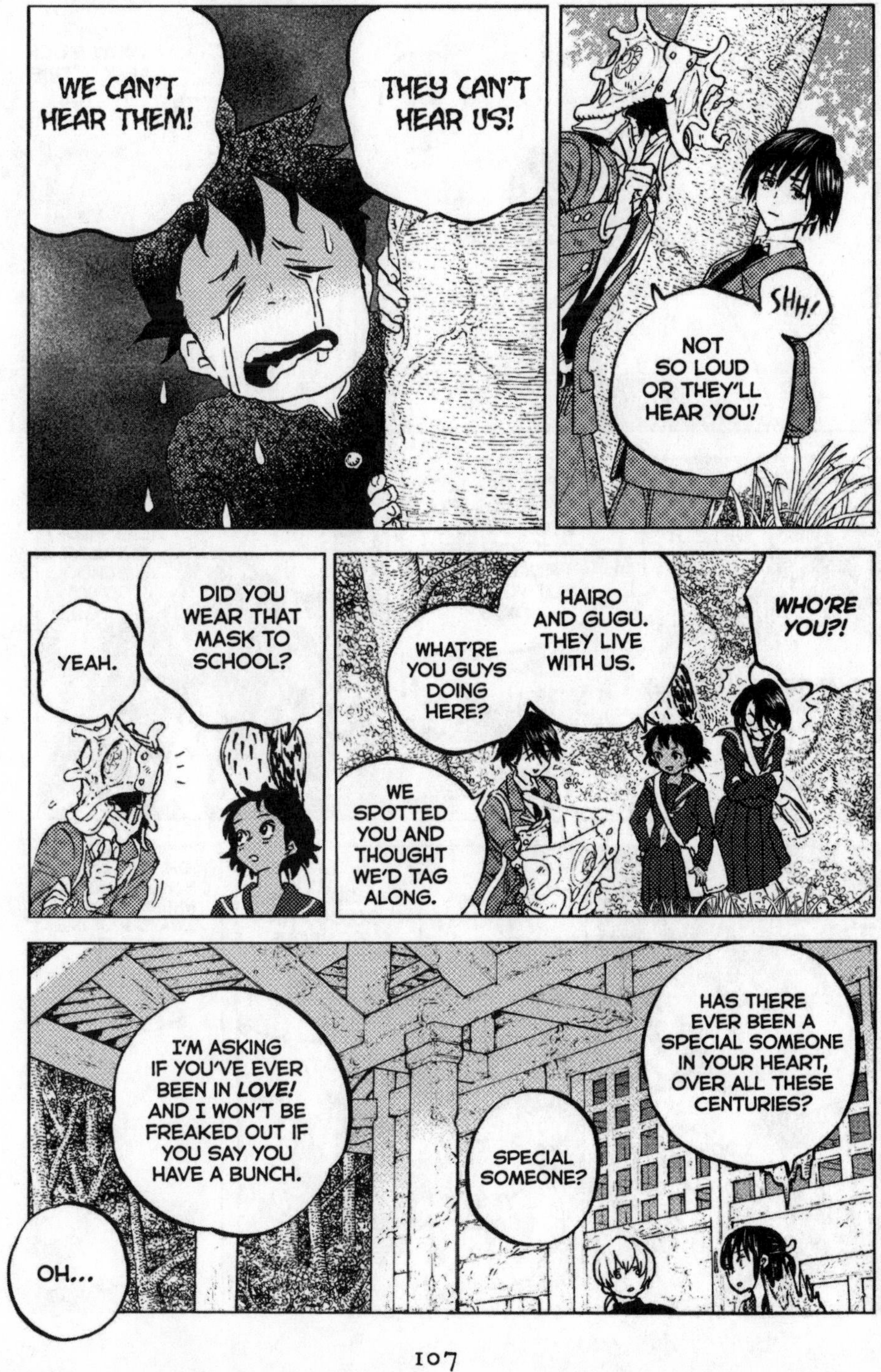
SHH!
NOT SO LOUD OR THEY'LL HEAR YOU!
THEY CAN'T HEAR US!
WE CAN'T HEAR THEM!
WHO'RE YOU?!
HAIRO AND GUGU. THEY LIVE WITH US.
WHAT'RE YOU GUYS DOING HERE?
WE SPOTTED YOU AND THOUGHT WE'D TAG ALONG.
DID YOU WEAR THAT MASK TO SCHOOL?
YEAH.
HAS THERE EVER BEEN A SPECIAL SOMEONE IN YOUR HEART, OVER ALL THESE CENTURIES?
SPECIAL SOMEONE?
I'M ASKING IF YOU'VE EVER BEEN IN *LOVE!* AND I WON'T BE FREAKED OUT IF YOU SAY YOU HAVE A BUNCH.
OH...

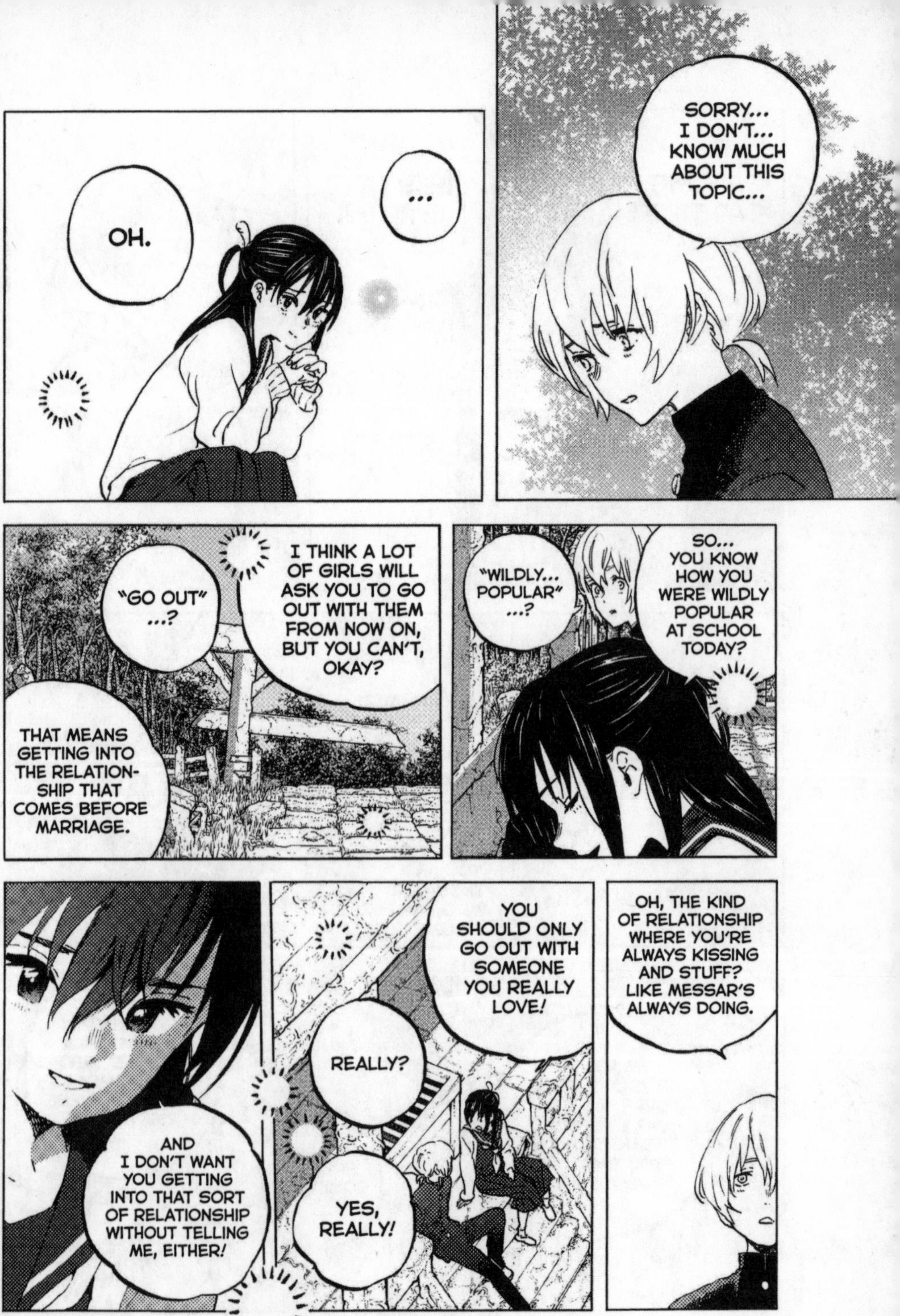
SORRY... I DON'T... KNOW MUCH ABOUT THIS TOPIC...
...
OH.
SO... YOU KNOW HOW YOU WERE WILDLY POPULAR AT SCHOOL TODAY?
"WILDLY... POPULAR" ...?
I THINK A LOT OF GIRLS WILL ASK YOU TO GO OUT WITH THEM FROM NOW ON, BUT YOU CAN'T, OKAY?
"GO OUT" ...?
THAT MEANS GETTING INTO THE RELATIONSHIP THAT COMES BEFORE MARRIAGE.
OH, THE KIND OF RELATIONSHIP WHERE YOU'RE ALWAYS KISSING AND STUFF? LIKE MESSAR'S ALWAYS DOING.
YOU SHOULD ONLY GO OUT WITH SOMEONE YOU REALLY LOVE!
REALLY?
YES, REALLY!
AND I DON'T WANT YOU GETTING INTO THAT SORT OF RELATIONSHIP WITHOUT TELLING ME, EITHER!

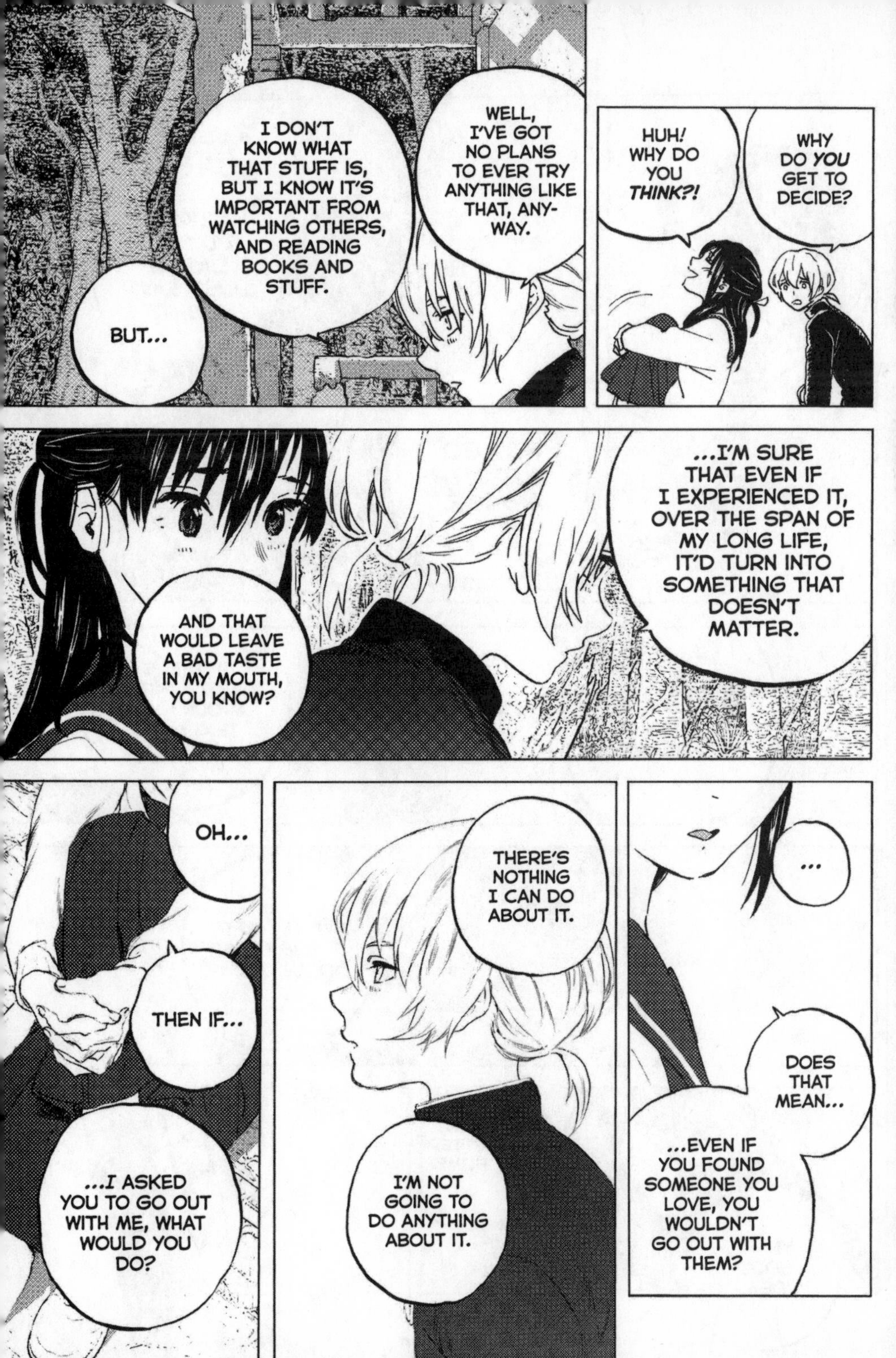
WHY DO *YOU* GET TO DECIDE?
HUH! WHY DO YOU *THINK?!*
WELL, I'VE GOT NO PLANS TO EVER TRY ANYTHING LIKE THAT, ANY-WAY.
I DON'T KNOW WHAT THAT STUFF IS, BUT I KNOW IT'S IMPORTANT FROM WATCHING OTHERS, AND READING BOOKS AND STUFF.
BUT...
...I'M SURE THAT EVEN IF I EXPERIENCED IT, OVER THE SPAN OF MY LONG LIFE, IT'D TURN INTO SOMETHING THAT DOESN'T MATTER.
AND THAT WOULD LEAVE A BAD TASTE IN MY MOUTH, YOU KNOW?
...
DOES THAT MEAN...
...EVEN IF YOU FOUND SOMEONE YOU LOVE, YOU WOULDN'T GO OUT WITH THEM?
THERE'S NOTHING I CAN DO ABOUT IT.
I'M NOT GOING TO DO ANYTHING ABOUT IT.
OH...
THEN IF...
...*I* ASKED YOU TO GO OUT WITH ME, WHAT WOULD YOU DO?

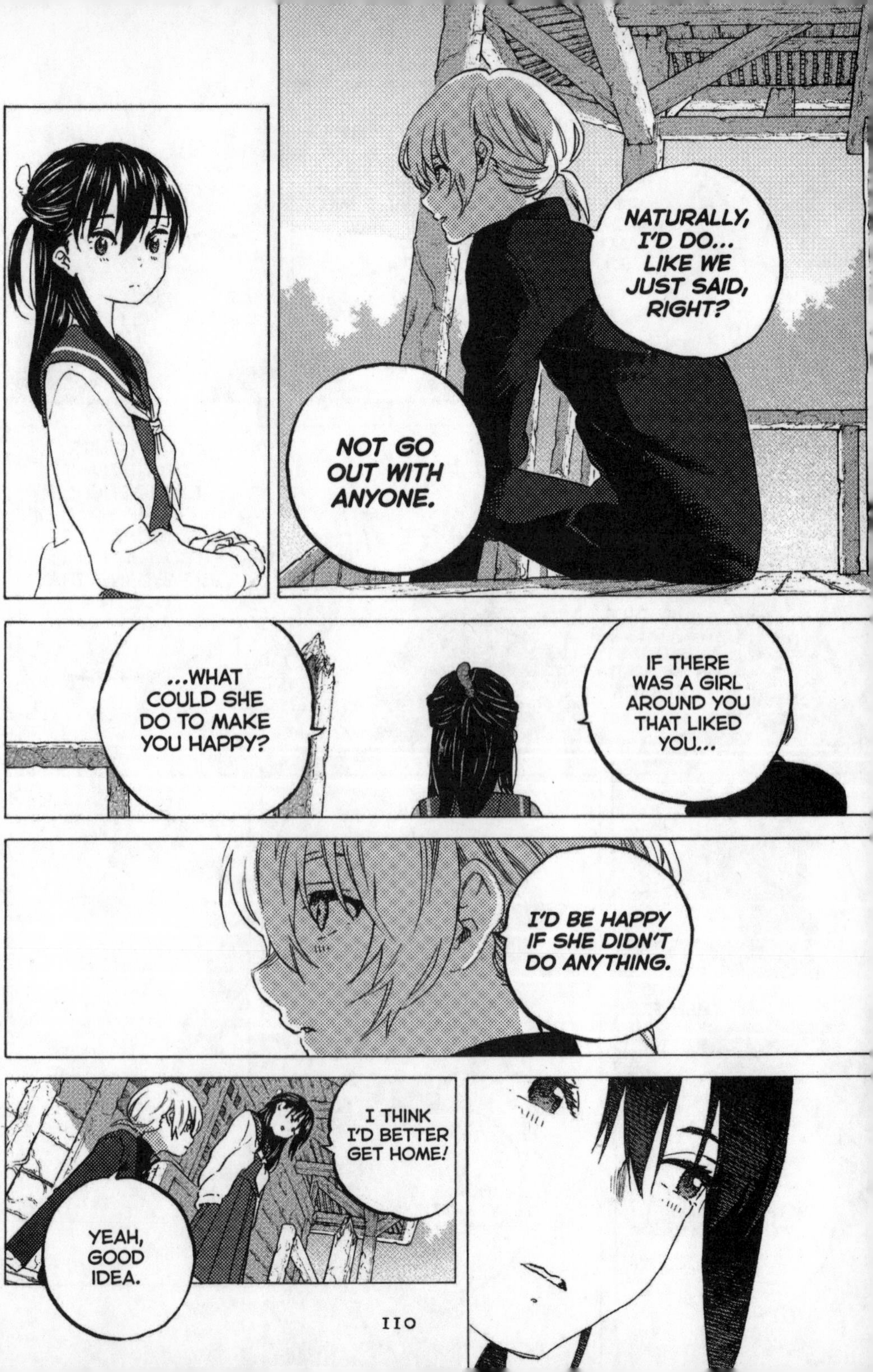
NATURALLY, I'D DO... LIKE WE JUST SAID, RIGHT?
NOT GO OUT WITH ANYONE.
IF THERE WAS A GIRL AROUND YOU THAT LIKED YOU...
...WHAT COULD SHE DO TO MAKE YOU HAPPY?
I'D BE HAPPY IF SHE DIDN'T DO ANYTHING.
I THINK I'D BETTER GET HOME!
YEAH, GOOD IDEA.

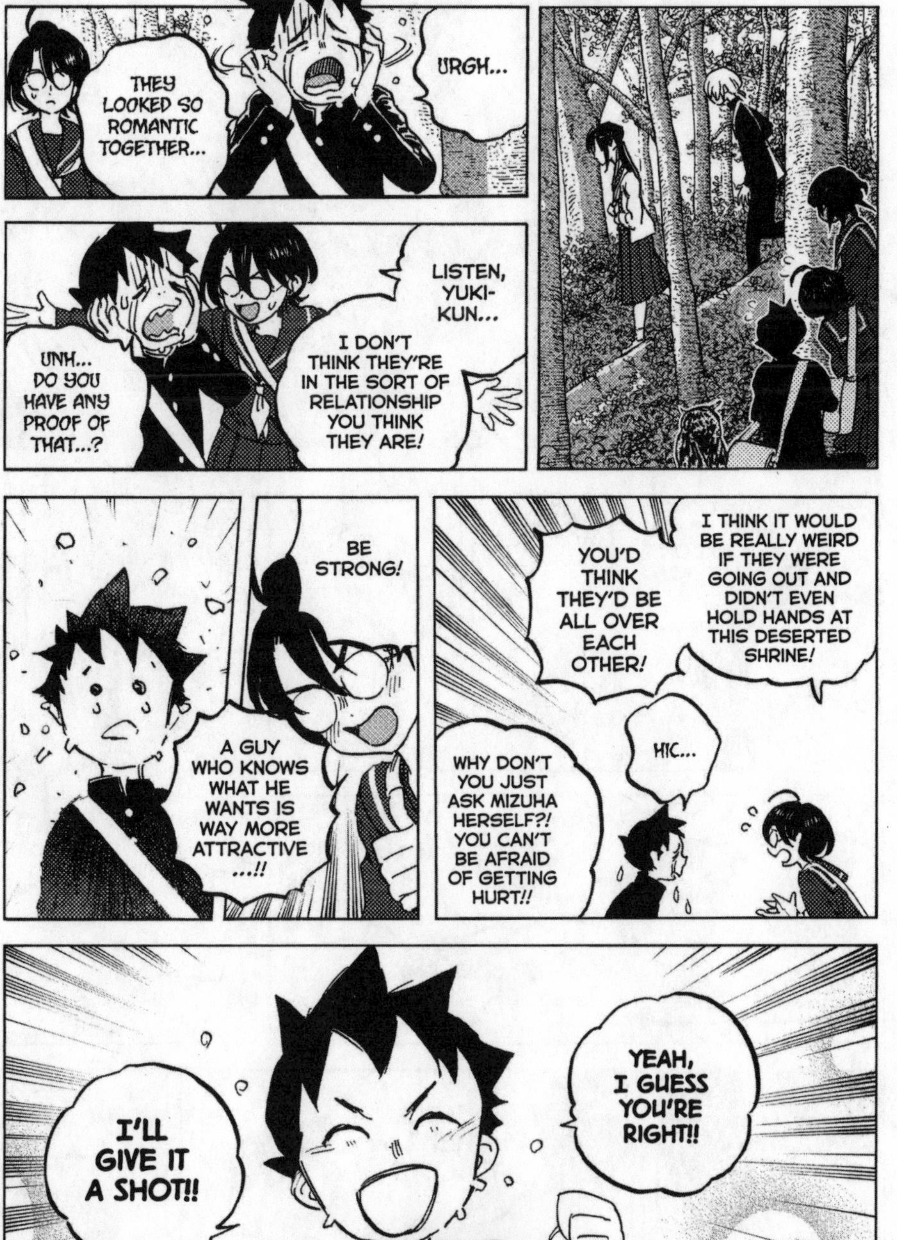
URGH...
THEY LOOKED SO ROMANTIC TOGETHER...
LISTEN, YUKI-KUN...
I DON'T THINK THEY'RE IN THE SORT OF RELATIONSHIP YOU THINK THEY ARE!
UNH... DO YOU HAVE ANY PROOF OF THAT...?
I THINK IT WOULD BE REALLY WEIRD IF THEY WERE GOING OUT AND DIDN'T EVEN HOLD HANDS AT THIS DESERTED SHRINE!
YOU'D THINK THEY'D BE ALL OVER EACH OTHER!
HIC...
WHY DON'T YOU JUST ASK MIZUHA HERSELF?! YOU CAN'T BE AFRAID OF GETTING HURT!!
BE STRONG!
A GUY WHO KNOWS WHAT HE WANTS IS WAY MORE ATTRACTIVE ...!!
YEAH, I GUESS YOU'RE RIGHT!!
I'LL GIVE IT A SHOT!!

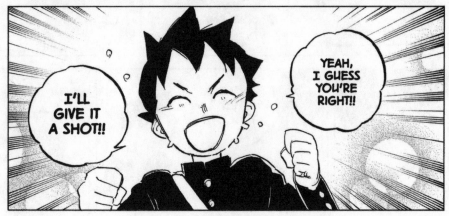

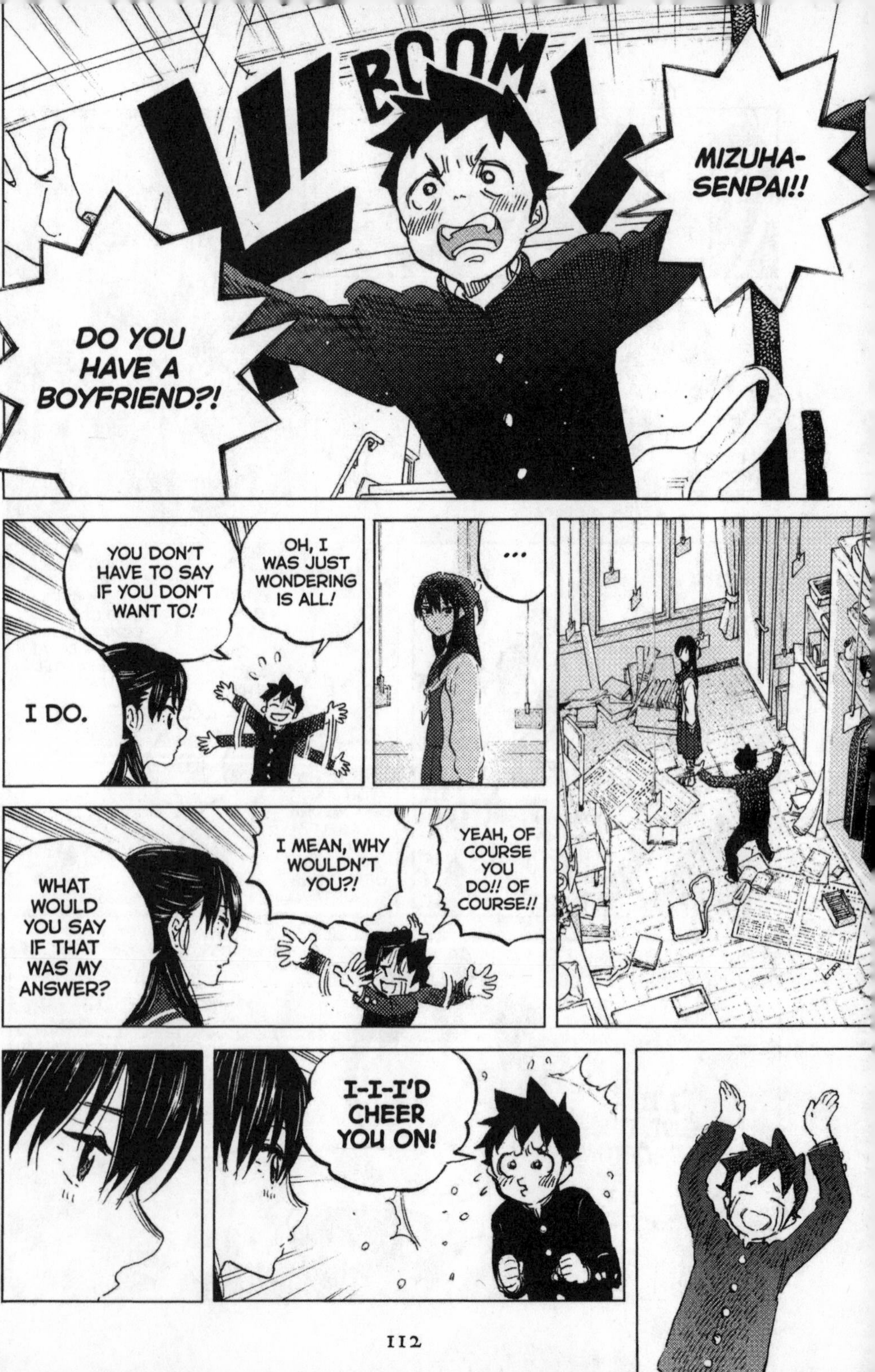
MIZUHA-SENPAI!!
BOOM!
DO YOU HAVE A BOYFRIEND?!
...
OH, I WAS JUST WONDERING IS ALL!
YOU DON'T HAVE TO SAY IF YOU DON'T WANT TO!
I DO.
YEAH, OF COURSE YOU DO!! OF COURSE!!
I MEAN, WHY WOULDN'T YOU?!
WHAT WOULD YOU SAY IF THAT WAS MY ANSWER?
I-I-I'D CHEER YOU ON!

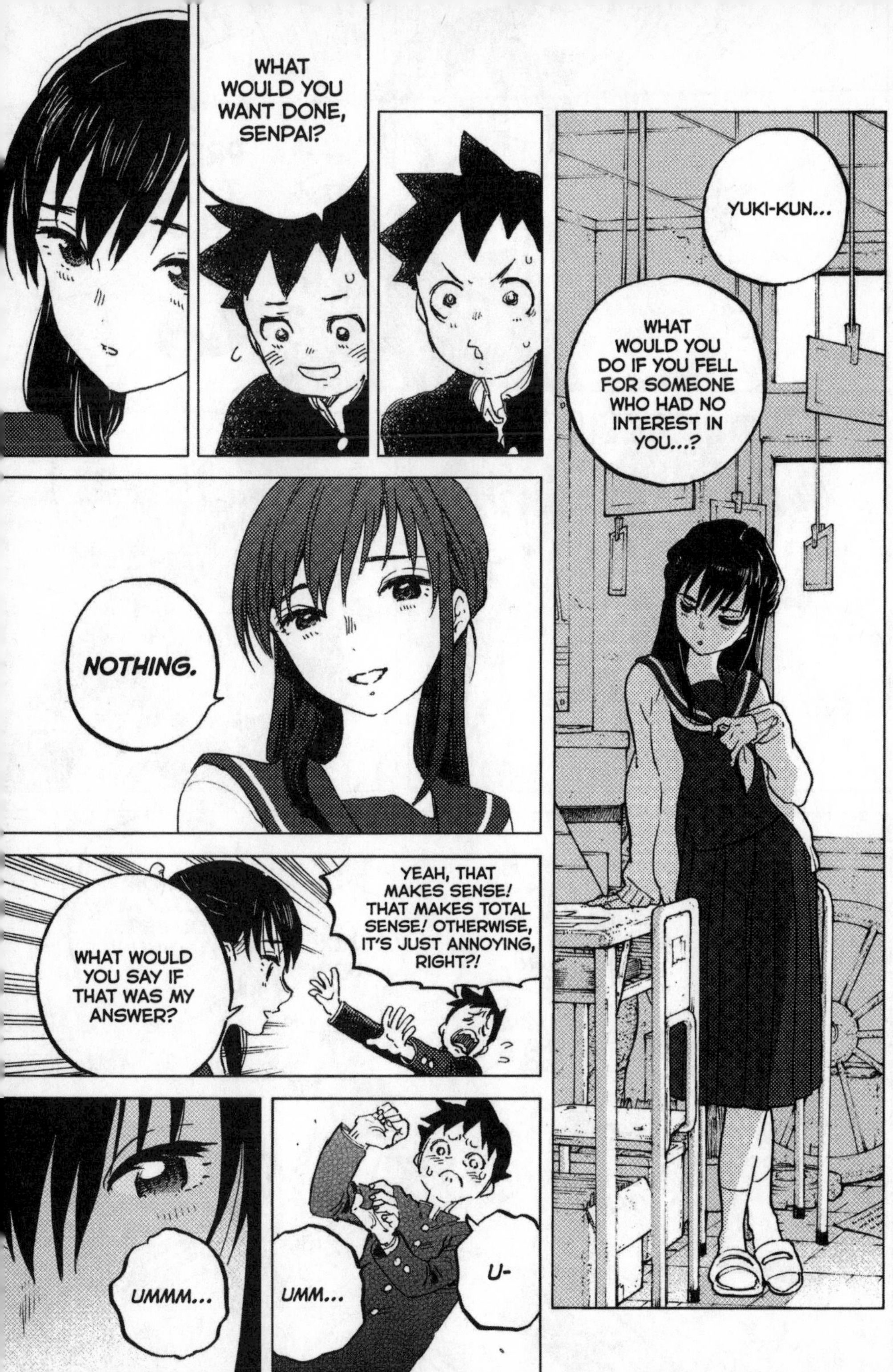
YUKI-KUN...
WHAT WOULD YOU DO IF YOU FELL FOR SOMEONE WHO HAD NO INTEREST IN YOU...?
WHAT WOULD YOU WANT DONE, SENPAI?
NOTHING.
YEAH, THAT MAKES SENSE! THAT MAKES TOTAL SENSE! OTHERWISE, IT'S JUST ANNOYING, RIGHT?!
WHAT WOULD YOU SAY IF THAT WAS MY ANSWER?
U-
UMM...
UMMM...

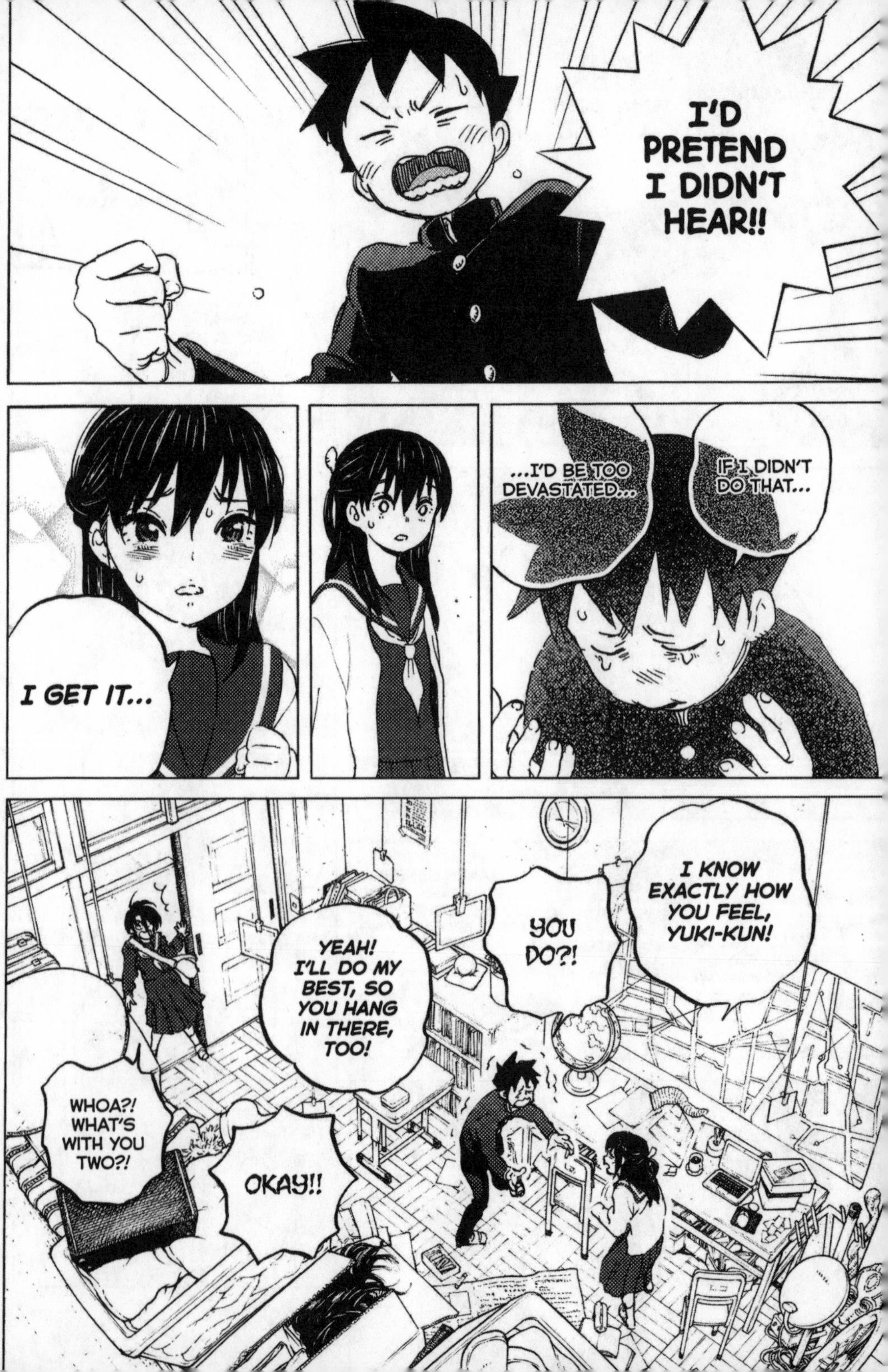
I'D PRETEND I DIDN'T HEAR!!
IF I DIDN'T DO THAT...
...I'D BE TOO DEVASTATED...
I GET IT...
I KNOW EXACTLY HOW YOU FEEL, YUKI-KUN!
YOU DO?!
YEAH! I'LL DO MY BEST, SO YOU HANG IN THERE, TOO!
OKAY!!
WHOA?! WHAT'S WITH YOU TWO?!

SEE YOU WHEN YOU GET BACK, MIZUHA.

WATCH OUT FOR CARS.

OKAY, MAMA!

MIZUHA'S FAKE MOM...

...ISN'T DOING ANYTHING UNUSUAL.

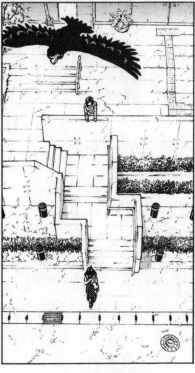

WE SHOULD BE ABLE TO GO TO SCHOOL WITHOUT ANY TROUBLE AGAIN TODAY.

*THE WORLD IS STILL AT PEACE.*

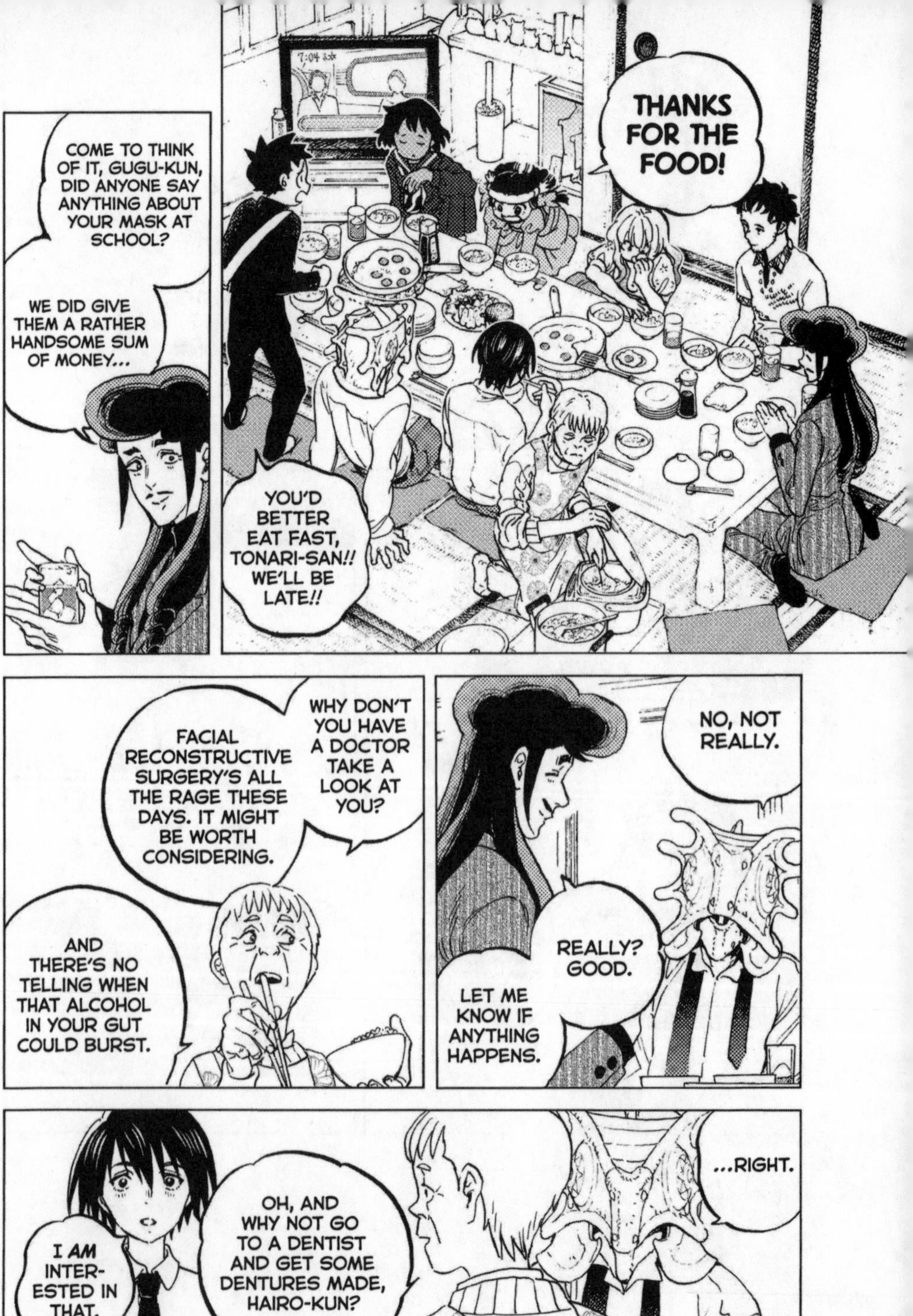
THANKS FOR THE FOOD!
YOU'D BETTER EAT FAST, TONARI-SAN!! WE'LL BE LATE!!
COME TO THINK OF IT, GUGU-KUN, DID ANYONE SAY ANYTHING ABOUT YOUR MASK AT SCHOOL?
WE DID GIVE THEM A RATHER HANDSOME SUM OF MONEY...
NO, NOT REALLY.
REALLY? GOOD.
LET ME KNOW IF ANYTHING HAPPENS.
WHY DON'T YOU HAVE A DOCTOR TAKE A LOOK AT YOU?
FACIAL RECONSTRUCTIVE SURGERY'S ALL THE RAGE THESE DAYS. IT MIGHT BE WORTH CONSIDERING.
AND THERE'S NO TELLING WHEN THAT ALCOHOL IN YOUR GUT COULD BURST.
...RIGHT.
OH, AND WHY NOT GO TO A DENTIST AND GET SOME DENTURES MADE, HAIRO-KUN?
I *AM* INTER-ESTED IN THAT.

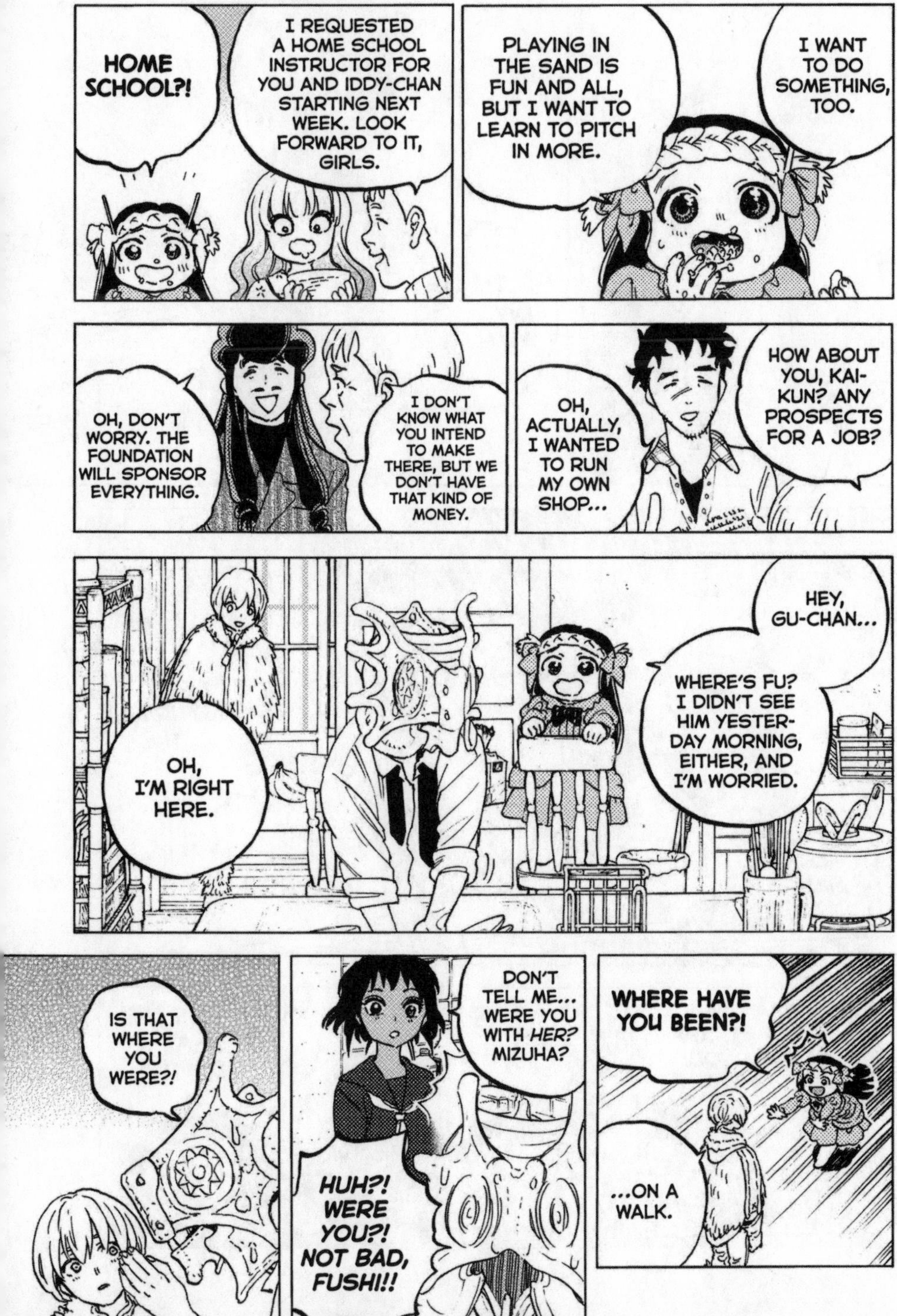
I WANT TO DO SOMETHING, TOO.
PLAYING IN THE SAND IS FUN AND ALL, BUT I WANT TO LEARN TO PITCH IN MORE.
I REQUESTED A HOME SCHOOL INSTRUCTOR FOR YOU AND IDDY-CHAN STARTING NEXT WEEK. LOOK FORWARD TO IT, GIRLS.
HOME SCHOOL?!
HOW ABOUT YOU, KAI-KUN? ANY PROSPECTS FOR A JOB?
OH, ACTUALLY, I WANTED TO RUN MY OWN SHOP...
I DON'T KNOW WHAT YOU INTEND TO MAKE THERE, BUT WE DON'T HAVE THAT KIND OF MONEY.
OH, DON'T WORRY. THE FOUNDATION WILL SPONSOR EVERYTHING.
HEY, GU-CHAN...
WHERE'S FU? I DIDN'T SEE HIM YESTERDAY MORNING, EITHER, AND I'M WORRIED.
OH, I'M RIGHT HERE.
WHERE HAVE YOU BEEN?!
...ON A WALK.
DON'T TELL ME... WERE YOU WITH *HER*? MIZUHA?
HUH?! WERE YOU?! NOT BAD, FUSHI!!
IS THAT WHERE YOU WERE?!

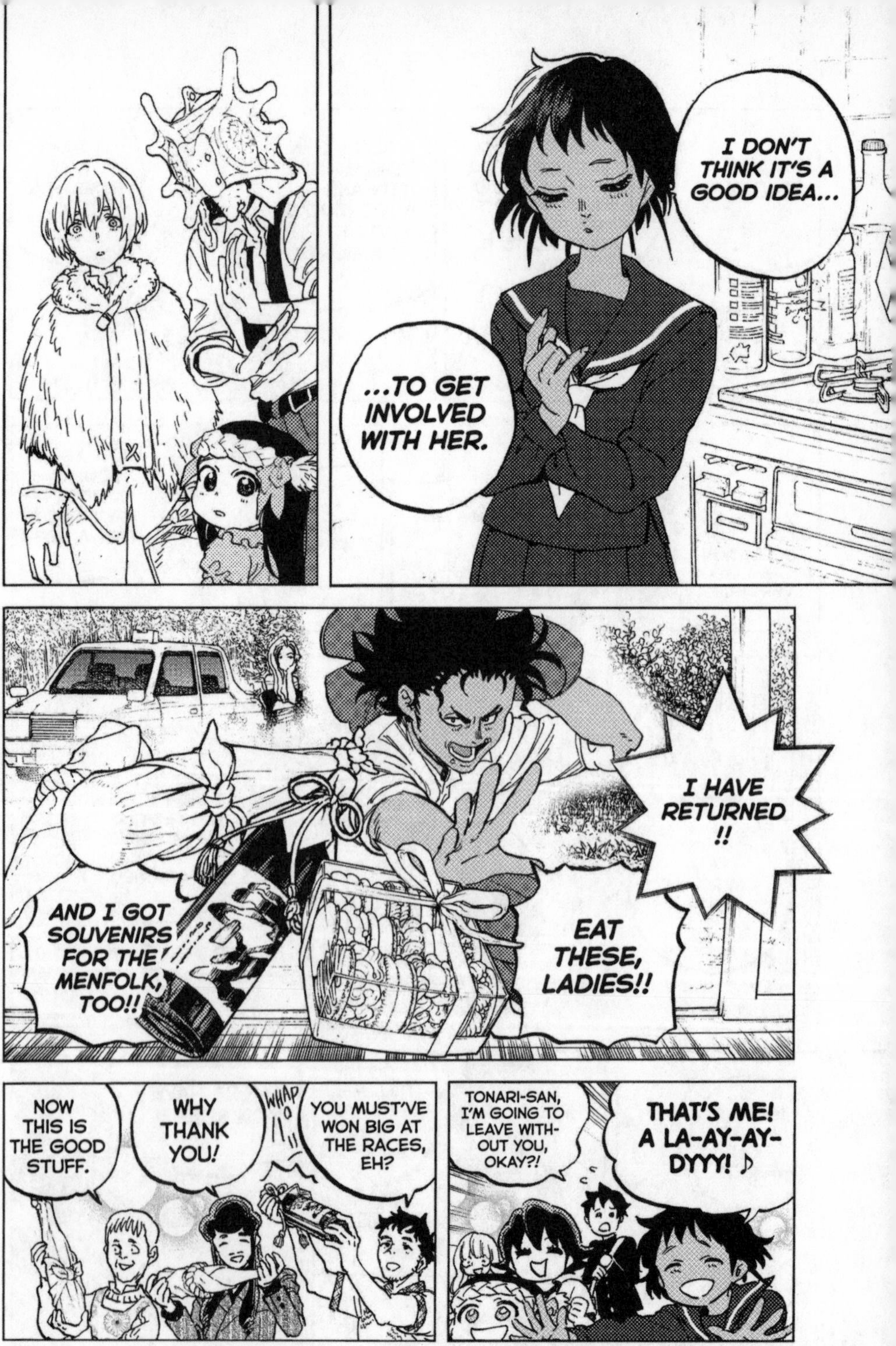
I DON'T THINK IT'S A GOOD IDEA...
...TO GET INVOLVED WITH HER.
I HAVE RETURNED !!
EAT THESE, LADIES!!
AND I GOT SOUVENIRS FOR THE MENFOLK, TOO!!
THAT'S ME! A LA-AY-AY-DYYY! ♪
TONARI-SAN, I'M GOING TO LEAVE WITH-OUT YOU, OKAY?!
YOU MUST'VE WON BIG AT THE RACES, EH?
WHAP
WHY THANK YOU!
NOW THIS IS THE GOOD STUFF.

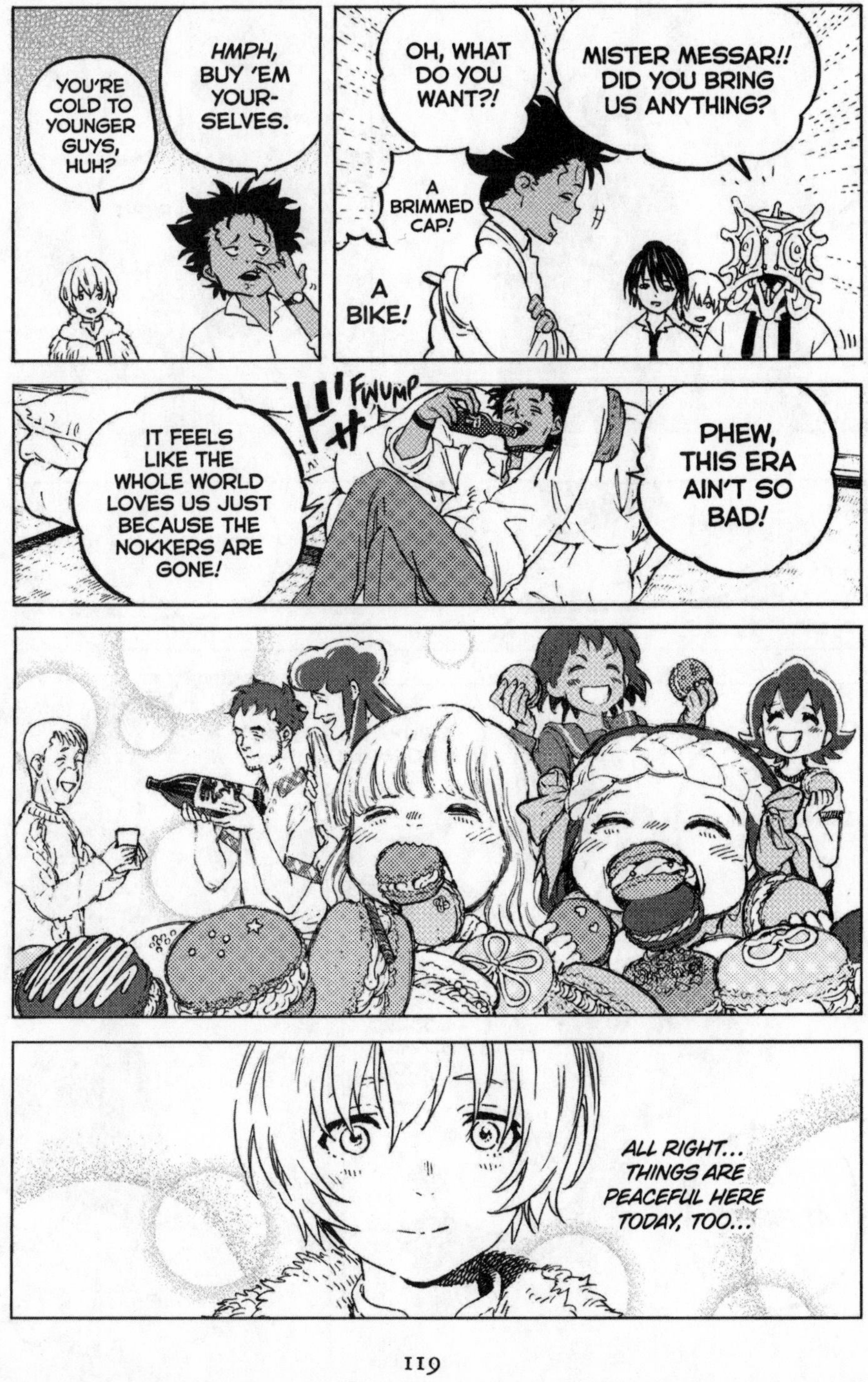
MISTER MESSAR!! DID YOU BRING US ANYTHING?
OH, WHAT DO YOU WANT?!
A BRIMMED CAP!
A BIKE!
HMPH, BUY 'EM YOURSELVES.
YOU'RE COLD TO YOUNGER GUYS, HUH?
PHEW, THIS ERA AIN'T SO BAD!
FWUMP
IT FEELS LIKE THE WHOLE WORLD LOVES US JUST BECAUSE THE NOKKERS ARE GONE!
ALL RIGHT... THINGS ARE PEACEFUL HERE TODAY, TOO...

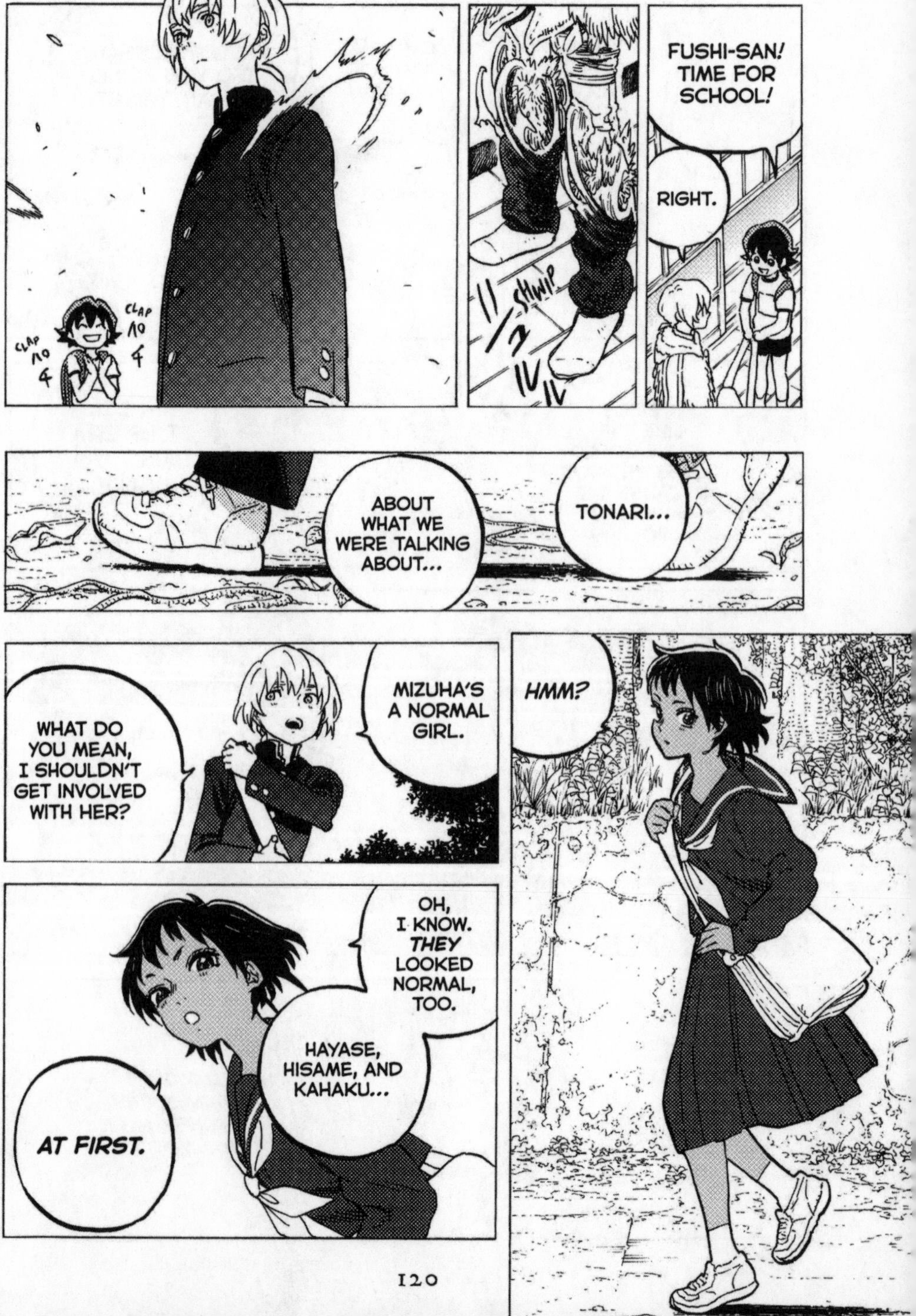
FUSHI-SAN! TIME FOR SCHOOL!
RIGHT.
SHWIP
CLAP
CLAP
TONARI...
ABOUT WHAT WE WERE TALKING ABOUT...
HMM?
MIZUHA'S A NORMAL GIRL.
WHAT DO YOU MEAN, I SHOULDN'T GET INVOLVED WITH HER?
OH, I KNOW. *THEY* LOOKED NORMAL, TOO.
HAYASE, HISAME, AND KAHAKU...
*AT FIRST.*

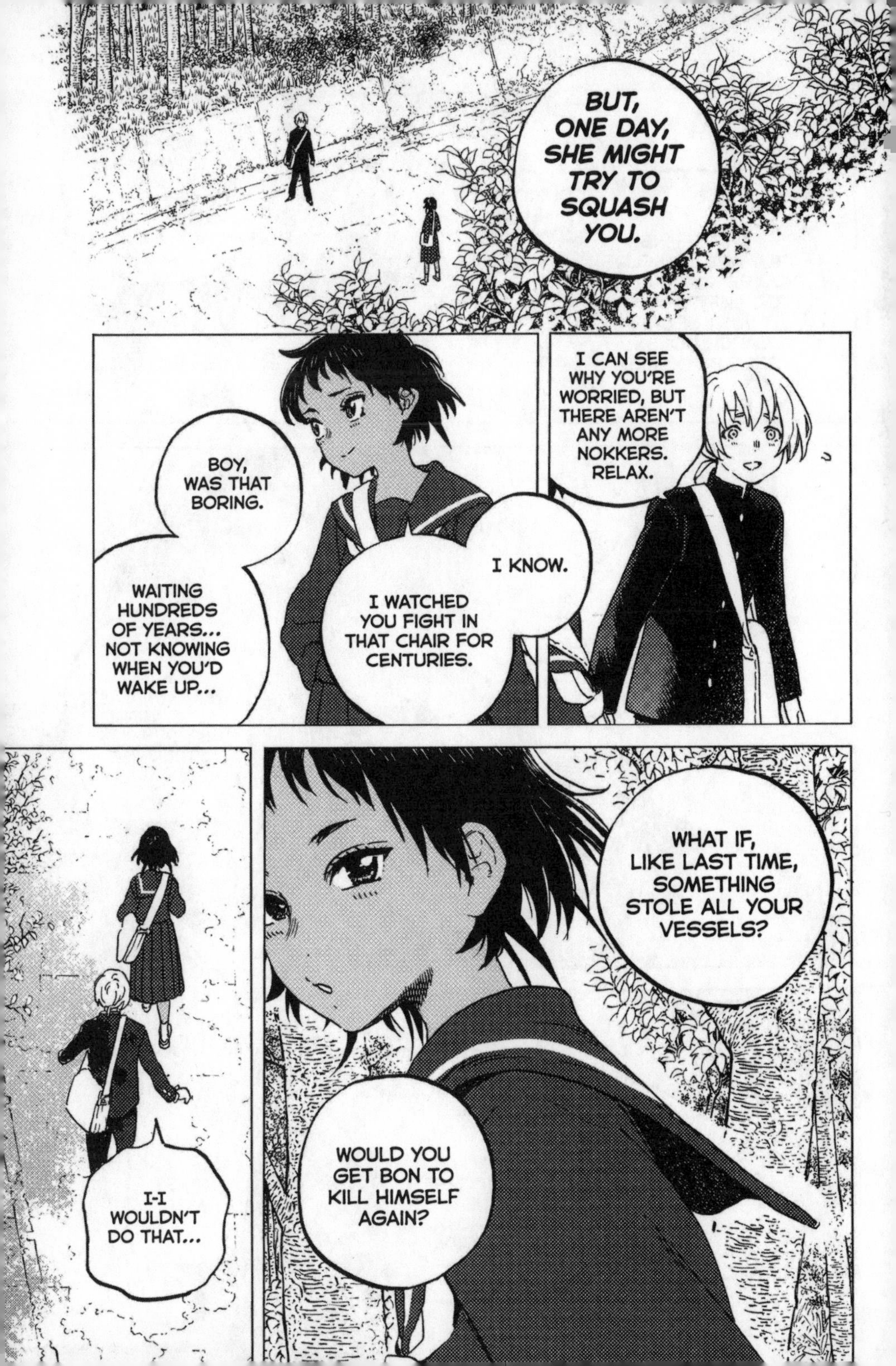
BUT, ONE DAY, SHE MIGHT TRY TO SQUASH YOU.
I CAN SEE WHY YOU'RE WORRIED, BUT THERE AREN'T ANY MORE NOKKERS. RELAX.
I KNOW.
I WATCHED YOU FIGHT IN THAT CHAIR FOR CENTURIES.
BOY, WAS THAT BORING.
WAITING HUNDREDS OF YEARS... NOT KNOWING WHEN YOU'D WAKE UP...
WHAT IF, LIKE LAST TIME, SOMETHING STOLE ALL YOUR VESSELS?
WOULD YOU GET BON TO KILL HIMSELF AGAIN?
I-I WOULDN'T DO THAT...

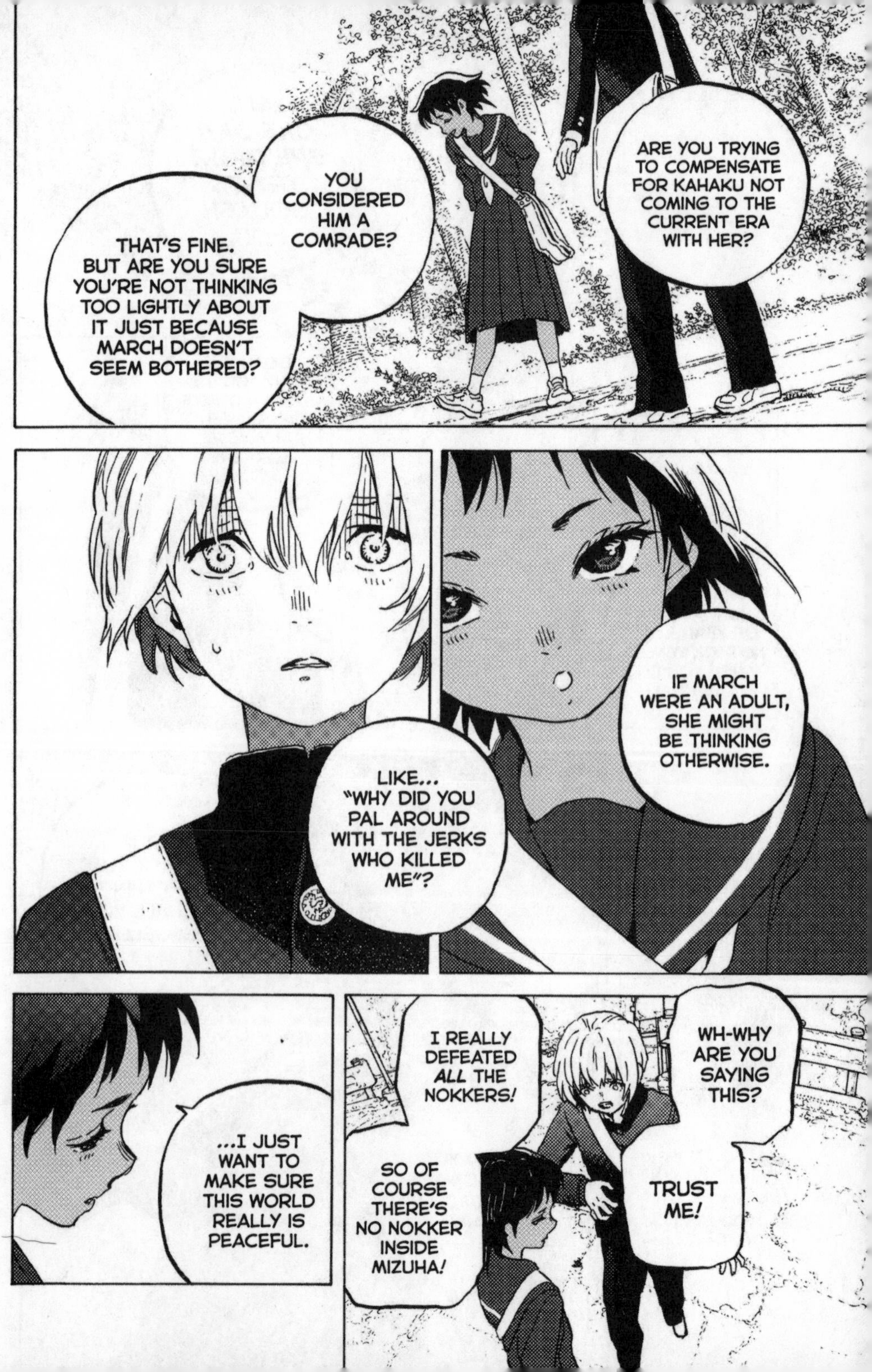
ARE YOU TRYING TO COMPENSATE FOR KAHAKU NOT COMING TO THE CURRENT ERA WITH HER?
YOU CONSIDERED HIM A COMRADE?
THAT'S FINE. BUT ARE YOU SURE YOU'RE NOT THINKING TOO LIGHTLY ABOUT IT JUST BECAUSE MARCH DOESN'T SEEM BOTHERED?
IF MARCH WERE AN ADULT, SHE MIGHT BE THINKING OTHERWISE.
LIKE... "WHY DID YOU PAL AROUND WITH THE JERKS WHO KILLED ME"?
WH-WHY ARE YOU SAYING THIS?
I REALLY DEFEATED *ALL* THE NOKKERS!
TRUST ME!
SO OF COURSE THERE'S NO NOKKER INSIDE MIZUHA!
...I JUST WANT TO MAKE SURE THIS WORLD REALLY IS PEACEFUL.

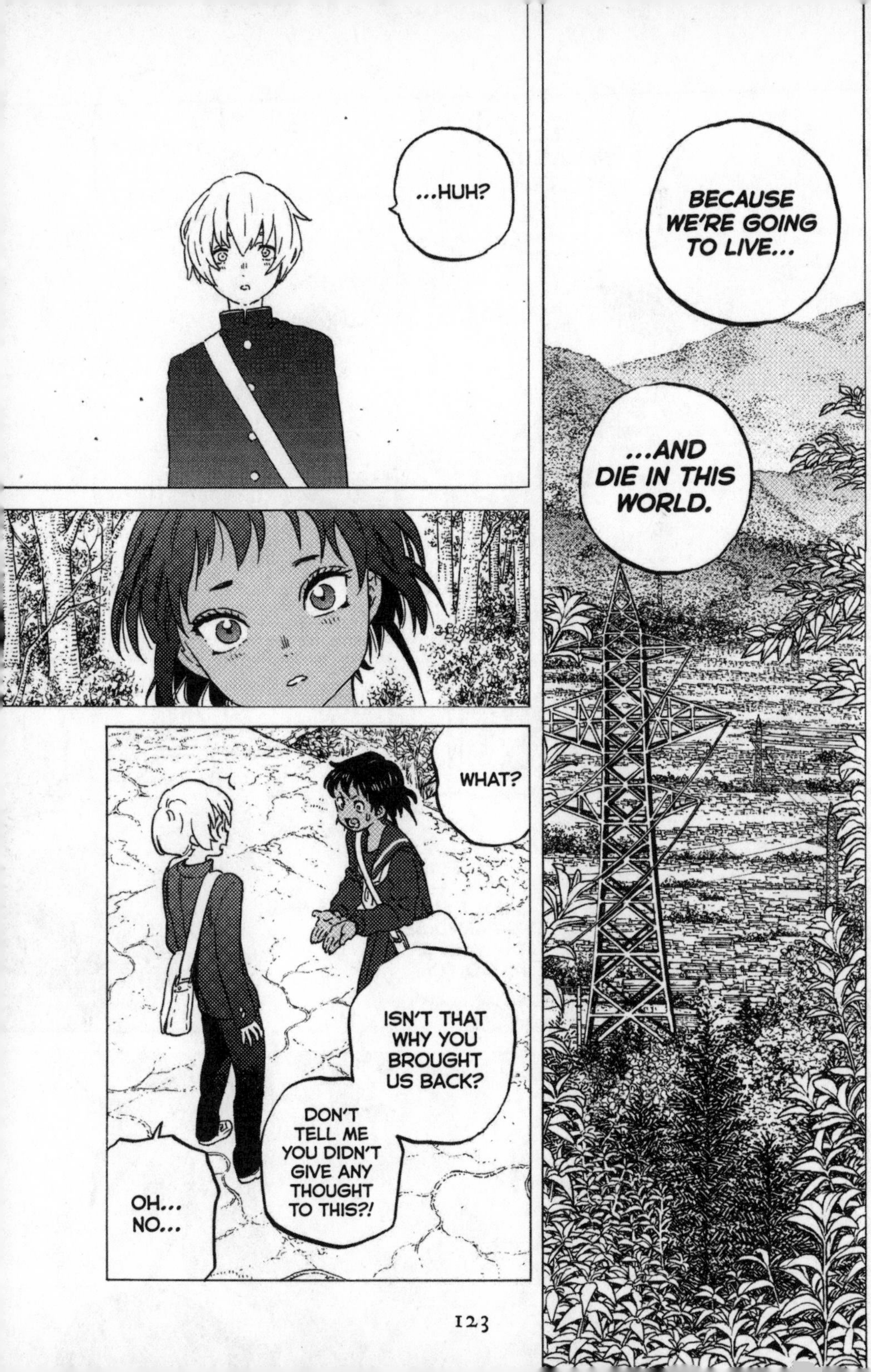
BECAUSE WE'RE GOING TO LIVE...
...AND DIE IN THIS WORLD.
...HUH?
WHAT?
ISN'T THAT WHY YOU BROUGHT US BACK?
DON'T TELL ME YOU DIDN'T GIVE ANY THOUGHT TO THIS?!
OH... NO...

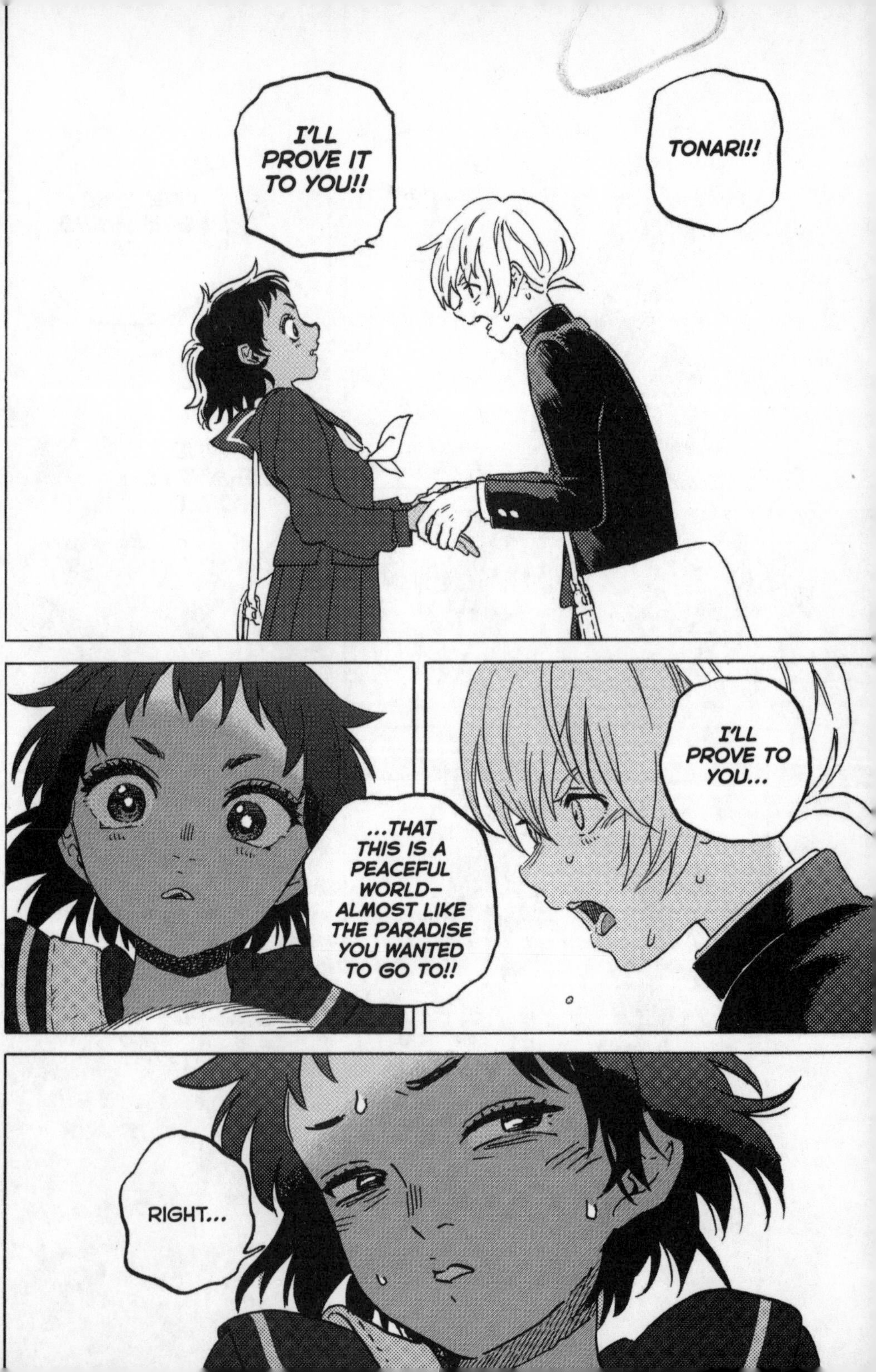
TONARI!!
I'LL PROVE IT TO YOU!!
I'LL PROVE TO YOU...
...THAT THIS IS A PEACEFUL WORLD—ALMOST LIKE THE PARADISE YOU WANTED TO GO TO!!
RIGHT...

TO YOUR

ETERNITY

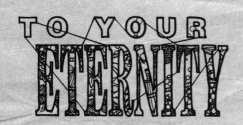

TO YOUR
ETERNITY

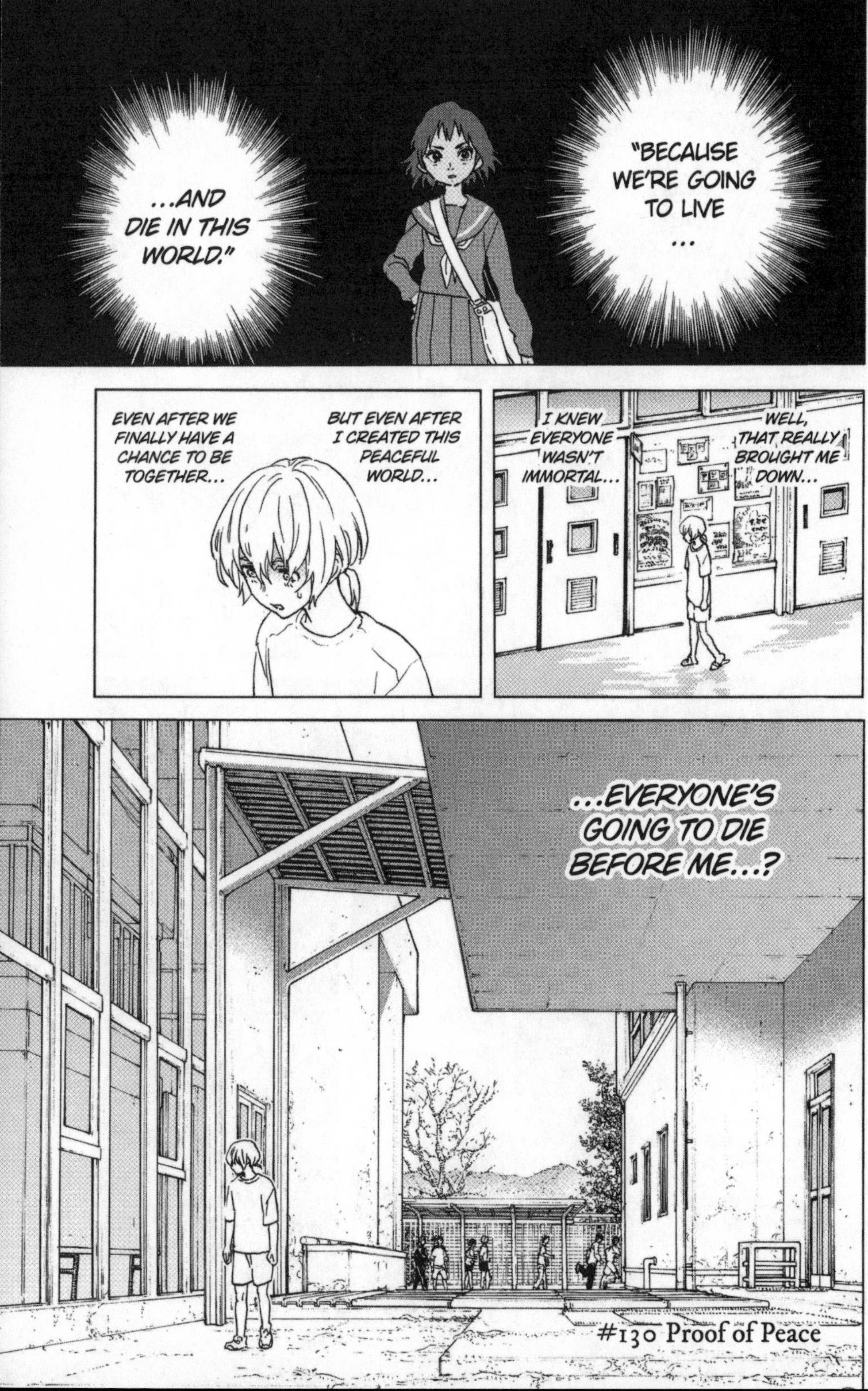
"BECAUSE WE'RE GOING TO LIVE ...
...AND DIE IN THIS WORLD."
WELL, THAT REALLY BROUGHT ME DOWN...
I KNEW EVERYONE WASN'T IMMORTAL...
BUT EVEN AFTER I CREATED THIS PEACEFUL WORLD...
EVEN AFTER WE FINALLY HAVE A CHANCE TO BE TOGETHER...
...EVERYONE'S GOING TO DIE BEFORE ME...?
#130 Proof of Peace

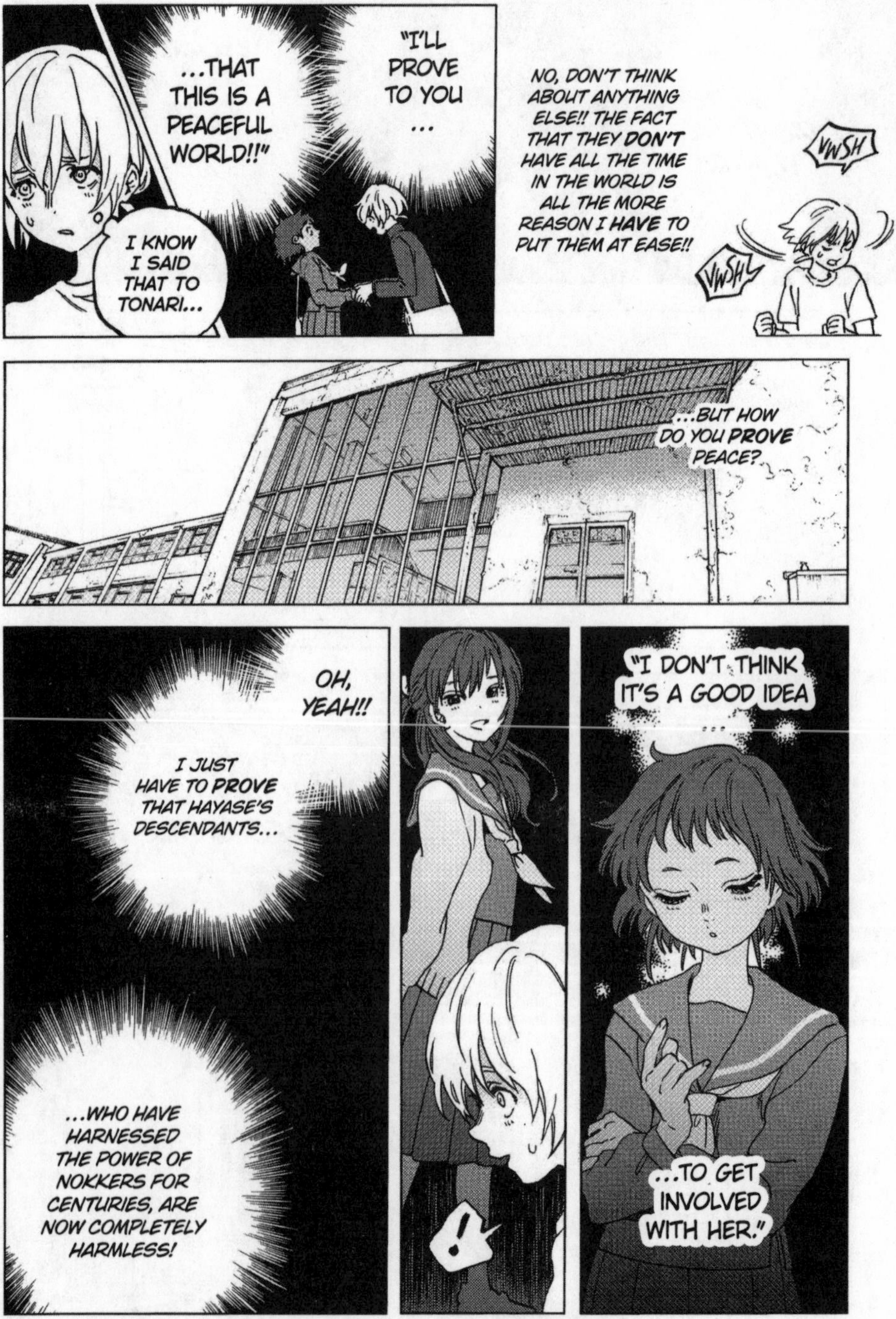
VWSH
NO, DON'T THINK ABOUT ANYTHING ELSE!! THE FACT THAT THEY DON'T HAVE ALL THE TIME IN THE WORLD IS ALL THE MORE REASON I HAVE TO PUT THEM AT EASE!!
VWSH
"I'LL PROVE TO YOU ...
...THAT THIS IS A PEACEFUL WORLD!!"
I KNOW I SAID THAT TO TONARI...
...BUT HOW DO YOU PROVE PEACE?
"I DON'T THINK IT'S A GOOD IDEA ...
...TO GET INVOLVED WITH HER."
!
OH, YEAH!!
I JUST HAVE TO PROVE THAT HAYASE'S DESCENDANTS...
...WHO HAVE HARNESSED THE POWER OF NOKKERS FOR CENTURIES, ARE NOW COMPLETELY HARMLESS!

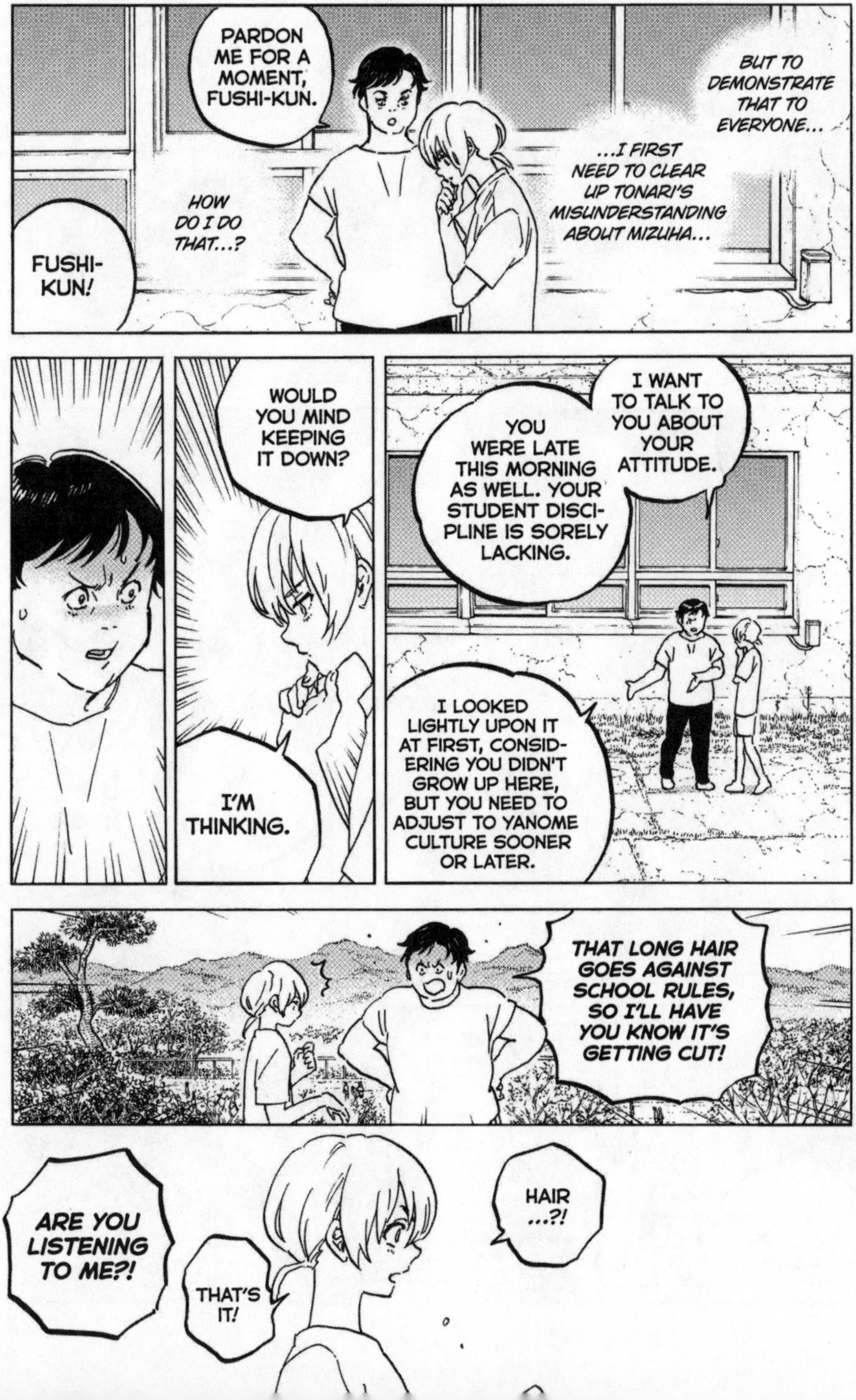
BUT TO DEMONSTRATE THAT TO EVERYONE...
...I FIRST NEED TO CLEAR UP TONARI'S MISUNDERSTANDING ABOUT MIZUHA...
PARDON ME FOR A MOMENT, FUSHI-KUN.
HOW DO I DO THAT...?
FUSHI-KUN!
I WANT TO TALK TO YOU ABOUT YOUR ATTITUDE.
YOU WERE LATE THIS MORNING AS WELL. YOUR STUDENT DISCIPLINE IS SORELY LACKING.
I LOOKED LIGHTLY UPON IT AT FIRST, CONSIDERING YOU DIDN'T GROW UP HERE, BUT YOU NEED TO ADJUST TO YANOME CULTURE SOONER OR LATER.
WOULD YOU MIND KEEPING IT DOWN?
I'M THINKING.
THAT LONG HAIR GOES AGAINST SCHOOL RULES, SO I'LL HAVE YOU KNOW IT'S GETTING CUT!
HAIR ...?!
THAT'S IT!
ARE YOU LISTENING TO ME?!

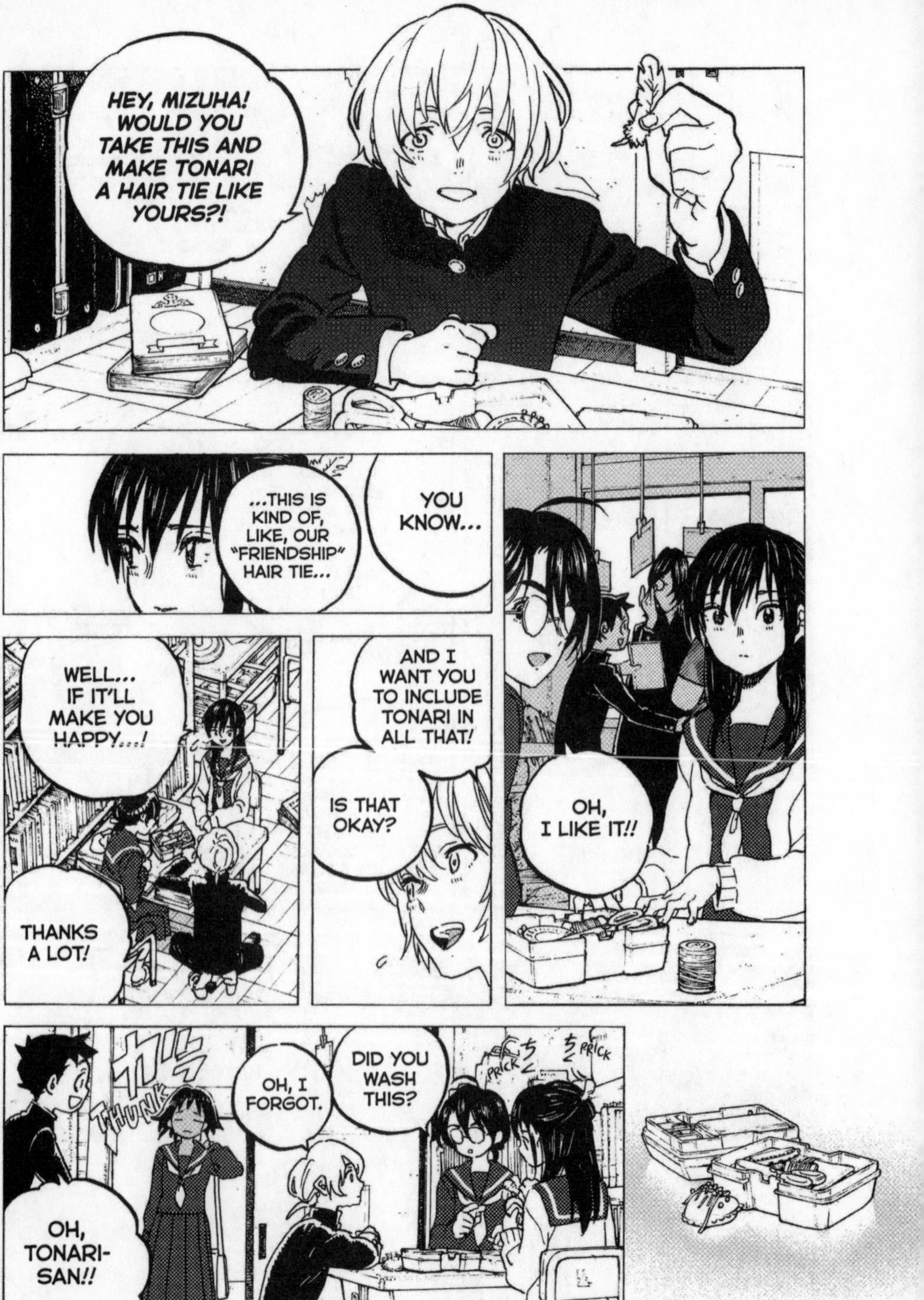
HEY, MIZUHA! WOULD YOU TAKE THIS AND MAKE TONARI A HAIR TIE LIKE YOURS?!
OH, I LIKE IT!!
YOU KNOW...
...THIS IS KIND OF, LIKE, OUR "FRIENDSHIP" HAIR TIE...
AND I WANT YOU TO INCLUDE TONARI IN ALL THAT!
IS THAT OKAY?
WELL... IF IT'LL MAKE YOU HAPPY...!
THANKS A LOT!
PRICK
PRICK
DID YOU WASH THIS?
OH, I FORGOT.
THUNK
OH, TONARI-SAN!!

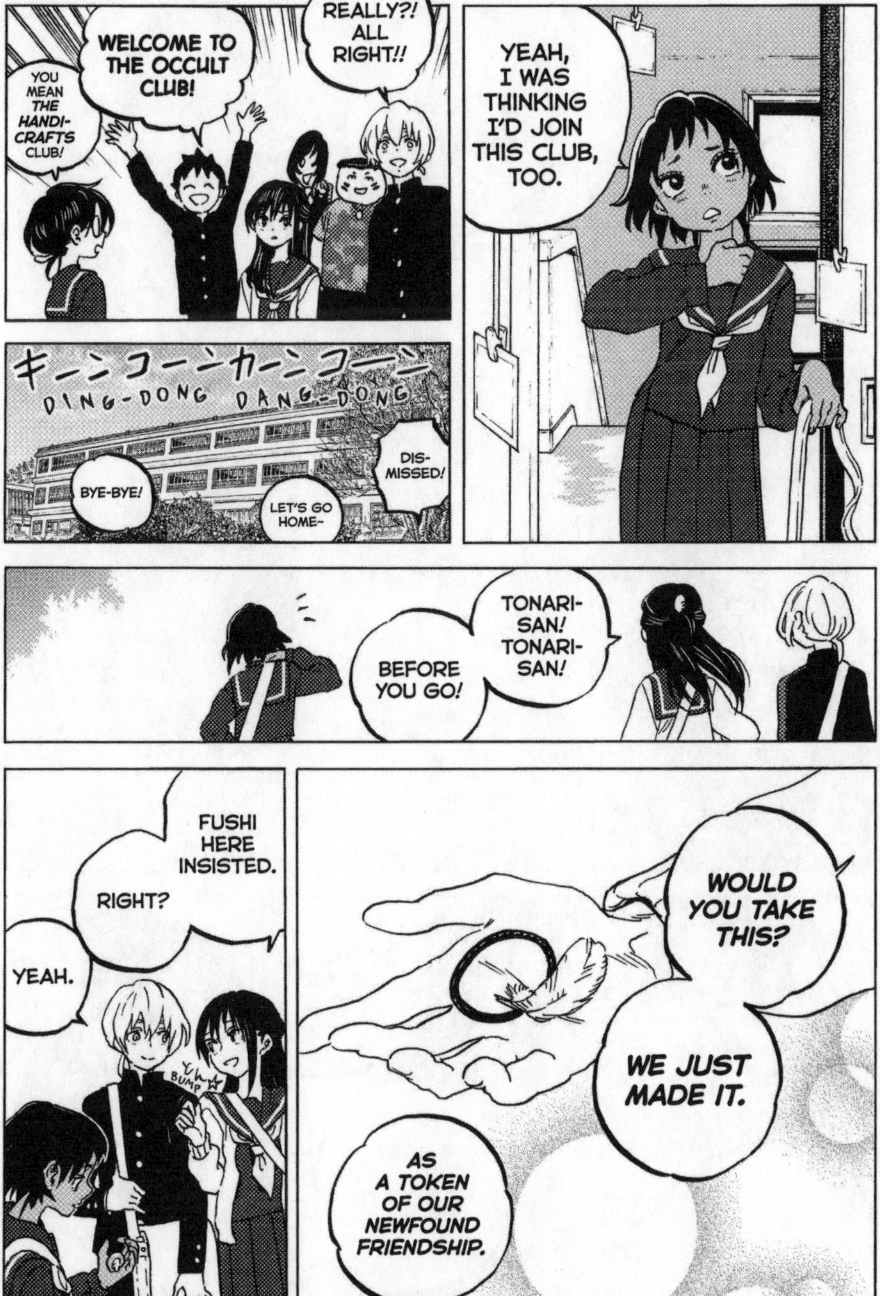
YEAH, I WAS THINKING I'D JOIN THIS CLUB, TOO.
REALLY?! ALL RIGHT!!
WELCOME TO THE OCCULT CLUB!
YOU MEAN THE HANDI-CRAFTS CLUB!
キーンコーンカーンコーン
DING-DONG DANG-DONG
DIS-MISSED!
LET'S GO HOME~
BYE-BYE!
TONARI-SAN! TONARI-SAN!
BEFORE YOU GO!
WOULD YOU TAKE THIS?
WE JUST MADE IT.
AS A TOKEN OF OUR NEWFOUND FRIENDSHIP.
FUSHI HERE INSISTED.
RIGHT?
YEAH.
BUMP

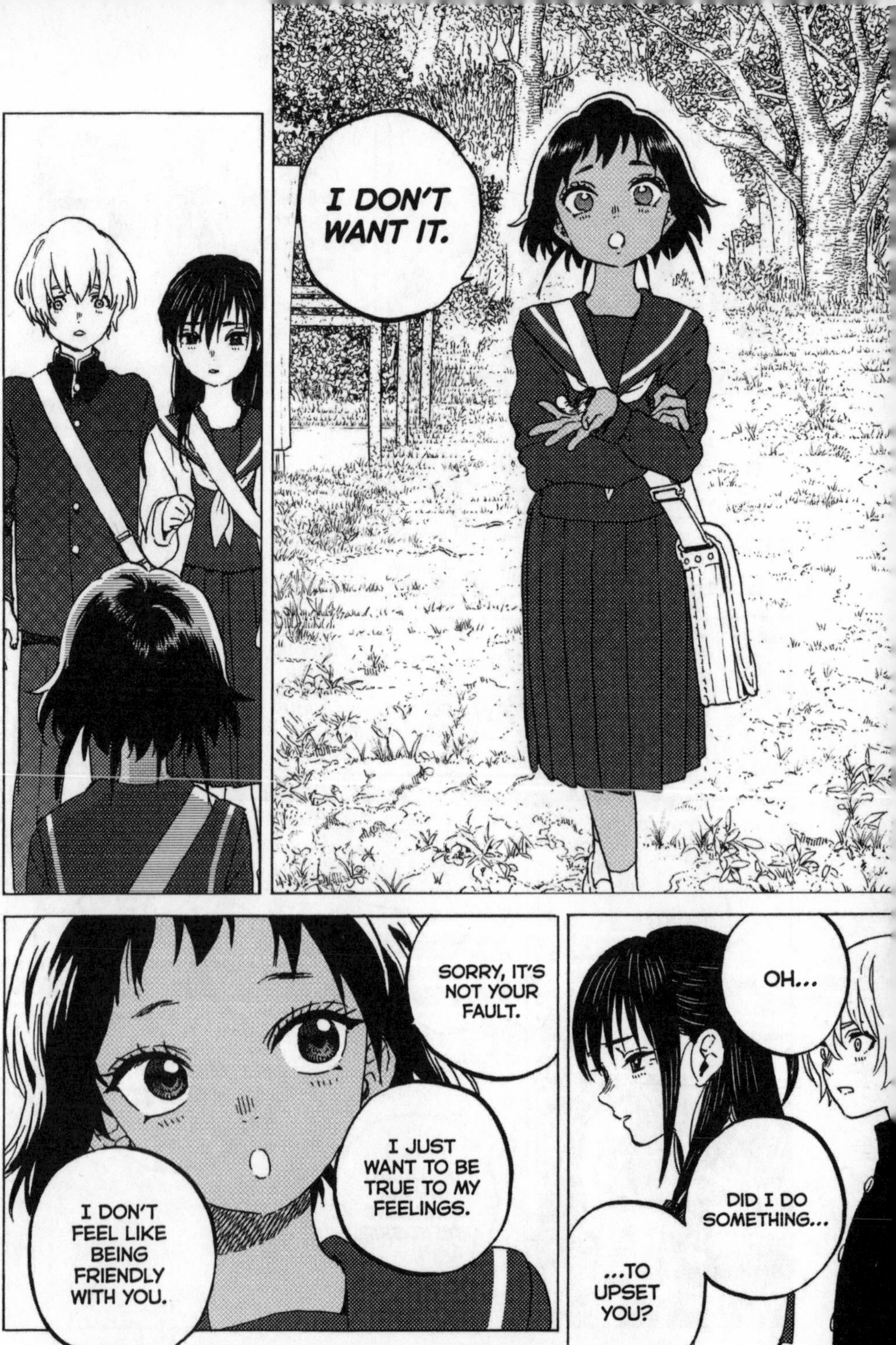
I DON'T WANT IT.
OH...
DID I DO SOMETHING...
...TO UPSET YOU?
SORRY, IT'S NOT YOUR FAULT.
I JUST WANT TO BE TRUE TO MY FEELINGS.
I DON'T FEEL LIKE BEING FRIENDLY WITH YOU.

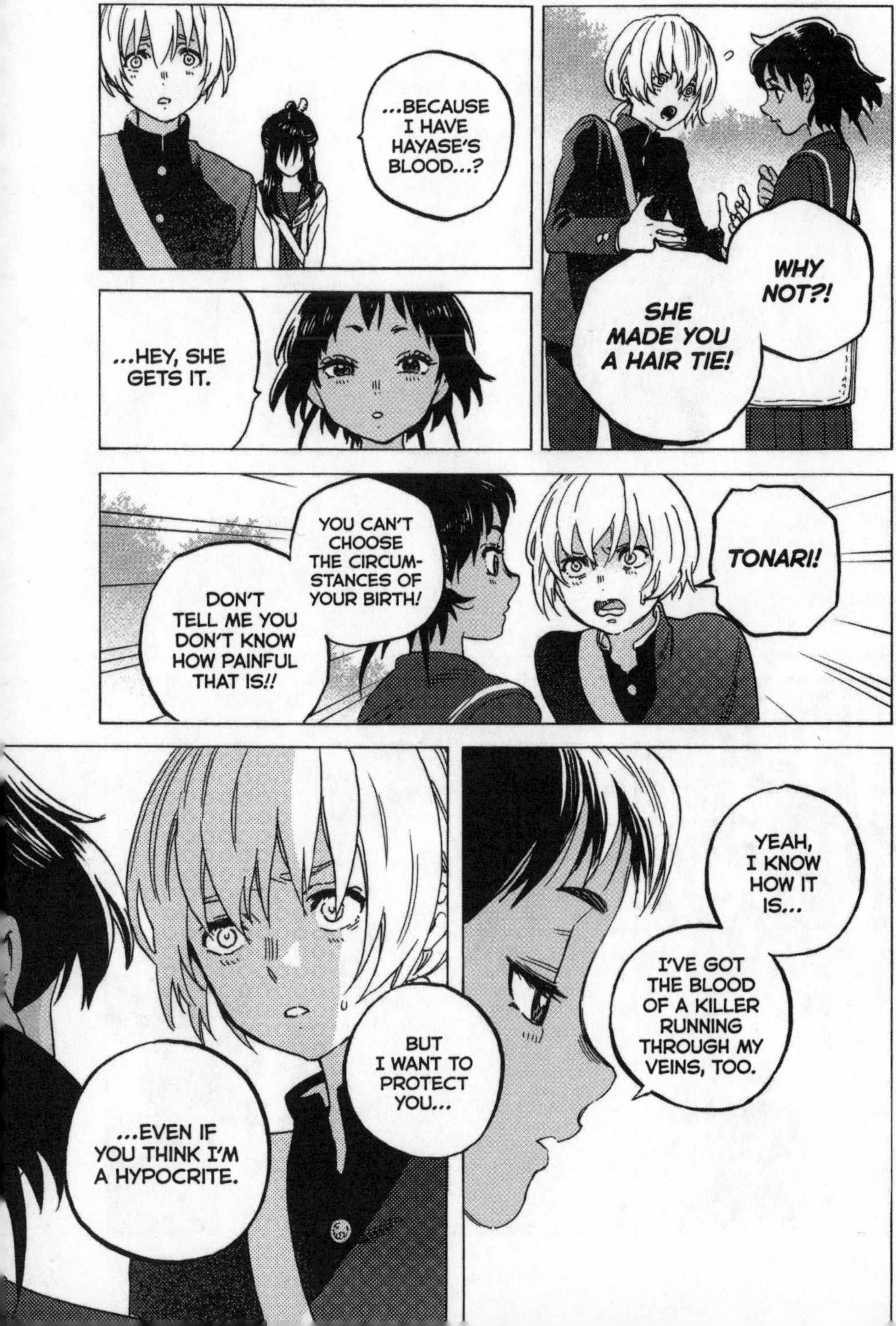
WHY NOT?!
SHE MADE YOU A HAIR TIE!
...BECAUSE I HAVE HAYASE'S BLOOD...?
...HEY, SHE GETS IT.
TONARI!
YOU CAN'T CHOOSE THE CIRCUM-STANCES OF YOUR BIRTH!
DON'T TELL ME YOU DON'T KNOW HOW PAINFUL THAT IS!!
YEAH, I KNOW HOW IT IS...
I'VE GOT THE BLOOD OF A KILLER RUNNING THROUGH MY VEINS, TOO.
BUT I WANT TO PROTECT YOU...
...EVEN IF YOU THINK I'M A HYPOCRITE.

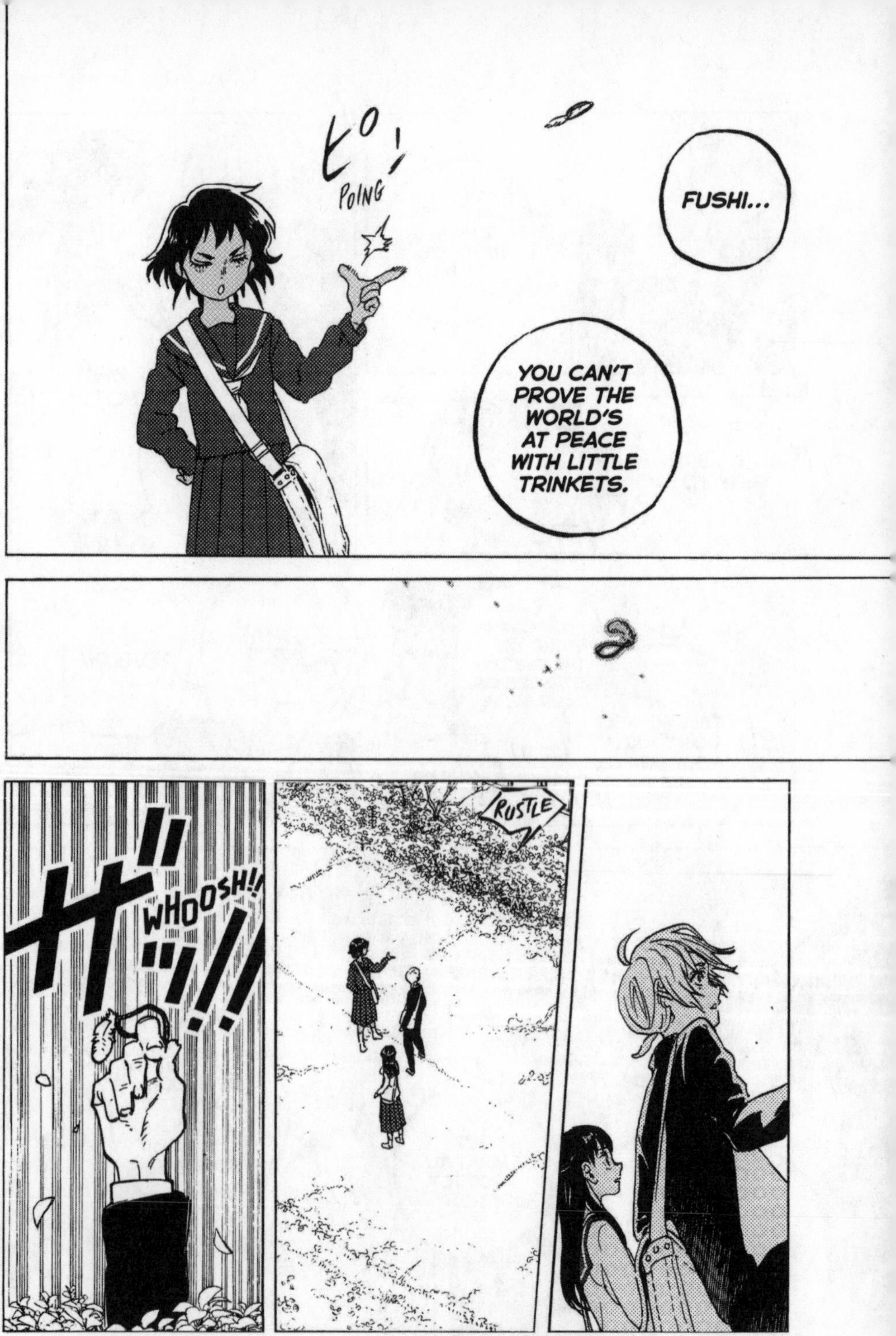
FUSHI...
POING
YOU CAN'T PROVE THE WORLD'S AT PEACE WITH LITTLE TRINKETS.
RUSTLE
WHOOSH!!

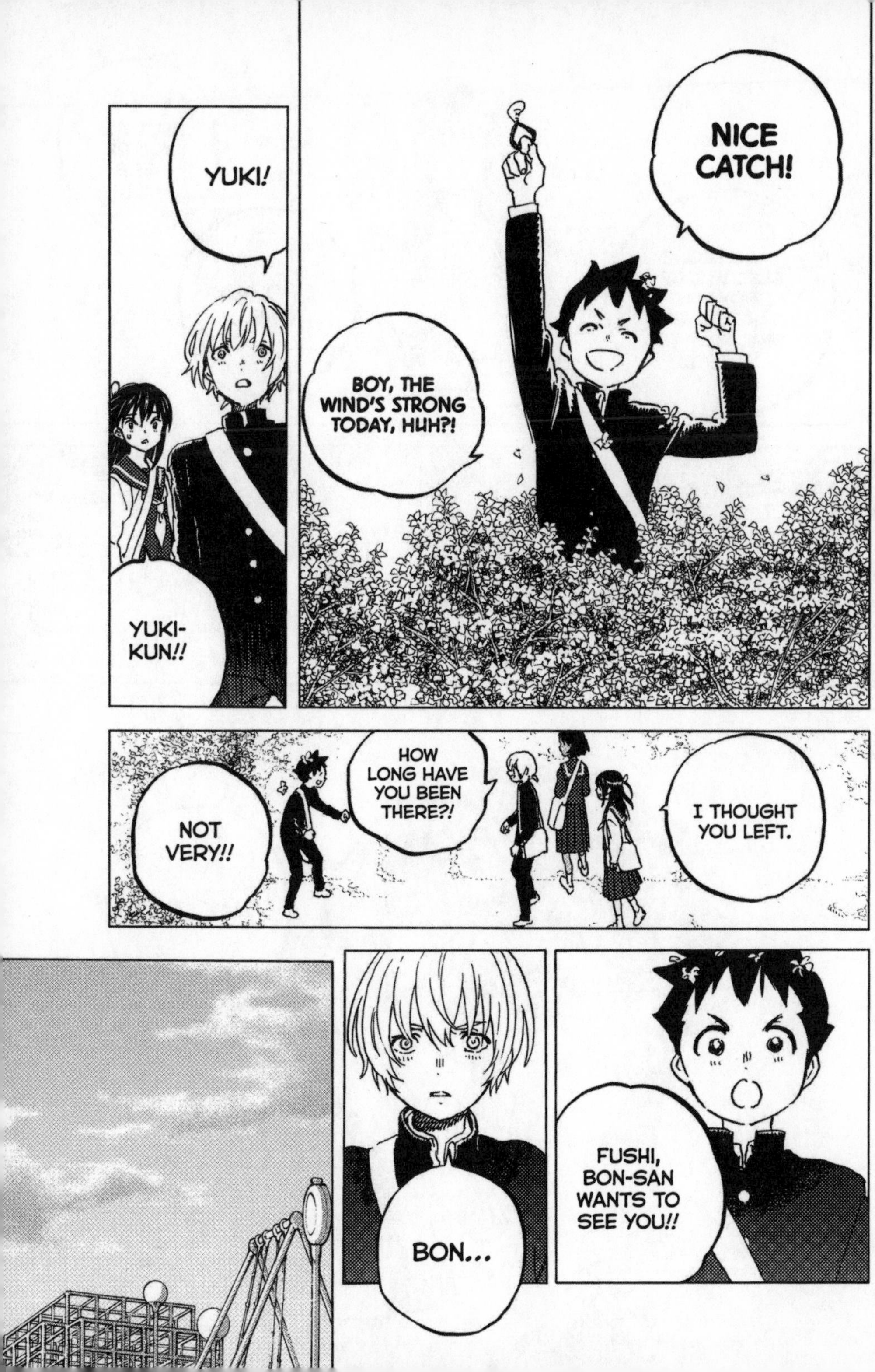
NICE CATCH!
BOY, THE WIND'S STRONG TODAY, HUH?!
YUKI!
YUKI-KUN!!
I THOUGHT YOU LEFT.
HOW LONG HAVE YOU BEEN THERE?!
NOT VERY!!
FUSHI, BON-SAN WANTS TO SEE YOU!!
BON...

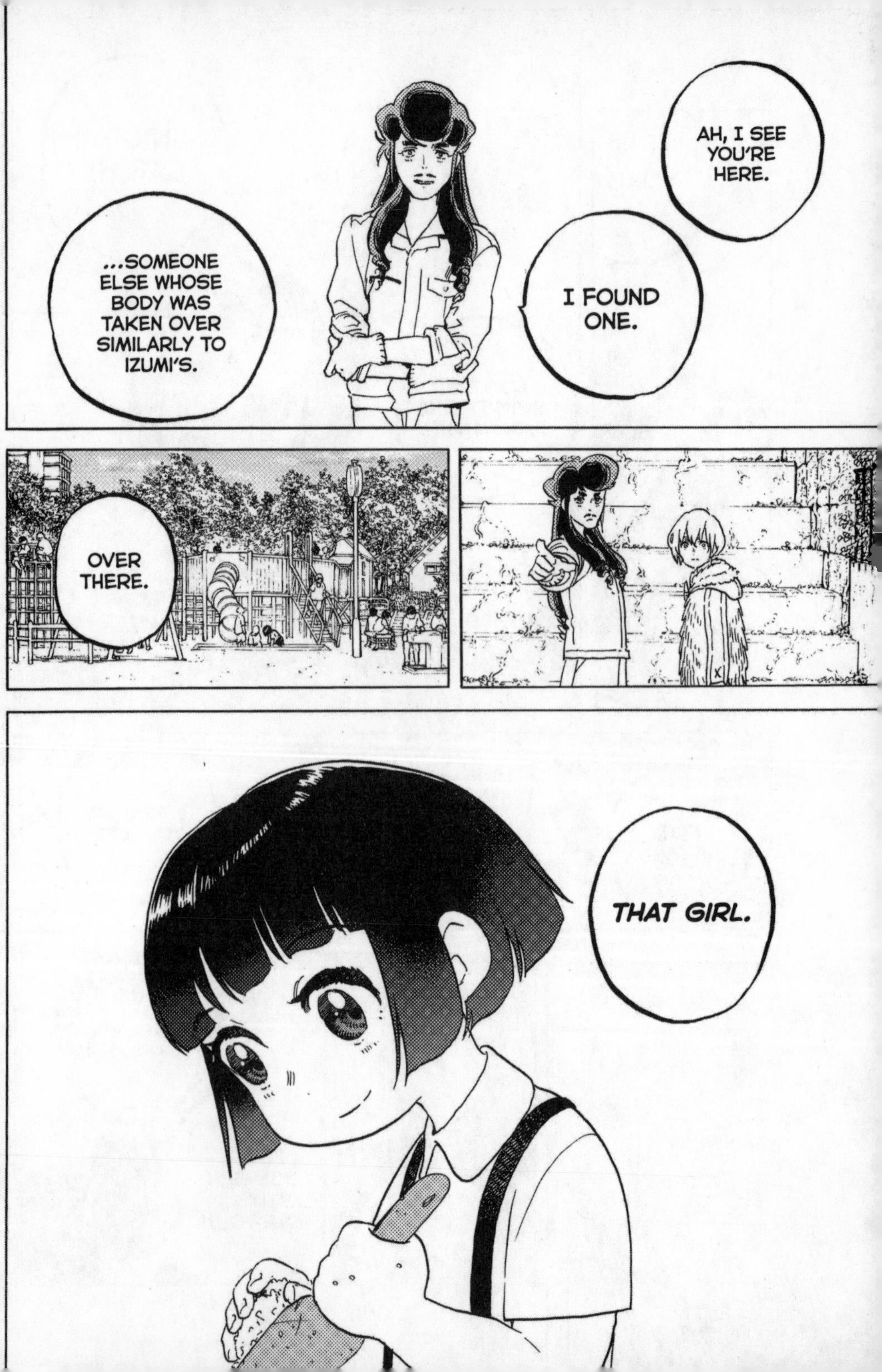
AH, I SEE YOU'RE HERE.
I FOUND ONE.
...SOMEONE ELSE WHOSE BODY WAS TAKEN OVER SIMILARLY TO IZUMI'S.
OVER THERE.
THAT GIRL.

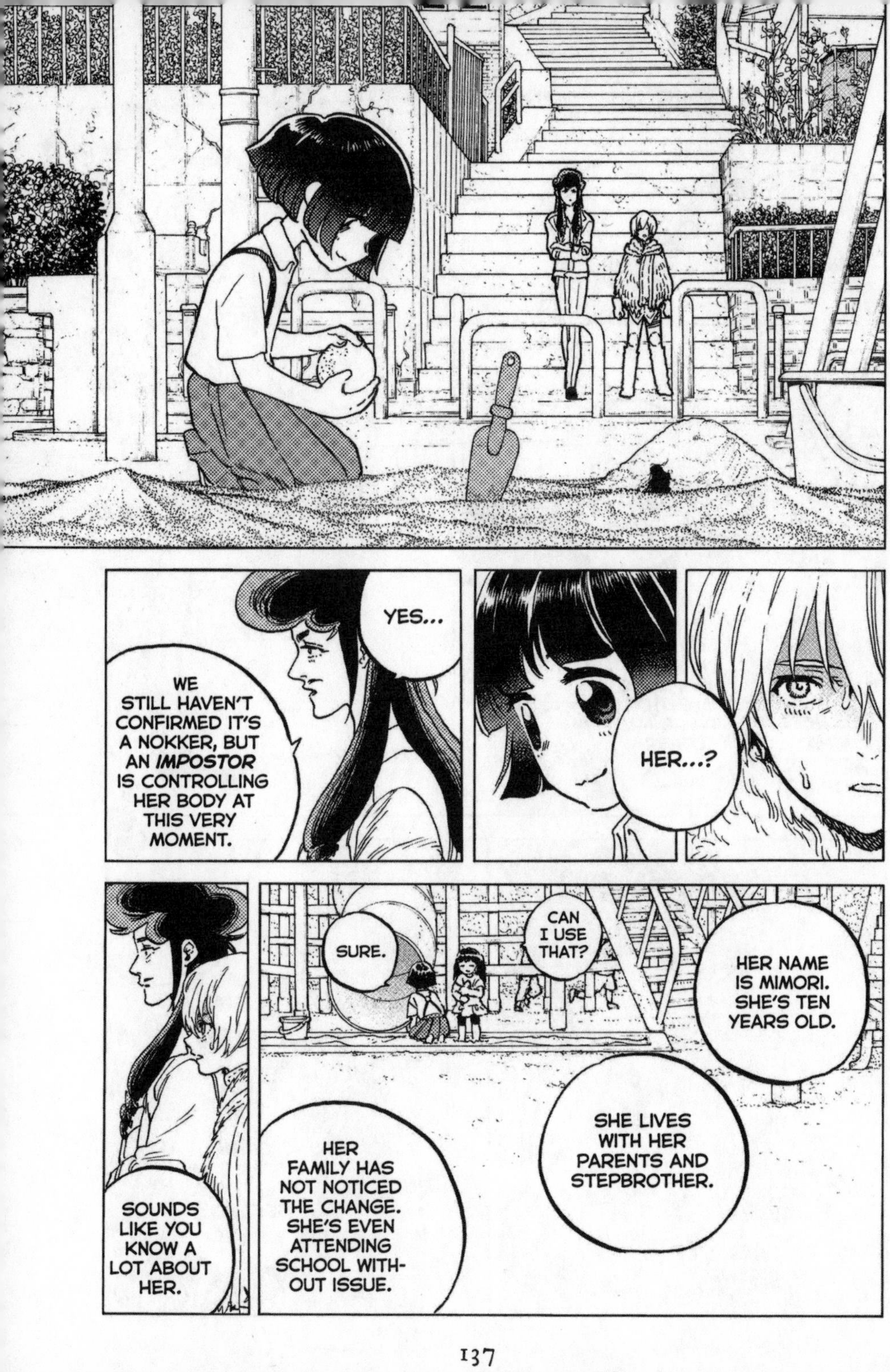
HER...?
YES...
WE STILL HAVEN'T CONFIRMED IT'S A NOKKER, BUT AN *IMPOSTOR* IS CONTROLLING HER BODY AT THIS VERY MOMENT.
HER NAME IS MIMORI. SHE'S TEN YEARS OLD.
CAN I USE THAT?
SURE.
SHE LIVES WITH HER PARENTS AND STEPBROTHER.
HER FAMILY HAS NOT NOTICED THE CHANGE. SHE'S EVEN ATTENDING SCHOOL WITH-OUT ISSUE.
SOUNDS LIKE YOU KNOW A LOT ABOUT HER.

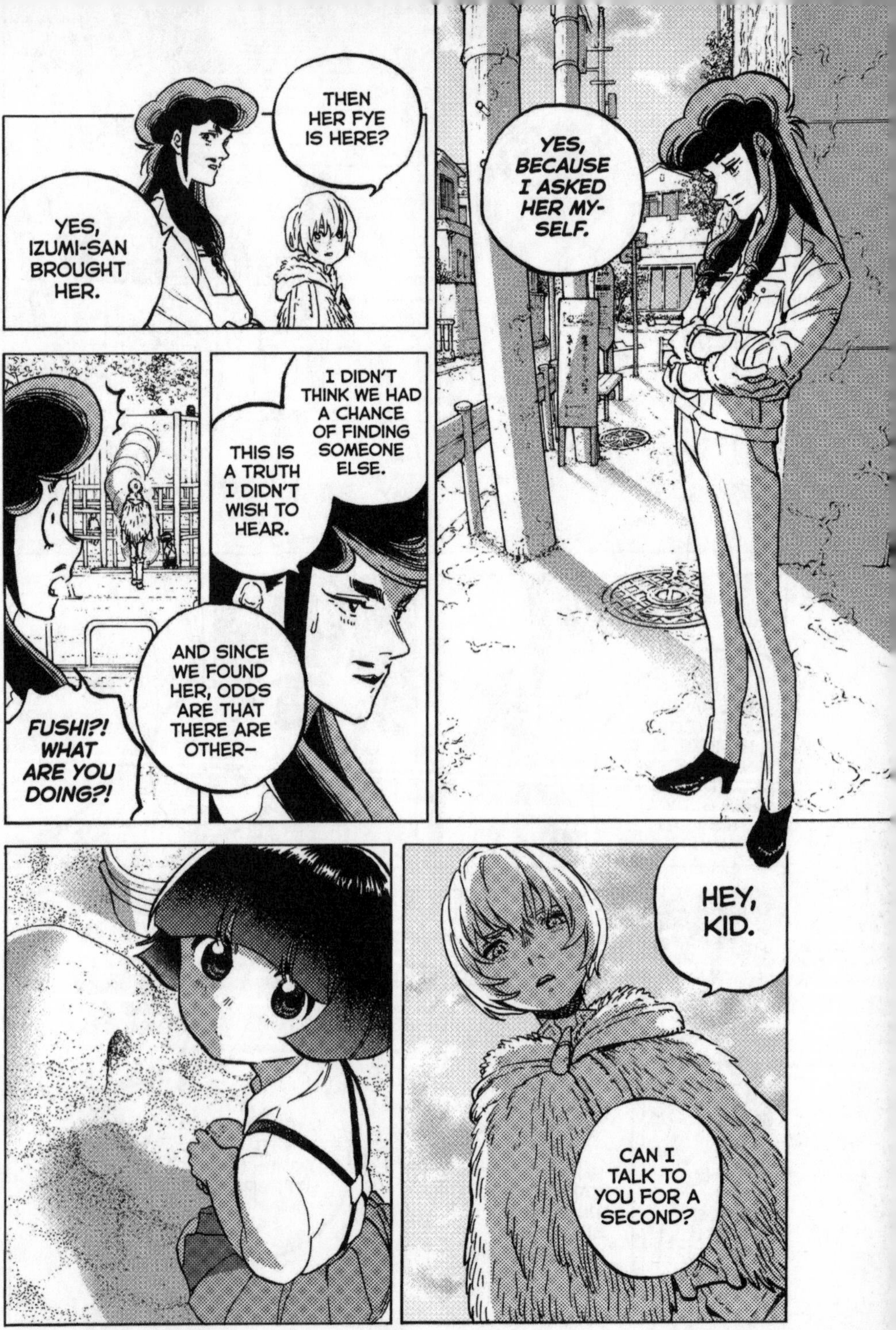
YES, BECAUSE I ASKED HER MY-SELF.
THEN HER FYE IS HERE?
YES, IZUMI-SAN BROUGHT HER.
I DIDN'T THINK WE HAD A CHANCE OF FINDING SOMEONE ELSE.
THIS IS A TRUTH I DIDN'T WISH TO HEAR.
AND SINCE WE FOUND HER, ODDS ARE THAT THERE ARE OTHER–
FUSHI?! WHAT ARE YOU DOING?!
HEY, KID.
CAN I TALK TO YOU FOR A SECOND?

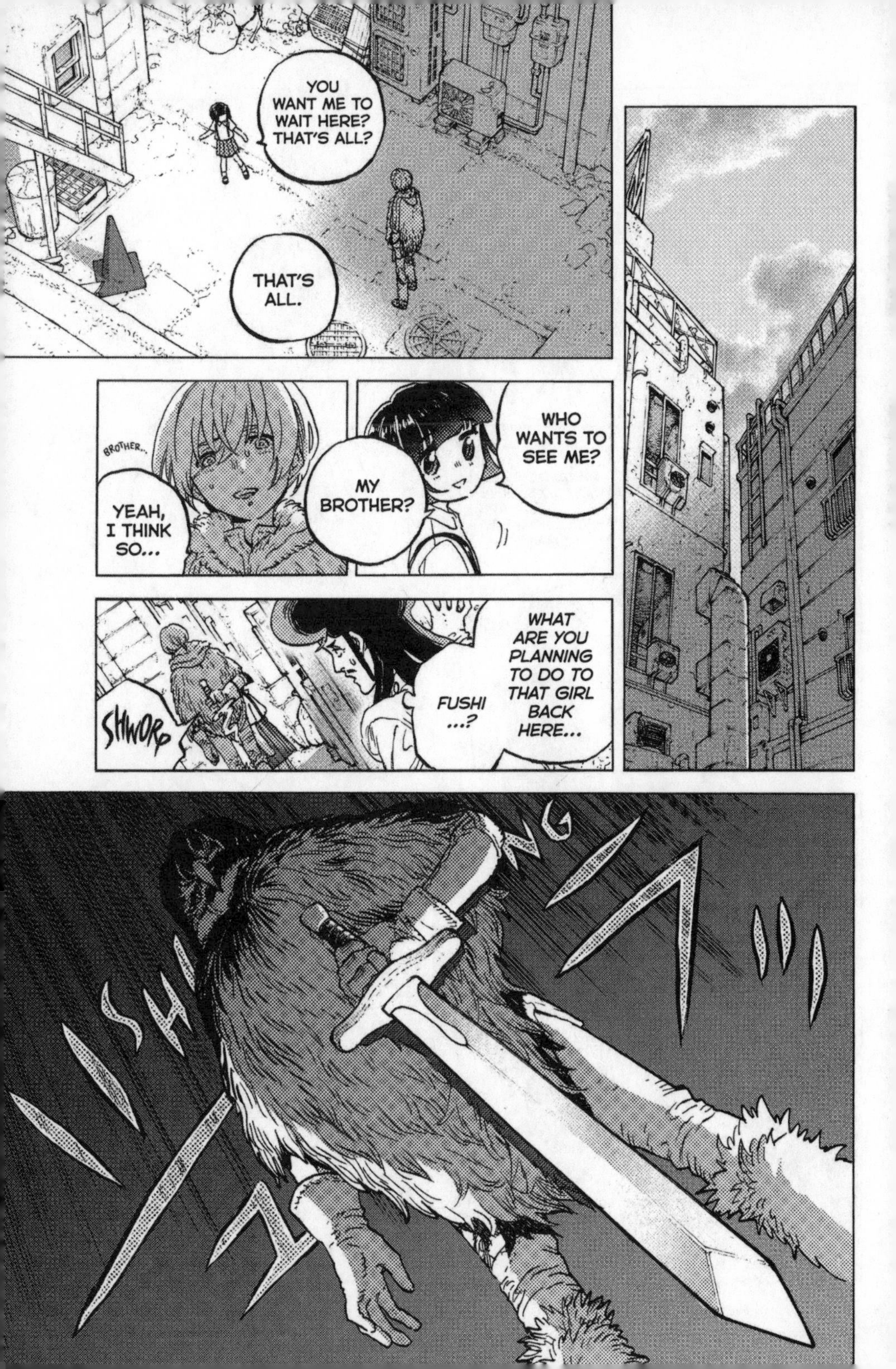
YOU WANT ME TO WAIT HERE? THAT'S ALL?
THAT'S ALL.
WHO WANTS TO SEE ME?
MY BROTHER?
BROTHER...
YEAH, I THINK SO...
WHAT ARE YOU PLANNING TO DO TO THAT GIRL BACK HERE...
FUSHI ...?
SHWORP
SHING

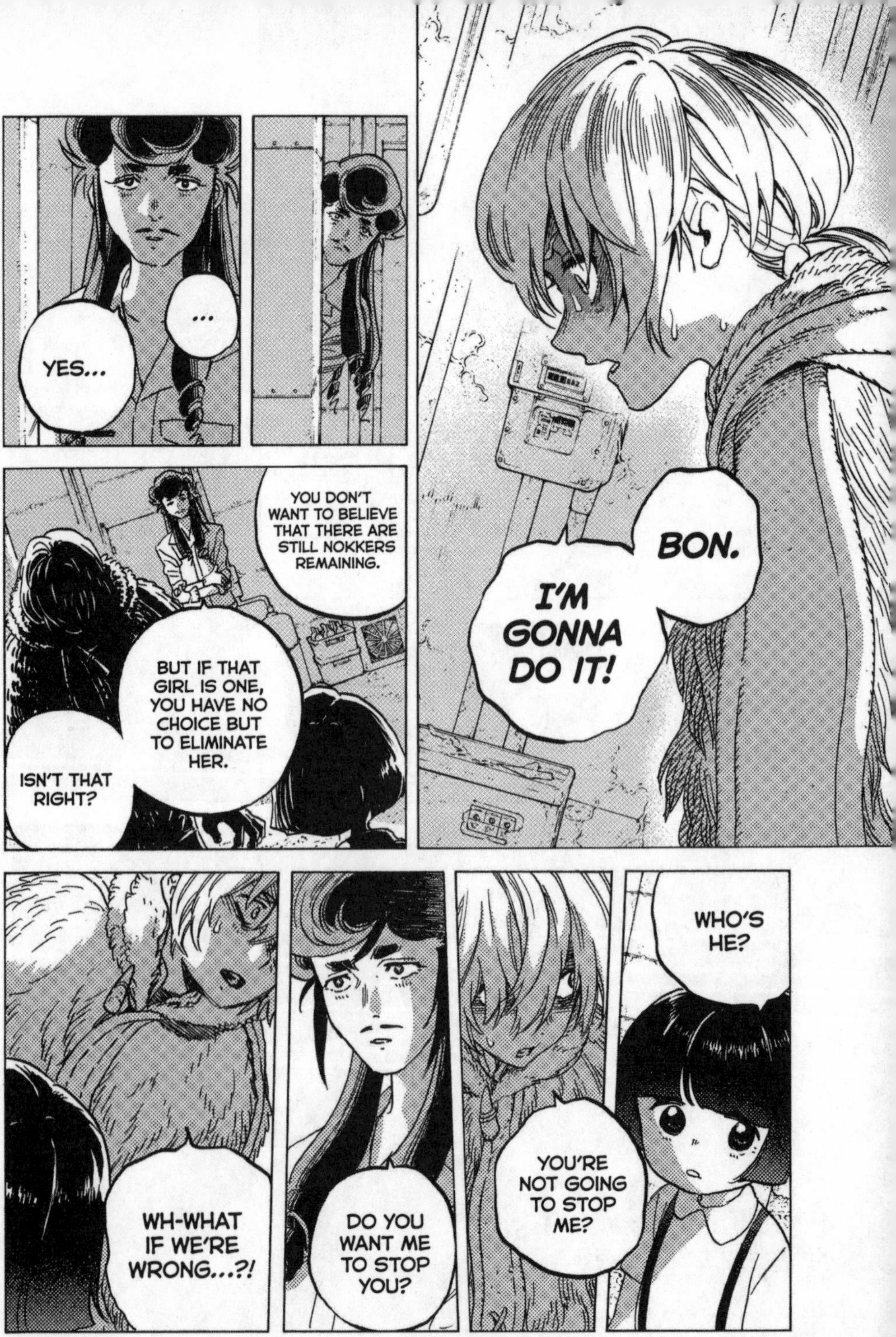
BON.
I'M GONNA DO IT!
...
YES...
YOU DON'T WANT TO BELIEVE THAT THERE ARE STILL NOKKERS REMAINING.
BUT IF THAT GIRL IS ONE, YOU HAVE NO CHOICE BUT TO ELIMINATE HER.
ISN'T THAT RIGHT?
WHO'S HE?
YOU'RE NOT GOING TO STOP ME?
DO YOU WANT ME TO STOP YOU?
WH-WHAT IF WE'RE WRONG...?!

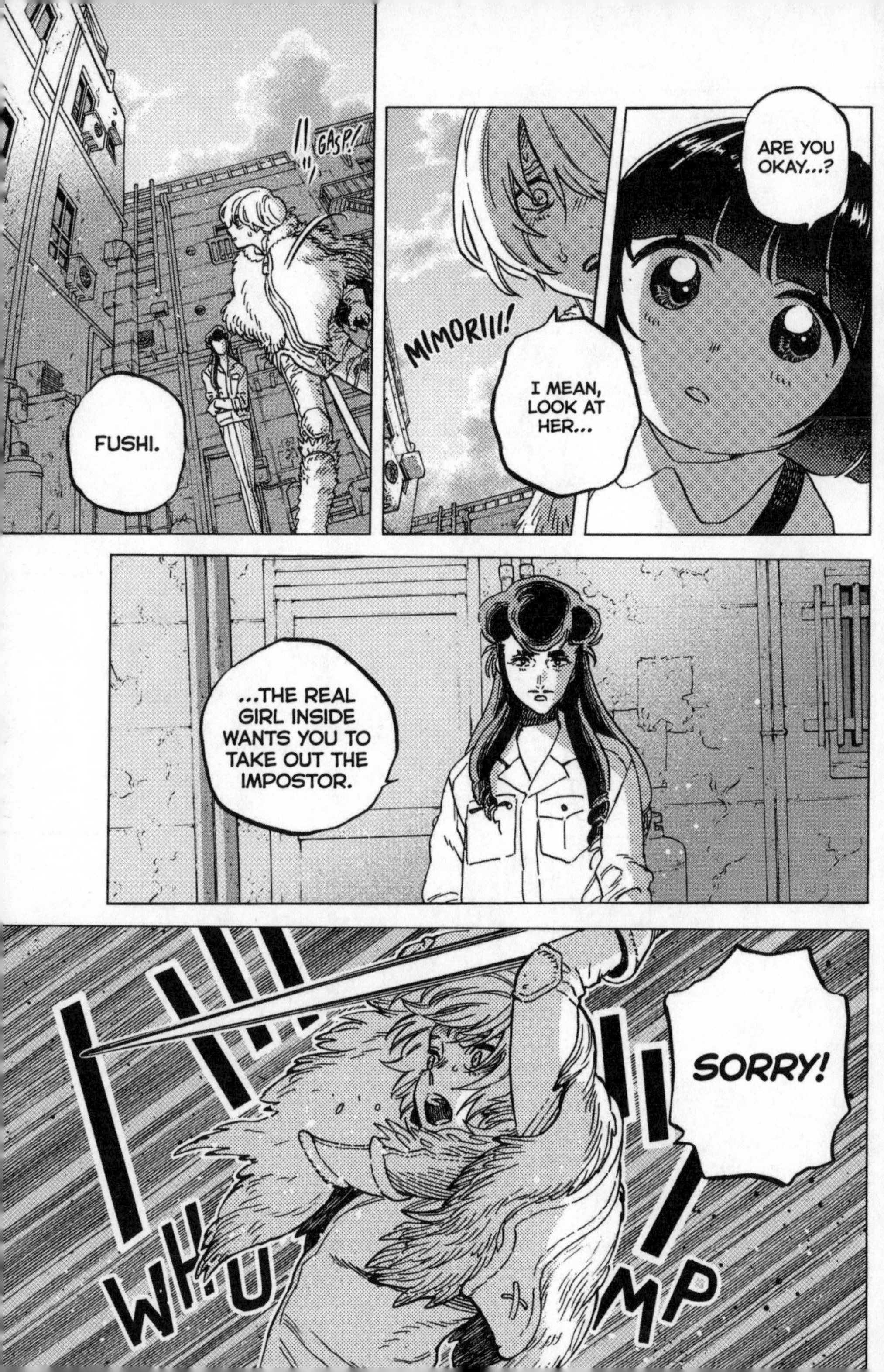
ARE YOU OKAY...?
MIMORIII!
I MEAN, LOOK AT HER...
GASP!
FUSHI.
...THE REAL GIRL INSIDE WANTS YOU TO TAKE OUT THE IMPOSTOR.
SORRY!
WHUMP

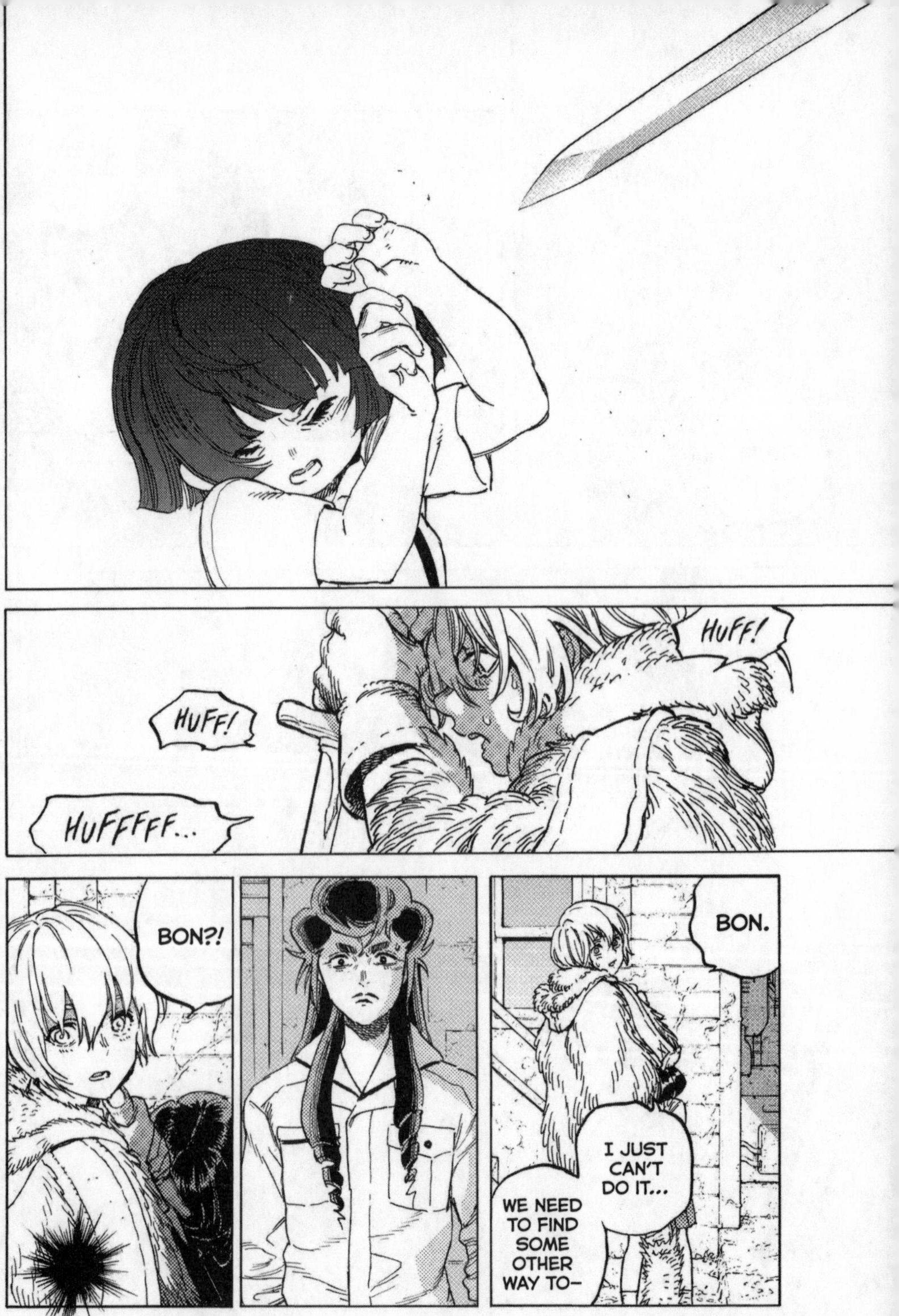
HUFF!
HUFF!
HUFFFFF...
BON.
I JUST CAN'T DO IT...
WE NEED TO FIND SOME OTHER WAY TO—
BON?!

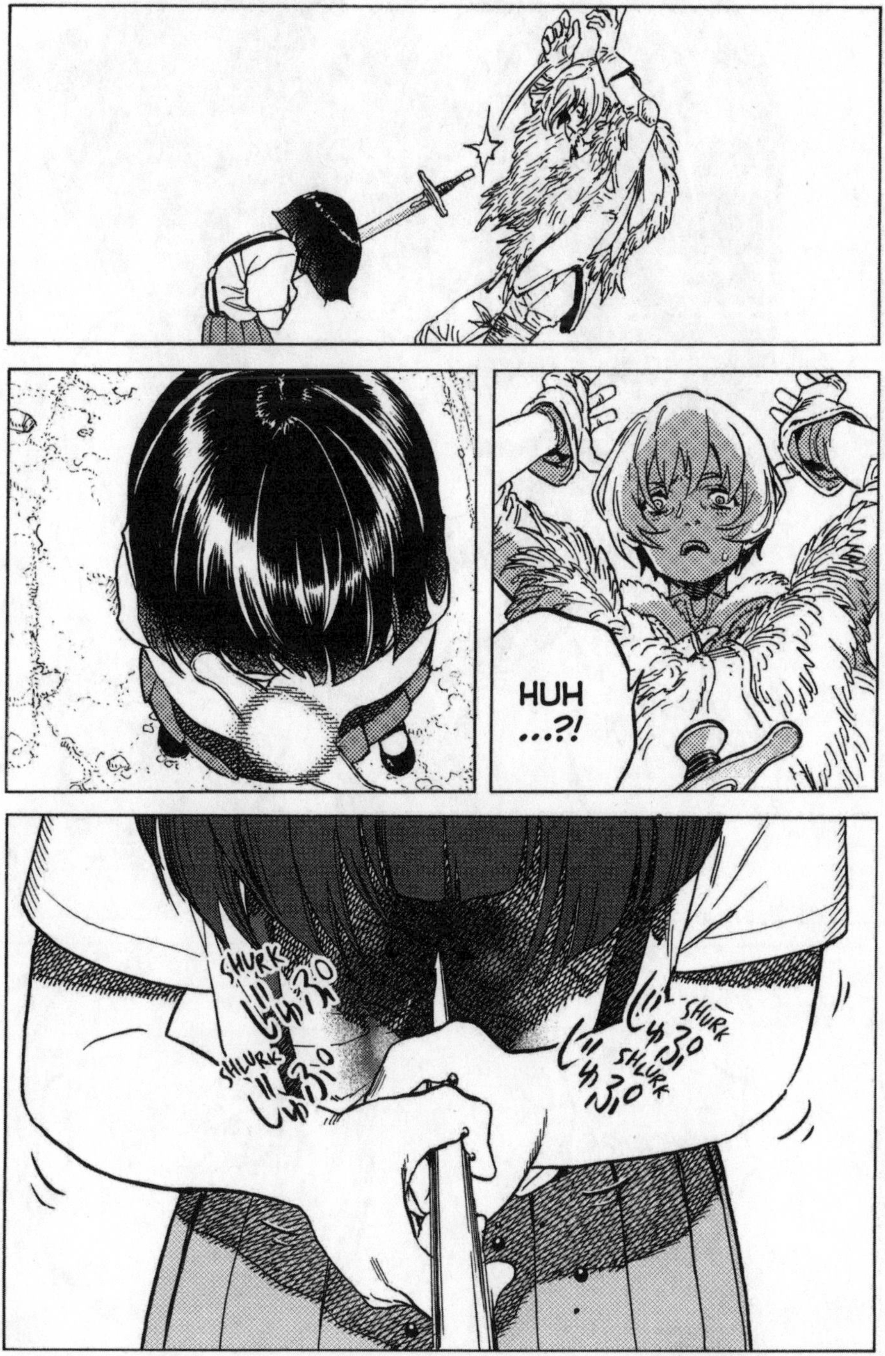

HUH ...?!
SHURK
SHLURK
SHURK
SHLURK

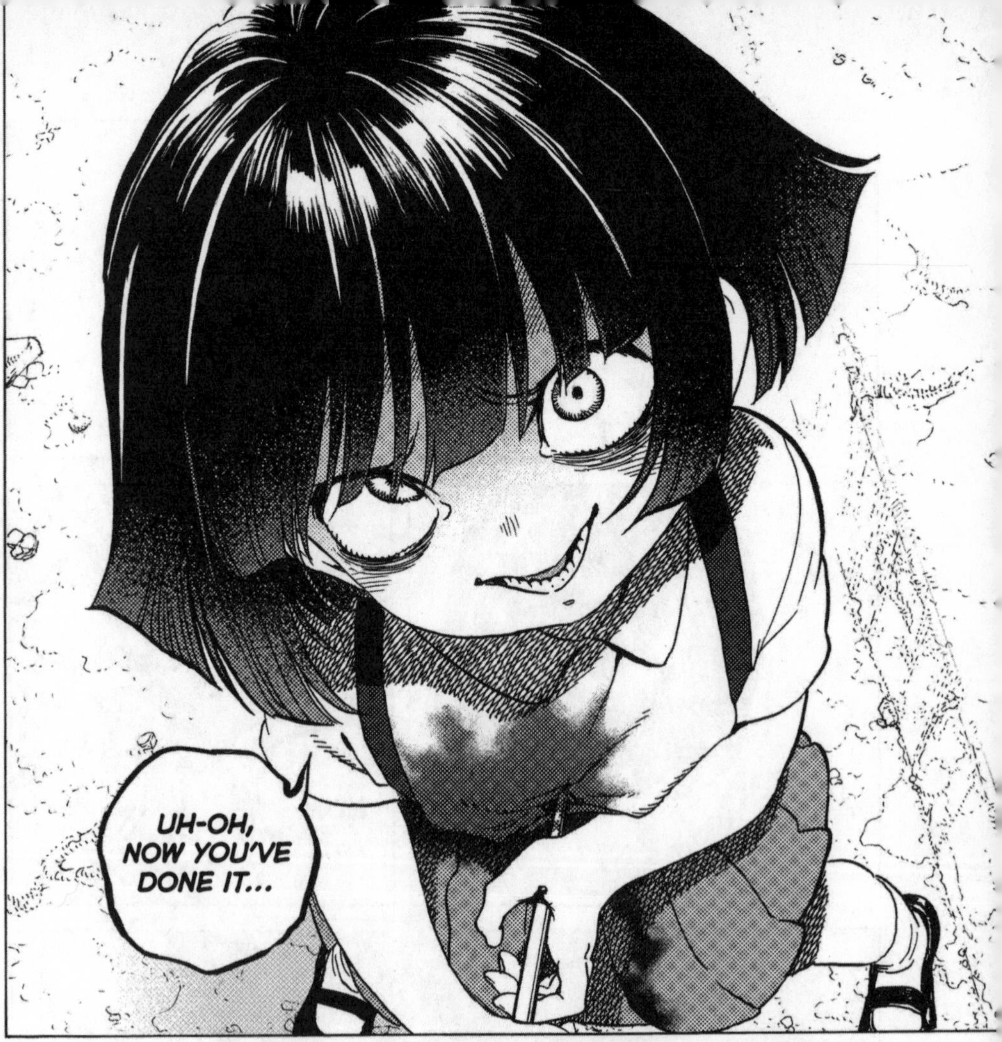
UH-OH, NOW YOU'VE DONE IT...
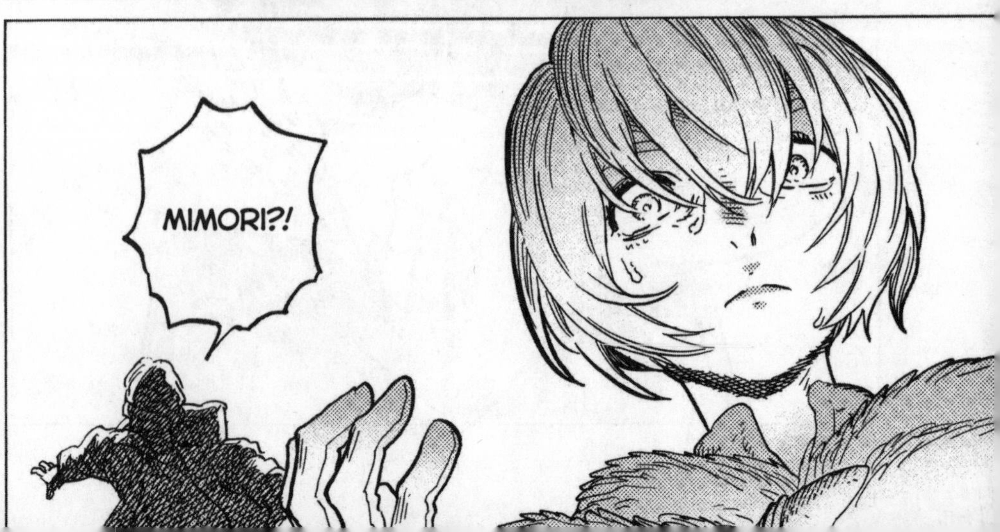
MIMORI?!

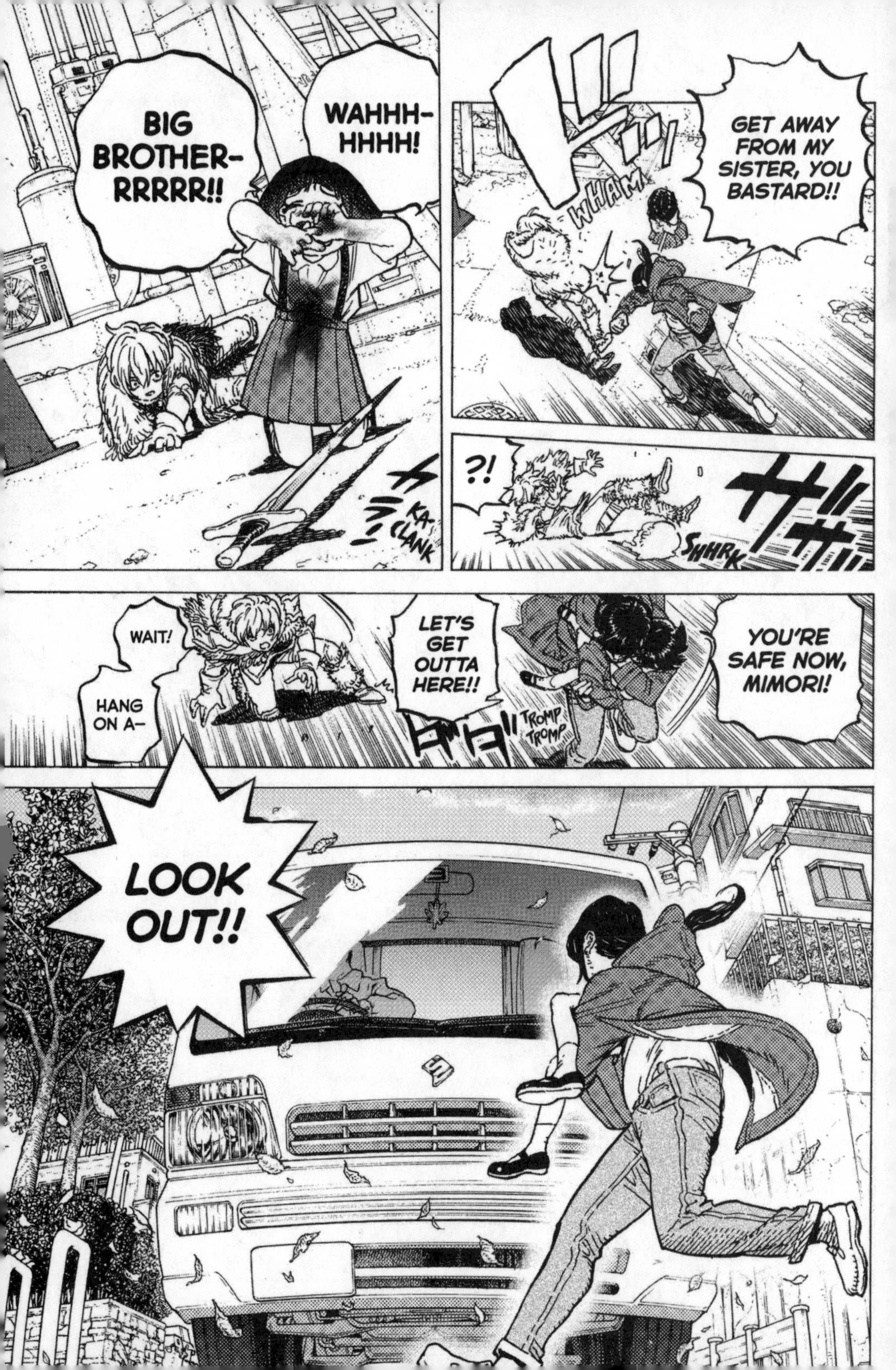

GET AWAY FROM MY SISTER, YOU BASTARD!!
WHAM
?!
SHHRK
WAHHHH-HHHH!
BIG BROTHER-RRRRR!!
KA-CLANK
YOU'RE SAFE NOW, MIMORI!
LET'S GET OUTTA HERE!!
TROMP TROMP
WAIT!
HANG ON A—
LOOK OUT!!

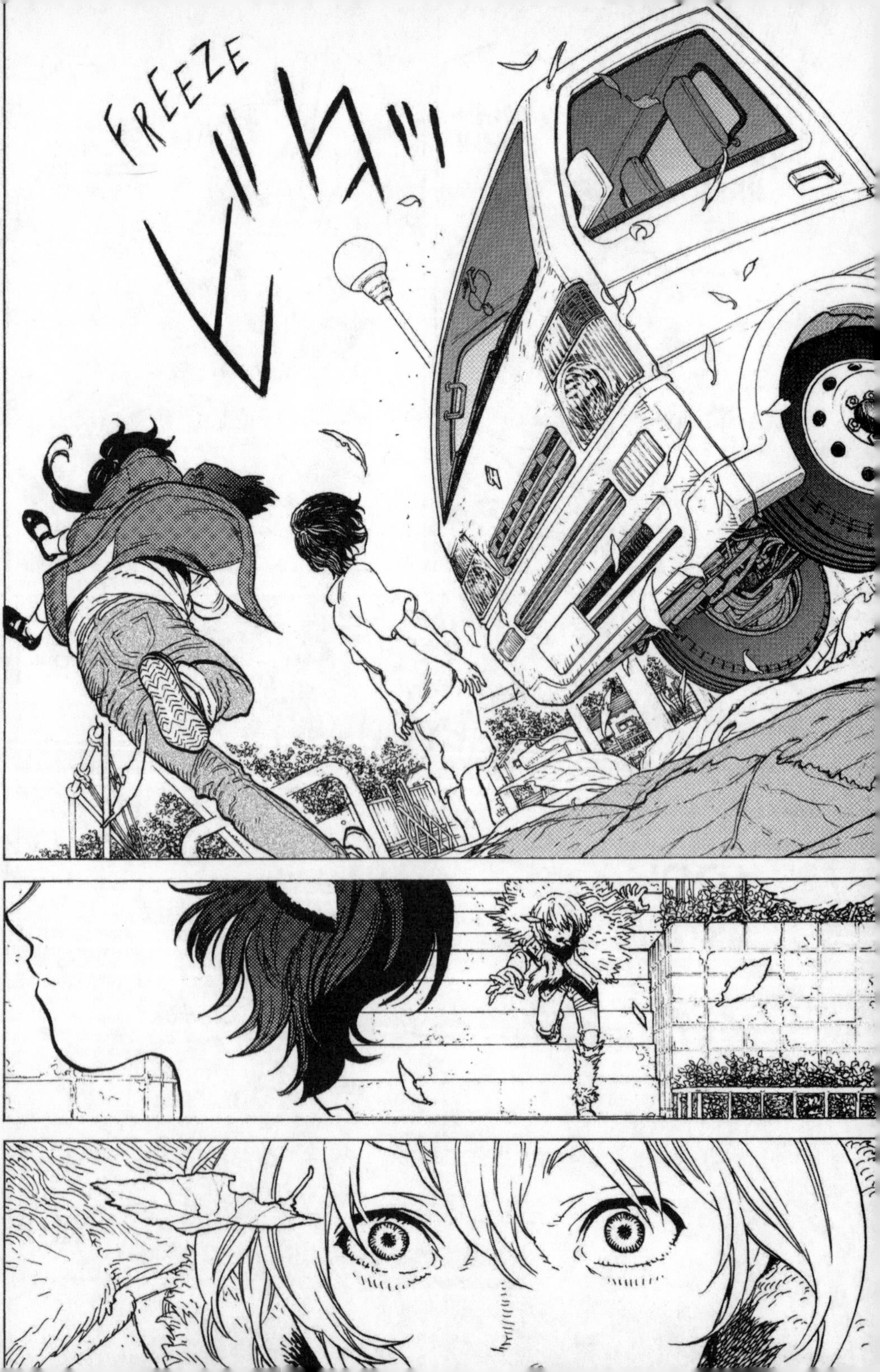

ビタッ
FREEZE

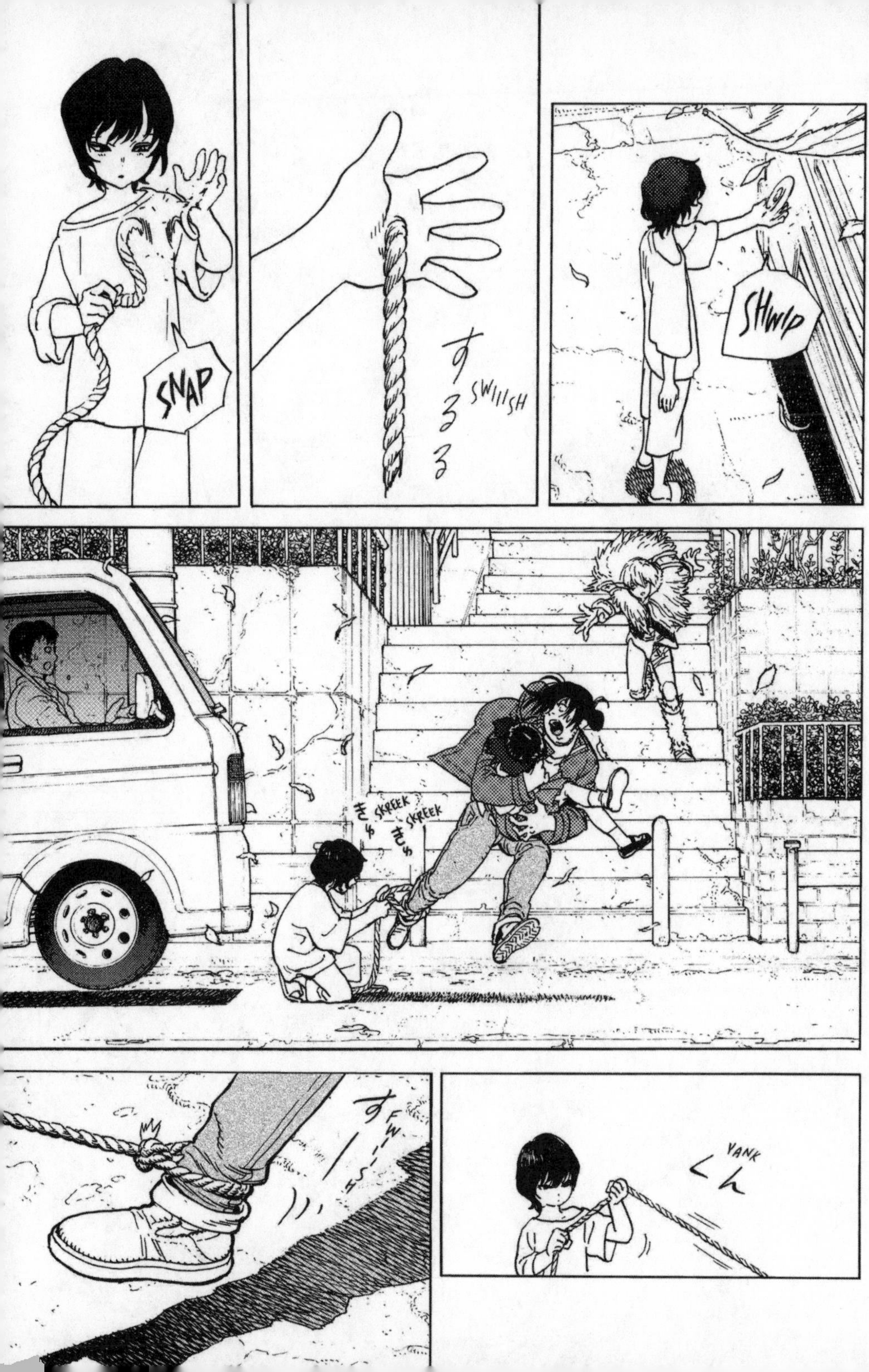
SHWIP
するる
SWIIISH
SNAP
きゅ
SKREEK
きゅ
SKREEK
くん
YANK
すー
FWIIISH

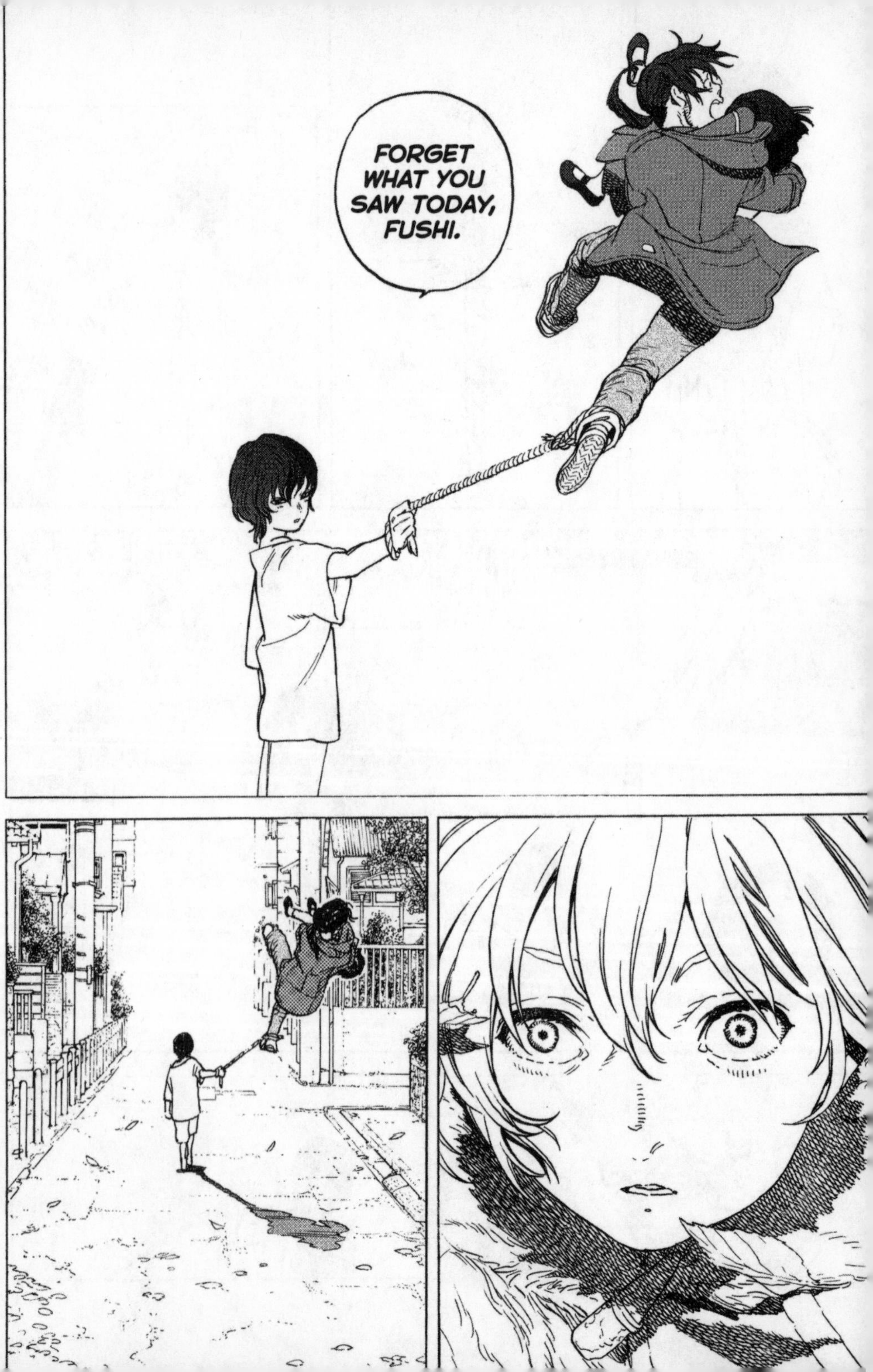
FORGET WHAT YOU SAW TODAY, FUSHI.

TO YOUR ETERNITY

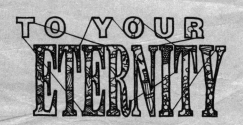

TO YOUR
ETERNITY

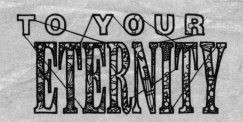

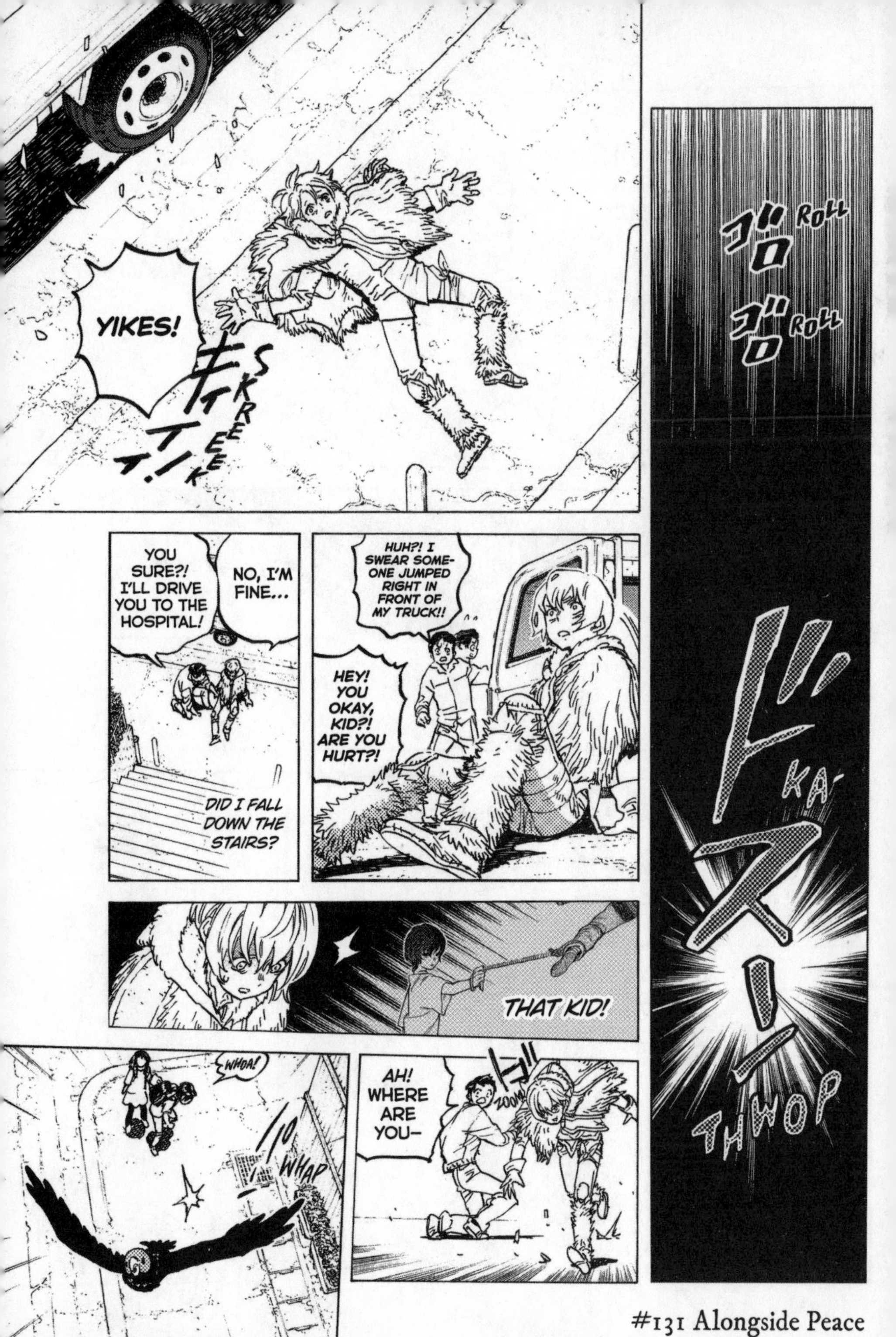
ROLL
ROLL
KA-
THWOP
YIKES!
SKREEEK
HUH?! I SWEAR SOMEONE JUMPED RIGHT IN FRONT OF MY TRUCK!!
HEY! YOU OKAY, KID?! ARE YOU HURT?!
NO, I'M FINE...
YOU SURE?! I'LL DRIVE YOU TO THE HOSPITAL!
DID I FALL DOWN THE STAIRS?
THAT KID!
AH! WHERE ARE YOU–
ZOOM
WHOA!
WHAP

#131 Alongside Peace

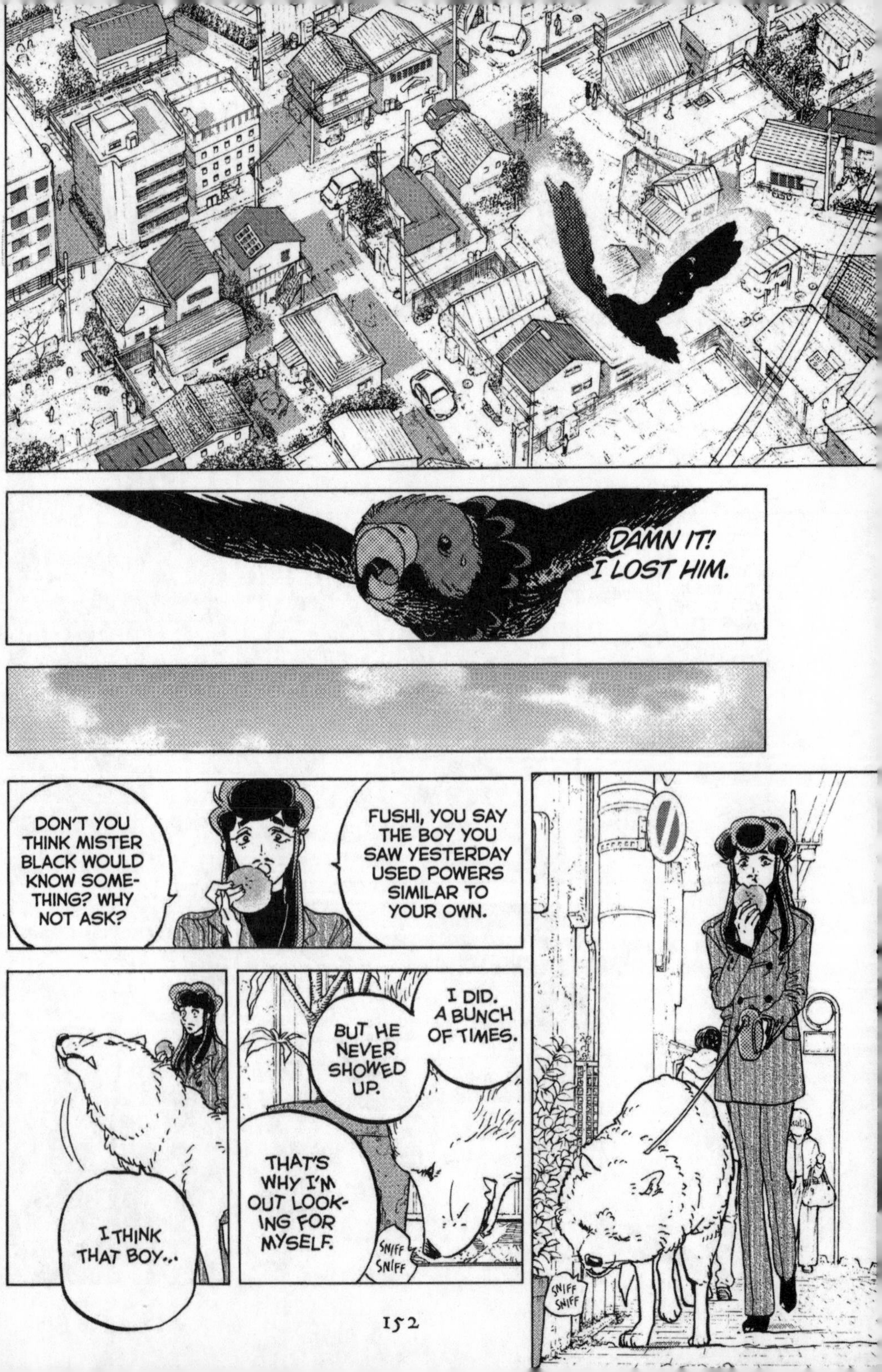
DAMN IT! I LOST HIM.
SNIFF SNIFF
FUSHI, YOU SAY THE BOY YOU SAW YESTERDAY USED POWERS SIMILAR TO YOUR OWN.
DON'T YOU THINK MISTER BLACK WOULD KNOW SOME-THING? WHY NOT ASK?
I DID. A BUNCH OF TIMES.
BUT HE NEVER SHOWED UP.
THAT'S WHY I'M OUT LOOK-ING FOR MYSELF.
SNIFF SNIFF
I THINK THAT BOY...

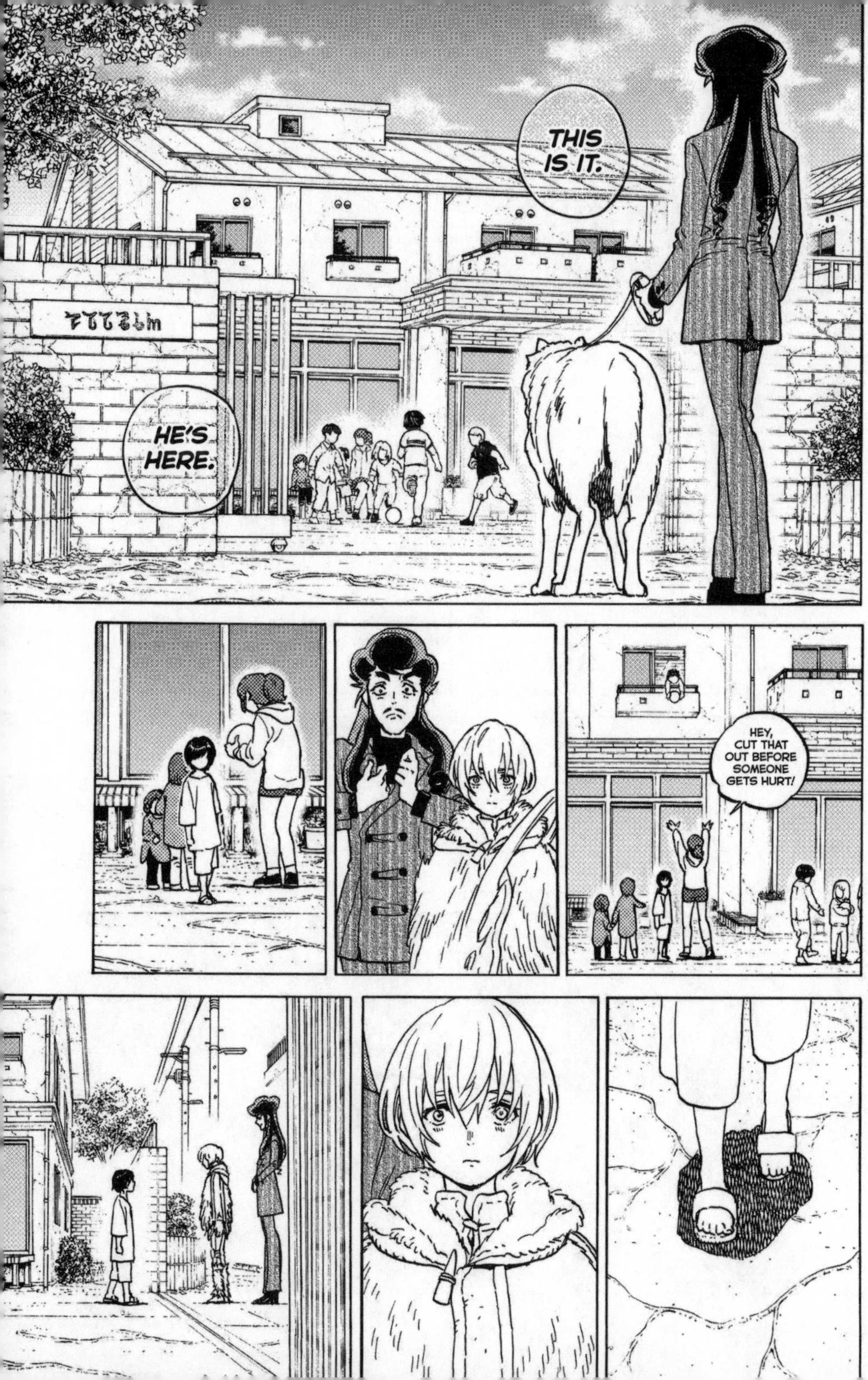
THIS IS IT.
HE'S HERE.
HEY, CUT THAT OUT BEFORE SOMEONE GETS HURT!

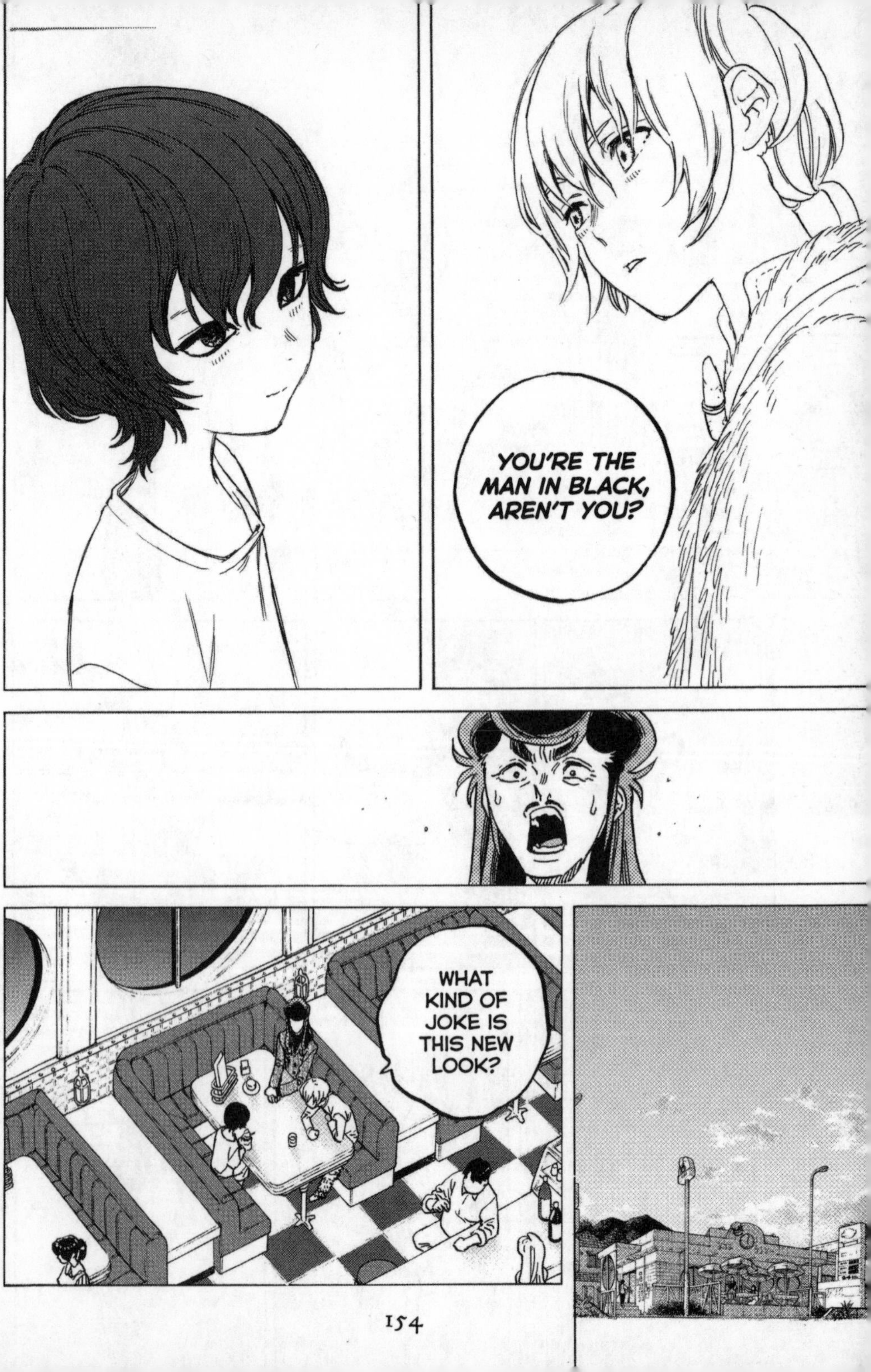
YOU'RE THE MAN IN BLACK, AREN'T YOU?
WHAT KIND OF JOKE IS THIS NEW LOOK?

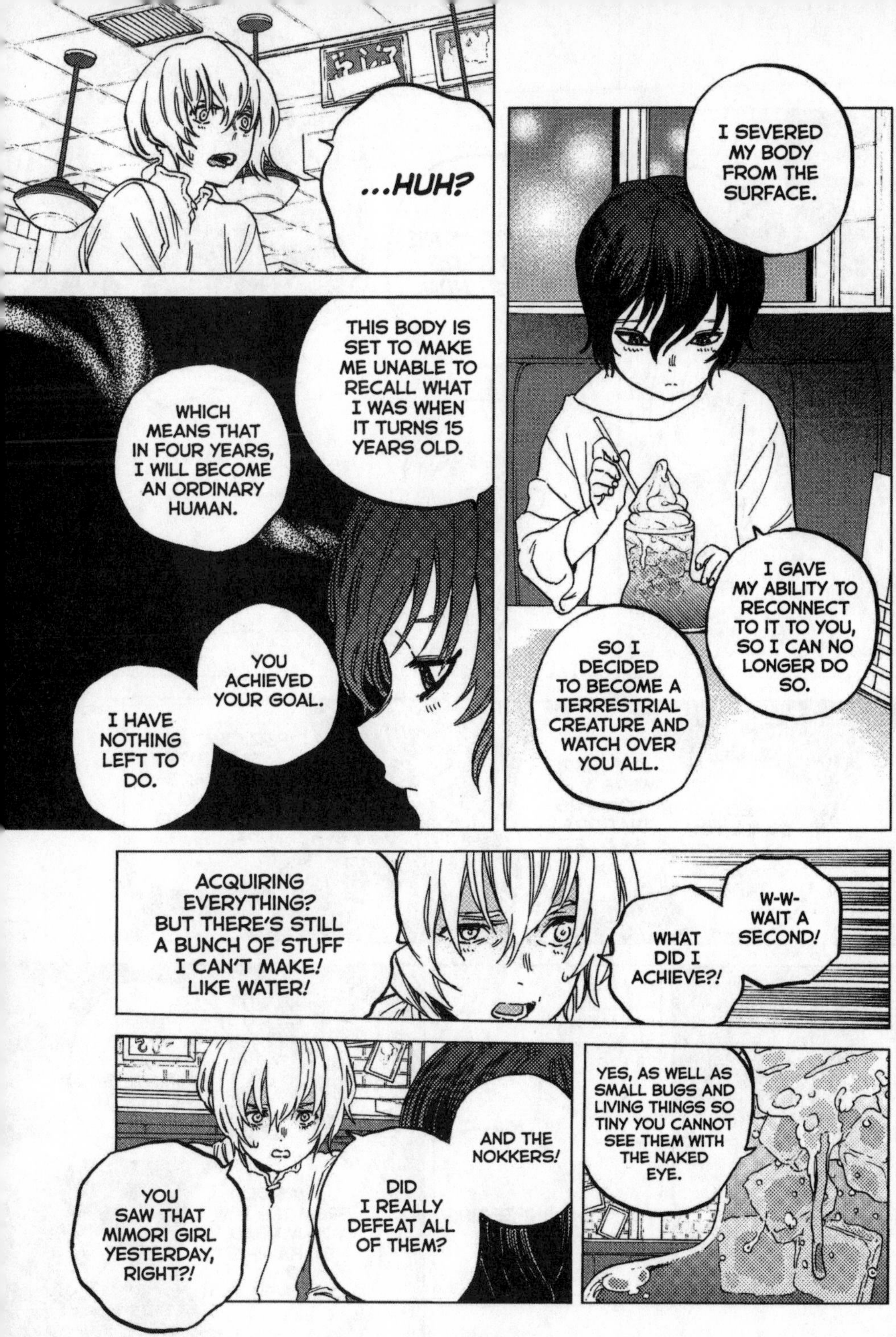
I SEVERED MY BODY FROM THE SURFACE.
I GAVE MY ABILITY TO RECONNECT TO IT TO YOU, SO I CAN NO LONGER DO SO.
SO I DECIDED TO BECOME A TERRESTRIAL CREATURE AND WATCH OVER YOU ALL.
...HUH?
THIS BODY IS SET TO MAKE ME UNABLE TO RECALL WHAT I WAS WHEN IT TURNS 15 YEARS OLD.
WHICH MEANS THAT IN FOUR YEARS, I WILL BECOME AN ORDINARY HUMAN.
YOU ACHIEVED YOUR GOAL.
I HAVE NOTHING LEFT TO DO.
W-W-WAIT A SECOND!
WHAT DID I ACHIEVE?!
ACQUIRING EVERYTHING? BUT THERE'S STILL A BUNCH OF STUFF I CAN'T MAKE! LIKE WATER!
YES, AS WELL AS SMALL BUGS AND LIVING THINGS SO TINY YOU CANNOT SEE THEM WITH THE NAKED EYE.
AND THE NOKKERS!
DID I REALLY DEFEAT ALL OF THEM?
YOU SAW THAT MIMORI GIRL YESTERDAY, RIGHT?!

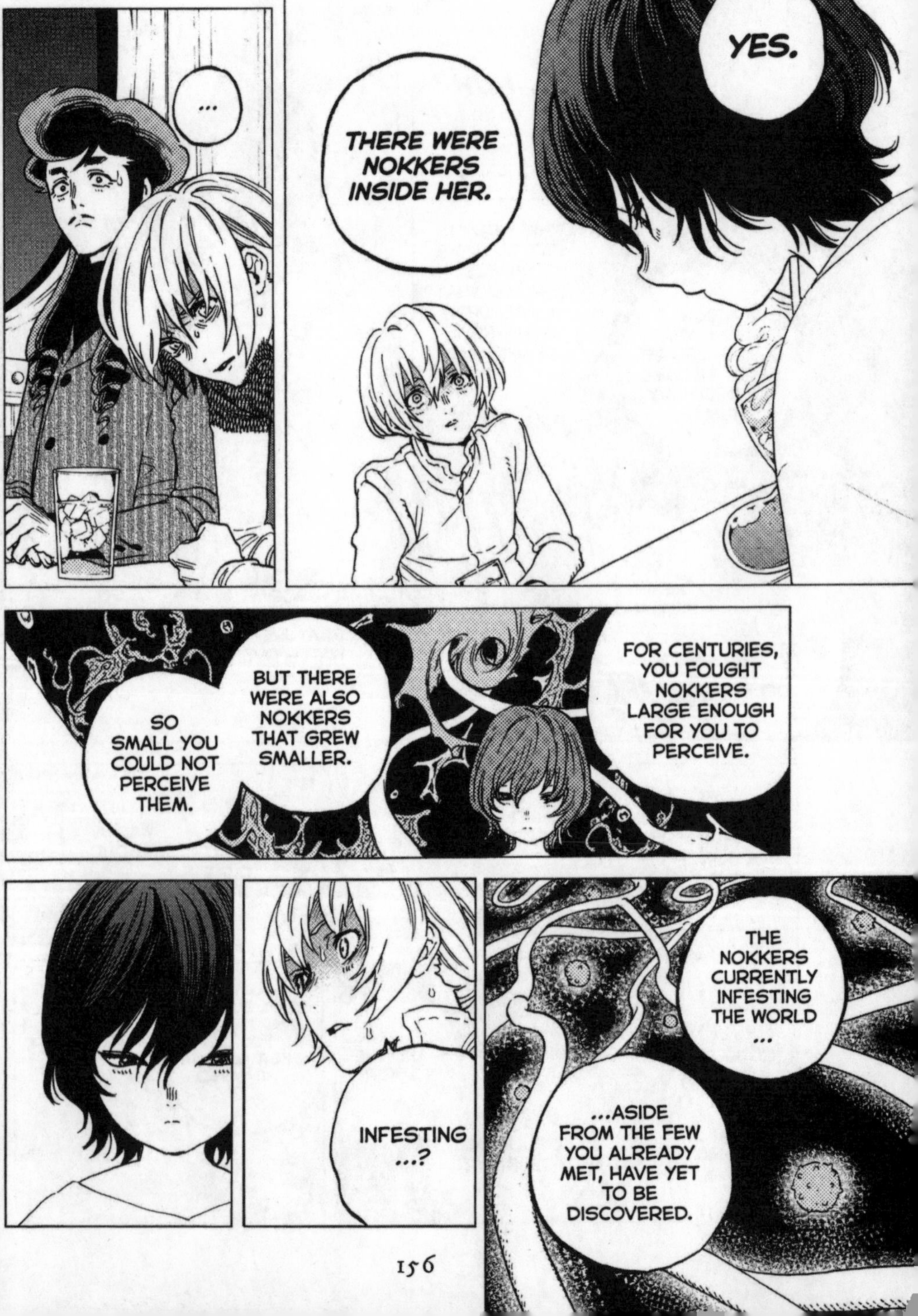
YES.
THERE WERE NOKKERS INSIDE HER.
...
FOR CENTURIES, YOU FOUGHT NOKKERS LARGE ENOUGH FOR YOU TO PERCEIVE.
BUT THERE WERE ALSO NOKKERS THAT GREW SMALLER.
SO SMALL YOU COULD NOT PERCEIVE THEM.
THE NOKKERS CURRENTLY INFESTING THE WORLD ...
...ASIDE FROM THE FEW YOU ALREADY MET, HAVE YET TO BE DISCOVERED.
INFESTING ...?

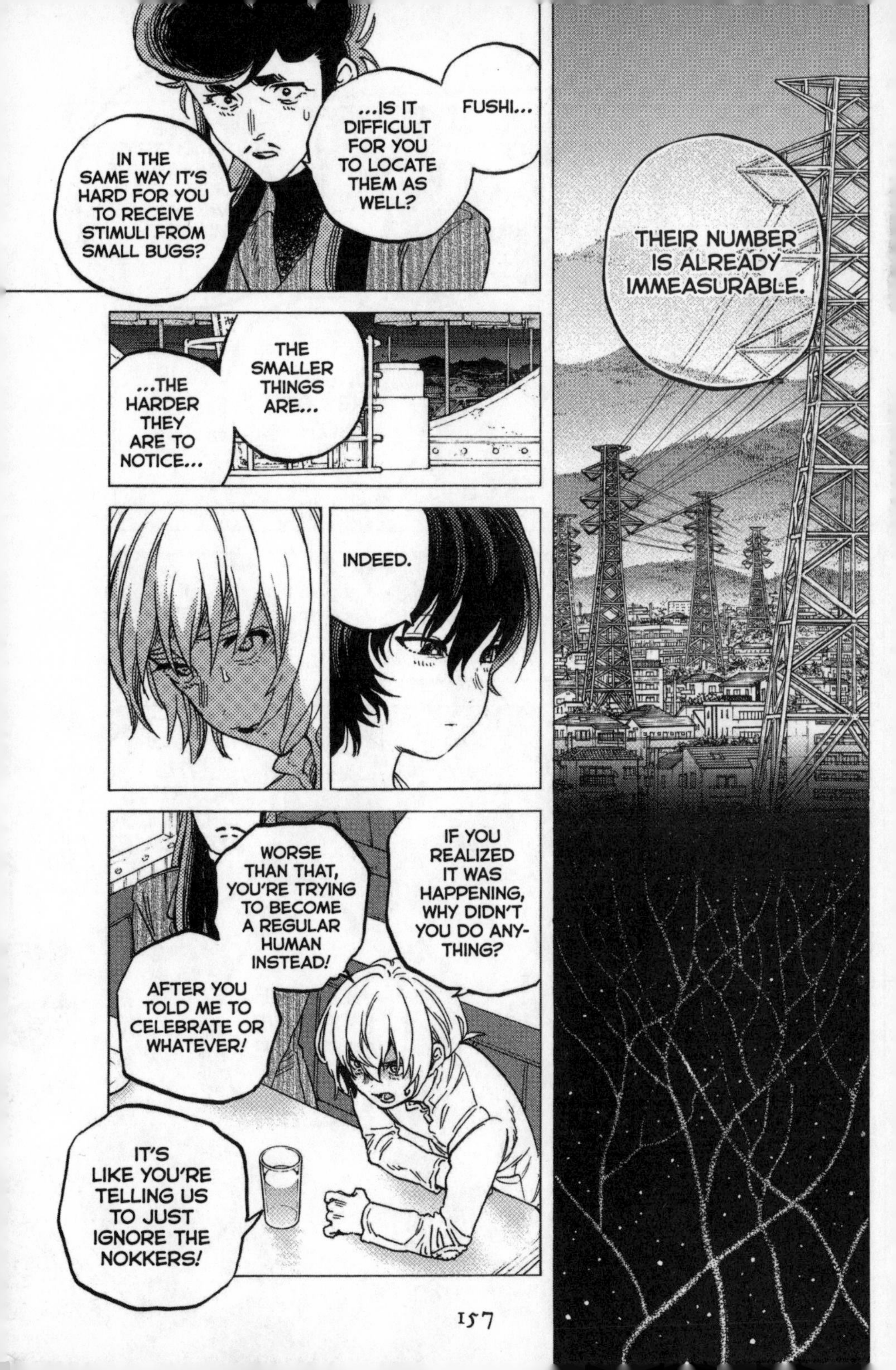
THEIR NUMBER IS ALREADY IMMEASURABLE.
FUSHI...
...IS IT DIFFICULT FOR YOU TO LOCATE THEM AS WELL?
IN THE SAME WAY IT'S HARD FOR YOU TO RECEIVE STIMULI FROM SMALL BUGS?
THE SMALLER THINGS ARE...
...THE HARDER THEY ARE TO NOTICE...
INDEED.
IF YOU REALIZED IT WAS HAPPENING, WHY DIDN'T YOU DO ANY-THING?
WORSE THAN THAT, YOU'RE TRYING TO BECOME A REGULAR HUMAN INSTEAD!
AFTER YOU TOLD ME TO CELEBRATE OR WHATEVER!
IT'S LIKE YOU'RE TELLING US TO JUST IGNORE THE NOKKERS!

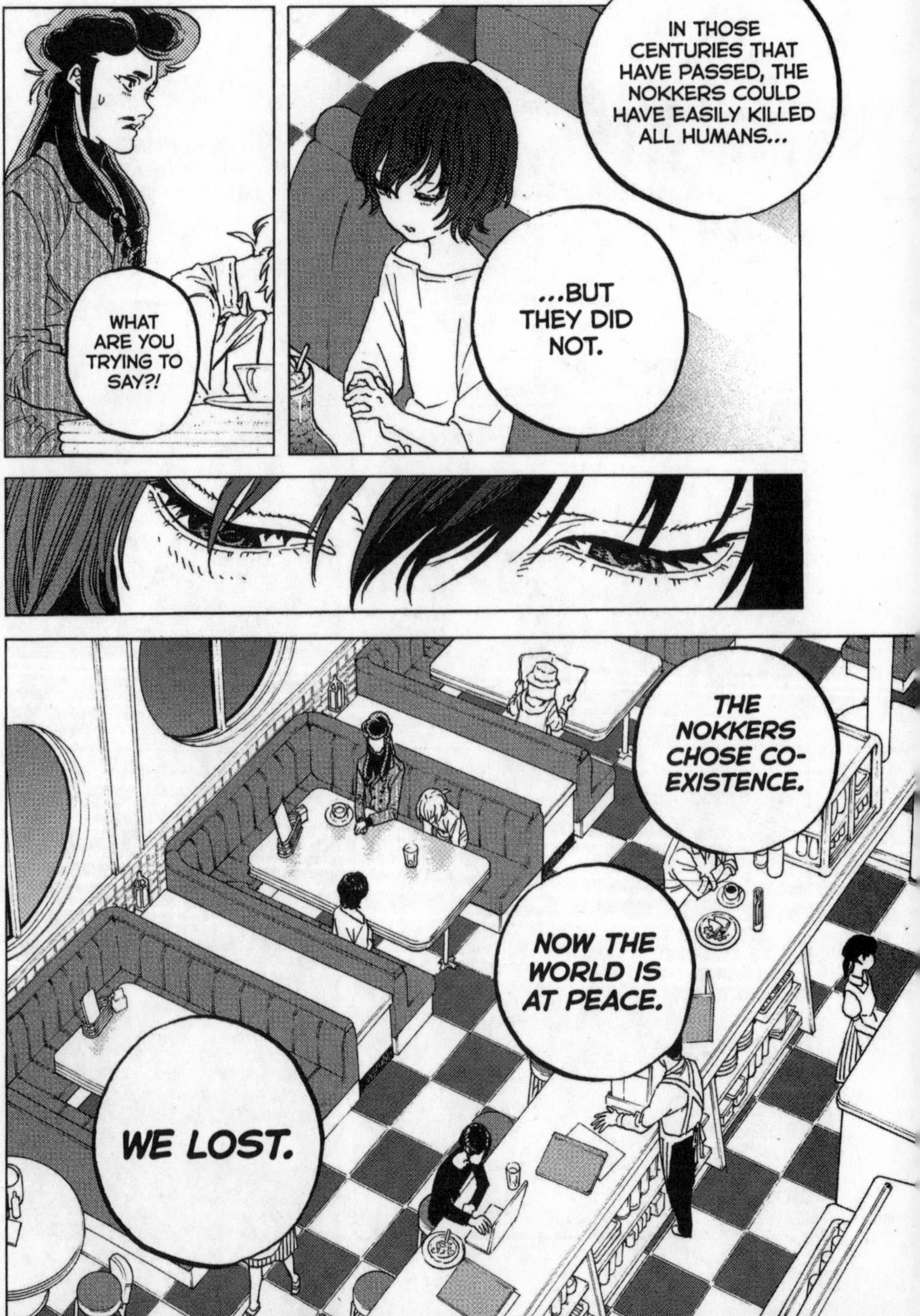
IN THOSE CENTURIES THAT HAVE PASSED, THE NOKKERS COULD HAVE EASILY KILLED ALL HUMANS...
...BUT THEY DID NOT.
WHAT ARE YOU TRYING TO SAY?!
THE NOKKERS CHOSE CO-EXISTENCE.
NOW THE WORLD IS AT PEACE.
WE LOST.

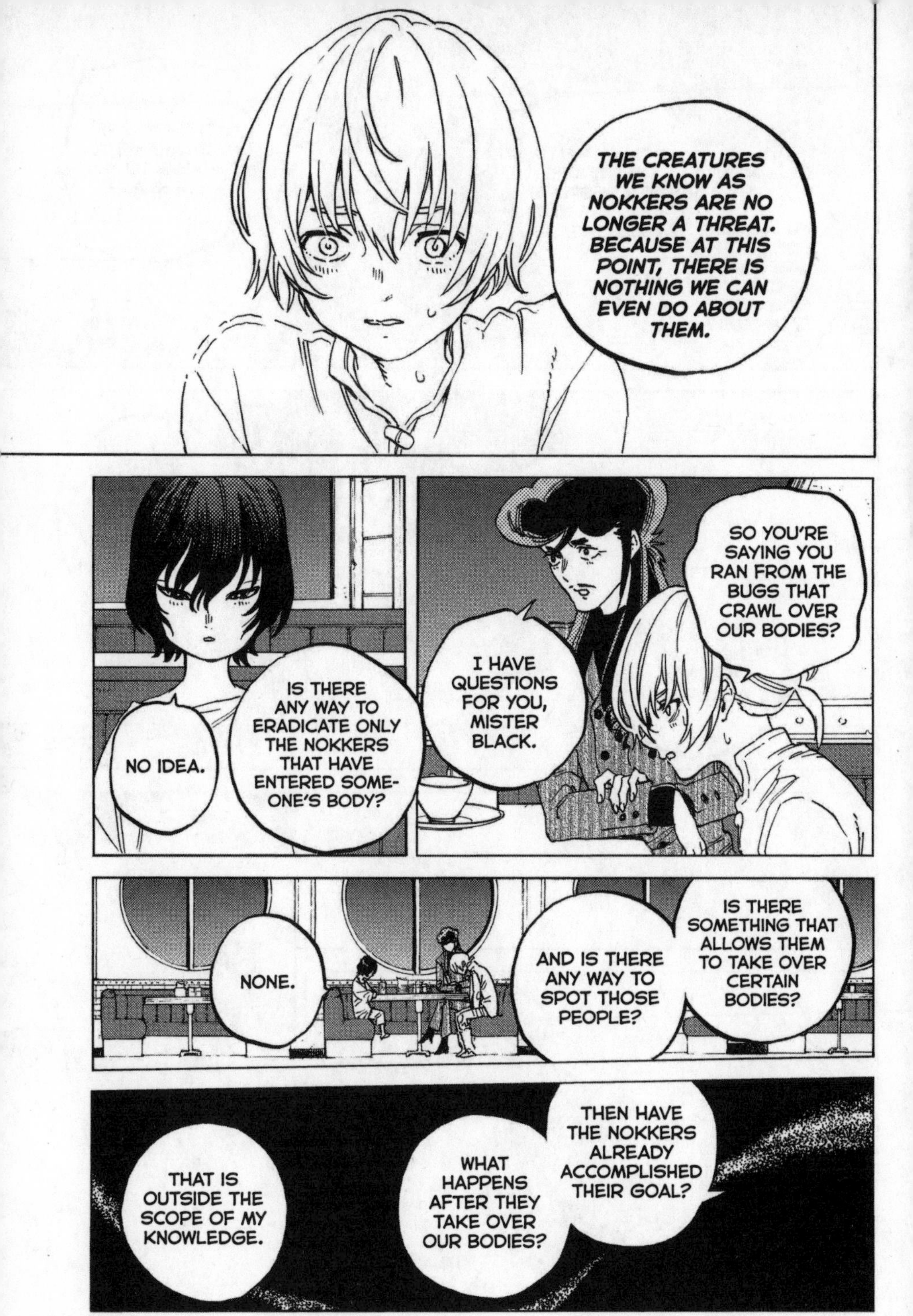
THE CREATURES WE KNOW AS NOKKERS ARE NO LONGER A THREAT. BECAUSE AT THIS POINT, THERE IS NOTHING WE CAN EVEN DO ABOUT THEM.
SO YOU'RE SAYING YOU RAN FROM THE BUGS THAT CRAWL OVER OUR BODIES?
I HAVE QUESTIONS FOR YOU, MISTER BLACK.
IS THERE ANY WAY TO ERADICATE ONLY THE NOKKERS THAT HAVE ENTERED SOME-ONE'S BODY?
NO IDEA.
IS THERE SOMETHING THAT ALLOWS THEM TO TAKE OVER CERTAIN BODIES?
AND IS THERE ANY WAY TO SPOT THOSE PEOPLE?
NONE.
THEN HAVE THE NOKKERS ALREADY ACCOMPLISHED THEIR GOAL?
WHAT HAPPENS AFTER THEY TAKE OVER OUR BODIES?
THAT IS OUTSIDE THE SCOPE OF MY KNOWLEDGE.

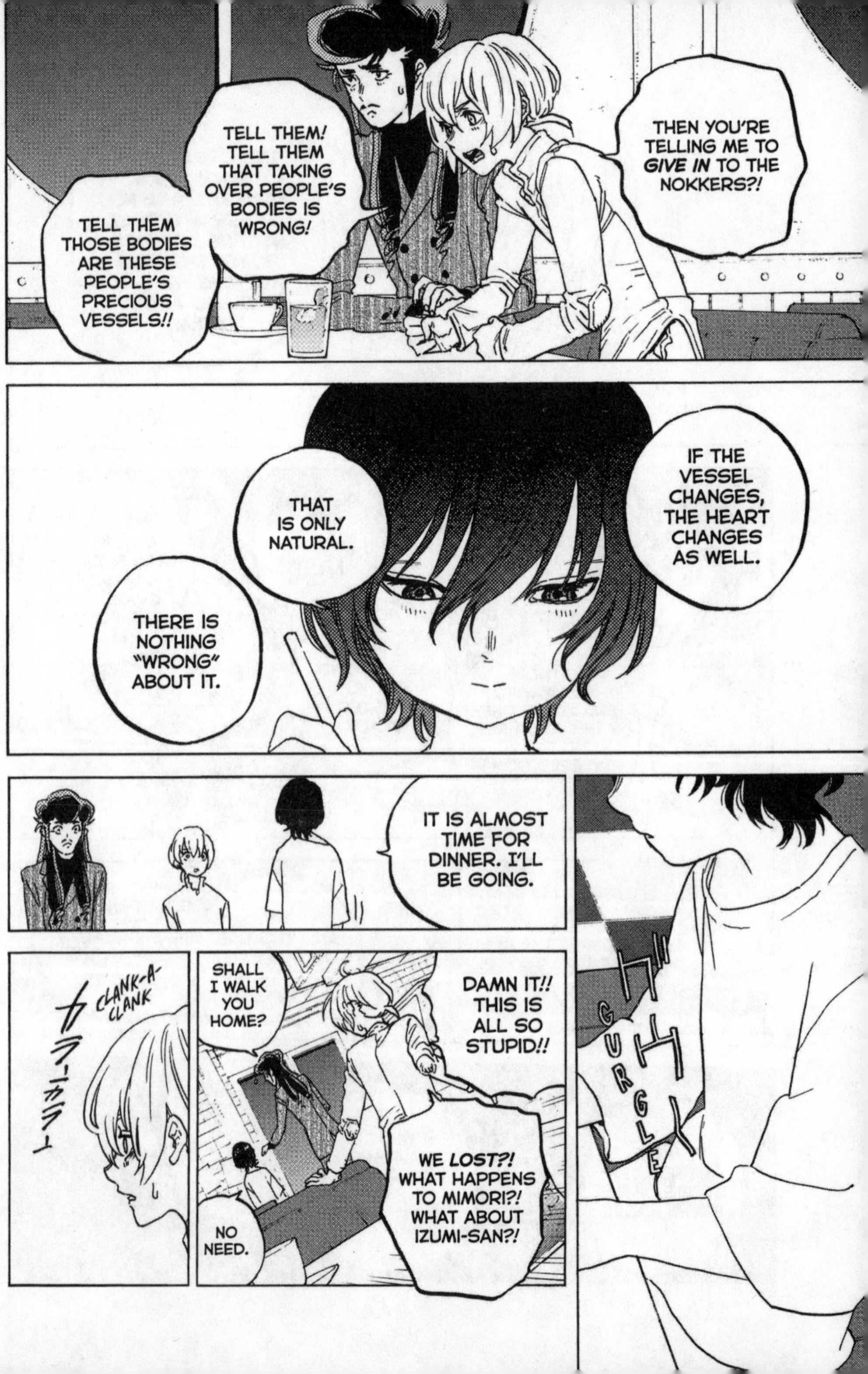
THEN YOU'RE TELLING ME TO *GIVE IN* TO THE NOKKERS?!
TELL THEM! TELL THEM THAT TAKING OVER PEOPLE'S BODIES IS WRONG!
TELL THEM THOSE BODIES ARE THESE PEOPLE'S PRECIOUS VESSELS!!
IF THE VESSEL CHANGES, THE HEART CHANGES AS WELL.
THAT IS ONLY NATURAL.
THERE IS NOTHING "WRONG" ABOUT IT.
GURGLE
IT IS ALMOST TIME FOR DINNER. I'LL BE GOING.
DAMN IT!! THIS IS ALL SO STUPID!!
SHALL I WALK YOU HOME?
WE *LOST?!* WHAT HAPPENS TO MIMORI?! WHAT ABOUT IZUMI-SAN?!
NO NEED.
CLANK-A-CLANK

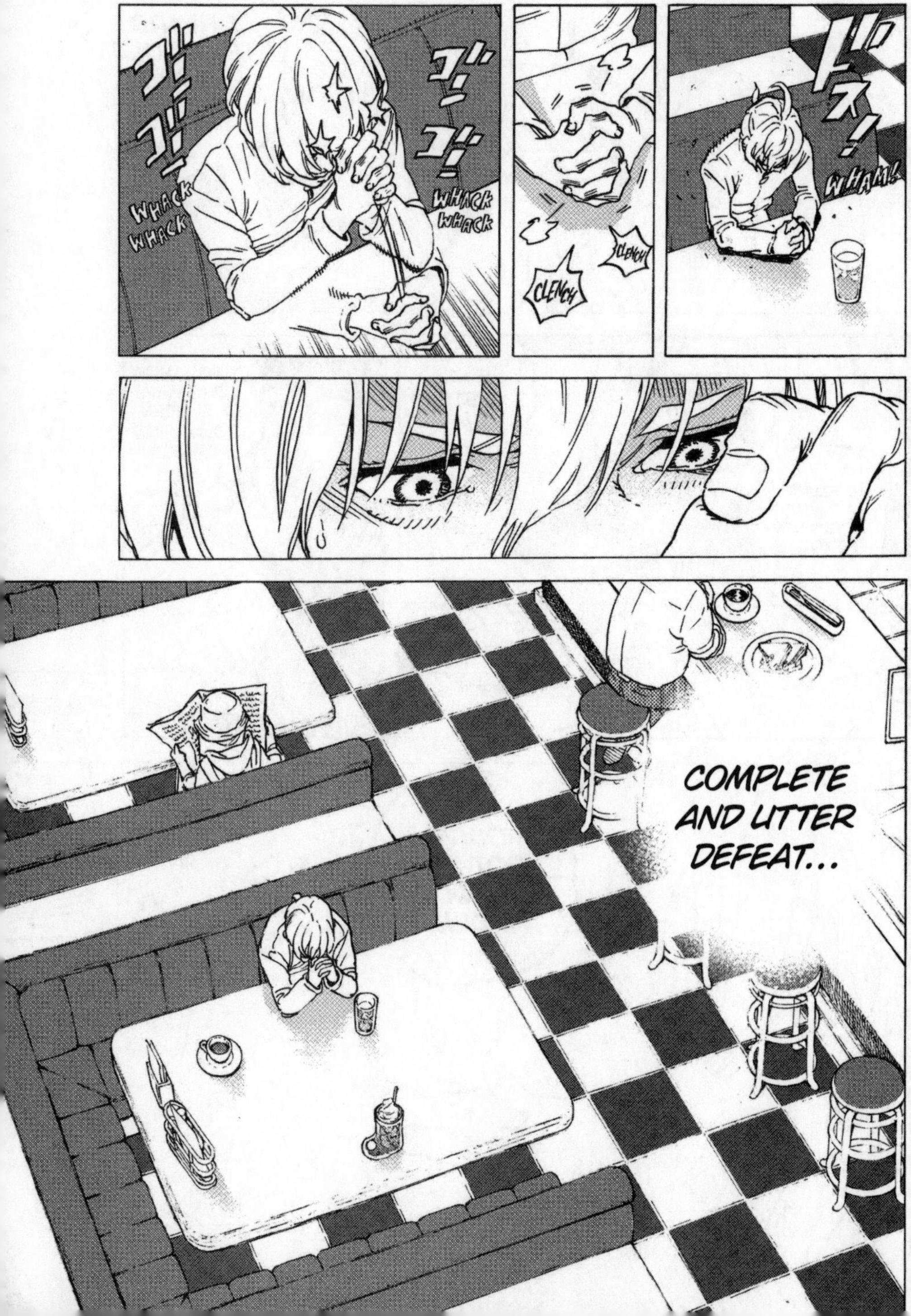
ドス!
WHAM!
CLENCH
CLENCH
WHACK WHACK
WHACK WHACK
COMPLETE AND UTTER DEFEAT…

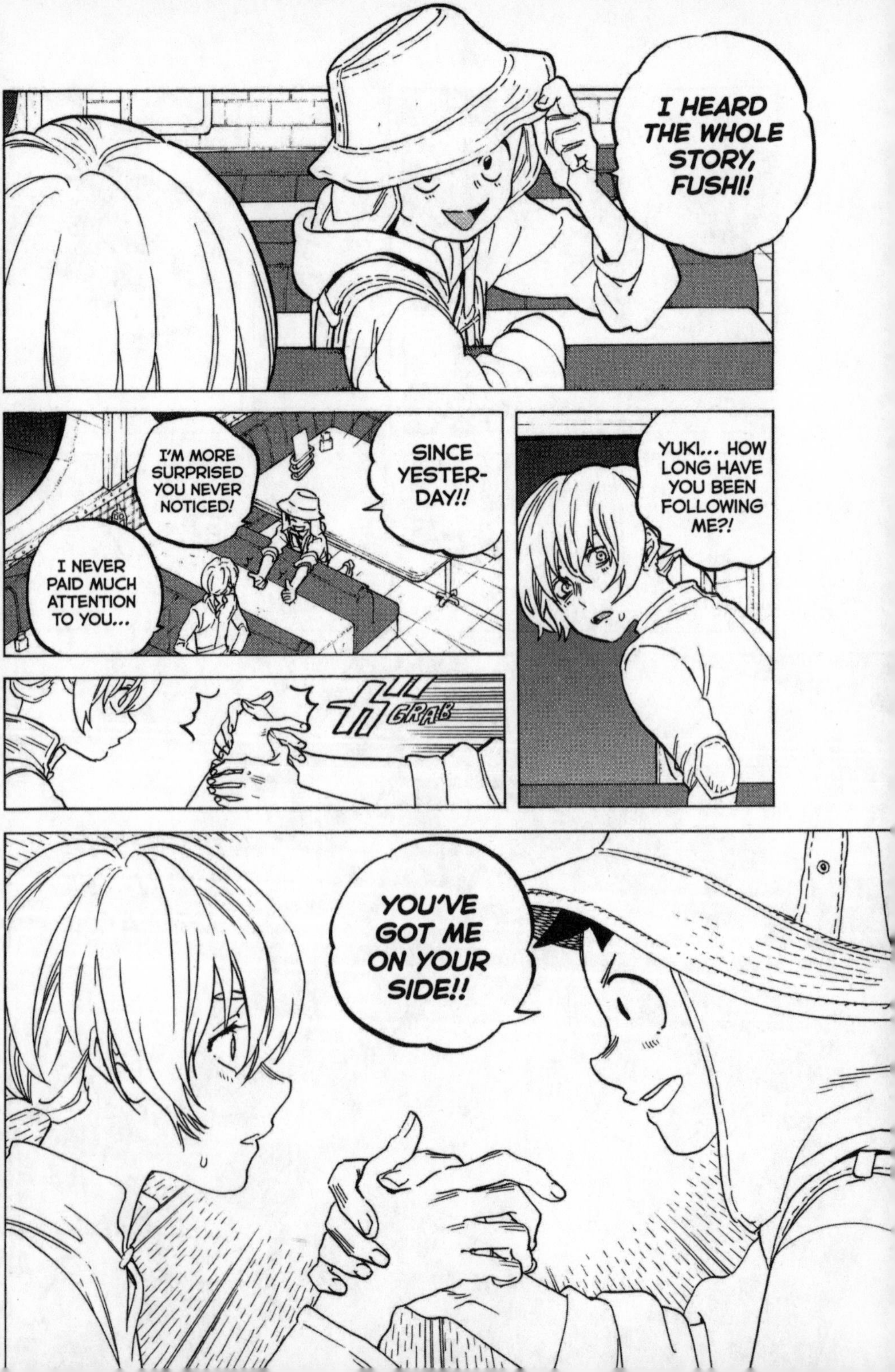
I HEARD THE WHOLE STORY, FUSHI!
YUKI... HOW LONG HAVE YOU BEEN FOLLOWING ME?!
SINCE YESTER-DAY!!
I'M MORE SURPRISED YOU NEVER NOTICED!
I NEVER PAID MUCH ATTENTION TO YOU...
GRAB
YOU'VE GOT ME ON YOUR SIDE!!

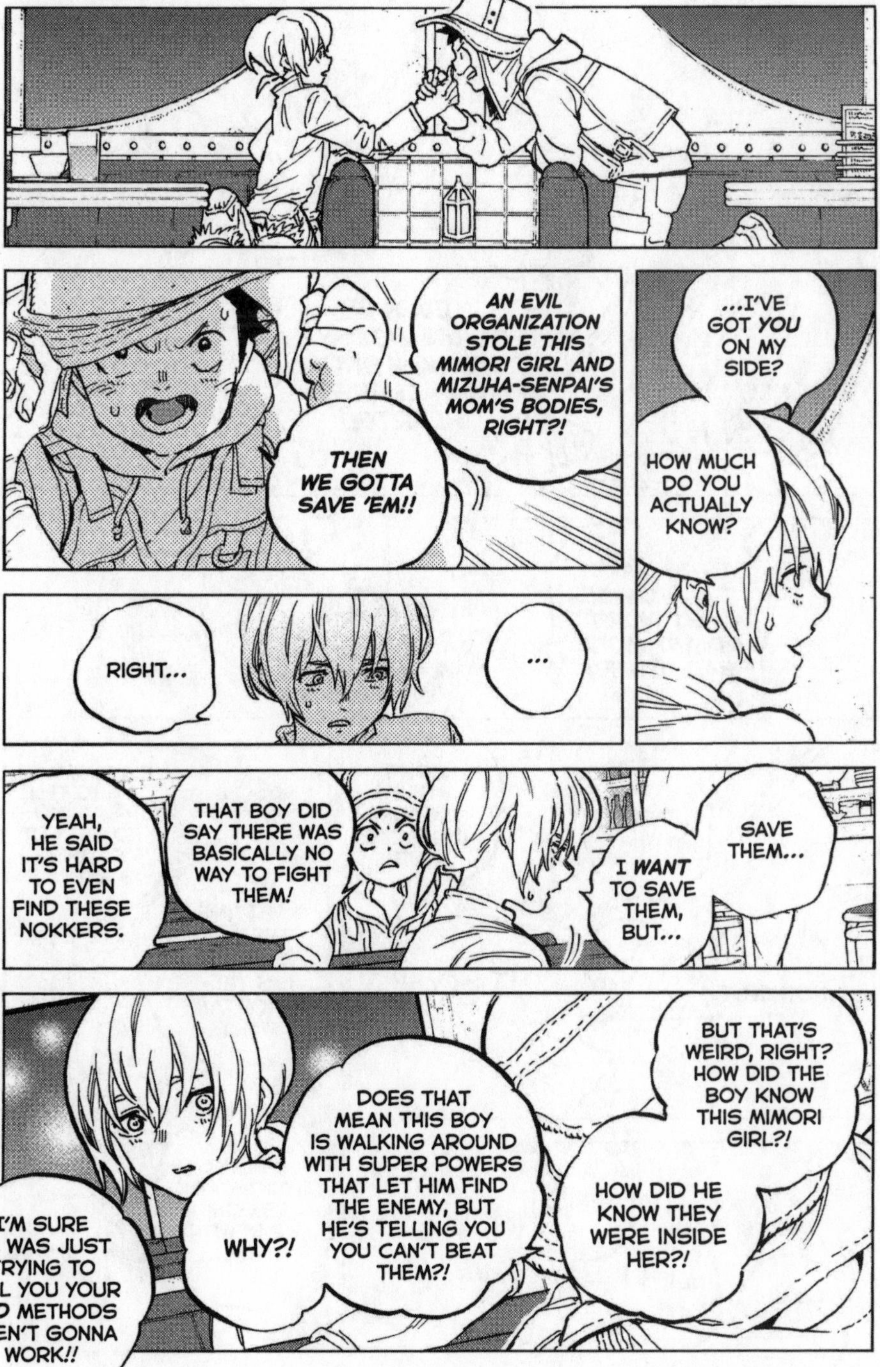
...I'VE GOT YOU ON MY SIDE?
HOW MUCH DO YOU ACTUALLY KNOW?
AN EVIL ORGANIZATION STOLE THIS MIMORI GIRL AND MIZUHA-SENPAI'S MOM'S BODIES, RIGHT?!
THEN WE GOTTA SAVE 'EM!!
...
RIGHT...
SAVE THEM...
I WANT TO SAVE THEM, BUT...
THAT BOY DID SAY THERE WAS BASICALLY NO WAY TO FIGHT THEM!
YEAH, HE SAID IT'S HARD TO EVEN FIND THESE NOKKERS.
BUT THAT'S WEIRD, RIGHT? HOW DID THE BOY KNOW THIS MIMORI GIRL?!
HOW DID HE KNOW THEY WERE INSIDE HER?!
DOES THAT MEAN THIS BOY IS WALKING AROUND WITH SUPER POWERS THAT LET HIM FIND THE ENEMY, BUT HE'S TELLING YOU YOU CAN'T BEAT THEM?!
WHY?!
I'M SURE HE WAS JUST TRYING TO TELL YOU YOUR OLD METHODS AREN'T GONNA WORK!!

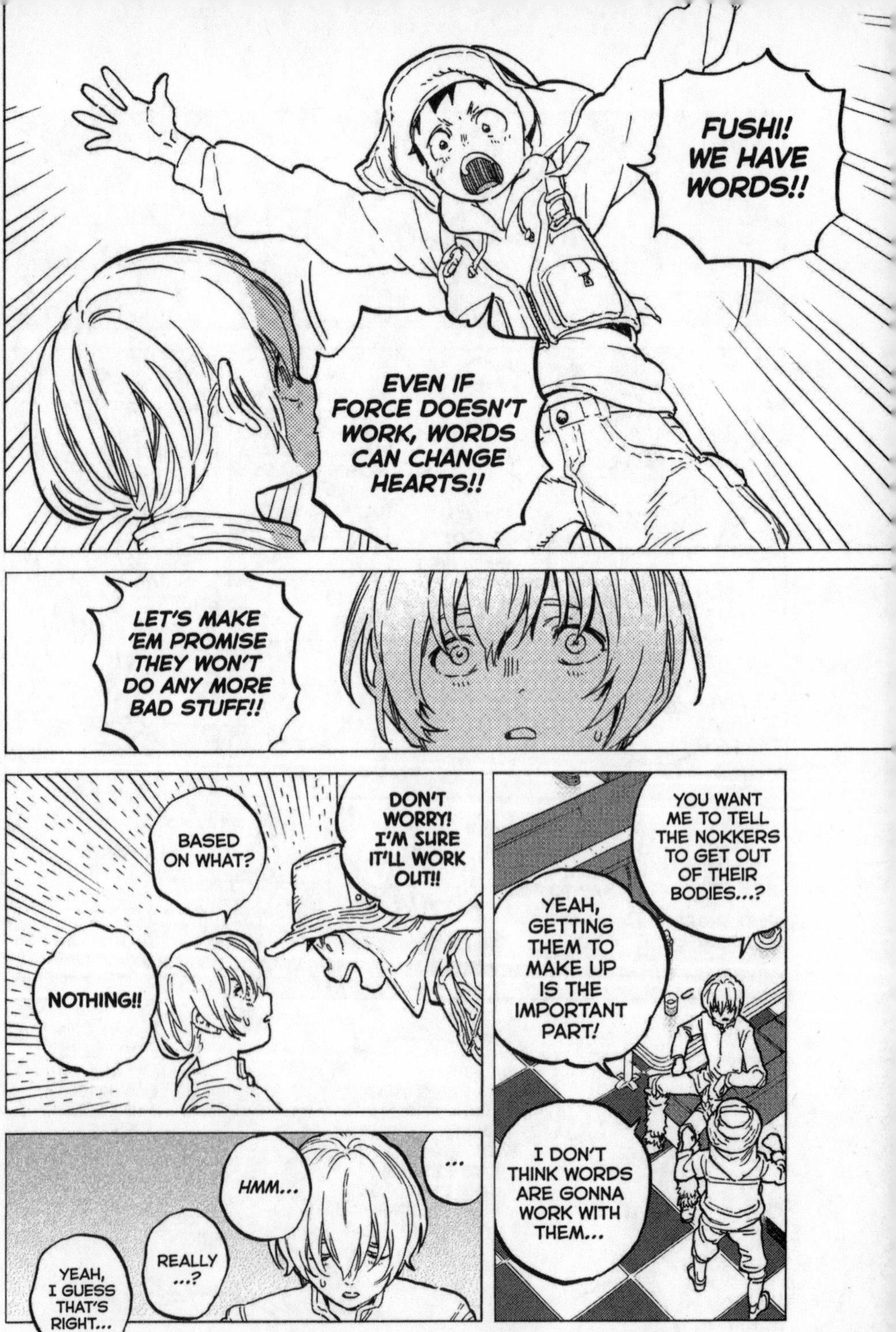
FUSHI! WE HAVE WORDS!!
EVEN IF FORCE DOESN'T WORK, WORDS CAN CHANGE HEARTS!!
LET'S MAKE 'EM PROMISE THEY WON'T DO ANY MORE BAD STUFF!!
YOU WANT ME TO TELL THE NOKKERS TO GET OUT OF THEIR BODIES...?
YEAH, GETTING THEM TO MAKE UP IS THE IMPORTANT PART!
I DON'T THINK WORDS ARE GONNA WORK WITH THEM...
DON'T WORRY! I'M SURE IT'LL WORK OUT!!
BASED ON WHAT?
NOTHING!!
...
HMM...
REALLY ...?
YEAH, I GUESS THAT'S RIGHT...

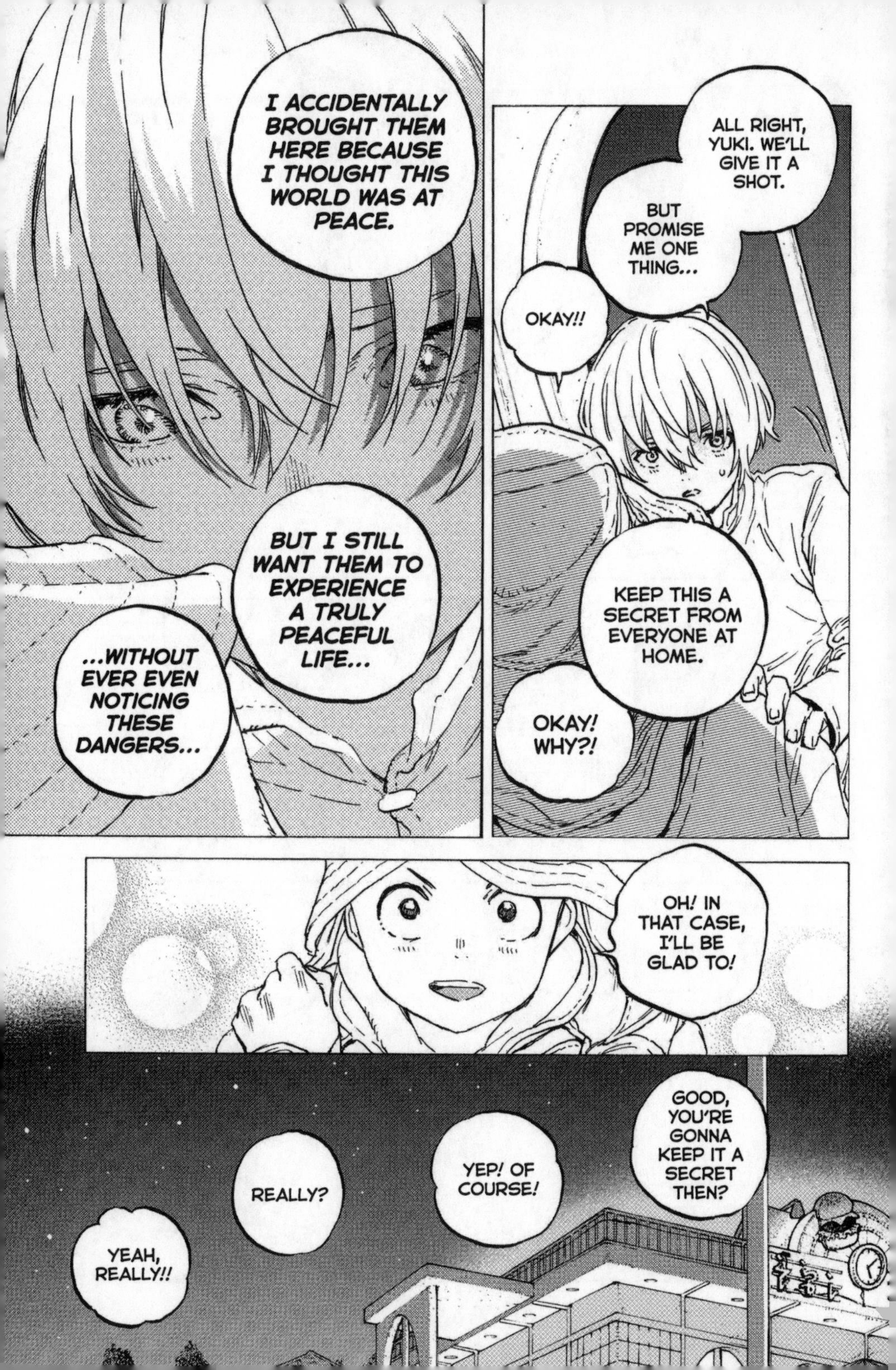
ALL RIGHT, YUKI. WE'LL GIVE IT A SHOT.
BUT PROMISE ME ONE THING...
OKAY!!
KEEP THIS A SECRET FROM EVERYONE AT HOME.
OKAY! WHY?!
I ACCIDENTALLY BROUGHT THEM HERE BECAUSE I THOUGHT THIS WORLD WAS AT PEACE.
BUT I STILL WANT THEM TO EXPERIENCE A TRULY PEACEFUL LIFE...
...WITHOUT EVER EVEN NOTICING THESE DANGERS...
OH! IN THAT CASE, I'LL BE GLAD TO!
GOOD, YOU'RE GONNA KEEP IT A SECRET THEN?
YEP! OF COURSE!
REALLY?
YEAH, REALLY!!

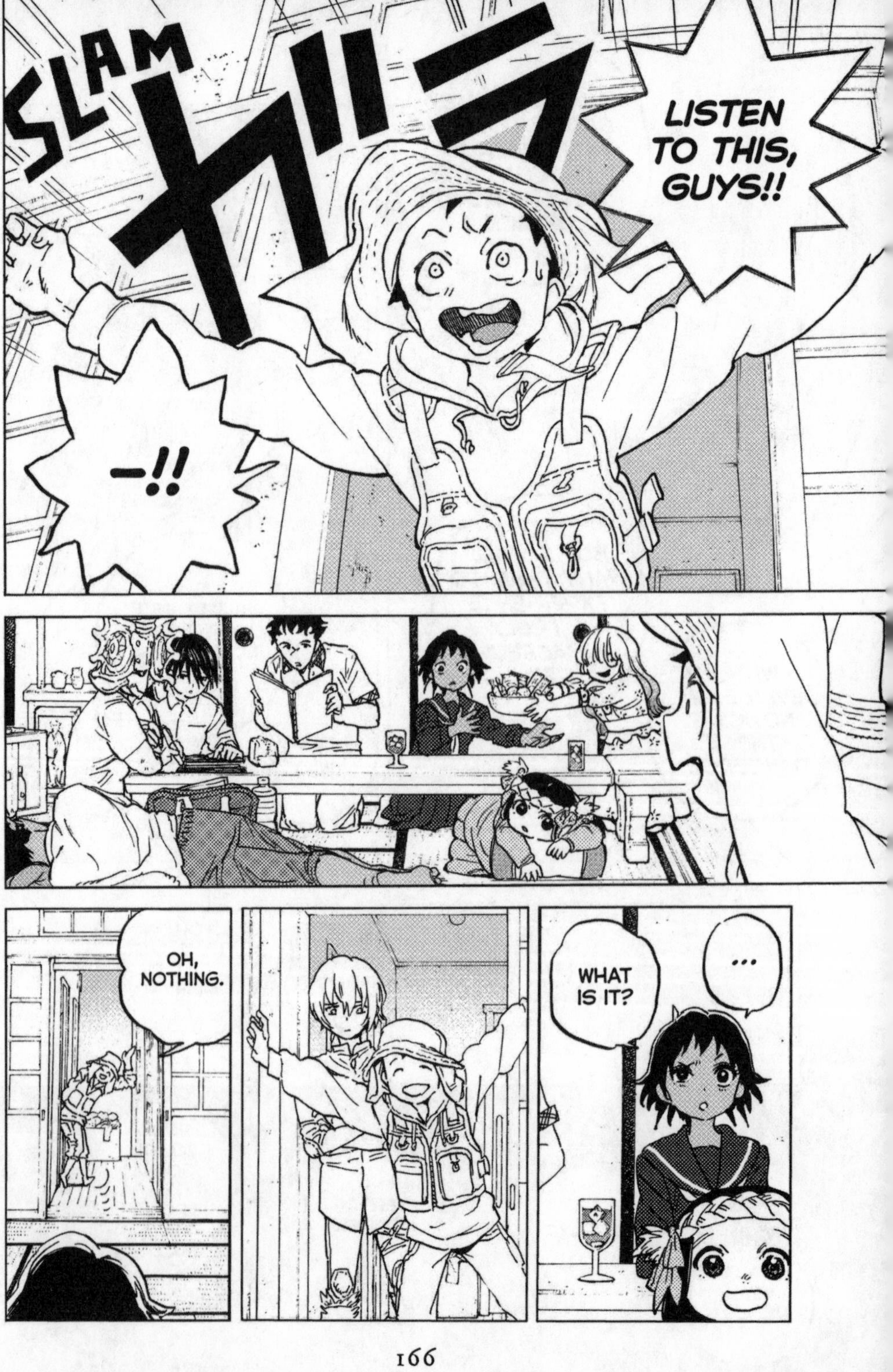
LISTEN TO THIS, GUYS!!
SLAM
—!!
...
WHAT IS IT?
OH, NOTHING.

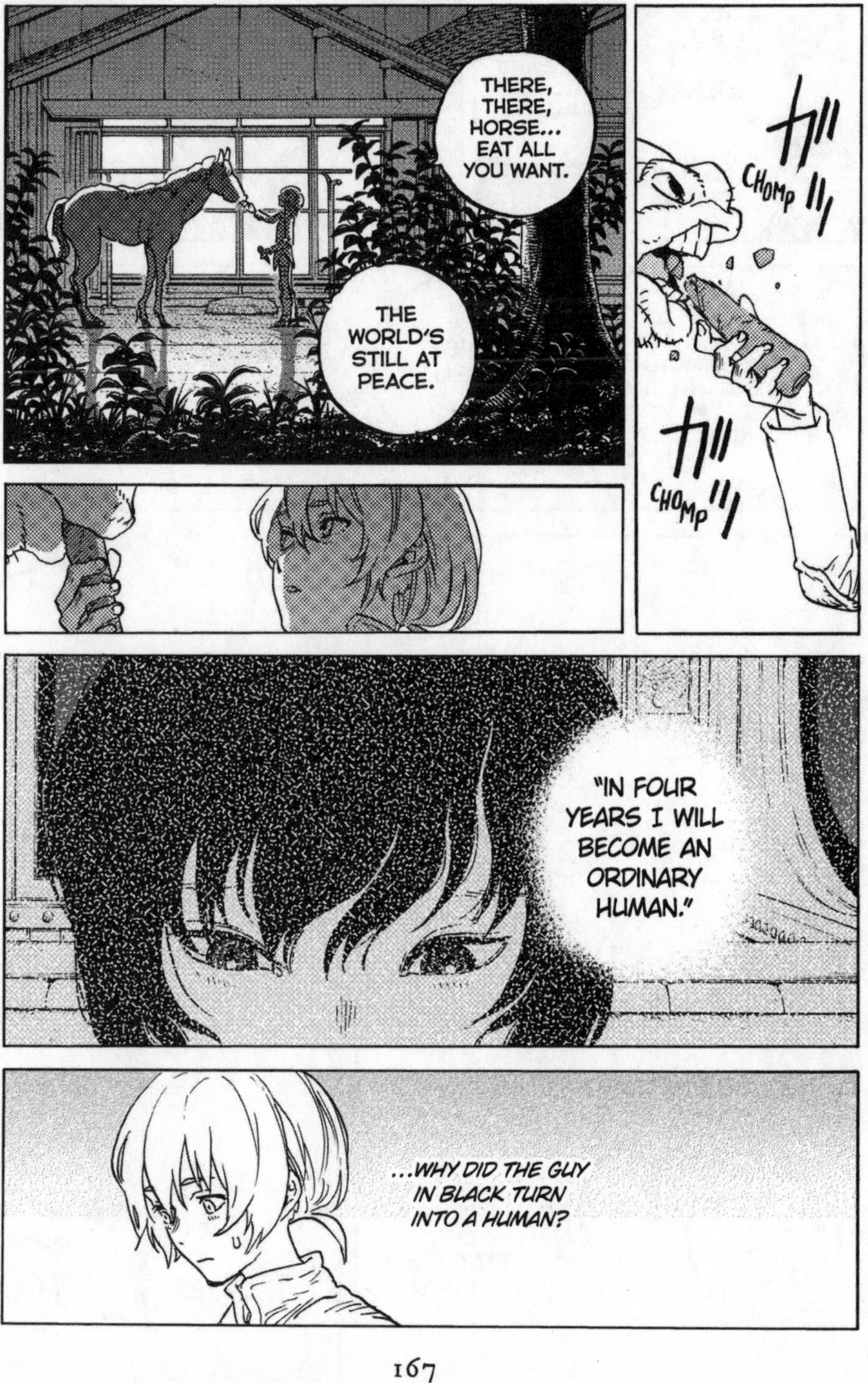
CHOMP
CHOMP
THERE, THERE, HORSE... EAT ALL YOU WANT.
THE WORLD'S STILL AT PEACE.
"IN FOUR YEARS I WILL BECOME AN ORDINARY HUMAN."
...WHY DID THE GUY IN BLACK TURN INTO A HUMAN?

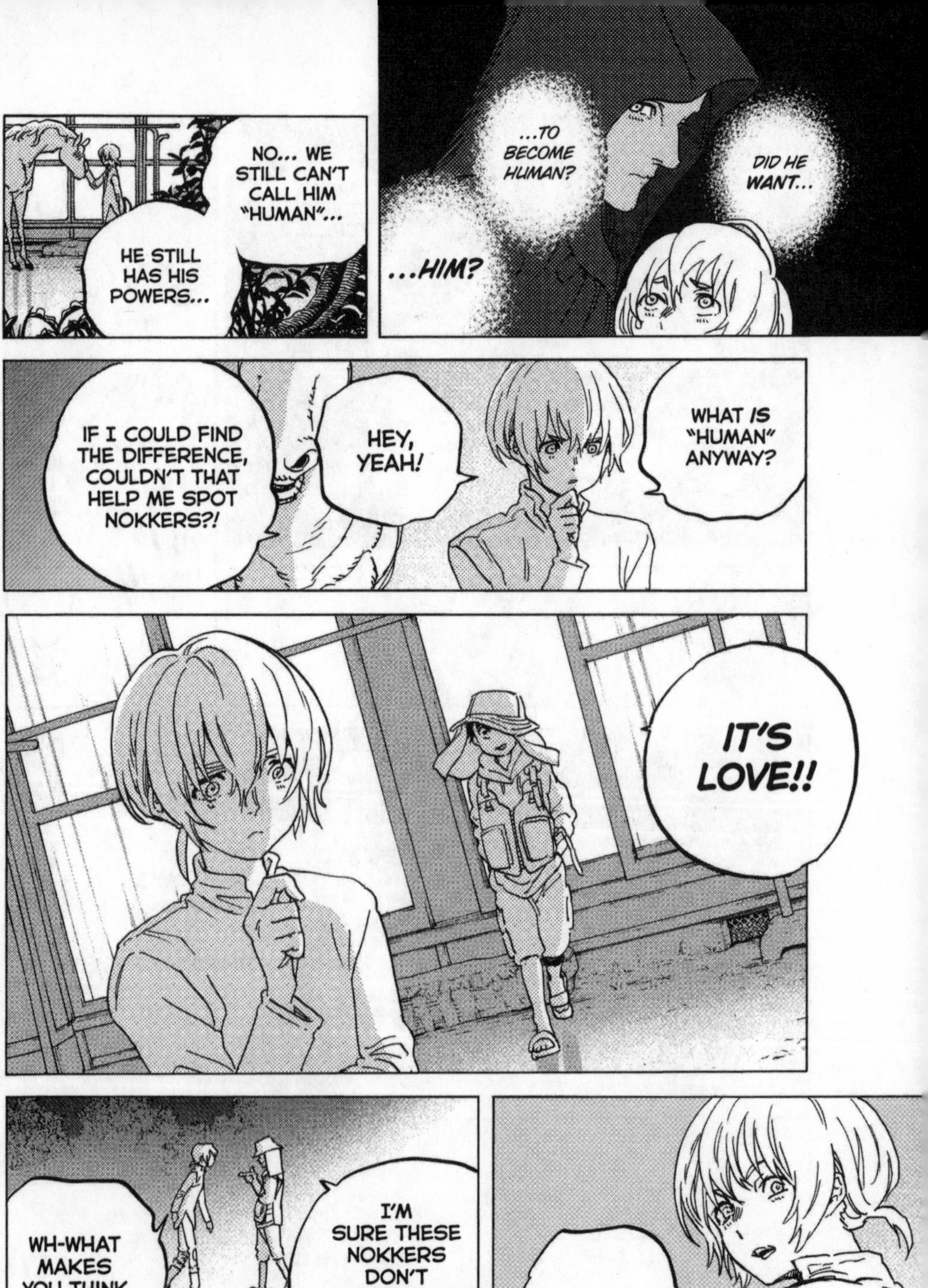
DID HE WANT...
...TO BECOME HUMAN?
...HIM?
NO... WE STILL CAN'T CALL HIM "HUMAN"...
HE STILL HAS HIS POWERS...
WHAT *IS* "HUMAN" ANYWAY?
HEY, YEAH!
IF I COULD FIND THE DIFFERENCE, COULDN'T THAT HELP ME SPOT NOKKERS?!
IT'S LOVE!!
...LOVE?
I'M SURE THESE NOKKERS DON'T EXPERIENCE LOVE!
WH-WHAT MAKES YOU THINK SO...?

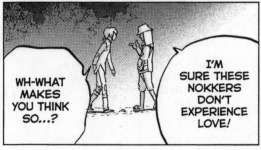

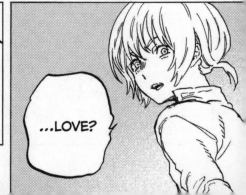

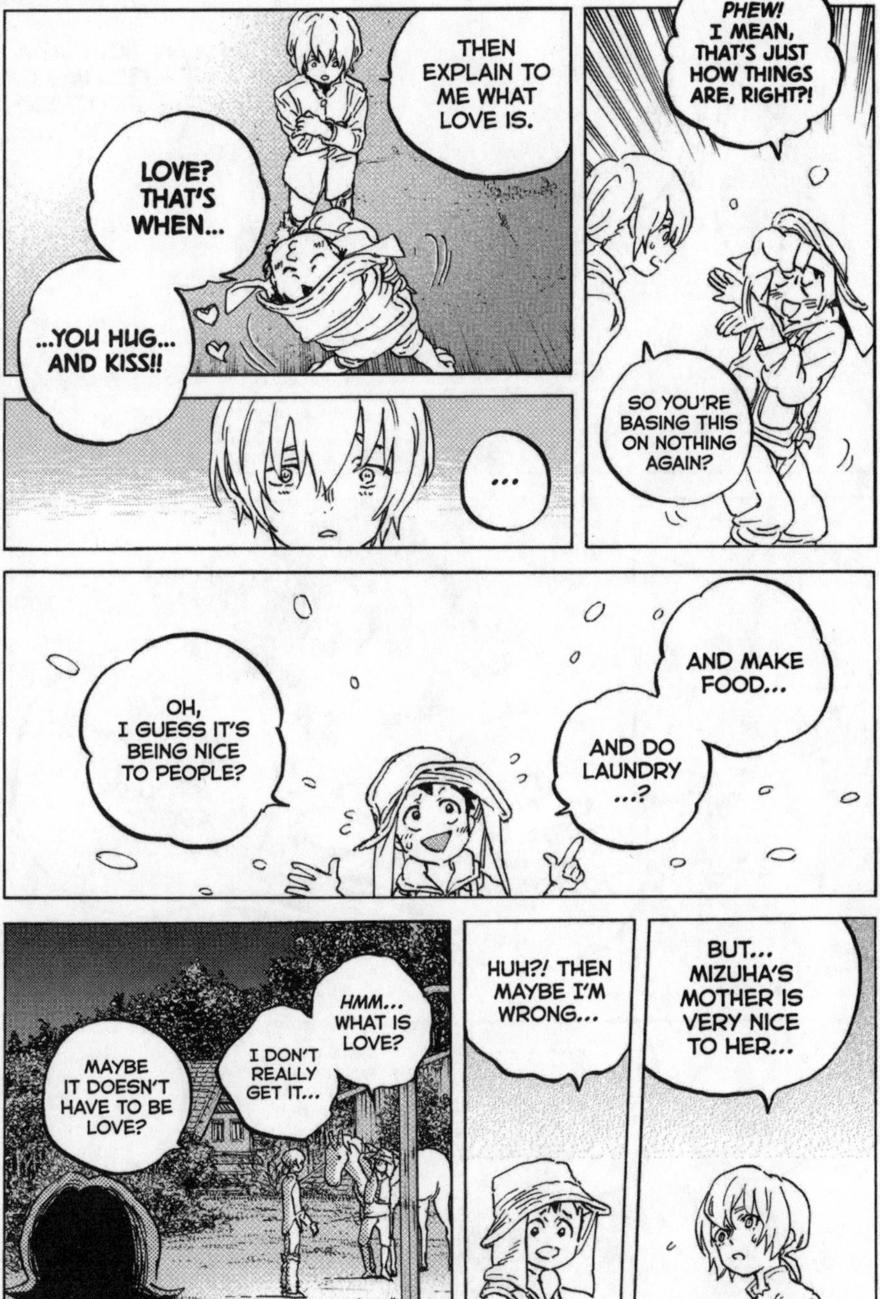
PHEW! I MEAN, THAT'S JUST HOW THINGS ARE, RIGHT?!
SO YOU'RE BASING THIS ON NOTHING AGAIN?
THEN EXPLAIN TO ME WHAT LOVE IS.
LOVE? THAT'S WHEN...
...YOU HUG... AND KISS!!
...
AND MAKE FOOD...
AND DO LAUNDRY ...?
OH, I GUESS IT'S BEING NICE TO PEOPLE?
BUT... MIZUHA'S MOTHER IS VERY NICE TO HER...
HUH?! THEN MAYBE I'M WRONG...
HMM... WHAT IS LOVE?
I DON'T REALLY GET IT...
MAYBE IT DOESN'T HAVE TO BE LOVE?

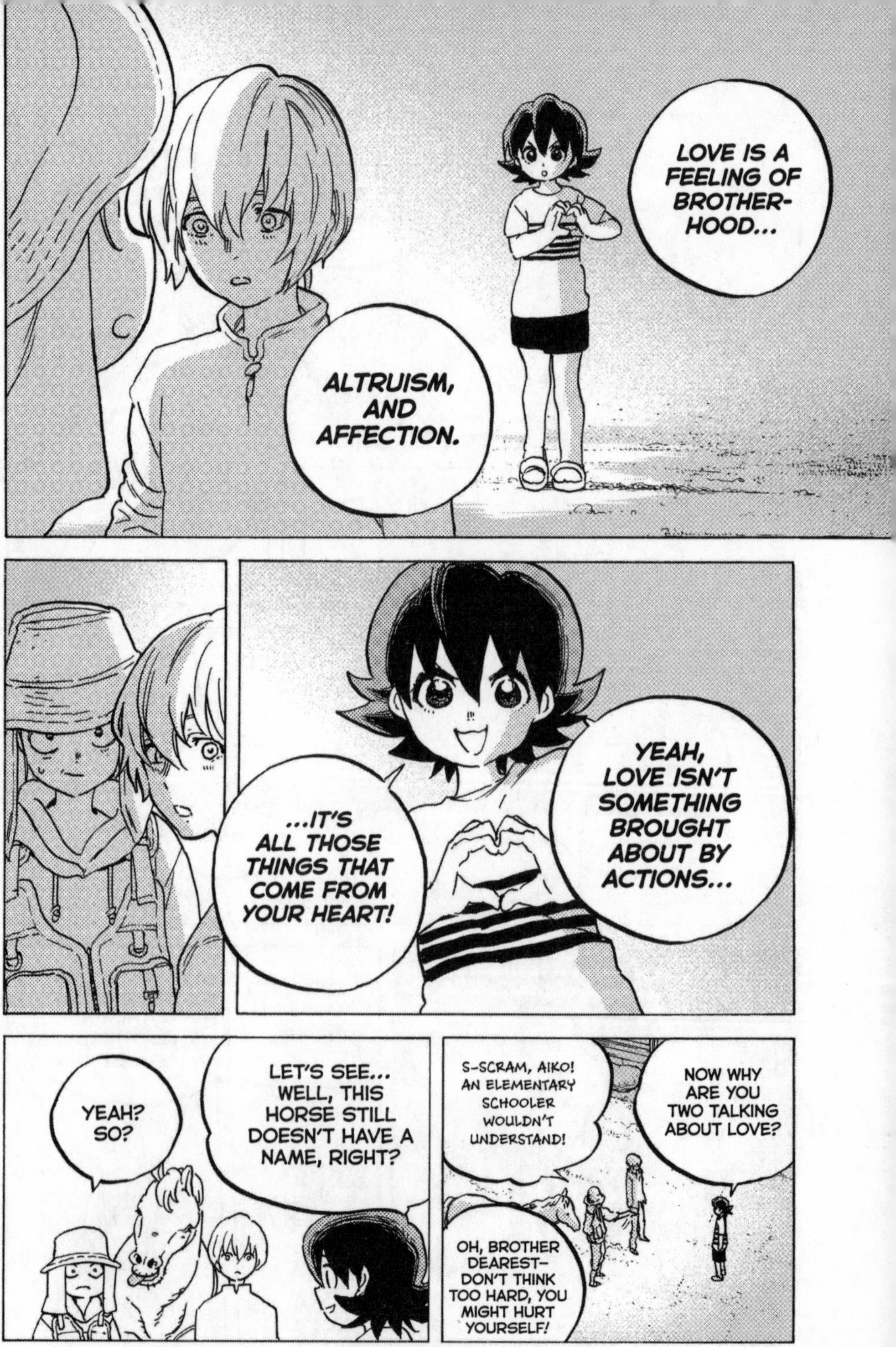
LOVE IS A FEELING OF BROTHER-HOOD...
ALTRUISM, AND AFFECTION.
YEAH, LOVE ISN'T SOMETHING BROUGHT ABOUT BY ACTIONS...
...IT'S ALL THOSE THINGS THAT COME FROM YOUR HEART!
NOW WHY ARE YOU TWO TALKING ABOUT LOVE?
S-SCRAM, AIKO! AN ELEMENTARY SCHOOLER WOULDN'T UNDERSTAND!
OH, BROTHER DEAREST— DON'T THINK TOO HARD, YOU MIGHT HURT YOURSELF!
LET'S SEE... WELL, THIS HORSE STILL DOESN'T HAVE A NAME, RIGHT?
YEAH? SO?

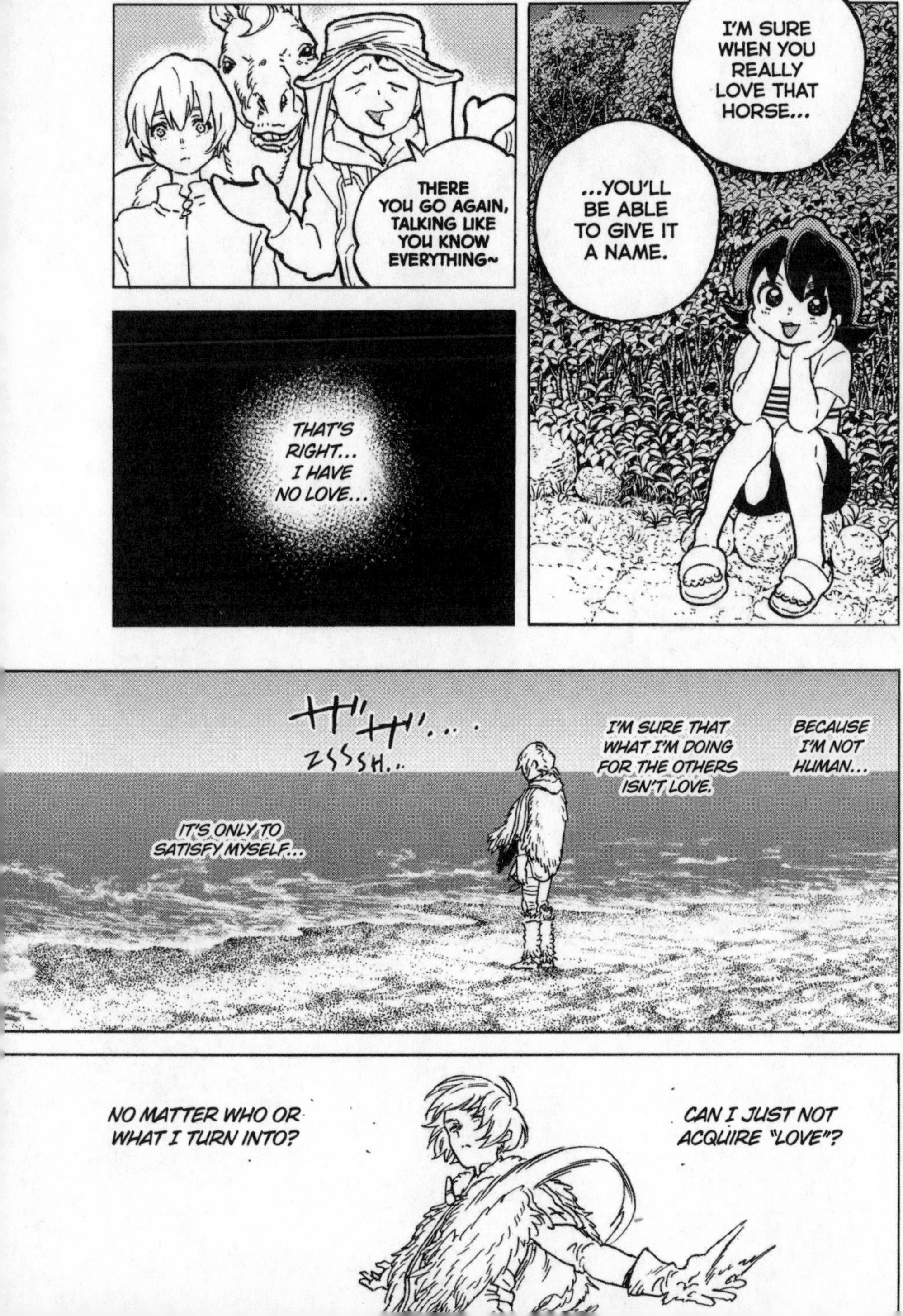
I'M SURE WHEN YOU REALLY LOVE THAT HORSE...
...YOU'LL BE ABLE TO GIVE IT A NAME.
THERE YOU GO AGAIN, TALKING LIKE YOU KNOW EVERYTHING~
THAT'S RIGHT... I HAVE NO LOVE...
BECAUSE I'M NOT HUMAN...
I'M SURE THAT WHAT I'M DOING FOR THE OTHERS ISN'T LOVE.
ZSSSH...
IT'S ONLY TO SATISFY MYSELF...
CAN I JUST NOT ACQUIRE "LOVE"?
NO MATTER WHO OR WHAT I TURN INTO?

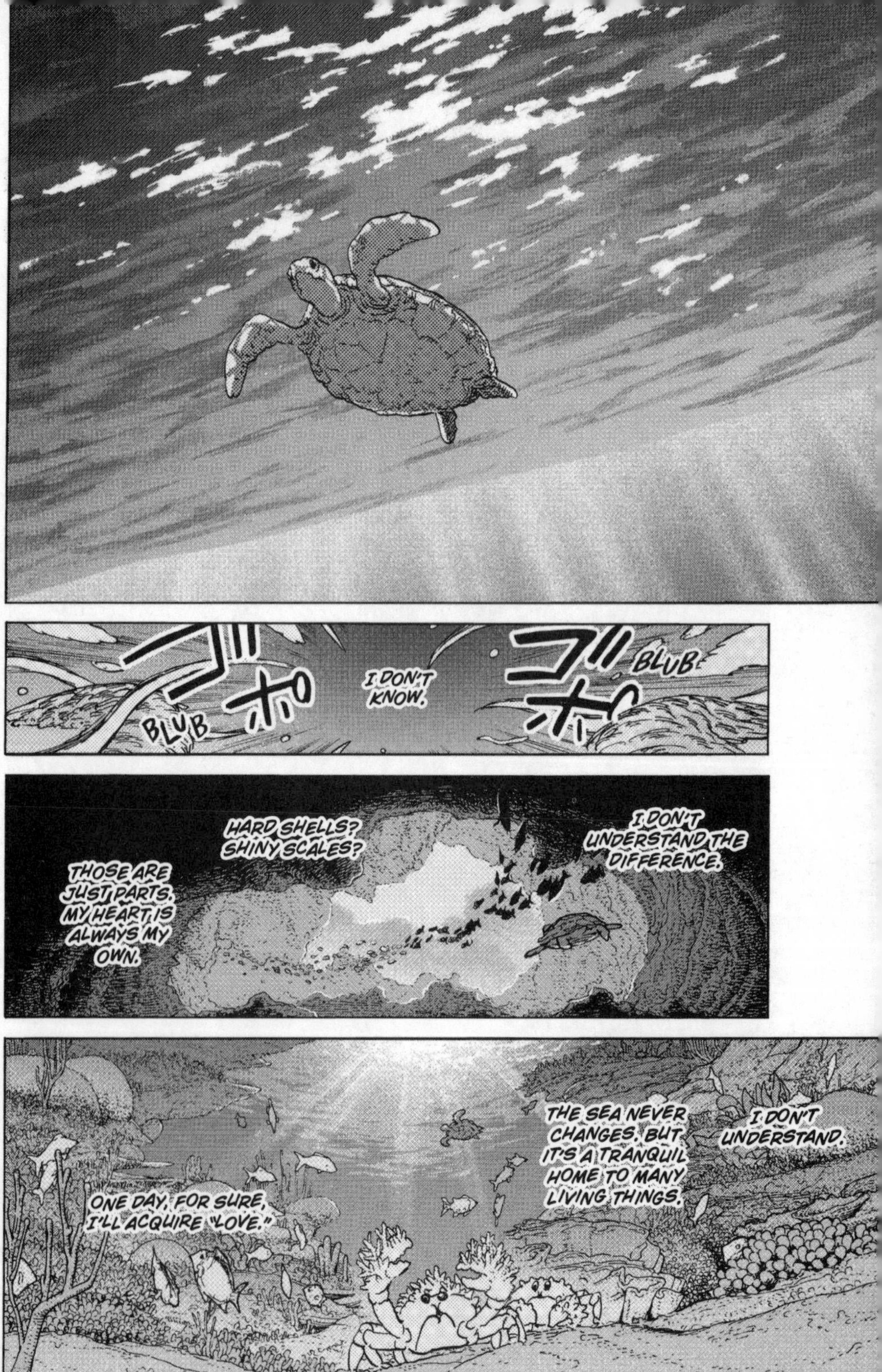
ゴポ
BLUB
I DON'T KNOW.
ゴポ
BLUB
I DON'T UNDERSTAND THE DIFFERENCE.
HARD SHELLS? SHINY SCALES?
THOSE ARE JUST PARTS. MY HEART IS ALWAYS MY OWN.
I DON'T UNDERSTAND.
THE SEA NEVER CHANGES. BUT IT'S A TRANQUIL HOME TO MANY LIVING THINGS.
ONE DAY, FOR SURE, I'LL ACQUIRE "LOVE."

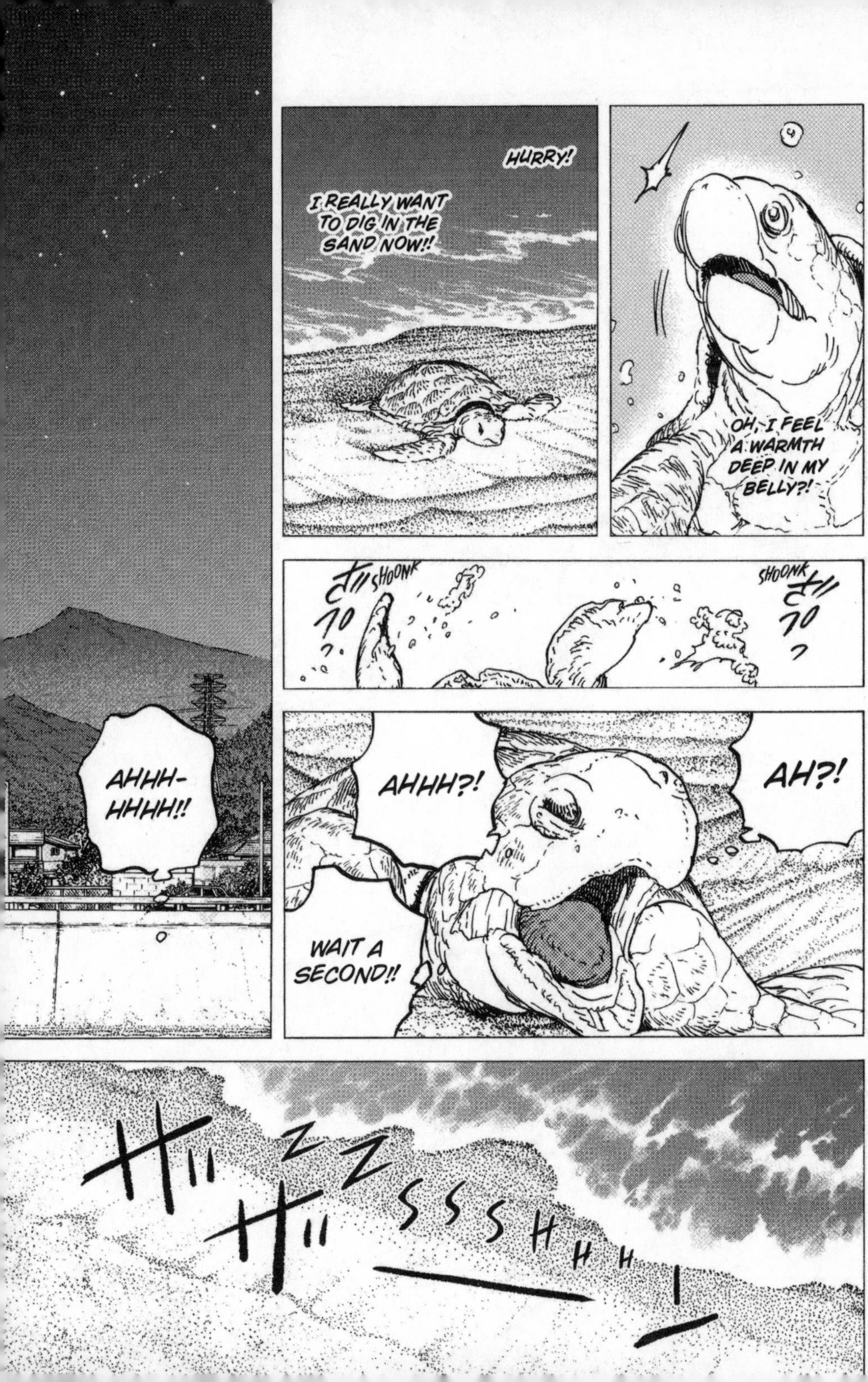
OH, I FEEL A WARMTH DEEP IN MY BELLY?!
HURRY!
I REALLY WANT TO DIG IN THE SAND NOW!!
SHOONK
SHOONK
AH?!
AHHH?!
WAIT A SECOND!!
AHHH-HHHH!!
ZZSSSHHH—!

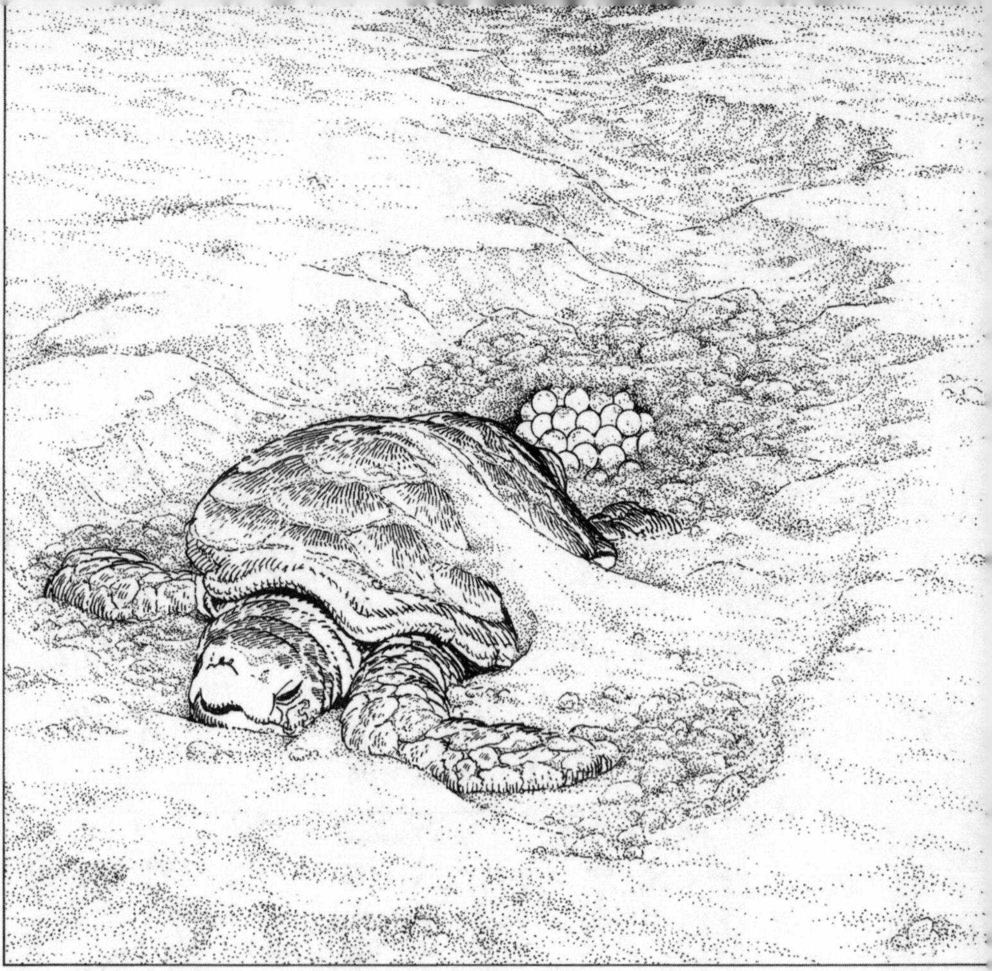

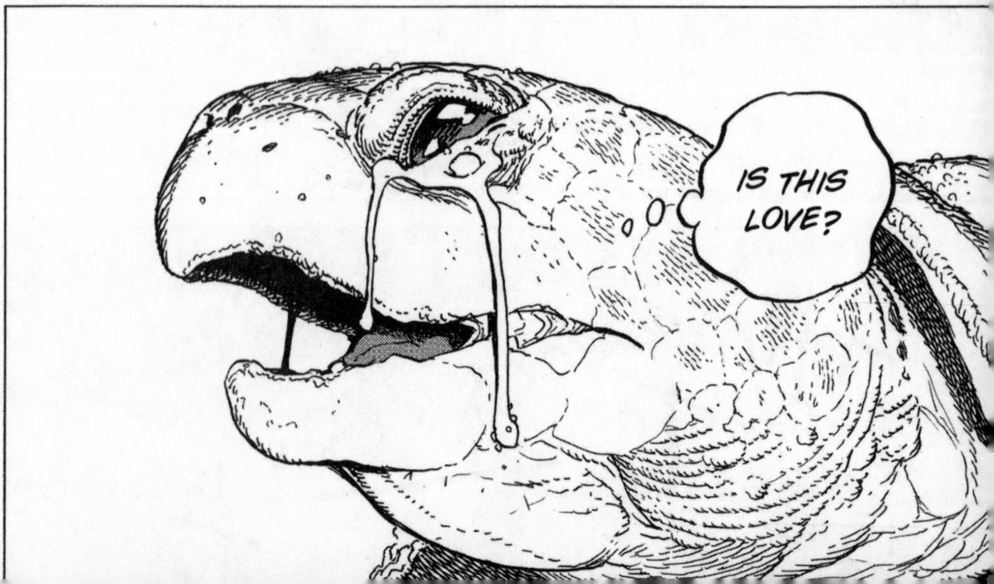

IS THIS
LOVE?

TO YOUR

ETERNITY

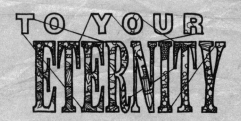

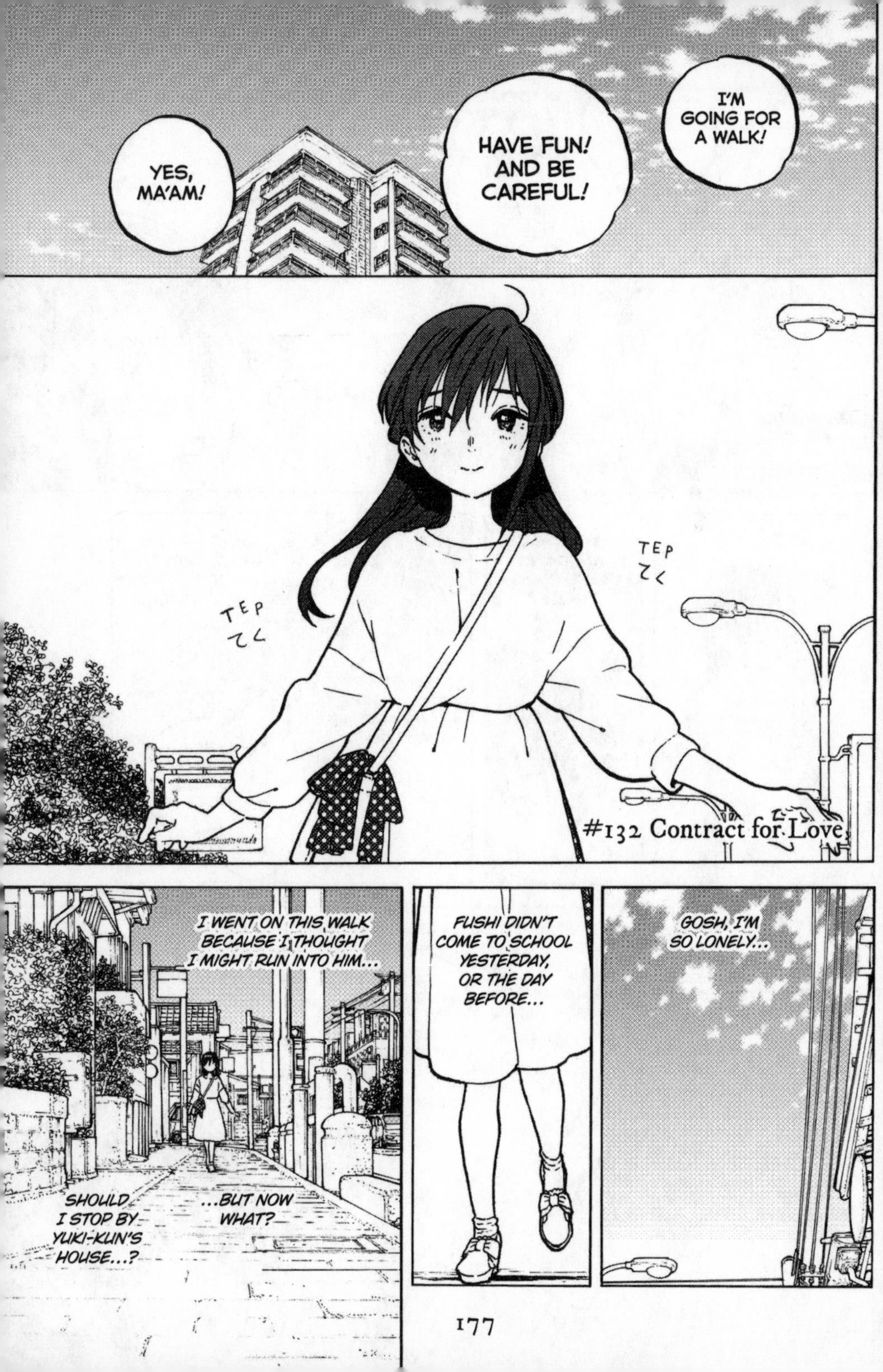

I'M GOING FOR A WALK!
HAVE FUN! AND BE CAREFUL!
YES, MA'AM!
TEP てく
TEP てく
#132 Contract for Love
GOSH, I'M SO LONELY...
FUSHI DIDN'T COME TO SCHOOL YESTERDAY, OR THE DAY BEFORE...
I WENT ON THIS WALK BECAUSE I THOUGHT I MIGHT RUN INTO HIM...
...BUT NOW WHAT?
SHOULD I STOP BY YUKI-KUN'S HOUSE...?

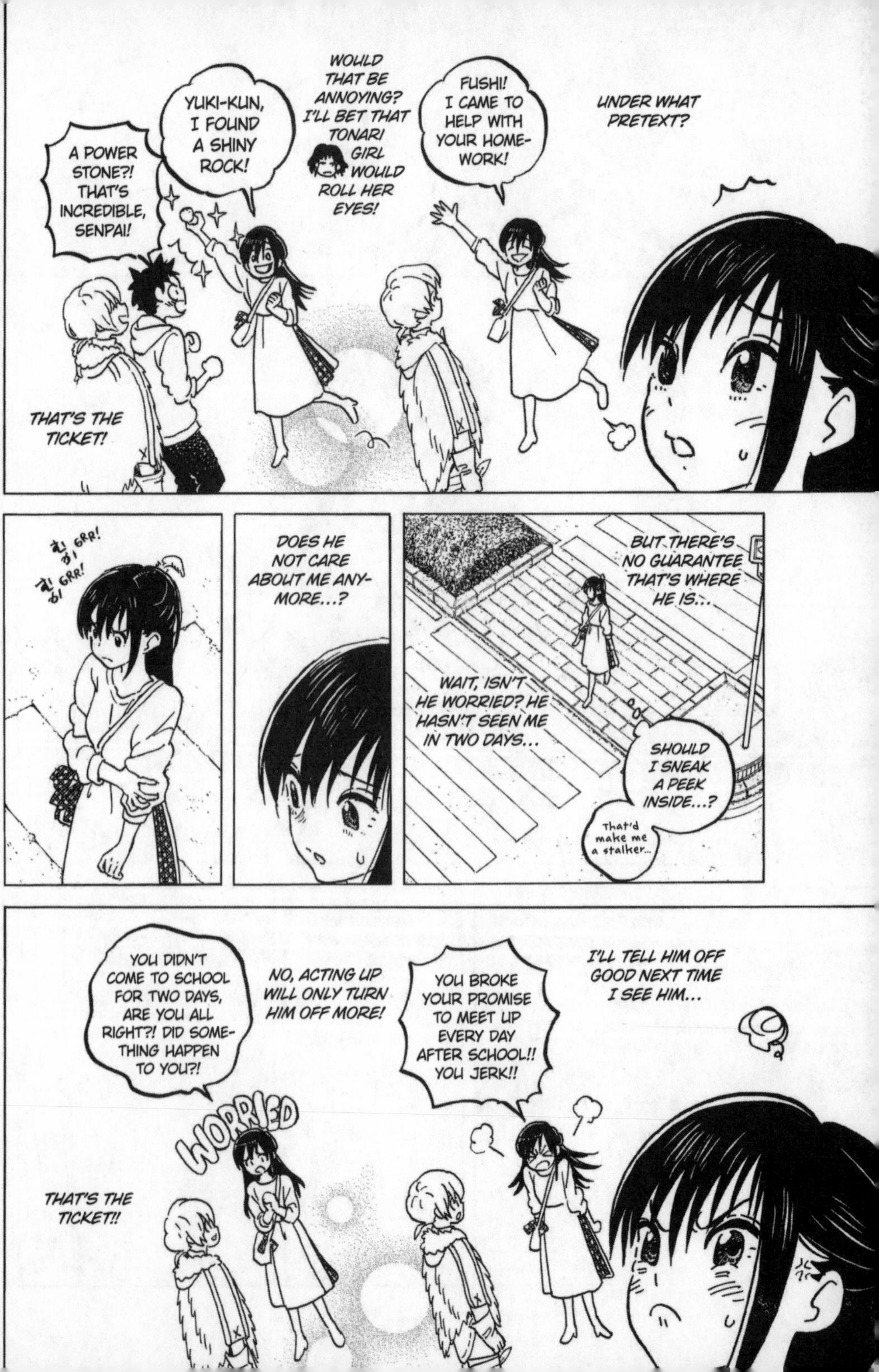
UNDER WHAT PRETEXT?
FUSHI! I CAME TO HELP WITH YOUR HOME-WORK!
WOULD THAT BE ANNOYING? I'LL BET THAT TONARI GIRL WOULD ROLL HER EYES!
YUKI-KUN, I FOUND A SHINY ROCK!
A POWER STONE?! THAT'S INCREDIBLE, SENPAI!
THAT'S THE TICKET!
BUT THERE'S NO GUARANTEE THAT'S WHERE HE IS...
WAIT, ISN'T HE WORRIED? HE HASN'T SEEN ME IN TWO DAYS...
SHOULD I SNEAK A PEEK INSIDE...?
That'd make me a stalker...
DOES HE NOT CARE ABOUT ME ANY-MORE...?
GRR!
GRR!
I'LL TELL HIM OFF GOOD NEXT TIME I SEE HIM...
YOU BROKE YOUR PROMISE TO MEET UP EVERY DAY AFTER SCHOOL!! YOU JERK!!
NO, ACTING UP WILL ONLY TURN HIM OFF MORE!
YOU DIDN'T COME TO SCHOOL FOR TWO DAYS, ARE YOU ALL RIGHT?! DID SOME-THING HAPPEN TO YOU?!
WORRIED
THAT'S THE TICKET!!

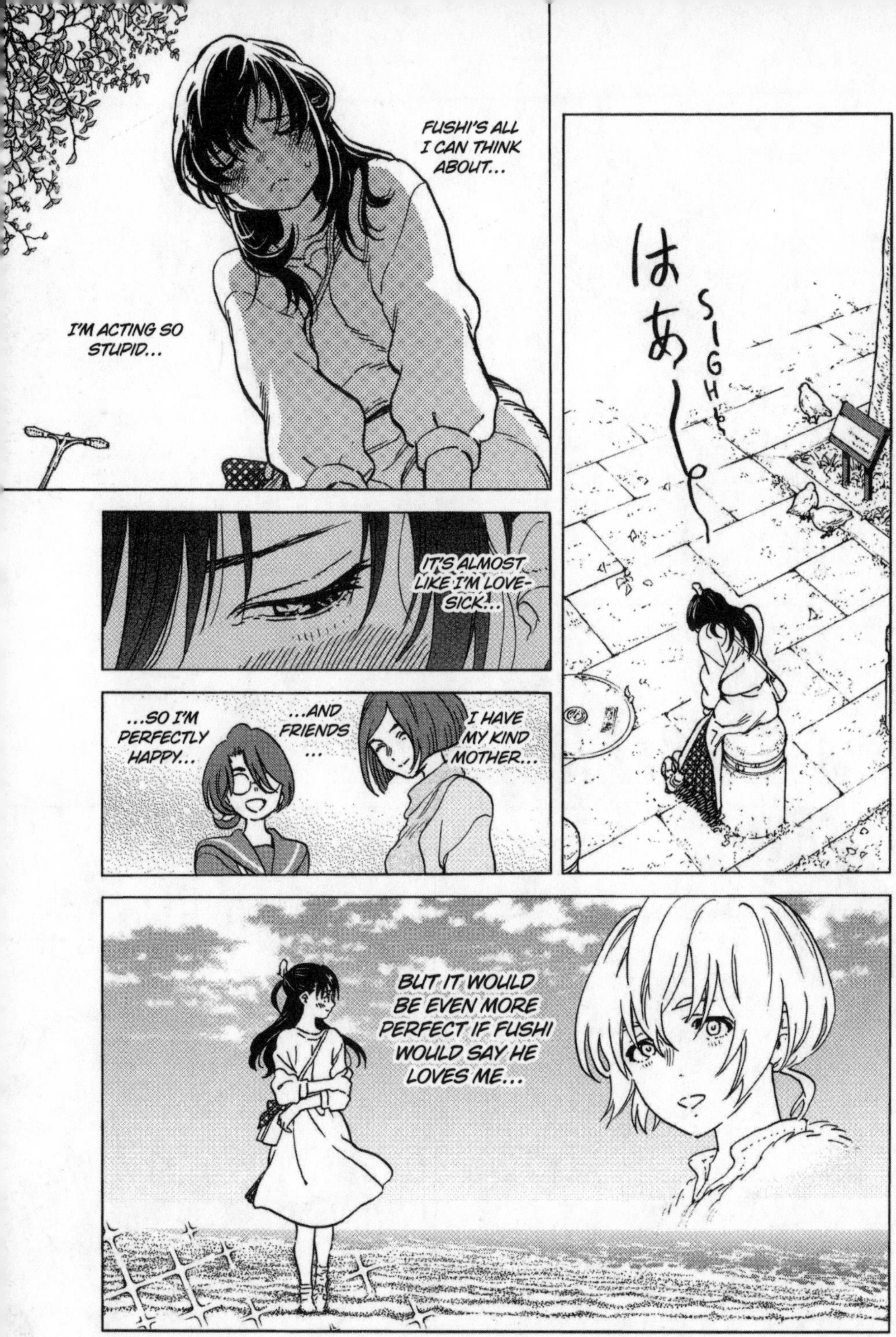
FUSHI'S ALL I CAN THINK ABOUT...
I'M ACTING SO STUPID...
はあ
SIGH
IT'S ALMOST LIKE I'M LOVE-SICK...
I HAVE MY KIND MOTHER...
...AND FRIENDS...
...SO I'M PERFECTLY HAPPY...
BUT IT WOULD BE EVEN MORE PERFECT IF FUSHI WOULD SAY HE LOVES ME...

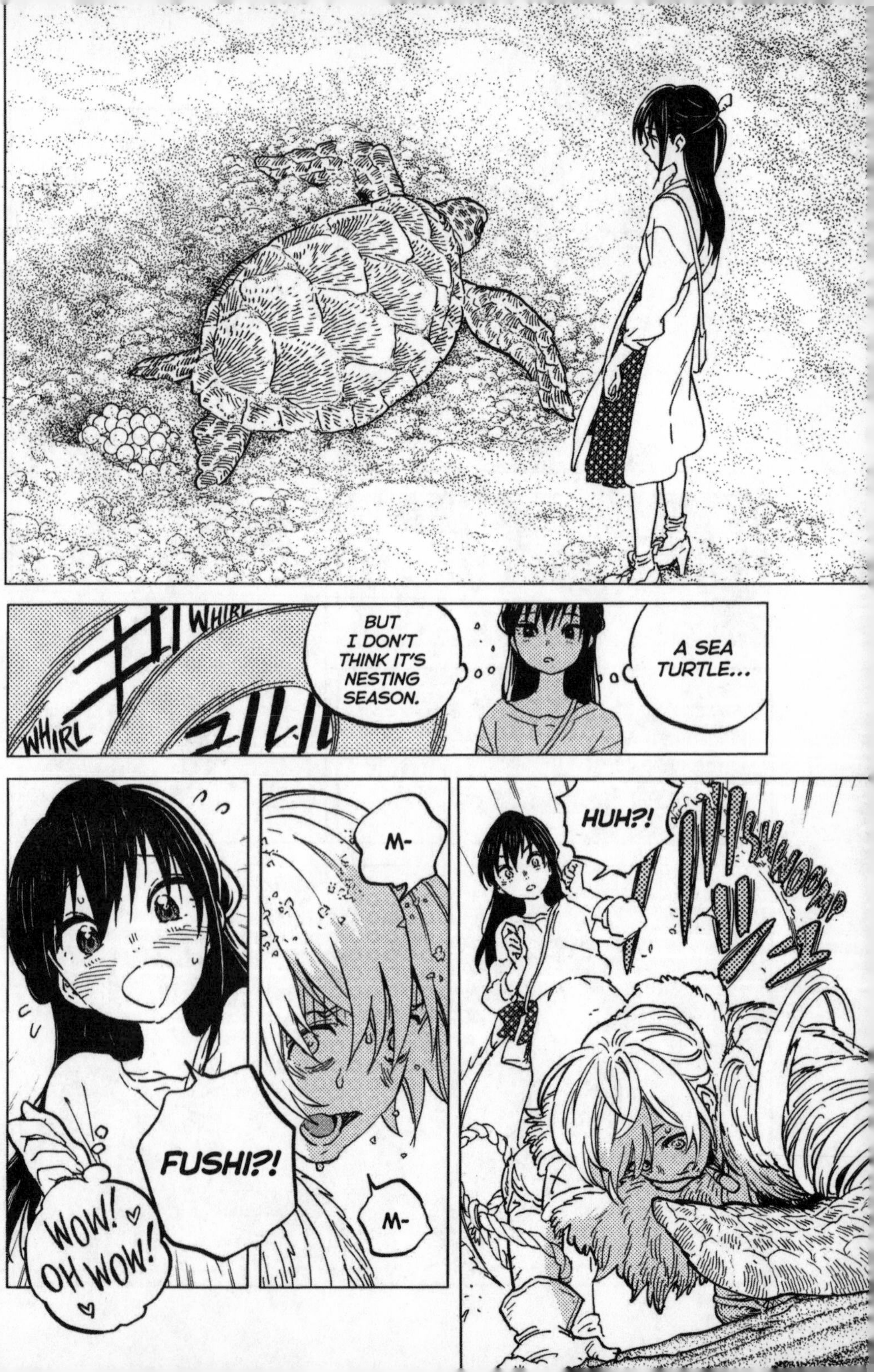
A SEA TURTLE...
BUT I DON'T THINK IT'S NESTING SEASON.
WHIRL
WHIRL
HUH?!
SHWOOMP
M-
M-
FUSHI?!
WOW! OH WOW!

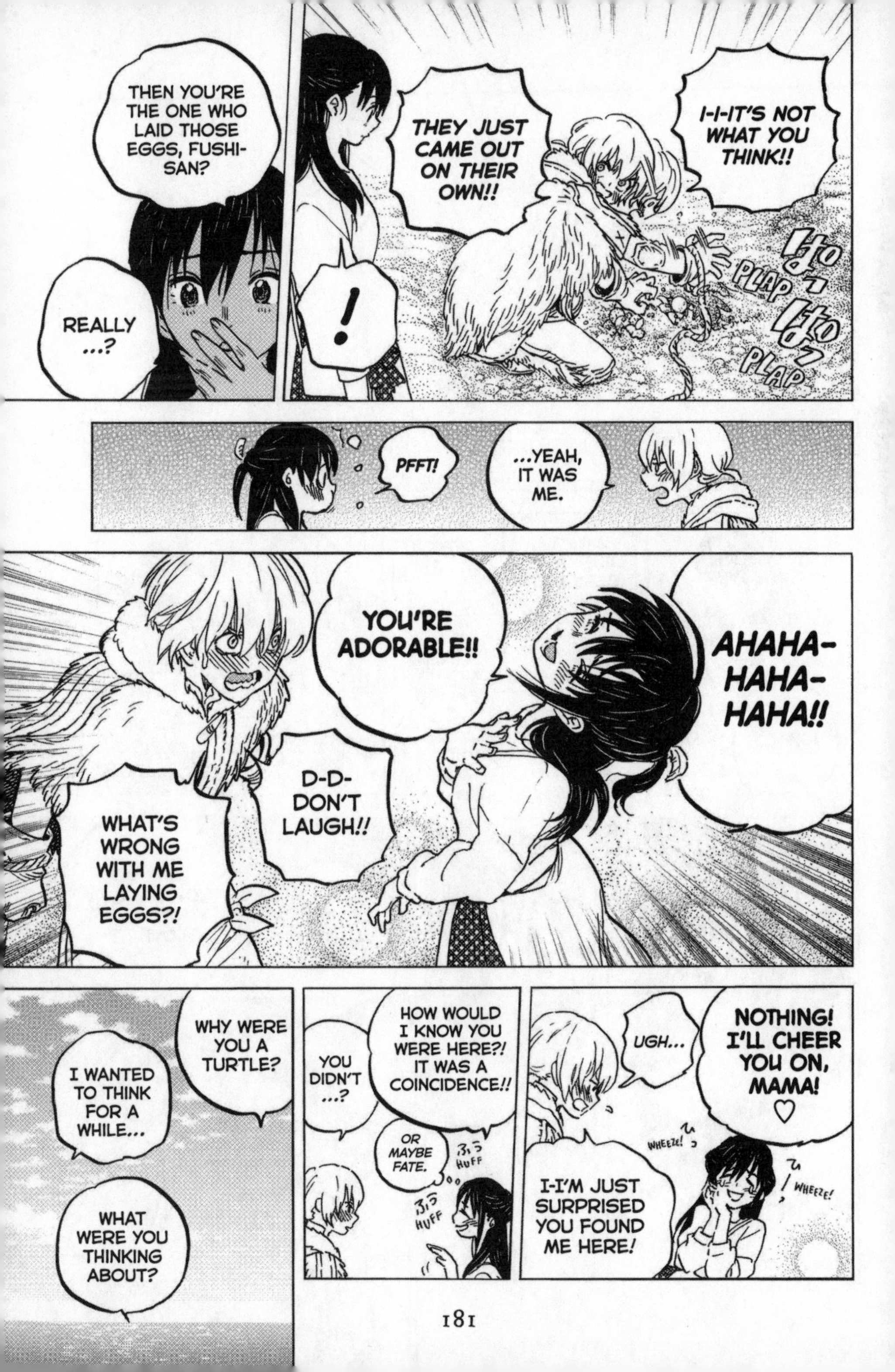
I-I-IT'S NOT WHAT YOU THINK!!
はっ PLAP はっ PLAP
THEY JUST CAME OUT ON THEIR OWN!!
!
THEN YOU'RE THE ONE WHO LAID THOSE EGGS, FUSHI-SAN?
REALLY ...?
...YEAH, IT WAS ME.
PFFT!
AHAHA-HAHA-HAHA!!
YOU'RE ADORABLE!!
D-D-DON'T LAUGH!!
WHAT'S WRONG WITH ME LAYING EGGS?!
NOTHING! I'LL CHEER YOU ON, MAMA! ♡
UGH...
ひっ WHEEZE!
I-I'M JUST SURPRISED YOU FOUND ME HERE!
ひっ WHEEZE!
HOW WOULD I KNOW YOU WERE HERE?! IT WAS A COINCIDENCE!!
YOU DIDN'T ...?
OR MAYBE FATE.
ふっ HUFF
ふっ HUFF
WHY WERE YOU A TURTLE?
I WANTED TO THINK FOR A WHILE...
WHAT WERE YOU THINKING ABOUT?

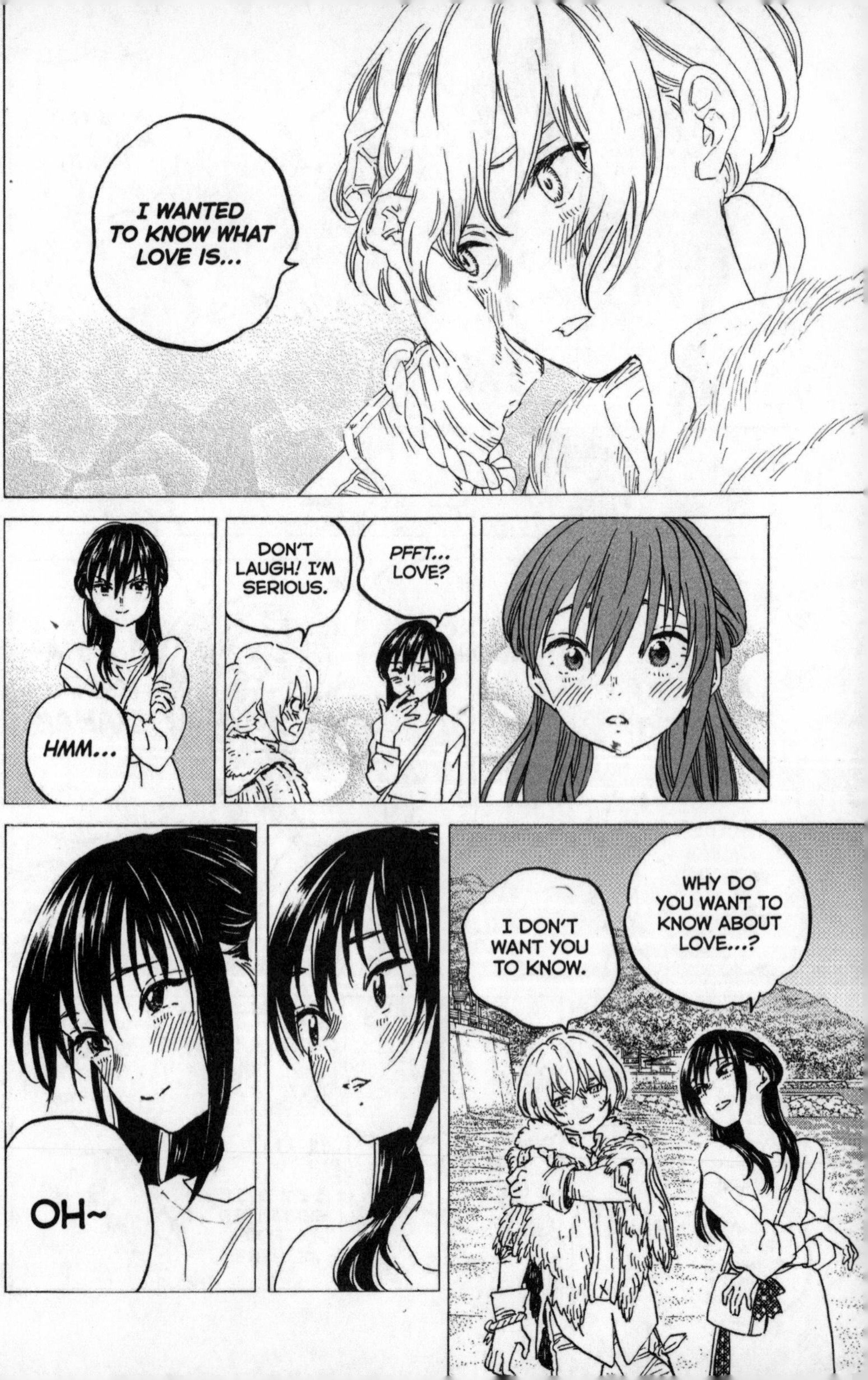
I WANTED TO KNOW WHAT LOVE IS...
PFFT... LOVE?
DON'T LAUGH! I'M SERIOUS.
HMM...
WHY DO YOU WANT TO KNOW ABOUT LOVE...?
I DON'T WANT YOU TO KNOW.
OH~

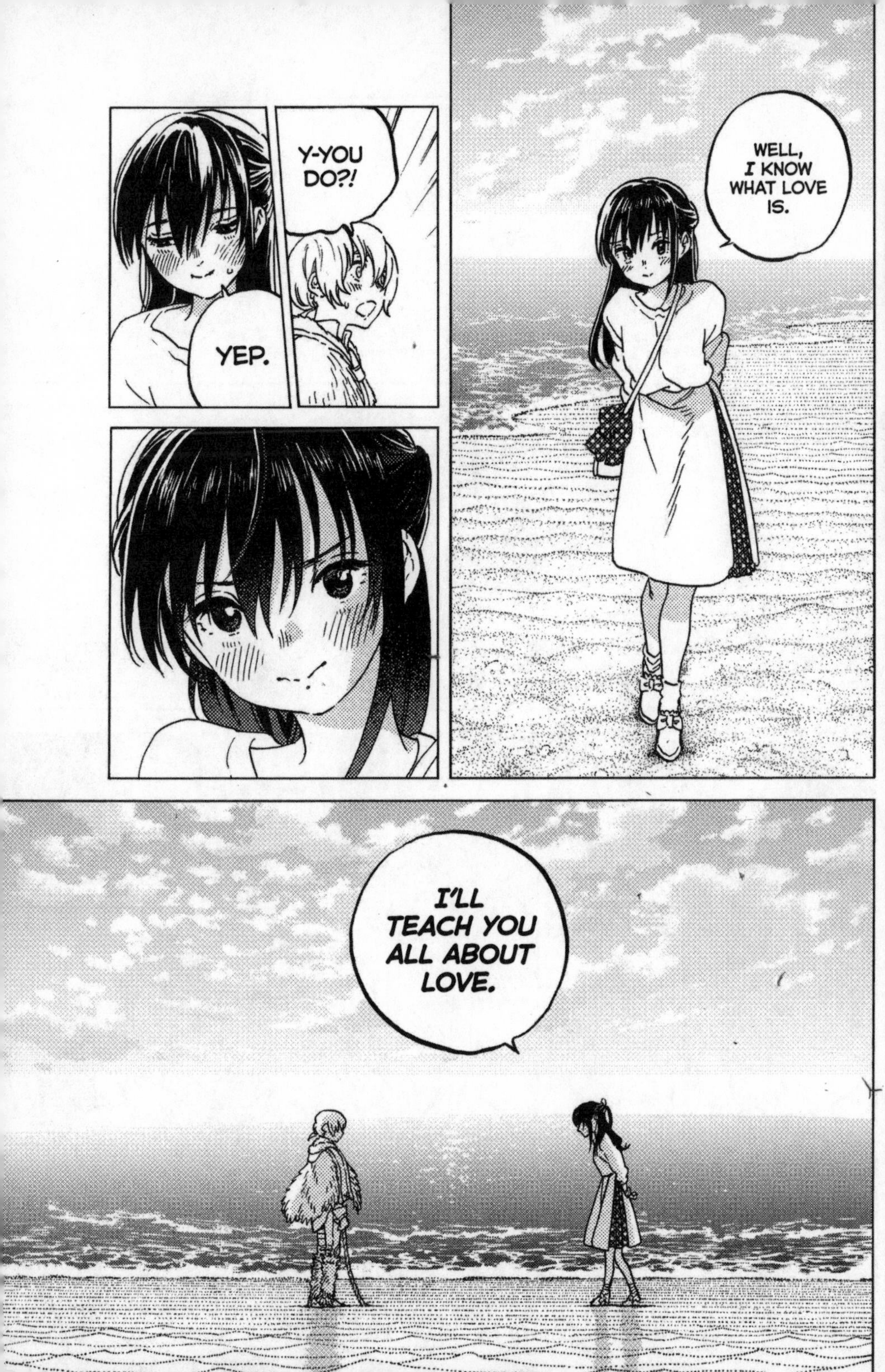
WELL, I KNOW WHAT LOVE IS.
Y-YOU DO?!
YEP.
I'LL TEACH YOU ALL ABOUT LOVE.

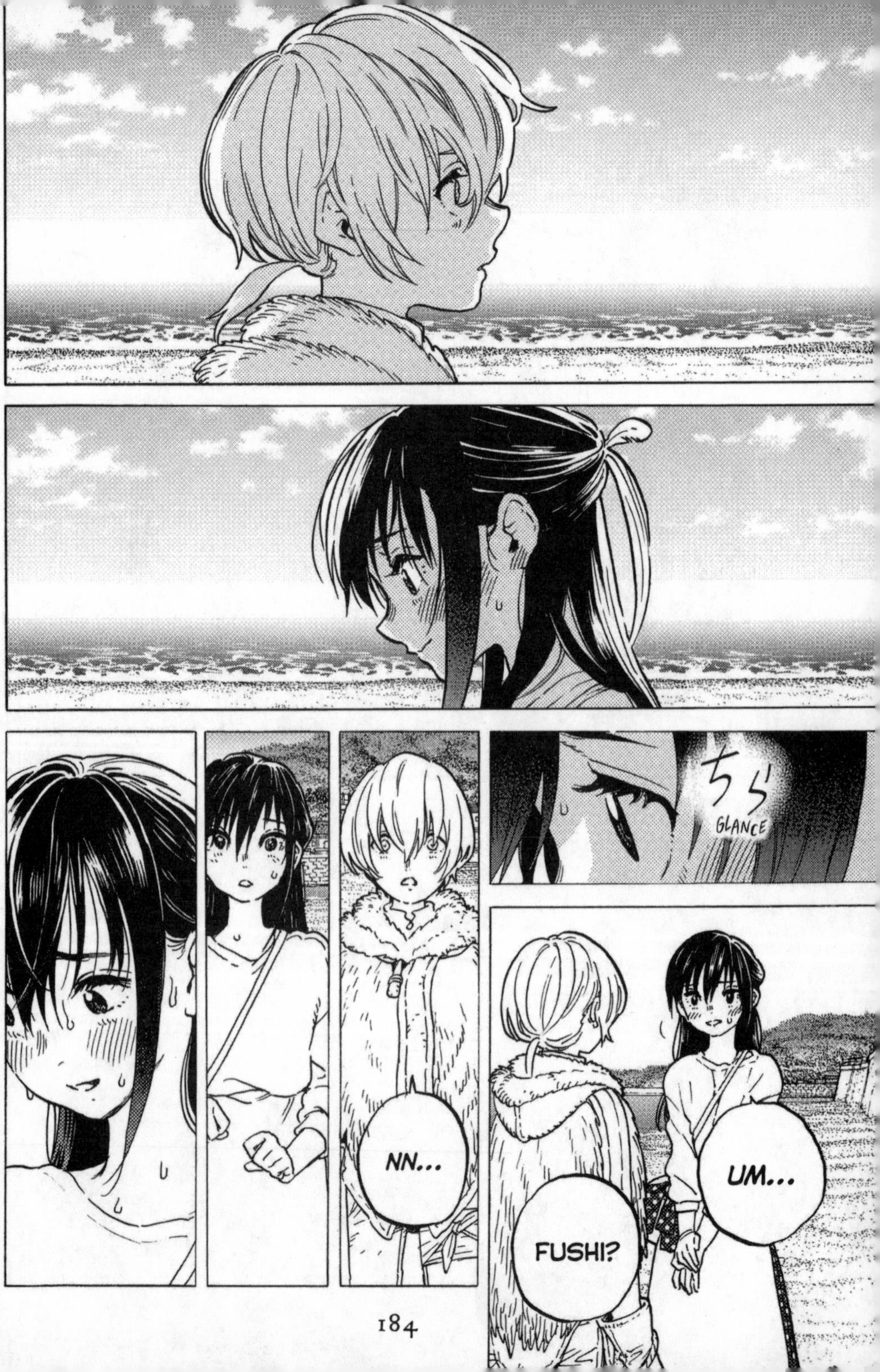
ちら
GLANCE
UM...
FUSHI?
NN...

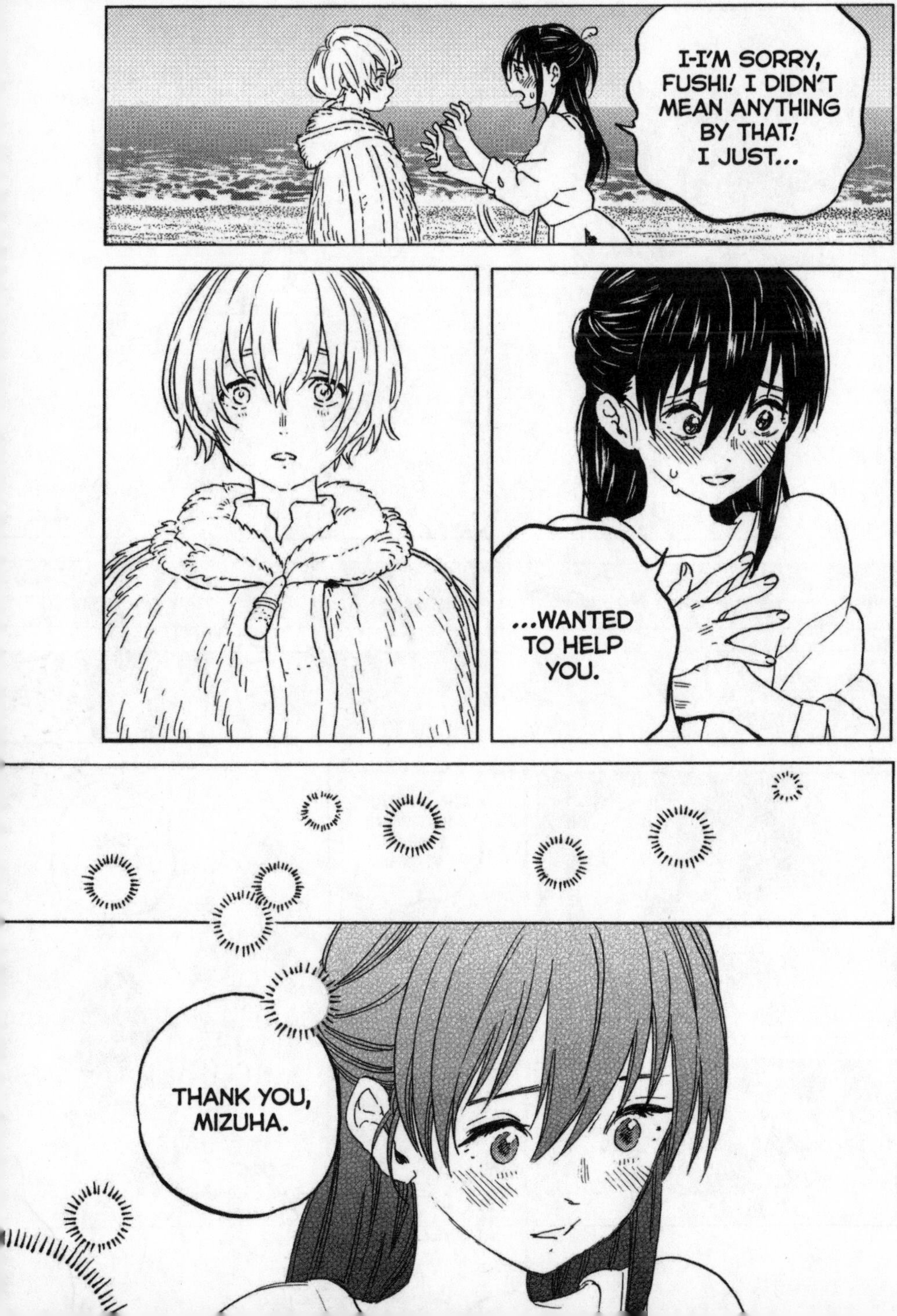
I-I'M SORRY, FUSHI! I DIDN'T MEAN ANYTHING BY THAT! I JUST...
...WANTED TO HELP YOU.
THANK YOU, MIZUHA.

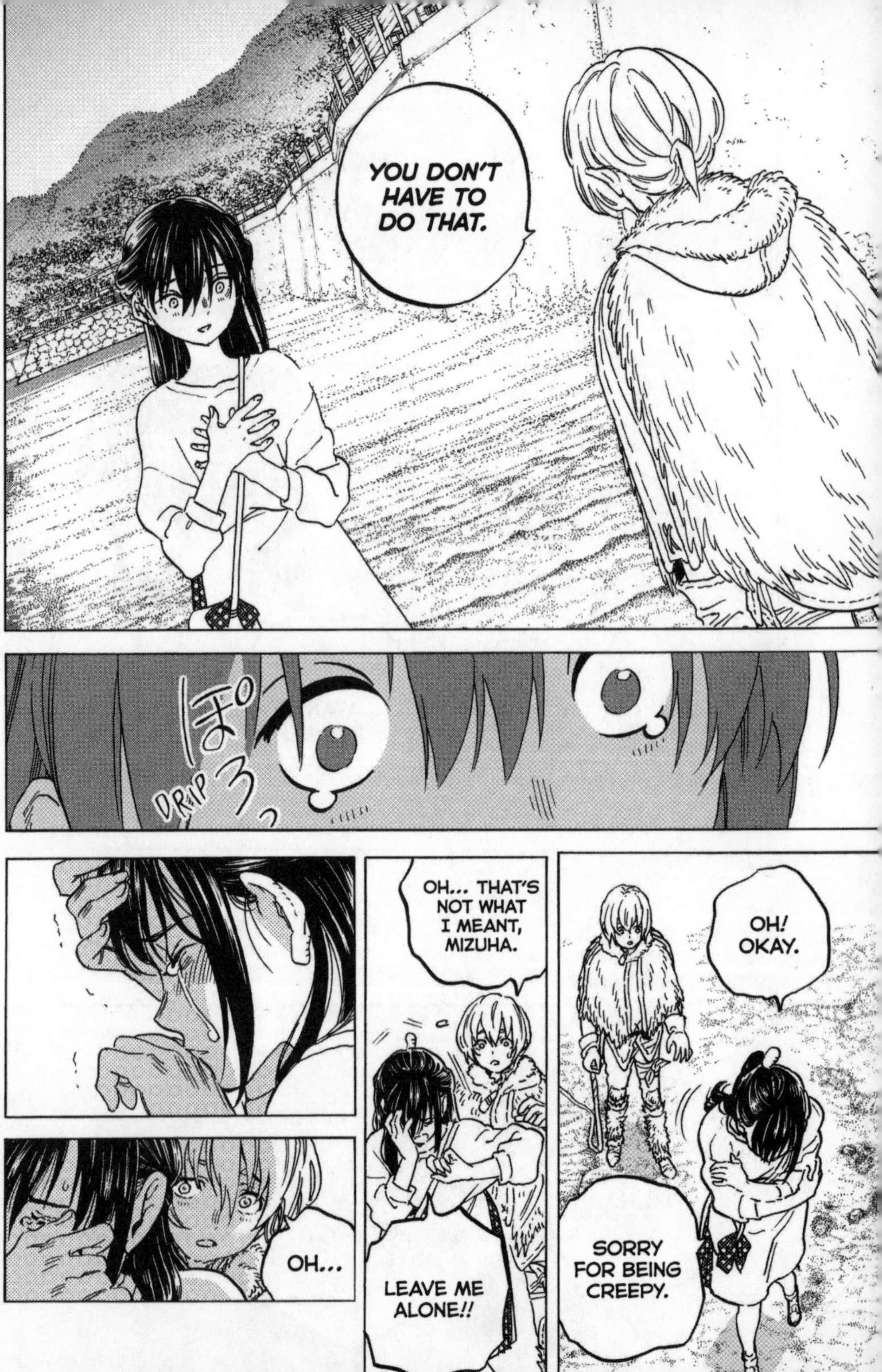
YOU DON'T HAVE TO DO THAT.
ぽろっ
DRIP
OH! OKAY.
SORRY FOR BEING CREEPY.
OH... THAT'S NOT WHAT I MEANT, MIZUHA.
LEAVE ME ALONE!!
OH...

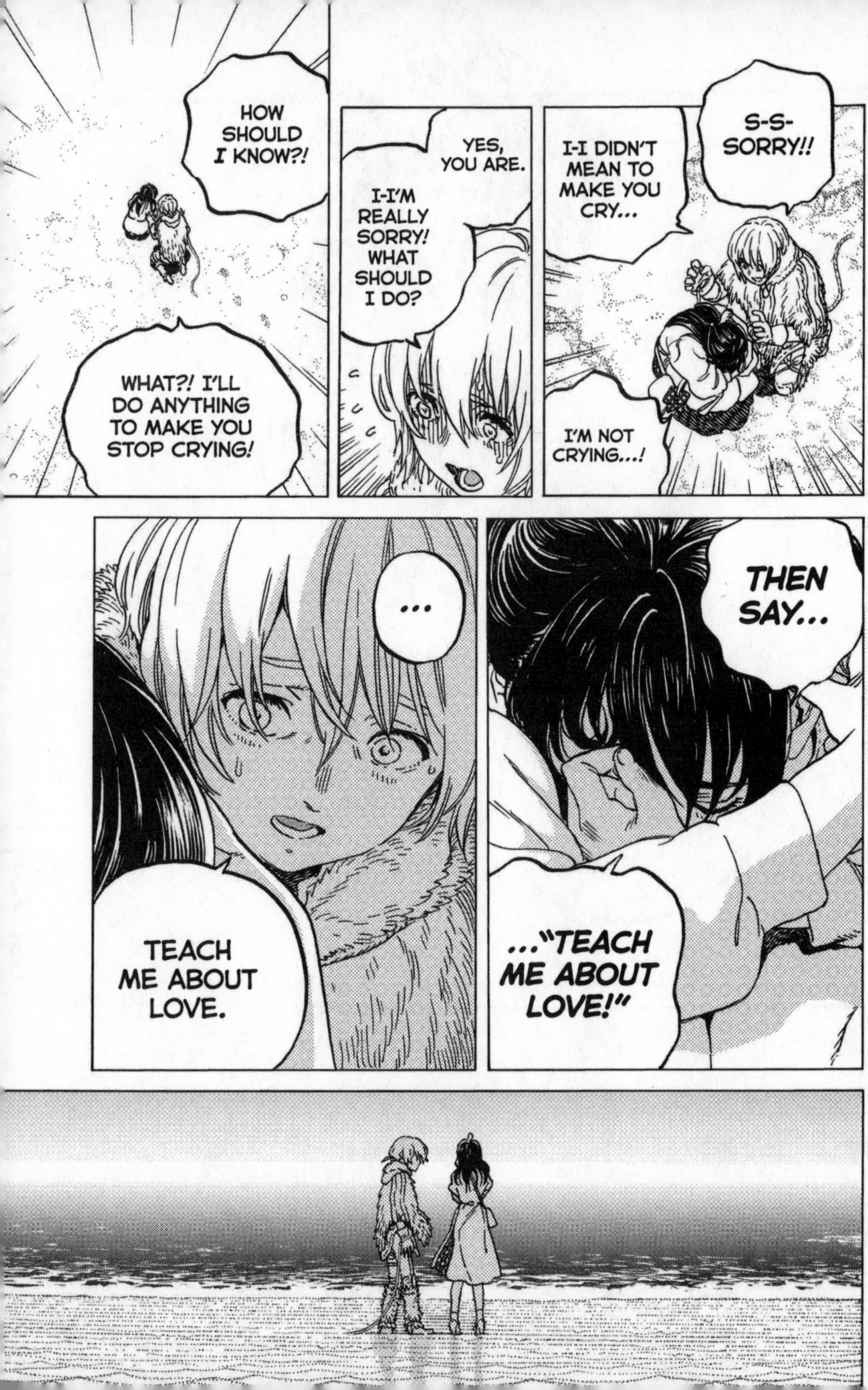
S-S-SORRY!!
I-I DIDN'T MEAN TO MAKE YOU CRY...
I'M NOT CRYING...!
YES, YOU ARE.
I-I'M REALLY SORRY! WHAT SHOULD I DO?
HOW SHOULD *I* KNOW?!
WHAT?! I'LL DO ANYTHING TO MAKE YOU STOP CRYING!
THEN SAY...
..."TEACH ME ABOUT LOVE!"
...
TEACH ME ABOUT LOVE.

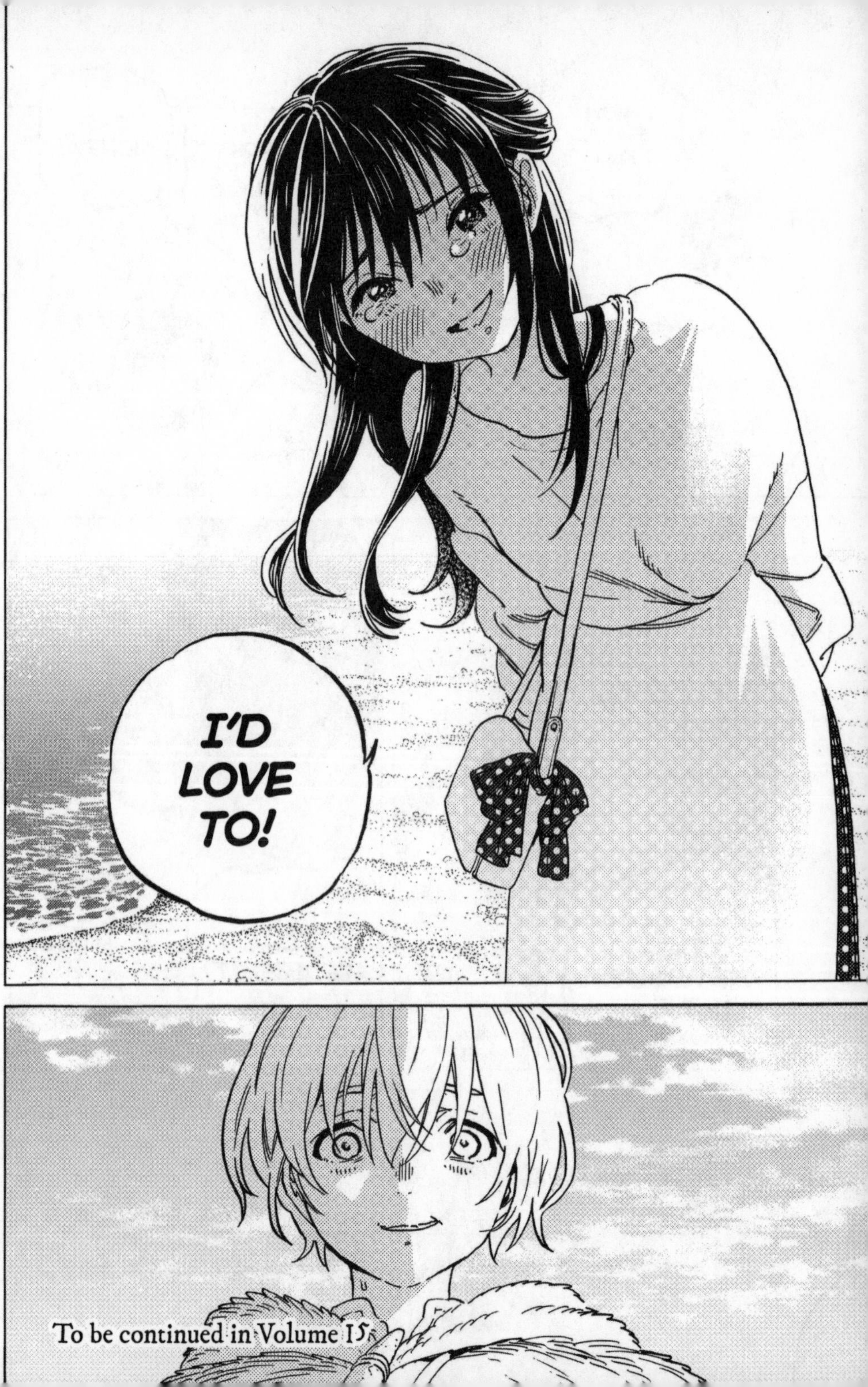
I'D LOVE TO!

To be continued in Volume 15

# TO YOUR ETERNITY

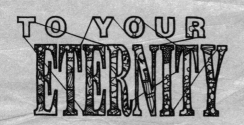

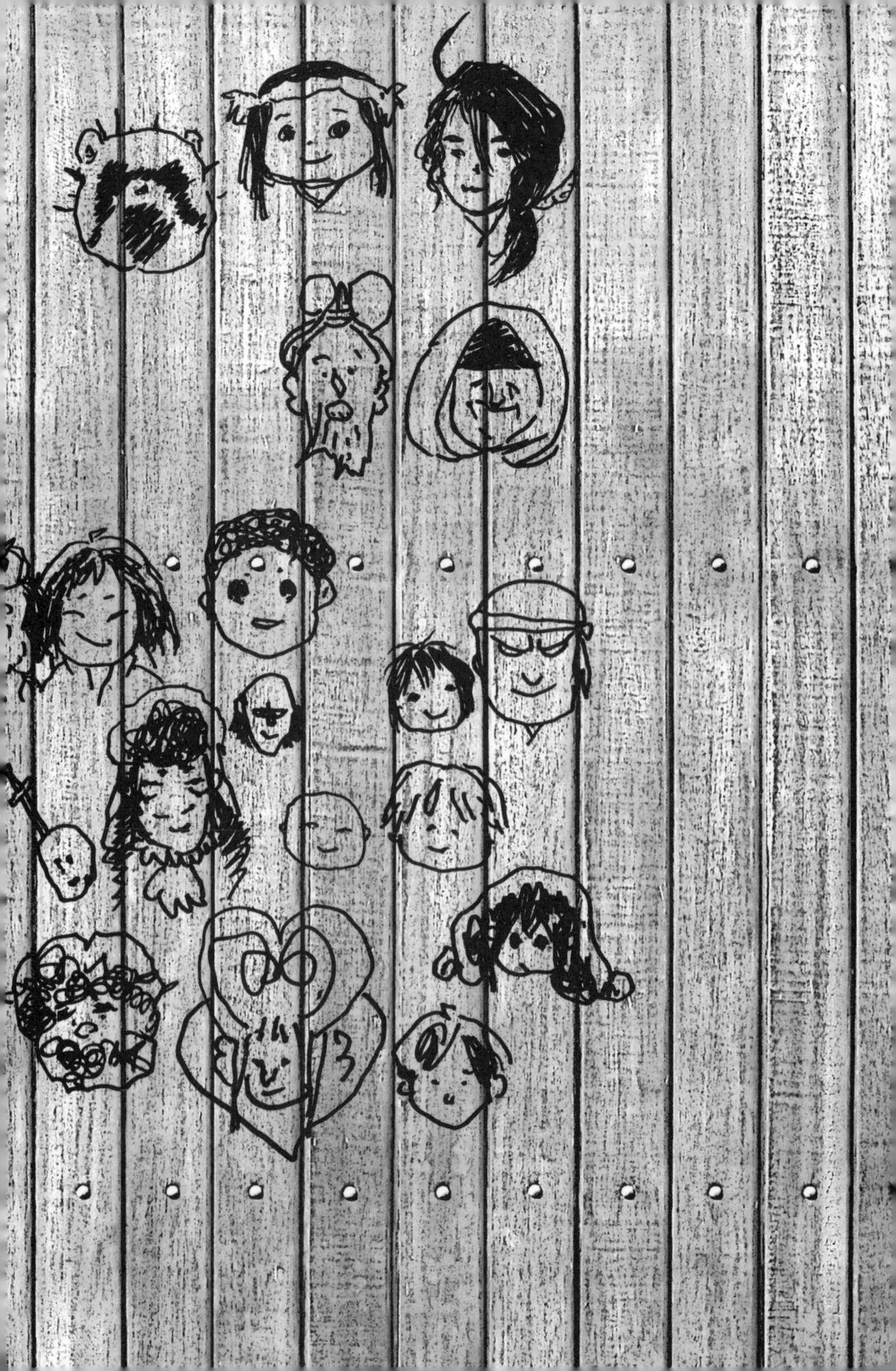

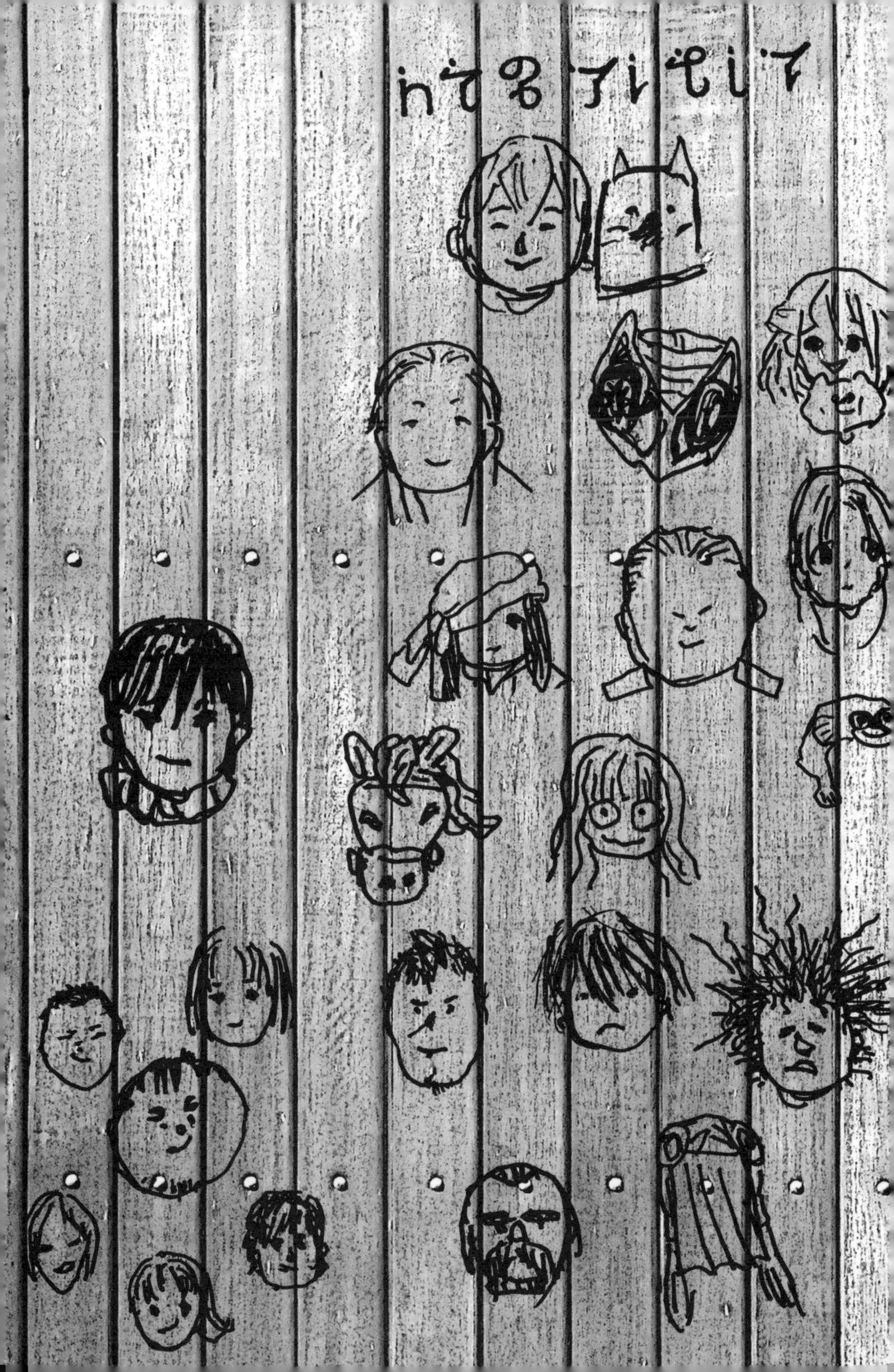

A Kodansha Comics Trade Paperback Original
*To Your Eternity* 14 copyright © 2020 Yoshitoki Oima
English translation copyright © 2021 Yoshitoki Oima

Published in the United States by Kodansha Comics, an imprint of Kodansha USA Publishing, LLC, New York.

Publication rights for this English edition arranged through Kodansha Ltd., Tokyo.

First published in Japan in 2020 by Kodansha Ltd., Tokyo as *Fumetsu no Anata e*, volume 14.

ISBN 978-1-64651-008-5

Cover Design: Tadashi Hisamochi (hive&co., Ltd.)
Title Logo Design: Shinobu Ohashi

Printed in the United States of America.

www.kodansha.us

9 8 7 6 5 4 3
Translation: Steven LeCroy
Lettering: Darren Smith
Editing: Haruko Hashimoto, Alexandra Swanson
Editorial Assistance: YKS Services LLC/SKY Japan, INC.
Kodansha Comics Edition Cover Design: Phil Balsman

Publisher: Kiichiro Sugawara

Director of publishing services: Ben Applegate
Associate director of operations: Stephen Pakula
Publishing services managing editors: Alanna Ruse, Madison Salters
Production managers: Emi Lotto, Angela Zurlo